Emotions and Multilingualism

How do bilinguals experience emotions? Do they perceive and express emotions similarly or differently in their respective languages? Does the first language remain forever the language of the heart? What role do emotions play in second language learning and in language attrition? Why do some writers prefer to write in their second language?

In this provocative and ground-breaking book, Pavlenko challenges the monolingual bias of modern linguistics and psychology and uses the lens of bi- and multilingualism to offer a fresh perspective on the relationship between language and emotions. Bringing together insights from the fields of linguistics, neurolinguistics, psychology, anthropology, psychoanalysis, and literary theory, Pavlenko offers a unique and comprehensive introduction to this cross-disciplinary movement. This is a highly readable and thought-provoking book that draws on empirical data and first-hand accounts and offers invaluable advice for novice researchers. It will appeal to scholars and researchers across many disciplines.

Dr. Aneta Pavlenko is Associate Professor of TESOL at the College of Education, Temple University, Philadelphia. She is the author of many articles and co-editor of *Multilingualism, Second Language Learning and Gender* (2001), *Negotiation of Identities in Multilingual Contexts* (2004), and *Gender and English Language Learners* (2004).

Emotions and Multilingualism

ANETA PAVLENKO
Temple University, Philadelphia

CAMBRIDGE UNIVERSITY PRESS
Cambridge, New York, Melbourne, Madrid, Cape Town, Singapore, São Paulo

Cambridge University Press
32 Avenue of the Americas, New York, NY 10013-2473, USA

www.cambridge.org
Information on this title: www.cambridge.org/9780521843614

First published 2005
This digitally printed version 2007

A catalog record for this publication is available from the British Library.

Library of Congress Cataloging in Publication data

Pavlenko, Aneta, 1963–
Emotions and multilingualism / Aneta Pavlenko.
    p. cm.
Includes bibliographical references.
ISBN 0-521-84361-8 (hardcopy)
1. Multilingualism.   2. Emotions.   3. Psycholinguistics.   4. Sociolinguistics.   I. Title.
P115.P385   2005
306.44´6 – dc22   2005011728

ISBN 978-0-521-84361-4 hardback
ISBN 978-0-521-04577-3 paperback

Contents

Tables

Preface

This book is written for many readers and also for just one. The one reader who was always on my mind as I was writing is a graduate student sitting silently and dejectedly in the library carrel, feeling – as I did many a time – that the academic world is not letting her or him on its major secrets. What areas of research are hotter than others? Which ones have been overexplored and which ones are underresearched? Which approaches are 'in' and which are considered outdated? Is it permissible to link one's own personal circumstances, such as one's bilingualism or childrearing experiences, with one's research topic? And how in the world does one come up with that research topic – or, for that matter, with an adequate research design?

If you have asked yourself any of these questions and have any interest in either bilingualism or emotion research, or, even better, both, this book is for you. Throughout, I have tried to be comprehensive in covering what has been done to date and to be detailed in discussing research designs and methods of analysis that 'go with' particular research directions and theoretical perspectives. I have also tried to be straightforward in explaining which approaches are outdated and why, outlining weaknesses of the currently accepted approaches and sketching out directions for new research. I have also sought to convey my own passion for using the multilingual lens for language research and the perspective of emotion in research on bilingualism. Most of all, I wanted this book to be seductive, so that the student reader in the library carrel would be intrigued enough to consider making a personal contribution to this field. I was also guided by my belief that writing about human beings should weave together the personal and the scholarly, the subjective and the objective. It is in the spirit of such a tapestry that I offer the story of where this book came from.

It was a beautiful sunny day in otherwise perennially foggy and rainy Ithaca. I was sitting in a graduate seminar room, basking in the sun and actively participating in the discussion, like the good girl that I was. It so happened that I asked our professor what a particular phenomenon we were discussing meant for second language acquisition. The professor lost it and blew up at me: "Aneta, not everything in life relates to second language acquisition!" Hmm. Really? I guess I must have pushed a little too hard this time.

As a doctoral student in linguistics, I spent several of my Cornell years taking core classes in syntax, semantics, phonology, and phonetics. At best, these classes highlighted several languages, as spoken by monolingual speakers. At worst, they focused predominantly on English. Alternately bored and puzzled, I tried to relate these classes to the world outside the classroom windows and to my own experiences as an immigrant woman trying to adjust to a new language, culture, and way of life, as a single mother trying to raise a child in two languages, as an English as a Second Language (ESL) teacher, and as a case worker trying to help incoming Russian, Ukrainian, and Bosnian refugees. Some of my professors may still remember my brazen questioning and insolent nagging, asking them to, please, relate the issues under consideration to second language acquisition and bilingualism. My advisor, Jim Lantolf, encouraged my questions. A few other professors patiently tried to answer them. Others dismissed them. One blew up. And when he did, I realized that perhaps it was not his job to use the 'multilingual lens' at every juncture – rather, it was mine, if I so choose. There and then I decided to spend the rest of my scholarly life proving him wrong, and showing that multilingualism, and yes, second language acquisition, have implications for every aspect of – if not life – then at least linguistics and for every phenomenon ever studied from an idealized monolingual point of view.

The present book is a part of this life-long project of rewriting 'monolingual' linguistics to fit the real world – messy, heteroglossic, and multilingual. Its main goal is to show what happens when a multilingual lens is applied to one specific field of study: language and emotions. One may ask what is the purpose of such an enterprise, especially as we already have healthy and productive fields of bi- and multilingualism and second language acquisition? My answer is, yes, these are indeed thriving fields – yet they are also marginal fields, at least in North American academia. Never core courses, always electives, they are always the recipients of theoretical knowledge from other fields, never the source. This situation will remain unchanged as long as the academic establishment believes that the focus of language-related inquiry should be on the minority of the world's population – monolingual or predominantly monolingual speakers – and that only when we find out how 'things work' in monolingual speakers-listeners will we be able to extend the findings to speakers of more than one language. I do not see this approach as valid, nor the status quo as either desirable or acceptable.

Importantly, this book is written not to blame scholars for being monolingual or insufficiently proficient in another language, nor to make them feel deficient. Rather, I blame the trend I perceive as militant monolingualism and argue that, considering that the majority of the world population is bi- or multilingual, the perspective that takes into consideration bilingualism, heteroglossia, and linguistic diversity is a much more productive orientation toward linguistic theory or, for that matter, any theory of the human mind, including language and emotions research. The reason for that is very simple. Rather than obstructing the view, the multilingual lens functions as a magnifying glass that highlights what happens when individuals have two or more affective repertoires or sets of emotion concepts: Do they still map onto a single set of unitary emotions?

As with any scholarly enterprise, this one was not a solitary journey, and thanks are due to many people and institutions. First thanks go to the editor of the series, Keith Oatley of the University of Toronto, and to Sarah Caro of Cambridge University Press for taking a chance on this book. Keith had been outstandingly prompt with feedback and unfailingly supportive – his wonderful insights have significantly improved the quality of the manuscript. I also consider myself lucky to have worked with an editor who shares not only my passion for research on language of emotions but also one for literature – he knew that all the discussions of bilingual writers are (hopefully) more than just gratuitous digressions. The writing of the book itself was enabled by a semester-long sabbatical granted to me by Temple University in the Spring of 2004 and by the unconditional support of my department chair, Dr. Thomas Walker. Much of the academic research was conducted in the Olin library of my alma mater, Cornell University. Working in the calm solitude of that library, listening to the Bell Tower chimes, eating lunch on the slopes, still remains my idea of the best vacation in the world.

Throughout the years of thinking and writing, I enjoyed the friendship and support of wonderful colleagues, many of whom became personal friends. Jean-Marc Dewaele has been an outstanding co-author, co-editor, and partner in our joint research on bilingualism and emotions, in numerous colloquia we organized together, and in special journal issues we co-edited. I am truly blessed by the gift of your friendship. I have also greatly benefited from the insights, support, and advice of many extraordinary colleagues from all over the world who contributed to this book both through their own research, through intense discussions we had in our colloquia and conferences, and through reading and commenting on various chapters. For the gift of their expertise, time, patience, and collegiality, I would like to thank Jeanette Altarriba, Colin Baker, Brian Goldstein, Cathy Harris, Celeste Kinginger, Michèle Koven, Michael McCarthy, Bonny Norton, Yumiko Ohara, Alexia Panayiotou, Ingrid Piller, Sanna Reynolds, Monika

Schmid, Elena Schmitt, Bob Schrauf, and Olga Stepanova. For sharing their experiences with us freely and generously, I would like to thank all contributors to the webquestionnaire. I would also like to thank my doctoral students and assistants at Temple, Eunhee Seo, Lydia Perez-Velez, Bei Zhou, and Youngkyoung Jong, for making endless trips to the library, tracking obscure sources, copying references, and being invariably cheerful and enthusiastic about the book. I am equally grateful to my doctoral advisee from the University of Toronto, Yasuhiro Imai, for his top-notch comments on the manuscript and for keeping me on my toes. Special thanks go to my wonderful friends, Betsy Hillman and Brenda Wickes, for holding my hand when I most needed it.

Real friends and colleagues were not the only people who helped me in the writing process – so did my imaginary friends. It so happened that December 15, 2003, the day I began to write this book, was also the day of the world premiere of the first Spanish-language telenovela produced and filmed in the United States, *Te amaré en silencio*. From then on, every weekday at nine the incomparable Eduardo Yañez and Ana Carolina da Fonseca accompanied me on my journey to the world of emotions in a language not my own. Watching the show through the lenses of the emerging book was a fascinating experience. It made me wonder time and again about emotions that might cross linguistic and cultural boundaries, about trials and tribulations of bilingual couples, about similarities and differences between emotional expression in natural communication and conventionalized expressions of emotions that make shows like this so easy to watch and so comprehensible to speakers of other languages.

Last but not least, behind many a scholarly book stand sacrifices on the part of the writer's family. My family is not an exception here – they lost me to the book for weeks at a time. For their extraordinary patience and unconditional love and support, I thank two very special men in my life: my son, Nik, and my partner, Doug. As I was finishing the book, I suffered the biggest loss any child could imagine – within the span of four months, I lost both of my parents. My dad was with me through every stage of this book – he was the only one in the family who always knew what chapter I was working on. Every one of our transatlantic conversations began with his questions about the progress I made. It will always hurt that he could not see the final result. The book is dedicated to his memory – with all my love and longing.

1

Language and emotions: What can a multilingual perspective contribute?

I had studied Fula for two years . . . but despite this indispensable apprenticeship I needed a year of life with the Fulani before I spoke fluently; today I continue to make many mistakes, and up until the last moment of our stay I was always learning new words and turns of speech. When I think of all that I have still to learn, I wonder how I could have written the pages which follow.

(Riesman, 1977: 3)

Jenny B. is a young, charming and enthusiastic doctoral student in linguistics, interested in the language of emotions. This year she was awarded a grant to conduct her field research in Karani, a language that has not been extensively studied before. After lots of bureaucratic complications, she had finally gotten her visa and airplane ticket, survived the flight (or rather an endless series of flights and rides), and at long last arrived in The Village, located at the heart of the Karani-speaking community. It took her a few days to settle in and then she was ready to begin her research in earnest.

Based on a few previous studies of languages related to Karani and on the remarks of anthropologists who had worked with Karani speakers before, Jenny hypothesized that Karani emotion terms might differ from their English counterparts. Prior to the trip she had taken an intensive, summer-long Karani course; upon arrival, she immediately began listening to conversations around her and taking notes. Unfortunately for her research, it appeared that the emotion terms known to her were used similarly to their English counterparts, which raised Jenny's apprehensions about her understanding of Karani and the validity of her initial assumptions.

Jenny's advisors knew that she would not be able to make definitive claims about Karani after six months of fieldwork based exclusively on her own proficiency, and reminded her repeatedly that she would have to work with local informants. This seemed like a good way to go. Jenny's courses in linguistic fieldwork gave her some basic knowledge of informant selection criteria, such as preferable age, gender, and psychological characteristics. A workshop offered at the Summer Institute in Linguistics also trained her in the basics of monolingual fieldwork. This approach seemed unnecessary, however, as Jenny also knew French, the local lingua franca. She had studied French in high school and college and practiced during the study-abroad semester in France. Jenny hoped that French would become the key to the mysteries of the Karani emotion lexicon.

And so she began scheduling meetings with informants, among them the local school teacher, Monsieur Robert, who spoke fluent French. Their first meeting took place in a sunny classroom that doubled as a library. Excited, Jenny got out her crumpled list of Karani emotion terms. Monsieur Robert nodded and benevolently translated the terms into French: "*Ah oui, c'est pareil à 'l'amour', et ça, c'est pareil à 'la haine.'*" (Ah yes, this is similar to 'love,' and this is similar to 'hate.') Jenny felt a frisson of panic – is that all there is to it? Is it possible that Karani terms function just like their English and French counterparts? Did she make a mistake coming here in search of cross-linguistic differences? Did she find universals instead? Or is she missing something in Karani conversations? Or perhaps miscommunicating with Monsieur Robert?

As her fieldwork goes on and her knowledge of Karani improves, Jenny undoubtedly will gain a better understanding of Karani emotion terms and then will be able to decide just how similar or different they are compared to their English translation equivalents. For now, however, her progress had been slowed not only by her limited competence in Karani but also by her lack of understanding of second language learning and bilingualism. She remembered that her stay with the French family during her semester abroad did wonders for her French fluency and expected the same outcome for Karani during her stay in The Village. She did not, however, consider the fact that prior to her visit to France she had studied French for several years, while all she had in Karani was one summer of intensive study. She also did not remember that even by the end of her stay in France she was unable to follow really rapid talk or conversations on complex topics, such as politics or philosophy. Nor did she think about ways in which her English influenced her learning and use of French or, for that matter, Karani. It is quite possible that her inability to pinpoint language-specific features of Karani emotion talk stemmed not only from her lack of competence in the language but also from semantic transfer, in other words the imposition of English semantic categories onto Karani. Monsieur Robert may have similarly imposed the categories of his native language, Karani, on French, and in reality the emotion terms in the two languages may not be as similar as he believes. Or, if Monsieur Robert spent a long time in France, his Karani categories may have shifted in the direction of their French counterparts.

Jenny is not thinking about her interactions with Monsieur Robert or Karani villagers from the perspective of bilingualism, though, and regrettably her attitude is far from unique. At present, most programs in linguistics, psychology, and anthropology espouse a 'monolingual' view of language advanced by Chomsky, whereby the only worthwhile form of a language is that spoken by 'idealized' monolingual native speakers. Student training in such programs ignores the fact that cross-cultural research is most often conducted through the medium of a second or third language, and that linguistic competencies and histories of researchers, informants, and translators may impact the research findings in profound and unexpected ways. When such possibility is acknowledged, students are simply told to stay away from bilingual speakers – because their competencies are deficient, their minds function in mysterious ways, or simply because they are not representative of their community.

The goal of this book is to offer a more nuanced and sophisticated understanding of bi- and multilingualism on the example of one field – language and emotions – in order to help students like Jenny understand what to expect from their own learning of other languages and from other speakers of more than one language. Consequently, the book has three interrelated aims: (a) to point to new and interesting questions bi- and multilingualism allow us to ask about the relationship between language and emotions; (b) to show how a deepened understanding of emotions as physical and conversational phenomena could enhance our understanding of bi- and multilingualism; and (c) to argue that reliability, validity, and true interdisciplinarity in cross-linguistic research require insights from the field of bilingualism.

I will approach these issues from two viewpoints: that of an audience familiar with research on language and emotions (but not necessarily on bilingualism), and that of an audience familiar with research on bilingualism and second language acquisition (but not necessarily on emotions). Chapter 1 will address the first contingent; Chapter 2 will argue for the need to see emotions in a more comprehensive manner in bilingualism research. In what follows, I begin with an argument against the monolingual bias in the study of language and emotions, followed by a short overview of the relevant terms, concepts, and findings in the field of bilingualism. Then I will highlight the role played by bi- and multilinguals in language and emotions research and show how assumptions made about second language learning, competence, and translation may serve as a deterrent in this research and may also bias its results.

1.1. The perils of the monolingual bias

In the past two decades, we have seen a great surge of interest in the relationship between language and emotions. That surge culminated in the appearance of several monographs, edited volumes, and state-of-the-art reviews in such diverse fields as cognitive linguistics (Athanasiadou & Tabakowska, 1998; Harkins & Wierzbicka, 2001; Kövecses, 1990, 2000; Wierzbicka, 1999), linguistic anthropology (Besnier, 1990; Lutz 1988; Lutz & Abu-Lughod, 1990), pragmatics (Arndt & Janney, 1991), communication sciences (Fussell, 2002; Planalp, 1999), and cognitive, cultural, social, and discursive psychology (Edwards, 1997; Russell, 1991a). However diverse their perspectives, all of these texts have one thing in common: They examine the relationship between language and emotions from a monolingual (meaning one language–one speaker) perspective. None considers the implications of bi- and multilingualism (for example, the representation and use of French, English, and Italian emotion terms in trilingual Canadians), nor, for that matter, the implications of language variation (for example, differences in French emotion terms in France, Canada, and Algeria).

This absence is not surprising: As I have argued earlier, the Chomskian view of language (which continues to dominate traditional linguistics and cognitive psychology) obliterates both language variation and bilingualism as uninteresting phenomena that have little if anything to contribute to the theories of language and mind. This attitude has translated into two common scholarly practices. First, researchers recruiting participants for language studies often try to avoid bi- and multilinguals, whose perceptions, intuitions, and performances might exhibit 'impure' knowledge of the language in question and thus skew the results. Secondly, when bi- and multilingual informants and participants do take part in language studies, their multiple linguistic competencies are often obscured in the reporting, as a fact irrelevant to their 'native speakerness.'

This monolingual bias is problematic for both the scope and the methodology of research in the field. In terms of methodology, the bias obscures the fact that the implicitly 'monolingual' cross-linguistic research is conducted by bi- and multilingual researchers (or at least with the help of multilingual assistants, informants, and translators), with participants who may be proficient in more than one language – all of which could potentially influence the results. In terms of scope, monolingual bias overlooks the fact that most of the world's population is bi- or multilingual, and that even those who view themselves as monolingual often have a long history of foreign language exposure. Yet theories of the relationship between language and emotions continue to privilege the one speaker–one language viewpoint, exhibiting an implicit assumption that whatever applies to monolinguals will also apply to bi- and multilinguals.

This assumption is tantamount to saying that whatever applies to men will also apply to women. Feminist scholars have exposed the bias behind such an assumption and have pointed to a variety of ways in which gender may impact human experiences, perceptions, and linguistic expression.

As a consequence, these days both ethnographers and experimental researchers are conscious of the gender distribution in their informant pools and participant samples. The present book aims to make the same argument with regard to bi- and multilingualism, exposing a pervasive monolingual bias in all areas of language research, including research on emotional expression. I argue that the monolingual bias legitimizes perceptions and experiences of a precious few, namely white middle-class monolingual college students, as normative, and leaves out as illegitimate speakers those who have been 'tainted' by another language. In doing so, researchers continue to privilege the knowledge and competencies of the monolingual minority, shying away from the complexity of bi- and multilingualism and segregating it into a marginal field of its own. How can this disparity be addressed?

1.2. Bi- and multilingualism

Feminist scholars arguing against gender bias in the social and medical sciences began by explaining gender and the difference it makes. I will follow their lead and begin with a short introduction to bi- and multilingualism. It is perhaps understandable that scholars who do not commonly work with bilingual participants are apprehensive about the multitude of factors to be considered in this research. Bilingualism has been studied less extensively than monolingualism. Theoretical models of bilingual development, competence, performance, and processing have not been sufficiently elaborated, and conceptual notions and definitions show a great deal of variability. As a result, empirical research may produce conflicting results, and it is not always clear what methodological considerations need to be taken into account in each particular case (Grosjean, 1998). The purpose of the following discussion and the book as a whole is to introduce readers unfamiliar with research on bi- and multilingualism to the key terms and findings in this area and to clarify what needs to be taken into account in emotions research with bi- and multilingual speakers.

Traditionally, the field of bilingualism studied the competence and performance of people who speak two or more languages, with the focus on the phenomenon of bilingualism. Recently, concerns about the limitations of this focus caused the field to significantly expand its boundaries and examine such phenomena as trilingual acquisition, third language acquisition, and the competence and performance of multilingual speakers (Cenoz, Hufeisen & Jessner, 2001, 2003). To reflect these new developments, I use *multilingualism* in the title of this book as the more inclusive term. To respect the history and traditions of the field, I use the term *bilingualism* in the body of the book to designate the field of research that examines both bi- and multilingualism (Baker, 2001; Baker & Prys Jones, 1997; Bhatia & Ritchie, 2004; Grosjean, 1982; Li Wei, 2000; Romaine, 1995). The term *bilingual,* unless specified otherwise, will be used to refer to speakers of two languages and the term *multilingual* to refer to speakers of more than two languages. *Majority language* will refer to the language used by the wider community and most often designated as its official language (for example, Spanish in Mexico or Estonian in Estonia). *Minority language* will refer to languages spoken by ethnic groups living in the wider community (for example, Spanish in the United States or Russian in Estonia). These somewhat problematic and dichotomizing terms are used not to draw attention to the numerical size of particular linguistic groups but to refer to situational differences in power, rights, and privileges (May, 2001; Pavlenko & Blackledge, 2004b; Piller, 2002a).

For lack of better commonly accepted terms, I also use the much-maligned terms 'competence,' 'performance,' and 'proficiency.' Following the current trend in the field of Second Language Acquisition (SLA), *competence* will designate the mostly unconscious knowledge a speaker has of the linguistic, sociolinguistic, and communicative principles that allow the interpretation and use of a particular language and that typically is deduced through metalinguistic tests/performance. Following recent developments in the field of linguistic anthropology, *performance* will refer not simply to language use but also to the creative construction of self and others, as in 'performance of affect.' (In the past two decades the competence/performance dichotomy repeatedly has come under fire, and rightfully so [cf. Duranti, 1997]. Nevertheless, I find the distinction between representational knowledge and language use helpful enough that I choose to maintain the dichotomy despite its problems and weaknesses.) Finally, *proficiency* will refer to the overall level of achievement in a particular language and the level of achievement in discrete skills, such as speaking or writing, measured through standardized tests or self-assessment.

Who is considered a bilingual these days for research purposes? A layperson definition posits that bilinguals are people who have similar levels of proficiency in two or more languages, typically learned from birth. In contrast, scholars in the field of bilingualism favor a use-based definition of *bi-* and *multilinguals* as speakers who use two or more languages or dialects in their everyday lives – be it simultaneously (in language contact situations) or consecutively (in the context of immigration). Research shows that these speakers rarely exhibit equal fluency in all language skills, due to the *complementarity principle* – that is, the fact that their multiple languages are usually acquired and used in different contexts, with different people, and for different purposes (Grosjean, 1998). Some of these languages may be undergoing the process of *attrition,* meaning inhibition or (temporary) loss of certain skills, lexical and structural elements, and linguistic and conceptual distinctions. The difference between proficiency-based and use-based definitions is an important one, as the latter involves a much larger group of people, including researchers and research participants who are not commonly viewed as bilinguals.

To differentiate between the various languages of multilingual individuals, scholars in bilingualism and SLA use such terms and abbreviations as 'first language' (L1), 'second language' (L2), 'third language' (L3), and so on. *Second language* often designates not only the language learned chronologically after the first, but any language learned later in life. Take, for instance, a speaker of Norwegian who studied English and German in secondary school and college, then married a French-speaker, moved to France, and began to study and use French for everyday purposes. A researcher interested in this speaker's acquisition of French might refer to it as an L2 in this case, even though technically it is an L4. A researcher interested in this speaker's English or German proficiency or attrition might also refer to the language in question as an L2. This is commonly the case when a study involves the L1 and one other language. If, on the other hand, the research design considers all languages an individual has studied, each will be referred to in sequential order as L1, L2, L3, and so forth. In accordance with the traditions of the field, in what follows, *first language*, or *L1*, will refer to the language or languages learned first, regardless of the speaker's current proficiency or dominance. *Second language*, or *L2*, will refer to a language learned later in life, whether or not it would be the second language in chronological terms. In discussions of speakers of three or more languages, I will also appeal to the term *LX*, which refers to any language but L1. *Linguistic repertoire*, a notion originally introduced by Gumperz (1964), will refer here to the totality of linguistic resources available to the individual.

SLA scholars also differentiate between *second (L2)* and *foreign (FL)* languages: The former refers to the language used in the speaker's daily life and the latter to the language studied in an educational context. (In other words, Japanese studying English in Japan are FL learners, and those who come to study it in the United States are L2 learners.) Albeit useful, this distinction is not always clear-cut: For instance, secondary and higher education establishments in the United States teach Spanish as a foreign language, while it is also the language of the largest linguistic minority in the country.

To distinguish between different types of engagement with language, Cook (1999, 2002) has advanced the notion of the *L2 user*. This term has a dual purpose: It avoids the notion of 'non-native speaker' and it offers a useful distinction between L2/FL learners (people who are in the process of learning a language in the classroom or by themselves) and L2 users (people who use a language learned later in life for real-life purposes). Accordingly, I will use the terms 'L2 learners' and 'FL learners' to refer to speakers who are studying a particular language but do not use it outside of the learning context, and the terms 'bilinguals,' 'multilinguals,' and 'L2 users' to refer to those who use the second language outside of the learning context, regardless of the level of proficiency they have in it.

Bi- and multilinguals can be subdivided further based on a number of factors. The three factors important for our purposes are age and context of acquisition and language dominance. In terms of dominance, *balanced* bilinguals are those who have a relatively similar proficiency in their languages, and *dominant* bilinguals are those who exhibit higher proficiency in one of the languages. Language dominance is a complex issue, as bilinguals may be balanced in some language areas and skills and dominant in others. For instance, many L2 users living in the L2 context are L2-dominant in their professional fields. They might experience difficulties when discussing or writing up professional matters in the L1 but still exhibit L1 dominance in other areas. Furthermore, dominance may not always mean higher proficiency: Speakers may have similar proficiency levels in two or more languages overall, but the one they use daily is much more easily activated and thus appears dominant.

In terms of the age of acquisition, *simultaneous* bilinguals are those who acquired two or more languages from birth, *childhood* bilinguals learned their additional language or languages in early or late childhood, and *late* or *post-puberty* bilinguals acquired additional languages as teenagers or adults. The age of acquisition is extremely important in understanding language learning outcomes. If all other factors, such as amount of exposure and interaction, are held equal, early, that is, simultaneous and childhood, bilinguals typically achieve higher levels of linguistic competence and proficiency than do late bilinguals.

In terms of the context of acquisition, we can talk about *coordinate* or *bicultural* bilinguals who learned their languages in distinct contexts, *compound* bilinguals who learned the languages in the same cultural and social context, and *subordinate* bilinguals who learned one language through the medium of another, most often in the classroom. In the past, these distinctions often appeared in discussions of bilingual memory, mental lexicon, and cognitive representations. It was suggested that coordinate bilinguals have fully distinct representations corresponding to their two languages, while compound bilinguals have two lexical items attached to one representation, and *subordinate* bilinguals attach a new lexical item to an already existing representation. Recent research has convincingly demonstrated that this was an oversimplified approach to the bilingual mental lexicon, and that different types of representations may coexist within the same lexicon, depending on the speaker's individual trajectory. At the same time, the distinction between naturalistic acquisition contexts and classroom contexts still holds, because only naturalistic exposure and second language socialization lead to development of coordinate – distinct and language-specific – representations, while classroom learning results in subordinate representation – mapping of new linguistic items onto the preexisting conceptual system.

This brief discussion does not and cannot do justice to the complex phenomenon of multilingualism, because human linguistic trajectories are extremely varied and intricate. The scholarship to date has focused predominantly on childhood and immigrant bilingualism, where adults move from one country to another. In reality, however, in the contemporary world of transcultural migration, individuals and groups of people often make multiple linguistic and cultural transitions that affect their linguistic repertoires. Russian Jews living in the Ukraine, for instance, grow up speaking Russian and may have some knowledge of Ukrainian, Yiddish, and a foreign language, most commonly English, French, or German. Upon emigration to Israel, their linguistic repertoire is transformed – they learn Hebrew, improve their English, and may also pick up some Arabic. Some may continue the immigrant journey out of Israel and into the United States, where their repertoire changes once again – they work in English and speak Russian to friends and family members, while Hebrew, Ukrainian, Yiddish, and Arabic undergo the process of attrition. What happens in the lives of many individuals, then, is the ongoing change in dominance, competence, and proficiency in all languages in question.

Traditionally, linguistics has treated L1 competence of individual speakers as a stable property, meaning that once the speaker's language system has 'matured,' linguistic competence would no longer be subject to change. A particularly strong version of this argument is presented in MacWhinney (1997), who suggests that once a local brain area "has been committed, it then begins to accept input data that lead toward a fine-tuning of the activation weights governing processing. If a second language is then to be imposed upon this pre-existing neural structure, it would directly interfere with the established set of weights. In fact, the use of transfer in second language learning allows the learner to avoid such catastrophic interference of L2 back upon L1" (p. 136). Recent research in SLA and bilingualism has challenged this assumption, demonstrating that L1 competence is a dynamic phenomenon that may be subject to both L2 influence and L1 attrition, evident in metalinguistic tasks and in L1 performance and processing (Cook, 2003; Pavlenko, 2000a; Schmid, 2002). Of particular importance is the fact that these effects may be visible even in learners and speakers of a foreign language who are still residing in their native language context (Kecskes & Papp, 2000; van Hell & Dijkstra, 2002).

These results have important implications for the typically homogeneous category of 'native speakers' that figures prominently in cross-linguistic research: The results indicate that people who know more than one language may perform differently from monolingual speakers in their L1, exhibiting different metalinguistic judgments and patterns of pronunciation, a slower rate of lexical processing, and more sophistication and

creativity in speaking and writing. The results also explain why many successful bi- and multilinguals judge themselves as not fully native-like in
all of their languages – they are measuring their own performance against
a monolingual yardstick (cf. Harris, 2004; Marx, 2003).

Not surprisingly, L2 competence and performance may also be distinct
from the monolingual speakers of the target language. L2 learners may
exhibit *L1 transfer*, that is, L1 influence on the acquisition and use of subsequent languages, including but not limited to incorporation of L1 structural
and lexical elements and perception of L2 input in terms of L1 categories.
The field of SLA has accumulated an impressive body of knowledge about
L1 transfer in phonology, morphosyntax, semantics, and pragmatics (Gass
& Selinker, 1992; Jarvis, 1998; Kellerman & Sharwood Smith, 1986; Odlin,
1989). The research suggests that L2 users may deviate from standard usage
in production, may impose L1 categories in perception and comprehension,
and may experience miscommunication when using the L2 both with other
L2 users and with speakers of the target language.

This is not to say that L2 users never approximate native speakers of
the language. Early research on the critical period hypothesis suggested
that ultimate (native-speaker-like) attainment was an insurmountable challenge for adult learners, at least in the area of syntax (Johnson & Newport,
1989). In contrast, recent research demonstrates that some late or post-
puberty bilinguals can perform within the native-speaker range in phonology (Bongaerts, 1999; Bongaerts et al., 1997; Hansen, 1995; Ioup et al., 1994),
morphosyntax (Birdsong, 1992; Ioup et al., 1994; White & Genesee, 1996),
sociolinguistic judgments (Ioup et al., 1994; Piller, 2002b), pragmatics (Ioup
et al., 1994), and conceptual framing (Pavlenko, 2003a). This means that on
a variety of tests and tasks some late bilinguals are indistinguishable from
native speakers and they can also pass for native speakers in some naturalistic contexts (Piller, 2002b).

Unfortunately, until recently the research on ultimate attainment has
focused predominantly on grammar and phonology, giving short shrift to
lexicon, semantics, pragmatics, and discourse. Indirectly, however, existence of a large contingent of writers, from Joseph Conrad to Ha Jin, who
write in a language they mastered in adulthood, suggests that native-
like mastery of the L2 lexicon, semantics, and discourse is also possible and that writing is an area where L2 users may at times be superior
to native speakers. Altogether, research on ultimate attainment suggests
that there is no conclusive support for the existence of a critical period
for second language learning. Rather, there exists an age-of-acquisition
effect that is mediated by the amount of exposure, interaction, motivation, and individual differences (Birdsong, 1999; Harley & Wang, 1997;
Marinova-Todd, Marshall & Snow, 2000). This effect is particularly pronounced in phonology and morphosyntax, and less visible in semantics
and pragmatics.

How long does it take to achieve a high level of proficiency in a second language? In view of tremendous variation in personal circumstances, motivation, educational settings, and living arrangements, there cannot be a definitive answer to this question. Research shows that linguistic minority children often require between four and eight years to achieve academic competence necessary to perform well in an L2 environment (Carrasquillo & Rodríguez, 2002). Similarly, adults may require three to seven years to achieve reasonable fluency in the second language (Birdsong, 1992, 1999; Larsen et al., 2002; Schrauf & Rubin, 2004).

Some adults may in fact reach an unusual level of proficiency in this time period. Jerzy Kosinski, later to become the first non-native speaker to win the National Book Award in Fiction, arrived in the United States in 1957 with little knowledge of English and published his first book in English less than three years later (Teicholz, 1993). His world-famous masterpiece *The Painted Bird* was published in 1965, eight years after his arrival. A year later, in 1966, another would-be American writer, Andrei Codrescu, landed on American soil, fresh from Romania and without any knowledge of English. His first book of English poetry appeared in 1970. Subsequently, Codrescu became an English professor, published dozens of volumes of poetry, fiction, essays, memoirs, and translations, and appeared on National Public Radio as an astute commentator on contemporary American mores. Undoubtedly, theirs are unique achievements, and most L2 learners do not aim to become a Kosinski or a Codrescu. Rather, numerous studies indicate that while successful second language acquisition is possible, it usually takes a long time and proceeds at different rates in different domains. It is common for L2 users to deviate from native speakers in performance and competence even after a decade or more in the target language context (Coppieters, 1987; Johnson & Newport, 1989), in particular if they continue to live their lives through the means of two or more languages.

More importantly, even in bi- and multilinguals who 'pass' for native speakers of more than one language, the two or more languages in the mental lexicon do not exist and function in a completely separate manner. Rather, there is a significant amount of positive and negative transfer between them, oftentimes referred to as bidirectional transfer (Pavlenko & Jarvis, 2002) or cross-linguistic influence (Cenoz et al., 2001; Odlin, 1989). In the presence of this cross-linguistic influence, even the most fluent bi- and multilinguals' metalinguistic judgments, conceptual representations, word associations, and language processing rates may be distinct from those of monolingual speakers.

To theorize this interaction between two or more languages, Cook (1991, 1992) proposed that people who know more than one language have a distinct compound state of mind – *multicompetence* – which is not equivalent to two monolingual states. A similar argument has been advanced by

Grosjean (1982, 1989, 1992, 1998), who repeatedly pointed out that a bilingual is not the sum of two complete or incomplete monolinguals in one body, but rather a specific speaker/hearer with a unique – but nevertheless complete – linguistic system. The competencies of this speaker/hearer are developed to the extent required by personal needs and the environment. The multicompetence view, now widely accepted in the field of bilingualism, will be adopted in this book. This framework will allow me to question assumptions made about bilingual participants and translators in cross-linguistic and cross-cultural research and to highlight the need to examine the judgments, perceptions, representations, and experiences of bi- and multilingual speakers in their own right.

1.3. Problems and challenges in cross-linguistic research on language and emotions

What are the implications of the findings discussed here for research on language and emotions? To begin with, they suggest that research findings may be impacted by the researcher's limited proficiency in the language in question or in the lingua franca. In his discussion of fieldwork in linguistic anthropology, Duranti (1997: 111) acknowledges this problem and cites an African anthropologist, Maxwell Owusu, who in 1978 had bitterly observed that Euro–Americans "continue to produce 'authoritative' monographs and essays on African cultures without seriously worrying about the degrading effects of their language deficiencies" (p. 327). And in research on language and emotions, it is not uncommon to see disagreements in cases where more than one anthropologist has worked on a particular language (Russell, 1991a).

Findings may also be affected by L1 transfer, where the categories of one's native language are imposed on the language in question. Russell (1991a) shows that in the past many ethnographers assumed the universality of emotions encoded in their own language and did not hesitate to attribute particular emotions to people they have observed. In some cases it is unclear whether categories 'discovered' by anthropologists were in any way meaningful for the speakers of a particular language. For instance, Levy (1973), whom Russell (1991a) interviewed about his work on emotions in Tahiti, admitted that he never attempted to find out whether his conclusions would be recognized as 'true' or even possible by Tahitians. In reporting, moreover – as Goddard (2002) insightfully points out – the practice of 'tagging' emotion concepts of other languages with single English glosses distorts the meanings of indigenous terms, equating them with English, and "excuses the analyst from engaging in deep conceptual analysis of English folk categories, which continue to be mistaken for objective categories of psychological reality" (p. 19).

Reliability of cross-linguistic research may also be affected by the idiosyncratic competencies of bilingual informants and translators. Take, for instance, Berlin and Kay's (1969) famous study of the color lexicon, which inspired the subsequent study of the emotion lexicon. The original color study relied on data from bilingual informants (typically one per language), from American linguists and anthropologists studying particular languages, and from obscure ethnographic studies, sometimes dating all the way to the beginning of the twentieth century. Many have since pointed out errors pertaining to less studied, less known languages. Yet even the data from languages like Russian, with a sizeable diaspora in the United States, sported several glaring errors, primarily because it was provided by a single English–Russian bilingual. For instance, 'orange' was translated as *kirpichnyi* (brick-like), a low-frequency term, rather than the basic term *oranzhevyi*, and 'purple' as *purpurnyi*, which is not only another low-frequency term but also a false cognate referring to 'blood-red' or 'dark-red' (the correct basic term being *fioletovyi*). Interestingly, Berlin and Kay (1969: 12) argued that they found it hard to believe that informants' bilingualism could distort the results, because it could not influence the placement of the color foci. By now we know that second language acquisition in adulthood may in fact influence color boundaries of the speakers (Andrews, 1994; Caskey-Sirmons & Hickerson, 1977). What is even more important is that single bilinguals and L2 users were relied on for information not just about the foci but also about 'basic' color terms and their meanings – and that as a result of this casual sloppiness, the data was flawed in a number of ways.[1]

Challenges to the reliability and validity of cross-linguistic research may also arise in the process of translation. As already mentioned earlier, reporting conventions in emotion research are beset with unacknowledged translation problems, among them the tendency to translate local emotion terms with single-word English glosses, as well as a lack of discussion of conceptual equivalence criteria for translation of emotion words in cross-linguistic projects (Goddard, 2002; Russell, 1991a; White, 1993). Russell (1991a) argues that a simple assurance from translators or collaborators about conceptual equivalence of the terms should not be considered sufficient, while Goddard (2002) offers several examples of misleading translations in large-scale emotion surveys.

Interesting evidence of multiple challenges also comes from studies of translation and interpretation in clinical contexts (Altarriba & Morier, 2004; Bolton, 2002; Drennan, Levett & Swartz, 1991; Erzinger, 1991; Marcos, 1979; Vasquez & Javier, 1991), where emotions function both as physical phenomena to be assessed (depression, for example) and as conversational phenomena that may interfere with the assessment (for example, Spanish-speaking patients' expectations for *simpatía* and *personalismo*, or conversational warmth). These studies reveal a number of potential error

---

[1] This example is offered not to question the credibility of an outstanding American psychologist who provided the authors with the terms, but to point to a problem with data elicited from any single informant, without an in-built verification procedure.

sources, including linguistic and conceptual non-equivalence and a mis-match in conversational assumptions. In the case of the latter, some respon-dents may espouse their own ideas of what is being sought (similar to Monsieur Robert, who believed that he was required to translate the Karani terms) and answer accordingly. In other cases, a lack of conversational cooperation prohibits respondents and patients from ever fully expressing their opinions and concerns (cf. Erzinger, 1991).

Furthermore, in both translation and interpretation, inaccuracies may stem from a power differential between doctors and patients and researchers and translators, or between researchers from Western and non-Western contexts, with the latter eager to collaborate on major research projects. In an insightful study of the production of a Xhosa version of the Beck Depression Inventory (BDI) in South Africa, Drennan, Levett, and Swartz (1991) show that translation is an intergroup enterprise fraught with potential conflict, where no amount of trusted procedures (such as back-translation, decentering, the bilingual approach, and the committee approach) would result in an adequate outcome. Of utmost concern to the researchers is the possibility that, to comply with the requirements, trans-lators may choose to avoid conflict and produce an instrument that glosses over translation problems. In the Drennan, Levett and Swartz study, back-translators from Xhosa to English did not acknowledge any problems in translation of BDI items such as 'I feel sad.' It turned out, however, that the suggested Xhosa equivalent of 'sad' (*khathazekile*) was back-translated as 'worried' by two translators and as 'depressed' by another. Further discus-sions with the translation committee members revealed that *khathazekile* was not necessarily the most appropriate translation equivalent, as it denotes worry with a connotation of depression, and that there are a num-ber of other Xhosa words that denote similar feelings, which needed to be discussed and compared before an appropriate equivalent could be chosen. More importantly, it also appeared that under the influence of English, the translators, urban speakers of Xhosa, had lost some conceptual distinctions found in the Xhosa spoken in rural locations.

Unfortunately, outside of the field of bilingualism, reporting of linguis-tic competence of both researchers and informants is not a common prac-tice in cross-linguistic research. This is not to say that it has never been acknowledged as an important issue. More than sixty years ago, a famous exchange on the use of native languages as fieldwork tools took place between Margaret Mead (1939) and Robert Lowie (1940). Mead pointed to a changing climate in the field, where more and more ethnographers were beginning to use the native language in their study rather than simply working through translators and interpreters. She also described her own experiences of linguistic fieldwork, where in some contexts she limited her investigation to contact with English-speaking informants, and in others combined work with informants with some use of the native language, studied through published grammars and dictionaries. Mead (1939: 192–193) cast suspicion on the fieldwork conducted exclusively through interpreters or in a contact language, pointing out numerous distortions that can come about, and argued that native languages must be used as a part of a field technique in ethnography. She paid particular attention to ways in which the use of an inappropriate lingua franca may heighten the power differential between researchers and informants, and stated that "it is reasonable that the fieldworker, when he uses only a contact language, should be asked to give an account of his contact language conditions in terms of its affect and implications" (1939: 194). Mead also offered a description of what, in her view, it meant to speak the native language. Discounting the need for 'linguistic virtuosity,' she put a premium on correct and idiomatic formulation of questions and instructions, establishment of rapport, and listening and understanding: "The field worker is not in the field to talk but to listen, not there to express complicated ideas of his own which will muddle and distort the natives' accounts" (Mead, 1939: 196).

Fully agreeing with the need to use native languages in fieldwork, Lowie vehemently objected to Mead's definition of language use. He pointed to the bias inherent in the assumption that a French civilization specialist should exhibit full mastery of French, but a scholar of an American Indian language could be satisfied with minimal competence. Drawing on his own fieldwork experiences in the Shoshone-speaking Lemhi reservation, he argued that while Mead was correct about the importance of understanding, she greatly underestimated the complexity of the task, for it is "one thing to grasp the simplified speech of an Indian trying to make himself clear to an ignorant outsider, but quite another to understand him in the midst of a rapid conversation of his peers" (Lowie, 1940: 82). Lowie is very clear that any adequate knowledge takes years of intensive study, and that ethnographers use interpreters not because they like to but because they have no other choice. In making these points, Lowie spoke from personal experience, as a German–English bilingual who arrived in the United States from Austria at the age of ten and as a result developed somewhat different competencies and representations in his two languages. (For an in-depth discussion, see Lowie, 1945.)

While disagreeing on how far an ethnographer should go in learning and using the native language, both Mead and Lowie were in complete agreement on the need to use native languages in research, on the fact that contact languages may bring in unexpected distortions and interferences, and on the need to discuss linguistic proficiency of both researchers and informants. Lowie (1940, 1945) also emphasized the challenges inherent in achieving both second language mastery and first language maintenance. Unfortunately, over the years the gist of the debate was lost in the fields engaged in cross-linguistic research. Researchers' language competence became, once again, a taboo topic, to surface only briefly when Mead's limited competence in Samoan gave rise to accusations that her informants misled her and performed a linguistic hoax, engaging in *tausuaga*, joking about sexual behavior, a speech act with which Mead was unfamiliar (Freeman, 1999).

Let us now consider briefly what assumptions are currently made about multicompetence and how it is reported in the three fields most engaged in research on language and emotions: anthropology, linguistics, and psychology.

Linguistic anthropologists typically conduct the fieldwork in the native language, with the help of monolingual, bilingual, and multilingual informants. In his excellent introduction to linguistic anthropology, Duranti (1997) underscores that accuracy and reliability of information are a major preoccupation for ethnographers. He criticizes the practice of underreporting, and in particular the lack of "an explicit discussion and documentation of the dialogical practices out of which descriptions are born" (p. 87). His text familiarizes students with several ethnographic methods of language data collection and verification and warns them to be cautious about ethnographies that are not accompanied by a discussion of data collection methods. (Similar concerns have been expressed over the years by Riesman [1977], White [1993], and others.)

Unfortunately, most existing anthropological work on language and emotions is written in a traditional manner, offering little if any information on how the data were analyzed and interpreted or on the researcher's and informants' multicompetence, as if to convey an aura of objectivity. Most existing ethnographies offer no information about the authors' own language competence and language choices made in the data collection procedure (cf. Besnier, 1995; Gerber, 1985; Myers, 1986; Schieffelin, 1976). Myers simply tells us that his fieldwork lasted altogether more than two years and that it took him a long time to understand what was said around him. Gerber offers a detailed discussion of the interviews with the informants, but does not mention what language or languages the interviews were conducted in. Lutz (1988) states that "the ethnographer's acquisition of language skills is the first and most significant way that access to local ethnopsychological knowledge is obtained" (p. 84), yet her own level of proficiency and understanding achieved at the end of a two-year period of ethnographic work on Ifaluk are not discussed anywhere in the book. Instead, Lutz offers a description of language areas – lexicon, metaphors, conversational assumptions – that can inform the inquiry into emotion talk (pp. 84–86), and a brief overview of methods – fieldnotes, participant observation, interviews, discourse, and definition elicitation – used in the process of data collection (pp. 43–46, 231). It remains unclear if the researcher always communicated in Ifaluk (and if so, how much miscommunication may have occurred), or if there was also a contact language involved in her investigation. Little discussion takes place of how the findings were verified with the local informants. (The fact that definitions of each term were collected from several individuals is disclosed only in a footnote, on p. 231.)

Importantly, this critique is offered not to cast doubt on the findings of the previous studies, nor to assert that native speakers have a privileged access to language. Rather, I argue for better reporting practices that offer readers more information on how the data were collected and verified, and what if any disagreements may have arisen in the interpretation of meanings of particular terms or practices. Excellent examples of such reporting are found in ethnographic studies by Briggs (1970), Heider (1991), Levy (1973), Riesman (1977), and Feld (1990) that offer detailed accounts of researchers' language learning experiences, levels of proficiency reached, and data collection and analysis. Levy and Riesman talk about investing two years in learning the local language and yet needing one more year in the local context to reach a reasonable level of proficiency. Feld reveals that by the end of his fieldwork he was able to compose his own songs in Kaluli and to manipulate various structural dimensions to test his hypotheses about constraints upon form. Heider offers both detailed accounts of his methodology and personal reflections on teaching anthropology courses in Indonesian. As we will see later, his study is also unique in highlighting the bilingualism of his participants.

In turn Briggs, who began her fieldwork without any knowledge of the language, offers an incomparable portrayal of the local community through the eyes of a linguistically incompetent adult whose speech blunders create opportunities for insight and understanding. Not many researchers followed in Briggs' footsteps in portraying themselves as blundering and incompetent, perhaps due to already deep-seated linguistic insecurities and anxieties. One of the leading scholars in the field of anthropology, James Clifford (1997: 22), likens talking about 'working in the local language' to opening a large can of worms:

Can one speak of *the* language, singular, as if there were only one? What does it mean to learn or use a language? How well can one learn a language in a few years? What about "stranger talk", specific kinds of discourse used with outsiders? What about many anthropologists' continuing reliance on translators and explicators for complex events, idioms, and texts? The subject deserves a full study, which I am not yet able to offer.

Instead of engaging in the kind of reflection called for by Clifford, the field has experienced a backlash against the push for better knowledge of the field language. For instance, Wikan, who studied emotional expression in Bali, argued that "it is not given that better language facility will necessarily improve the quality of our accounts or our understanding. There is even a danger it may have the opposite effect" (1993: 206).

This is precisely the position taken in the field of linguistics, where most fieldwork methods courses and textbooks begin with the assumption that competence in the target language is not required and that the researcher and the informant will speak a common language, either the researcher's language or a lingua franca. Budding linguists are offered an array of field methods developed to elicit information and intuitions from native speakers of the language (Burling, 1984; Newman & Ratliff, 2001a; Samarin, 1967; Vaux & Cooper, 1999). They are also told that professional training is more important than language fluency and that fieldworkers are superior to native speakers in their ability to define particular terms (cf. Samarin, 1967; for a dissenting voice, see Hale, 1969). Vaux and Cooper, for instance, teach beginning linguistics students that semantic and pragmatic distinctions can be easily discovered through interviews with informants where "the linguist will ask questions, the informant will answer them, and everything will go smoothly" (p. 51). As a result of such training, students are often satisfied working in a lingua franca and do not aim for conversational fluency in the target language. Newman recalls that when he was working on his dissertation on Tera, a Chadic language spoken in northern Nigeria, it never occurred to him that he ought to learn to speak the language. Instead, he carried out his elicitation work through Hausa, of which he had some rudimentary knowledge (Newman & Ratliff, 2001b).

Over the years, several scholars questioned the role and the use of the native speaker in linguistic research (Coulmas, 1981; Hale, 1969; Paikeday, 1985). Recently, a collection by Newman and Ratliff (2001a) brought these issues into the spotlight, pointing to cross-linguistic influence that may occur in bilingual informants' responses and to difficulties inherent in the use of a contact language in which both the researcher and the informant may have limited competence (Everett, 2001; McLaughlin & Sall, 2001). So far, however, these discussions have had little influence on reporting practices: At present, linguistic publications still lack information on data collection and verification methods or on the multicompetence of researchers and informants. To give a personal example, as one of the two Russian-speaking students in a linguistics program I was often contacted by my colleagues and classmates to offer 'native-speaker intuitions' on Russian. Not a single person asked me about my full linguistic repertoire (which in fact includes not only English and Russian but also Ukrainian, Polish, French, and Spanish) or wondered if my multilingualism and shifting dominance could impact these judgments. Not surprisingly, I have never found any acknowledgment of the bilingualism of 'native-speaking' informants in resulting publications on 'how Russian works.'

The field of psychology is perhaps most noteworthy for its detailed reporting of research design and methodology and the use of verification procedures, yet it functions similarly to the other two fields in terms of how little attention is paid to issues of multicompetence (outside of research on

bilingualism per se), and how much 'glossing over' the process of translation takes place. Cross-cultural emotion research on specific languages continues to rely on translated and back-translated research instruments, with
little if any attention being paid to the details of the translation procedure.
(For critiques, see Goddard, 2002; Shweder, 1994.) A noteworthy exception is Brandt & Boucher's (1986) cross-linguistic study, where extreme
care was taken to describe the translation procedure and to ensure the balance between translators, so that English would be the L1 for half of them
and the L2 for the other half.

Many studies also continue to treat bi- and multilingual collaborators,
interpreters, and participants as 'monolingual-like' speakers of the language or languages in question. For example, in a study by Tapia (2001),
an Emotional Intelligence Inventory was administered to Spanish–English
and English–Spanish bilinguals in Mexico City schools, yet we never learn
what language the Inventory was administered in (presumably English) or
whether there were any differences between the two groups of bilinguals,
who are simply treated as 'adolescents.' Based on what we know so far
about bilinguals' performance, one could expect different performances
on this self-report measure between the two groups of bilinguals, between
the groups responding in English and Spanish, and, possibly, between
monolingual and bilingual participants, considering that bilinguals often
exhibit higher metalinguistic and sociolinguistic awareness and superior
attention control (cf. Bialystok, 2001). Unfortunately, with the bilingual
population treated as if it were monolingual, these inquiry possibilities
remained unexplored.

The possibilities are similarly lost when bilinguals are treated as 'two
monolinguals in one body.' For instance, Davitz's (1969) classic study of
emotional experiences reported by Ugandan and American adolescents
did take advantage of the bilingualism of the Ugandan participants in
Luganda and English and asked whether the language of report made a
difference. The results indicated that it did not, and led Davitz to conclude
that definitions of emotional states "are not as susceptible to linguistic
influences as one might have expected" (p. 189). What he did not take into
consideration was that his informants were subordinate bilinguals, whose
knowledge of English piggybacked on Lugandan concepts, and thus they
were not likely to exhibit distinct types of knowledge in the two languages.

An equally problematic approach is to exclude non-native speakers of
the language as unrepresentative speakers. The most recent example of
this trend is offered in a study of French emotion terms by Niedenthal
and associates (2004) that excluded from the final analysis responses from
the L2 users of French, as well as responses from respondents who had
learned French after the age of five (p. 294), rather than considering these
speakers in separate categories as being distinct but equally interesting and
legitimate speakers of French.

We see, then, that research conducted in these diverse fields may be framed differently in theoretical and methodological terms, yet it is similar in neglecting both the multicompetence of researchers and participants and also the problems inherent in the processes of translation and interpretation. Current studies of language and emotion offer little if any explicit information on the researchers' proficiency in the language or languages in question, the degree and kind of bilingualism of the informants and translators, and the methods of verification used in data elicitation and translation. These studies lack any discussion of how linguistic histories and competencies of the people involved in the research process could impact the findings. At best, we are told that collection instruments were subject to the back-translation procedure, which is supposed to make them fully reliable. (See, however, Drennan et al., 1991; Goddard, 2002.) This glossing over of the linguistic aspect of cross-linguistic research is quite striking given the attention paid to other aspects of research design and data analysis, including elicitation procedures, assessment measures, and statistical methods. Yet it is not surprising: In Western (and in particular North American) academia, this failure is born out of deep discomfort – perhaps even insecurity – concerning second-language proficiency, oftentimes coupled with linguistic arrogance.

This contradictory combination of linguistic arrogance and insecurity is particularly visible in the double standard applied to the learning of a language by immigrants and guest workers as compared to the language competence of linguistic fieldworkers. Immigrants are shown to take decades to move out of the so-called basic variety of their adopted language to an intermediate or advanced level of proficiency (Perdue, 1993). In linguistic fieldwork, by contrast, it is commonly assumed that the level of proficiency necessary for competent research can be reached in six months or so (Everett, 2001). In other words, while non-native speakers in general are commonly viewed as speakers with 'incomplete competence' and faulty metalinguistic judgments (cf. Johnson & Newport, 1989), linguists and linguistic anthropologists are assumed to have a privileged status with regard to other languages. In reality, however, observers with limited degrees of proficiency in another language may be quite perceptive of the vocal cues or facial expressions of fluent speakers, but they cannot fully evaluate the intricacies of the lexicon and categorization systems of the language and thus become dependent on the judgments of their monolingual and bilingual informants. Yet this human dimension of cross-linguistic inquiry into emotion concepts remains in the shadows – perhaps because it is ill-mannered to question the linguistic proficiency of ethnographers who at times take significant personal risks to pursue their topics, or because it is impolite to point to the monolingualism of linguists or psychologists conducting large cross-linguistic studies. It is also possible that because cross-linguistic inquiry into emotion talk is still in its early stages – with methodologies still being bandied about – discussion of these issues has been premature until now. The time has come, however, to consider how the data comes to be, and what factors may impact the validity and reliability of the data on emotion lexicon and discourse.

1.4. Conclusions

I would like to underscore that my goal is not to be irreverent or disrespectful of other scholars' efforts, nor to argue that native speakers have unique and privileged insights. To the contrary, if anything I assert 'the non-native speaker privilege' (Kramsch, 1997) – the privilege of L2 users, bi- and multilinguals with a skewed or double vision – as critical for cross-linguistic research. This privilege was recognized more than sixty years ago by Robert Lowie (1945), who stated that while the bilingual may be the sociologist's 'marginal man' with shortcomings in both languages, "by compensation he has insights not granted in quite so vivid a manner to others. He cannot help constantly comparing modes of expression; and what others recognize as an abstract principle is to him an ever-recurring vital experience – the incommensurability of different languages" (p. 257).

Just as I aim to validate, not discount, bilingual researchers, I argue for future inclusion of bi- and multilingual participants who should not be viewed as speakers with 'compromised competence.' Instead, variation stemming from speakers' linguistic histories has to be taken into account in research on language, just as are differences stemming from age, gender, or socioeconomic background. Rather than being an afterthought, bilinguals' perspectives can come to the foreground of emotions research, complementing semantic and conceptual analyses with insights derived from subjective experiences (Wierzbicka, 2004).

I also advocate the use of better reporting practices, because the cross-linguistic data we discuss and the cross-linguistic analyses we conduct are only as good as the bilingualism of the informants and analysts, the communication between them, and the verification procedure used. Similarly, I advocate the use of more sensitive translation procedures that would go beyond the 'tagging' of indigenous concepts with English glosses or the use of closest single-word equivalents. I will return to these methodological issues in my final chapter and make specific recommendations for future research on emotional expression.

It is my hope that this book will offer novice researchers useful guidance and advice on how we can 'factor' bilingualism into emotions research both as a topic and as a method. What is at issue here is not the boundary around the 'idealized monolingual competence' and the right and ability to study it, but something much more fundamental – a consideration of how we conduct our research in the increasingly multilingual world.

2

Emotions in the study of multilingualism: Framing the questions

> Languages not only inspire loyalty, they also provoke fear, hatred, resentment, jealousy, love, euphoria – the entire gamut of human emotion. From the undergraduate whose difficulties with *ser* and *estar* make him complain that he "hates Spanish", to the exile who clasps her mother tongue in a tight embrace, tongue ties are every bit as knotty as our other affections.
>
> (Pérez Firmat, 2003: 3)

In his beautiful literary treatise on bilingual Spanish and Hispanic writers, Pérez Firmat, a bilingual writer himself, raises several questions that are crucial to a full understanding of the phenomenon of bilingualism and yet are unexamined in the scholarly field that studies it. What is the nature of the emotional bonds that tie individuals to their languages? How do these ties influence self-expression? What are the consequences of living in exile, away not only from one's country but also from one's language? What happens when one falls in love across a language boundary?

These questions resonate profoundly with me, a Russian Jewish immigrant who has lived for more than a decade in the United States. The words of my native language, Russian, brim with intimacy and familiarity. They are permeated with memories of my childhood and youth, friendships and intimate relationships, happiness and disappointments. For me, Russian has no neutral words – each one channels voices, each one inspires feelings. Yet it is also a language that attempted to constrain and obliterate me as a Jew, to tie me down as a woman, to render me voiceless, a mute slave to a hated regime. To abandon Russian means to embrace freedom. I can talk and write without hearing echoes of things I should not be saying. I can be me. English is a language that offered me that freedom, and yet it is also my second language, whose words – in the unforgettable terms of another fellow bilingual, Julia Kristeva – make us strangers to ourselves.

Each language, in Pérez Firmat's words, ties me differently, with bonds I cannot shake loose. And so, on a daily basis, I have no choice but to use both English and Russian when talking about emotions. "I love you," I whisper to my English-speaking partner. "*Babulechka, ia tak skuchaiu po tebe* (Grandma, I miss you so much)," I tenderly say on the phone to my Russian-speaking grandmother. In these, as in many other cases, my language choices are determined by the proficiency of my interlocutors. Yet many of my interlocutors are also bilingual, and in these cases my emotion talk becomes bilingual as well. "Who is my sweet little *zaichik* (bunny)?" I coo to my son. "*Mne nuzhna* (I need) privacy, can we talk later?" I snap at my mother. What factors govern this code-switching in emotion talk? Are emotion and emotion-laden terms in bilinguals' languages perfectly equivalent or are they represented differently? Do bilinguals have different emotional reactions to their respective languages? Do their emotional linguistic bonds influence their language choices? Are their actual feelings affected by the language they speak? I argued in Chapter 1 that considering multilingualism as a theoretical and methodological issue would enrich the interdisciplinary research on language and emotions. In this chapter I aim to show that a similar need exists in the fields of second language acquisition and bilingualism, where emotions and emotional expression have not yet been comprehensively considered.

To be adequately studied, any scientific problem must be adequately formulated. This chapter surveys several attempts that have been made throughout the twentieth century to relate emotions and multilingualism. I begin with the early trend to pathologize bilingualism by linking it to feelings of anomie and shame and to problems in emotional development. Then I discuss classic studies in polyglot psychoanalysis that have connected emotions, language, and memory, giving birth to contemporary studies of bilingual autobiographic memory and bilingual behaviors in therapy. Next, I look at studies that linked emotions to second language learning outcomes through affective factors such as attitudes and anxiety. I argue that the extremely narrow understanding of the relationship between emotions and multilingualism, still prevalent in the study of second language acquisition and bilingualism, makes it impossible to answer the questions raised in the beginning of this chapter and I point to a few studies that over the years attempted to steer the research into new directions. Then I describe a study of bilingualism and emotions conducted by myself jointly with Jean-Marc Dewaele (Dewaele & Pavlenko, 2001–2003), the findings of which will be invoked in several chapters. I end this chapter by outlining the structure of the rest of the book.

2.1. Bilingualism and psychopathology

A worldwide phenomenon common for the human condition since antiquity, bi- and multilingualism continues to elicit a variety of reactions, depending on time and place. In multilingual societies, speaking more than one language is viewed as part of everyday life, not worthy of further consideration. In traditionally monolingual communities, on the other hand, bilinguals are often viewed with suspicion either as linguistic and cultural hybrids who may be in conflict with themselves, or as individuals whose shifting linguistic allegiances imply shifting political allegiances and moral commitments. These divergent attitudes were apparent throughout the twentieth century as the field of bilingualism came into existence. In his 1899 treatise *Language and Linguistic Method*, Laurie asserted:

If it were possible for a child or boy to live in two languages at once equally well, so much the worse for him. His intellectual and spiritual growth would not thereby be doubled, but halved. Unity of mind and character would have great difficulty in asserting itself in such circumstances. (p. 18)

This eloquent statement, which predated and informed most of the twentieth-century bilingualism debates, exposes the locus of the problem – a deep and pervasive belief that bilinguals are people with two conflicting personalities who thus are at a mental and emotional disadvantage. Interestingly, this view rarely applied to all bi- and multilinguals. Rather, from the moment of their inception, the fields of linguistics and psychology (and later bilingualism) were characterized by a double standard, both in Europe and in North America. 'Elite bilingualism' – that is, bilingualism of the upper and middle classes – was typically presented as a positive phenomenon. This attitude is seen in the encouragement of bi- and multilingualism among the children of the elite, and in European research on childhood bilingualism and second language learning (Epstein, 1915; Pavlovitch, 1920; Ronjat, 1913).

In contrast, bilingualism of immigrant and linguistic minority children was commonly associated with mental retardation, moral inferiority, split identity, and linguistic shortcomings. For example, studies of Welsh–English bilingual children demonstrated that they performed worse on a variety of tasks than monolingual children of the same age, particularly in rural areas (Saer, 1924; Saer, Smith & Hughes, 1924; Smith, 1923). To explain these results, Saer (1924) posited affective differences between rural children (who experienced an emotional conflict between Welsh and English) and urban children (who resolved this conflict at an early age). Smith (1923) echoing Laurie, further argued that because words are steeped in emotions and a life to be lived – and because we have not two lives but one – we can have only one language.

The conflicting attitudes toward bilingualism are also visible in the U.S. debates on foreign language education that took place during and after World War I. The nineteenth and early twentieth centuries in the United States were marked by tolerance toward linguistic diversity and bilingual education establishments, which allowed immigrants, in particular German–Americans, to maintain their native languages and to transmit them to their children and grandchildren. With the advent of the Great Migration wave of 1880–1924 and in particular with the United States entry in World War I, this complacent attitude gave way to a xenophobic movement that framed bilingualism as an un-American phenomenon and required incoming immigrants to not only learn English but also to abandon their native languages if they wanted to be 'real Americans,' because the United States could have but one language (Pavlenko, 2002a, 2003b). Nowhere did the double standard come across as clearly as in the address given at the War Time conference of Modern Language Teachers by Marian Whitney, a Vassar College professor. She stated:

In so far as teaching foreign languages in our elementary schools has been a means of keeping a child of foreign birth in the language and ideals of his family and tradition, I think it a bad thing; but to teach young Americans French, German or Spanish at an age when their oral and verbal memory is keen and when languages come easily, is a good thing. (Whitney, 1918: 11–12)

With time, the negative view of bilingualism permeated North American linguistics, psychology, education, and sociology. Scholars came to consider the bilingual to be a 'marginal man' (Bossard, 1945; Goldberg, 1941) and pointed to adverse effects of bilingualism on children's cognitive, linguistic, and emotional development (Anastasi & Cordova, 1953; Bossard, 1945; Smith, 1931, 1939; Spoerl, 1943; Yoshioka, 1929; for a dissenting opinion see Arsenian, 1937, 1945).

In Germany, with the rise of the Nazi regime which extolled the superiority of German to all other languages, bilingualism acquired a similarly negative connotation and became associated exclusively with Jews and other ethnic minorities (Henss, 1931; Müller, 1934; Sander, 1934; Schmidt-Rohr, 1932, 1933, 1936; Weisgerber, 1929, 1933). Thus, in a paper entitled *Bilingualism as a pedagogical problem*, Henss (1931) contended that bilinguals experience a pathological inner split and that in their struggle to become one they suffer intellectual and moral deterioration. Müller (1934) wrote that the Polish–German population of Upper Silesia suffered from mental inferiority as a result of their bilingualism. Sander (1934) referred to the 'bilinguality of feelings' and the 'mercenary relativism' of bilinguals who switch principles and values as they switch languages.

As seen in these examples, early writings on bilingualism underscored its negative effects not only for intelligence and cognition but also for emotional well-being. They attempted to pathologize bilingualism (at least in immigrants and linguistic minorities) and link it to feelings of anomie, alienation, apathy, cognitive dissonance, and emotional vulnerability. *Anomie*, the term originally introduced by the French sociologist Durkheim (1897), connotes the feelings of anxiety, social isolation, personal disorientation, and rootlessness experienced by people who are in transition from one social group to another. Originally the term was used to describe the temporary condition of social deregulation experienced by those who move from one social strata to another or suffer from widowhood, separation, or divorce. Child's (1943) study of the Italian–American community in New York suggested that the notion of emotional conflict also applies to the children of immigrants, who experience frustration and bewilderment brought on by conflicting linguistic and cultural loyalties. Spoerl's (1943) study of college students similarly attributed the emotional maladjustment of bilingual students to culture conflicts experienced by the children of immigrants and to resulting family disharmony and social frustration. Bossard (1945) noted that "under the most fortunate circumstances, the bilingual situation appears to involve a nervous strain" (p. 701), in terms of both language production and family relationships, with children experiencing resentment or even hatred toward the parents who can't keep pace in the use of English.

Notably, while Saer (1924), Smith (1931), and others argued that bilingualism creates an internal mental and emotional conflict, Child (1943), Spoerl (1943), and Bossard (1945) shifted the locus of the problem outside the individual, stating that "the emotional maladjustment of the bilingual student is environmentally determined and is not the result of mental conflict" (Spoerl, 1943: 56). This perspective was maintained in the later part of the century. For instance, Diebold (1968) reviewed several studies that linked early bilingualism to emotional maladjustment and concluded that the observed crisis in social and personal identity is brought on by pressures from the "sociologically dominant monolingual society within which the bicultural community is stigmatized as socially inferior and to which its bilingualism (historically viewed) is itself an assimilative response" (p. 239).

The relationship between anomie and bilingualism was extensively researched by Lambert and associates (Lambert, 1967; Lambert & Aellen, 1969). They expanded the meaning of the term *anomie* to denote not only the immigrant's frustration, but also the chagrin or regret bilinguals experience as they lose their ties to one group, and the fearful anticipation they experience upon entering a relatively new one (Lambert, Just, & Segalowitz, 1970: 274). To give an example, Lambert (1967) discussed the case of American students in a six-week intensive French program who began to experience anomie as they became more skilled in the language. As a result, they attempted to seek out occasions to use English, even though they had pledged to use only French until the end of the course. Echoing Diebold's (1968) conclusions, the work by Lambert and associates suggested that anomie has social and not linguistic origins and that long-term anomie would be experienced only in contexts where the speakers' two languages and cultures are not valued and dual allegiances are not possible.

The view of bilingualism as a problem of split identity or two incompatible identities is also invoked in another set of terms used to refer to bilinguals – schizoglossia and schizophrenia. Baetens Beardsmore (1982) borrows Haugen's (1962) term *schizoglossia* – which originally referred to the linguistic insecurity of speakers of more than one linguistic variety – to refer to bilinguals' apprehension and anxiety about non-normative linguistic elements in their own speech as compared to the imaginary standard. *Schizophrenia*, used metaphorically, refers to the problems brought on by culture shock, by cognitive, linguistic, and cultural dissonance, by conflicting definitions of reality, and by different social roles occupied by bicultural bilinguals (Amati-Mehler, Argentieri & Canestri, 1993; Clarke, 1976; Todorov, 1994).

Clarke (1976) offers an expanded version of this argument, framing second language learning as "a clash of consciousness, in which double bind phenomena are viewed as the result of differences between culturally determined definitions of reality" (p. 382). Clarke's discussion likens foreign students in the United States to schizophrenic patients, in that their low levels of communicative competence result in threatening and anxiety-producing social encounters and force them to employ defense mechanisms to reduce the trauma. In Clarke's view this conflict stems from the fact that the students typically come from more traditional societies and have trouble adjusting to modernity, progress, and the bewildering pace of American life. Notably, this ethnocentric explanation does not consider the xenophobia and discrimination foreign students are likely to encounter.

It is important to underscore here that the negative view of bilingualism was not the only perspective either in Europe or in North America in the early and mid-twentieth century. In many settings, bi- and multilingualism was viewed as a positive phenomenon or simply as the norm. Rather, I argue that in the first half of the century, the negative perspective was most commonly taken in theorizing the relationship between bilingualism and emotions or for that matter, cognition. As time went by and evidence accumulated, the attempts to pathologize bilingualism in scholarly work became fewer and farther between. Most of these attempts stemmed from a monolingual view of bilinguals as two individuals in one body, in conflict with each other. A growing realization of the pervasiveness of bi- and multilingualism and hybridity – and of the fact that many bilinguals interact predominantly with other bilinguals and thus are not pulled in different directions by monolingual worlds – resulted in rejection of an essentialized link between bilingualism and affective disturbances.

The current consensus in the field, based on decades of research, is that bilingualism per se is not the cause of problems in emotional and social adjustment of immigrant and linguistic-minority children (Baker, 2000: 78). It is fair to point out, however, that the opposite view is still alive and well outside of the field and that the terms 'anomie' and 'schizophrenia' pop up time and again in anti-immigration and anti-bilingualism discourses. For instance, British Home Secretary David Blunkett (2002) has recently argued that the use of English – rather than the native language – in Asian–British households would help "overcome the schizophrenia which bedevils generational relationships" in immigrant families.

2.2. Polyglot psychoanalysis

A somewhat different understanding of the relationship between individuals' emotions and multiple languages emerged in the field of psychoanalysis. The interest in multilingualism in this field is not surprising: Psychoanalysis was founded in multilingual Europe and many of the early psychoanalysts (including Freud and his disciples) underwent and practiced analysis in more than one language, commonly considering dilemmas presented by multilingual patients. Ferenczi (1916) pointed to differences in bilinguals' perceptions of obscene words in a mother tongue versus a second language. Freud (1893; Breuer & Freud, 1895) had written extensively about the mysterious case of Anna O., who lost her mother tongue German for eighteen months, and communicated exclusively in her other languages, English, French, and Italian. Freud and his followers also analyzed and discussed the case of the Wolf Man, a Russian prince who grew up speaking Russian, English, and German and whose analysis took place in German (Amati-Mehler et al., 1993).

Interest in the emotional and cognitive underpinnings of multilingualism was shared by psychoanalysts around the world. In Palestine, Velikovsky (1934) examined the multilingual wordplay in the dreams of his patients who spoke Hebrew in combination with Arabic, German, Yiddish, Russian, Ukrainian, and a variety of other languages. In England, Stengel (1939) considered both the influence of second language learning on thought and the differences in representation of translation equivalents in bilinguals' languages. And in France, Bonaparte (1945), one of Freud's favorite disciples, revealed that as a child she wrote stories in her second language, English, to put some distance between herself and traumatic events she witnessed.

These reflections took a new turn at the end of World War II when, as a result of an unprecedented wave of displacement and global migration, many German analysts found themselves working in English or Spanish with equally multilingual patients. For instance, Eduardo Krapf (1955), working in Argentina, practiced psychoanalysis in Spanish, English, German, and French, with a working knowledge of Italian and Portuguese thrown into the mix. He and others began to wonder about the distinct relationships patients formed with their languages and about ways in which language choice in psychoanalysis can affect the outcome. This inquiry resulted in three classic papers that laid the foundation of the current understanding of the relationship between language and emotions in bilingual psychoanalysis.

In the first of these papers, German–English bilingual Edith Buxbaum (1949) demonstrated that the mother tongue was the deep-seated root of anxiety for two of her patients, Anna and Bertha, who were born in Germany and came to the United States as adolescents. Both women chose to undergo analysis in English, but it was the use of German that allowed the analyst to uncover the reasons for their anxieties. In Anna's associations, 'sausages' played a major part. Yet only when the word was translated into German as *Blutwurst* was she able to remember several sexual incidents and psychic traumas of her childhood. Similarly, in Bertha's case, the use of German – and in particular the words *Fenster* (window) and *fensterln* (a courting custom in which a young man appears beneath the window of a girl of his choice) – brought back feelings and desires Bertha tried to repress by switching into English. In the analyst's view, both women refused to speak their native tongue because it "contained the keywords to their repressed fantasies and memories" (p. 287). They used the new language, English, as a mechanism of defense.

Buxbaum's conclusions echoed an earlier remark by Erikson (1946), who suggested that persistent use of a second language by the patient in a multilingual analytic relationship may reflect an attempt to repress a past ego identity. A similar situation was described by Greenson (1950), whose patient, an immigrant to the United States from Austria, refused to discuss her mother in German. Initially, upon encountering linguistic difficulties in English, she was quite willing to switch to German, but with time she became reluctant to do so. She admitted to her therapist: "I am afraid. I don't want to talk German. I have the feeling that talking in German I shall have to remember something I wanted to forget" (p. 19). Eventually, the use of German led her to recapture her feelings about her mother, whom she found a "loathsome creature" (p. 19). Her anxieties translated into a sense of a dual self: "In German I am a scared, dirty child; in English I am a nervous, refined woman" (p. 19). Greenson agreed with Buxbaum that the use of the native language in therapy serves to break through the patient's emotional defenses, while the use of a second language allows the patient to create a new persona and build up a system of defense against childhood memories and experiences.

Krapf (1955) criticized the arguments of the two analysts, pointing out that their patients lived in the United States, where they experienced high pressure to assimilate both culturally and linguistically. Consequently, their language choices may not have been fully voluntary. In contrast, in Argentina where he himself practiced, cosmopolitan tolerance and multilingualism were the way of life, and immigrants could continue to use their native languages "without being ostracized as alien, queer, or disloyal" (Krapf, 1955: 345). Using more than one language during psychoanalysis was accepted practice among multilingual analysts and patients, and one could be confident that the patients' choices were individual rather than socially imposed decisions. Krapf's observations led him to agree with Buxbaum that patients often appeal to the second or third language to resist anxiety and to avoid talking about painful, traumatizing, or embarrassing topics. At the same time, he disagreed with the usefulness of returning to the first learned language and illustrated his argument with two clinical cases where an identity created in a second language was a healthy one for his patients. Despite some differences in interpretation, early psychoanalysts were in agreement on the main premise – that the very condition of bi- and multilingualism is a cause of a potential identity split. Working from a classical drive/conflict model, they posited that the native language functions as a vehicle for reviving the past, while the second language offers a ready defense system and allows patients to repress negative feelings associated with early life (Foster, 1996a).

A different interplay between the two languages was posited in psychoanalytic approaches to the study of second language acquisition. Guiora and associates (Guiora, Brannon & Dull, 1972; Guiora et al., 1972; Guiora et al., 1980) advanced an account of second language learning driven by a *language ego*, which evolves during native language development. They argued that children learn languages in an easy manner because their language ego is still flexible. After puberty, the ego becomes protective and defensive and may become 'threatened' by the new language – a phenomenon that makes second language learning essentially a traumatic experience and accounts for difficulties experienced by adults in the process of L2 learning and acquisition of a second identity.

These arguments made a significant impact on the field of foreign and second language teaching, where efforts have been made to reduce the learners' defenses and barriers. These efforts have been particularly pronounced in the counseling learning approach, developed in the United States by Charles Curran (1976), and in *Suggestopedia*, developed in Bulgaria by psychologist Georgi Lozanov (1979) and popular in Eastern Europe and in the West in the 1970s and 1980s. At the same time, the language ego hypothesis did not make a lasting impact on theory development in bilingualism and second language acquisition. (See, however, Arnold, 1999; Ehrman, 1996.) In contrast, Buxbaum's (1949), Greenson's (1950), and Krapf's (1955) case studies exerted a profound effect on bilingualism and emotions research, firmly establishing the view of the first language as the language of emotions and the second as the language of distance and detachment, a view that would dominate clinical and psychological studies in the later part of the century. This view and the metaphor of a 'split identity,' an identity 'in-between,' continue to pervade contemporary scholarly and personal writing on second language learning and bilingualism (Amati-Mehler et al., 1993; Hoffman, 1989; Todorov, 1994; Zhengdao Ye, 2004). In Chapters 5, 6, and 7, I will revisit these metaphors and reexamine them in view of the findings of recent research in autobiographic memory, psycholinguistics, and discursive psychology.

2.3. Language attitudes

From the perspective of research on bilingualism and emotions, the early psychoanalytic investigations – while innovative and intriguing – lacked a larger sociopolitical, sociocultural, and socioeconomic context where multilinguals' languages acquired different meanings and values. In their close adherence to the classic Freudian paradigm, the three psychoanalysts did not mention that their patients' reluctance to use German may have been affected not only by sex-related events from early childhood but also by war traumas and by the anti-German atmosphere in the United States. (Krapf, 1955, made a brief reference to the war in discussing a Jewish patient of his.) The 'language attitudes' approach, which emerged in the fields of bilingualism and sociolinguistics, took a closer look at the individual attitudes and tied them to language learning outcomes.

Gardner and Lambert (1959) were the first to demonstrate a positive and statistically significant relationship between motivation, positive attitudes toward the L2 and its speakers, and mastery of L2 aspects that are less susceptible to conscious manipulation (for instance, phonology). Carroll (1962) showed that, after aptitude, attitudes were the second most important set of variables for predicting L2 learning achievement. As time went by, language attitudes emerged as one of the key affective variables that explained L2 learning outcomes through their links to motivation. *Attitudes* are commonly understood as underlying psychological predispositions to act or evaluate behavior in a certain way, and *motivation* as the combination of desire and effort to achieve a particular goal, which linked individuals' rationales for particular activities with the range of behaviors and degree of effort employed in achieving their goals (Gardner, 1985). Gardner and Lambert (1972) distinguished between two types of attitudes and the resulting motivation: *integrative* with the learner being motivated by his or her desire to identify with the L2 group, and *instrumental* with the learner being motivated to learn the L2 for utilitarian, practical purposes. The authors suggested that integrative attitudes or a combination of integrative and instrumental attitudes will lead to better results in the long run.

Several models of second language acquisition incorporated attitudes as an important affective factor that can account for differences in L2 learning outcomes (Baker, 1992; Gardner, 1980, 1985, 1988; Gardner & Lambert, 1972; Krashen, 1977; Schumann, 1978). The best known among them is the Monitor Model (Krashen, 1977, 1981, 1994), the first comprehensive theory of second language acquisition. One of the five components of the Monitor Model is the Affective Filter, which comprises such factors as attitudes, motivation, and anxiety. The Affective Filter Hypothesis states that affective factors do not impact language acquisition directly, but that they either facilitate or prevent input from reaching the language acquisition device (Krashen, 1994). Learners with positive attitudes and low anxiety will have a 'low filter' and will thus reach high proficiency, while learners with negative attitudes and high anxiety will have a 'high filter' that will impede the input and, consequently, the L2 learning.

Over the years, several researchers questioned the linear relationship between attitudes, motivation, and L2 learning outcomes, arguing that in some cases instrumental motivation may be stronger than integrative and in others the L2 may be successfully appropriated despite the negative attitudes toward its speakers (Baker, 1992; Ellis, 1994; Larsen-Freeman & Long, 1991). Larsen-Freeman (2001) pointed out that attitudes are socially constructed and cannot be understood as individual constructs, and the relationship between attitudes and achievement may be reciprocal rather than unidirectional. Both Baker (1992) and Husband and Saifullah-Khan (1982) argued that language attitudes are neither unitary nor stable and need to be analyzed at different levels of social organization, taking into consideration historical processes and power relationships. Critics also questioned the reliability and validity of questionnaire-based methodologies in language attitudes research (Gass & Selinker, 1994; Larsen-Freeman & Long, 1991). The definitions of various constructs, and the questions that resulted, were both deemed ambiguous, making it unclear what was being measured in a particular case.

Current research has addressed some of these criticisms, approaching attitudes and motivation as dynamic phenomena (cf. Dörnyei, 2001), but it has not yet made sufficient links with language ideology research to advance a comprehensive account of sociocultural and sociopolitical construction of FL and L2 learning attitudes and motivation. (For an expanded version of this argument, see Kubota, Austin & Saito-Abbott, 2003; Pavlenko, 2002b.) In Chapter 7, I will revisit research on affective variables, to argue that the narrow constructs of 'motivation' and 'attitudes' do not capture the diversity of affective tongue ties and the range of emotions elicited by the languages we speak and those that speak to us. I will offer an alternative approach that links the social and the personal and highlights the impact of societal ideologies of language and identity on individual linguistic decision making.

2.4. Language learning and anxiety

Several early authors, among them Stengel (1939), Bossard (1945), and Gardner and Lambert (1959), acknowledged that second language learning and use are also linked to feelings of anxiety, shame, and embarassment. With time, anxiety came to occupy the leading position among affective factors in second language acquisition as the one emotion that most pervasively influences the learning process (Arnold, 1999; Chastain, 1975; Gardner & MacIntyre, 1993; Scovel, 1978). *Affective factors* in SLA began to be defined as factors that involve "emotional reactions and motivations of the learner; they signal the arousal of the limbic system and its direct intervention in the task of learning" (Scovel, 1978: 131). *Anxiety* is commonly seen as a state of apprehension and vague fear linked only indirectly to the object in question, be it the language itself or the learning situation (Scovel, 1978).

Researchers differentiate between *facilitating* and *debilitating* anxiety, with the former motivating the learner 'to fight' the learning task and the latter 'to flee,' that is, to postpone homework, engage in escapist activities, or cut classes (Bailey, 1983; Chastain, 1975; Kleinmann, 1977; Scovel, 1978). They also distinguish between *trait anxiety*, a stable personality characteristic, and *state anxiety*, a transient, situation-specific response to a particular anxiety-provoking stimulus. Until recently, research has mainly focused on state anxiety, defining *foreign language learning anxiety* as "the feeling of tension and apprehension specifically associated with second language contexts, including speaking, listening, and learning" (MacIntyre & Gardner, 1994: 284). This feeling stems from perceived threats to the student's sense of security or self-esteem, and from fear of failure, fear of negative evaluation, and apprehensions about communicating in a language in which one may appear incompetent or ridiculous. Richard Watson (1995), an American philosopher who at a mature age embarked on a journey to learn French, offers an incomparable description of foreign language learning anxiety:

I was more tense [in class] than I have ever been in my life or ever want to be again.The first time I ever climbed a mountain wall with hundreds of feet of exposure below me, that time we arrived back at the entrance of a cave to find a wall of water roaring in and had to crawl downstream as fast as we could for a long distance to clamber up into passages above water level, my Ph.D. oral exam – none of those times could begin to compete with the state of tension I was enduring now. And how am I to characterize or express adequately my sensations when with every indication of justified anger and disgust, The Professor called me an idiot and an imbecile? (Watson, 1995: 39)

SLA scholars developed a number of scales to measure foreign language anxieties, for example the French Class Anxiety Scale (Gardner, 1985; Gardner & Smythe, 1975), the Foreign Language Classroom Anxiety Scale (Horwitz, Horwitz, & Cope, 1986), or the Spanish Use Anxiety Scale (Muchnick & Wolfe, 1982). Several studies using these scales found correlations between students' anxiety levels and achievement (Gardner & MacIntyre, 1993; Horwitz, 1986, 2001; Horwitz, Horwitz, & Cope, 1986; MacIntyre & Gardner, 1989). Gardner and MacIntyre (1993) reported that language anxiety is the best single correlate of foreign language achievement.

To explain how anxiety functions at different stages in the learning process, MacIntyre and Gardner (1994) advanced a three-stage model of foreign language learning anxiety, suggesting that: (a) at the beginning or input stage, anxiety may have detrimental effects on language processing; (b) at the processing stage it may negatively impact memory and thus internalization of new grammar rules or vocabulary; and (c) at the output stage it may negatively affect retrieval and thus L2 production. While both MacIntyre and Gardner (1994) and Horwitz (2001) postulate a causal relationship between anxiety and achievement, Sparks and Ganshow (2001) argue that anxiety may be the outcome, rather than the cause, of the difficulties in the learning process, reflecting differences in language learning abilities. Agreeing that this may indeed be the case for some learners, Horwitz (2001) points out that anxious language learners worry even when their objective language learning abilities are adequate.

These individual differences in levels of communicative anxiety, or trait anxiety, became the topic of recent research in the field (Dewaele, 2002a,b; Dewaele & Furnham, 1999, 2000). The findings suggest that introverts and extroverts differ in levels of arousal: Extroverts are under-aroused and tend to compensate by choosing more arousing tasks with greater sensory stimulation; introverts are over-aroused and compensate by avoiding over-arousing situations. Dewaele (2002b) argues that the extroverts' low autonomic arousability makes them less anxiety-prone and thus better able to cope with the stressful situation of L2 speech production. Introverts' excessive levels of dopamine and norepinephrine associated with high arousal make them more anxiety prone and negatively affect their L2 perfomance.

Overall, we can see that the fields of bilingualism and SLA have acknowledged the contribution of affective factors to the process of language learning. At the same time, they developed a rather narrow understanding of the affective domain. Rather than considering what Pérez-Firmat (2003) calls 'the entire gamut of human emotions' inspired by languages, theorists reduce emotions to a laundry list of decontextualized and oftentimes poorly defined sociopsychological constructs such as attitudes, motivation, anxiety, self-esteem, empathy, risk taking, and tolerance of ambiguity (Arnold, 1999; Brown, 1987; Ehrman, 1996; Oxford, 2002; Richard-Amato, 1988).

It is not surprising that this individualistic and cognitive view of the affective domain emerged in North American academia, where individuals are viewed as autonomous selves and monolingualism rules as the norm. Language learning anxiety as a key explanatory factor in L2 learning outcomes can thrive only in classrooms populated by more or less monolingual speakers who grew up with a deep conviction that FL learning is a challenging process in which one can never really succeed – and more importantly, in which one does not need to succeed in a globalized

English-speaking world. To perform in the target language, these learners require fun-filled classrooms and 'caring and sharing' activities that aim to enhance their self-esteem more than the actual knowledge of the L2. (For examples of such activities, see Arnold, 1999; Moskowitz, 1978, 1999; Richard-Amato, 1988.)

The reason the constructs of anxiety, risk taking, and motivation are of limited use in the study of bilingualism is that they best reflect the experiences of white middle-class North American students learning foreign languages in the classroom. They are less reflective of experiences of immigrants and guestworkers, who strive to join the global marketplace and whose fears are fueled not by test-taking anxiety but by gatekeeping practices and power relationships that prevent them from accessing the target language community and resources (Bremer et al., 1996; Norton Peirce, 1995; Norton, 2000, 2001; Pavlenko, 2000b, 2002b). One cannot help but wonder how anxiety-reducing activities such as writing fortune cookie messages would allow FL learners to acquire the vocabulary they will need in situations where real threats are present – where they are discriminated against on the basis of their gender, race, ethnicity, or sexuality, and need to stand up for themselves (Polanyi, 1995; Talburt & Stewart, 1999; Twombly, 1995). The constructs of either anxiety or risk taking are also inapplicable in multilingual environments such as Southeast Asia or the Northwestern Amazon, where people continue to learn languages throughout their lives, without ever stopping to think about 'the fear of failure.' Nor do these constructs cast light on dilemmas experienced by bilingual writers whose contradictory affections and allegiances result, in Pérez-Firmat's (2003) words, in 'knotty tongue ties.'

I do not deny that many L2 learners and users experience a very real feeling of anxiety using the L2 both in and outside of the language classroom. But I also want to underscore the social causes of this anxiety, including language ideologies that construct second language learning as a challenging and perhaps impossible task, and instances of linguistic, ethnic, racial, and gender discrimination (Bremer et al., 1996; Norton, 2001; Polanyi, 1995; Talburt & Stewart, 1999). To push the thinking in the field beyond a single and reductive construct, I will return in Chapters 6 and 7 to the notion of anxiety, to incorporate it into a more compehensive and inclusive framework of emotional experience in language learning and use.

2.5. Emotions and multilingualism

My discussion so far demonstrates that emotions remain undertheorized in the study of bilingualism and SLA, and that the questions asked about the role of emotions in additional language learning and use are extremely limited. Researchers also continue to frame the issue as the relationship between languages *and* emotions, leaving out languages *of* emotions, or multilingual performance of affect. Consequently, just as I argued earlier for the importance of considering multicompetence in cross-linguistic research on language and emotions, now I emphasize the need to bring a broad understanding of emotions into the scholarship on bilingualism and SLA. I do not want to take full credit for reframing the discussion, though: Several attempts in a similar vein have been made in the past. Each time, however, the researcher remained a lone voice with agendas and approaches that were not taken up by others.

Arsenian (1945) was the first to offer a more comprehensive agenda for the study of bilingualism, one that included examination of affective values of single words as well as whole languages. Among the questions he posed were the following:

What are the extent and nature of the emotional values of words and expressions in a language native to one and foreign to the other person? In what kind of cultural juxtaposition do equilateral, competitive or superior-inferior feelings as to language show themselves? (p. 85)

Weinreich (1953), in his foundational text *Languages in Contact*, remarked that bilinguals may have distinct emotional attachments to their languages, and that emotional involvements of later life – such as love affairs, friendships, or pride in one's new country – are likely to result in affective bonds that may conflict with or even supersede those established with the mother tongue. He also underscored the importance of language loyalties and resistance in language transfer phenomena and urged researchers to examine *affective borrowing*, that is, the use of lexical and grammatical categories of one language to signal affect when speaking another.

Only two researchers proceeded to examine these and related issues in the next few decades. The first, Susan Ervin-Tripp (1954, 1964, 1967), examined bilinguals' affective repertoires, and the second, Věroboj Vildomec (1963), bi- and multilinguals' emotional investments in their languages. In her studies, Ervin-Tripp asked the participants, typically coordinate bilinguals, to perform a sentence-completion task and a Thematic Apperception Test (which requires participants to describe a set of pictures), with sessions in their two languages taking place six weeks apart.

The first of the studies examined responses in Japanese and English from a Japanese–English bilingual who was born in the United States into a Japanese-speaking family and educated in Japan between the ages of eight and fourteen (Ervin, 1954). The researcher found that Japanese stories elicited by the pictures were much more emotional than the ones told in English. In the Japanese stories, people went mad with grief, cried aloud with pain, and wept over lost love. In contrast, in the English responses to the same pictures, a young man was robbed by a hypnotist, a woman came home drunk, and a girl was trying to complete a sewing project. Eight of the Japanese stories involved family relationships and two more a love relationship, while only three of the English stories involved people related by emotional or family ties. The most common conflict in the Japanese stories was a child's debt to parents, with ensuing guilt or fear of disappointing them, while in the corresponding English stories such themes did not appear at all. The results of the sentence-completion task mirrored the TAT results: The English sentences appeared abstract and cold, while the Japanese ones involved feelings. The researcher explained her results through differences in the emotional relationships formed in the two languages of the bilingual individual, she also referred to Buxbaum's (1949) study to support her findings.

Ervin's (1964) second study used the same procedure with 64 French–English bilinguals, all of whom had lived in the United States for more than 4 years (mean n = 12) and learned English primarily from Americans. Forty of them were or had been married to Americans. The responses in both languages were coded by two independent coders and analyzed both qualitatively and quantitatively in terms of dominant themes and main characters. To avoid scoring biases, one of each subject's stories was translated into the other language and evaluated again. The analysis of variance pointed to differences in two emotional themes: French stories described more verbal aggression toward peers and more withdrawal and autonomy. The author explained these differences through the emphasis on verbal argument in French culture and education, and the cultural emphasis on withdrawal as a dominant mode of response after a disagreement. In Ervin-Tripp's view, the differences suggested that the participants told stories that were language- and culture-appropriate and reflected dominant cultural themes and values.

Similar results were achieved in another study conducted with Japanese–English bilingual women (Ervin-Tripp, 1967). Thirty-six women participated in the study, all of them war brides brought home by American servicemen. In addition to sentence completion and the TAT Test, they were also asked to provide word associations. The results were compared to those obtained from monolingual English speakers and a sample of second-generation Japanese–Americans who returned to Japan for education. The findings show that both Japanese groups shifted associations and responses when they shifted the language. For instance, Japanese women more often said, "What I want most in life is . . . peace," while Americans said ". . . happiness." Completing the sentence, "When I am with men . . . ," Japanese women more often said "uncomfortable," whereas American women said "contented." This study, too, pointed to the presence of distinct cultural associations and emotion discourses in the two languages of the speakers.

While Ervin-Tripp's work raised the possibility that bicultural bilinguals may have distinct affective repertoires, narratives, and ways of relating to others in their languages, Vildomec (1963) showed that they also have distinct emotional attachments to the languages. Vildomec criticized the early writing on multilingualism for neglecting the emotional values of languages, in particular the positive values of the mother tongue and the negative values of languages of the so-called enemy nations. To rectify the situation, he sent out three questionnaires, composed in French, to 470 potential study participants in international colleges in a number of European countries, including France and Denmark. The first, most general, questionnaire elicited data on the speakers' age, gender, occupation, language history, and attitudes. It also inquired about languages the speakers prefer or detest. The second questionnaire asked about advantages and disadvantages of multilingualism, and about factors that may influence participants' responses. The third questionnaire elicited judgments as to the emotional value of the speakers' languages at different periods in their lives and opinions about factors that influenced their attitudes toward particular languages.

Only 61 among the 470 prospective participants responded to the questionnaire, and even then, not all the questions were always answered. As a result, only 40 questionnaires were considered in the final analysis. Among these respondents were 24 men and 16 women. (Vildomec notes that women sent in fewer completed questionnaires.) The participants were between the ages of 20 and 70, most were well-educated middle-class individuals, among them several university professors, teachers, and lecturers. Among their first languages were English, Alsatian, Dutch, French, German, Czech, Romanian, Arabic, Estonian, Russian, and Flemish.

Of the 36 participants who responded to the question about preferred languages, 22 favored the L1, at least as one of the preferred languages. For instance, one respondent noted that when she is excited, she finds it difficult to express her thoughts entirely in her L3 German and appeals to Gallicisms (L1) and Alsatianisms (L2). Not surprisingly, the participants who exhibited emotional preference for the L2 were also ones who stated that they speak the L2 better than L1. One, in fact, admitted disliking her L1 Alsatian. Among the reasons for the preference of one language over others, the participants offered language dominance, beauty, expressivity, and family associations. Reasons for disliking particular languages included ugliness, difficulty, and personal and political associations. German emerged as a particularly disliked language due to its ties to respondents' experiences during World War II. Importantly, neither the questionnaire results nor subsequent interviews and correspondence with the participants showed any negative emotional consequences of either language attrition or the transfer of emotional attachment from L1 to another language.

Working in different fields and at somewhat different points in time, Arsenian (1945), Weinreich (1953), Vildomec (1963), and Ervin-Tripp (1954, 1964, 1967) had all noticed the need for an inquiry on emotions and affective repertoires in the study of bilingualism that would go beyond the issues of attitudes and motivation. Nevertheless, their research and questions did not inspire subsequent studies, perhaps for the simple reason that the time had not come for emotions research in general. A 'soft' subject, for a long time emotions remained in the background not only in the field of bilingualism, but also in psychology and linguistics, where transformational and later universal grammar ruled and the cognitive revolution was underway. In the late 1960s and 1970s the pendulum shifted once again and the fields of psychology, linguistics, and anthropology opened up to the study of human emotions (Ekman, 1980; Izard, 1977) and their interaction with the linguistic system (Davitz, 1964, 1969; Levy, 1973; Riesman, 1977; Schieffelin, 1976). As a result, at present we have a large and still exponentially growing body of emotions research that offers fertile ground for future studies of emotions and multilingualism.

2.6. Webquestionnaire study "Bilingualism and Emotions"

In the rest of this book, I will discuss research conducted in a variety of fields, from psycholinguistics to psychotherapy to literary studies, that illuminates the relationship between emotions and multilingualism. I will also draw on my own work, in particular a webquestionnaire study Jean-Marc Dewaele and I conducted (Dewaele & Pavlenko, 2001–2003) to elicit bi- and multilinguals' own views and perceptions of the connections between their languages and emotions. While the study did not inform us about the particularities of actual language use, it succeeded in eliciting subjective experiences and beliefs of an unprecedentedly large group of multilinguals. The analysis of their responses helped us to understand how and why multilingual speakers select particular languages for emotional expression (Dewaele, 2004a,b,c, in press; Pavlenko, 2004a, in press) and to formulate questions and agendas for future research. Because references to the questionnaire, the studies based on it, and the quotes from the respondents will appear in more than one chapter, I found it appropriate to discuss its methodology once, prior to its multiple appearances.

The webquestionnaire "Bilingualism and Emotions"[1] (see Appendix A) was created in 2001 by the two authors and maintained on the Birkbeck College website until December 2003. Prior to posting the questionnaire, we piloted several versions with our students at Birkbeck College and Temple University, respectively. The final version of the questionnaire contained 34 questions and was divided into two parts. The first part consisted of closed questions with 5-point Likert scales; the second contained open-ended questions where the participants had to write a response. The balance between close-ended and open-ended questions aimed to ensure the reliability and validity of the questionnaire, whereby baseline data contained in Likert scale responses would be examined against the

[1] Here, bilingualism refers to both bi- and multilingualism.

participants' open-ended comments. The questionnaire collected the following sociobiographical information from the participants: gender, age, education level, ethnic group, occupation, languages known, dominant language(s), chronological order of language acquisition, context of acquisition, age of onset, frequency of use, typical interlocutors, and self-rated proficiency scores for speaking, comprehending, reading, and writing in the languages in question. Language choice was determined for self- and other-directed speech, and for emotional and non-emotional speech.

The questionnaire was advertised through several listservs and informal contacts with colleagues around the world. The use of an on-line questionnaire allowed us to gather an unprecedented amount of data from a large and diverse population of bi- and multilingual speakers of different ages and from a variety of linguistic backgrounds. At the same time, the reliance on the internet introduced its own methodological limitations: The sample was skewed toward individuals literate in English (the language of the questionnaire), with easy access to the internet, and possessing a degree of metalinguistic awareness necessary to respond to the questions. The on-line data collection procedure also did not allow us to control the demographics of the sample.

A total of 1,039 bi- and multilinguals[2] contributed to the database (731 females, 308 males). The ages of the respondents ranged between 16 and 70 years of age (mean = 35.6; SD = 11.3). The respondents were generally well-educated: high school diploma or less – 115 (11%), Bachelor's degree – 273 (26%), Master's degree – 308 (30%), PhD – 338 (33%). (Five participants chose not to answer the question.) A majority (n = 837) reported working in a language-related area. Clearly, these respondents are not representative of the more general bi- and multilingual population: The overwhelming majority are well-educated 'elite bilinguals' who have time and resources to invest in searching for information about and reflecting upon issues in bilingualism. The overrepresentation of well-educated professionals is easily explained by the advertising procedure. Our informal contacts were other PhDs who in turn knew other language professionals; similarly, the listservs we advertised on were most likely to be read by well-educated individuals who knew how to find these resources. The dominance of female respondents is perhaps best explained by the preponderance of women in education and language-related professions, as well as by the topic itself – as a group, women may be more comfortable discussing emotions, parenting, and relationships. Interestingly, in Vildomec's (1963) study, female respondents were in a minority. It is possible that the present reversal reflects the increased presence of women in the public sphere.

---

[2] While the overall number of respondents is somewhat higher we have deleted incomplete responses, doubled responses, as well as responses that looked less than serious.

The overrepresentation of women and PhDs undoubtedly skews the sample and suggests the need for better balance in the future. This potential pitfall is inevitable with a web-based questionnaire whose distribution one cannot control, and it needs to be kept in mind when interpreting the patterns, because results might be different for a sample of working-class males with high school education. To partially remedy the problem, additional data was collected in the London area through a printed version of the questionnaire from about 50 multilinguals who did not finish high school. Statistical analyses did not reveal significant differences between this group and the rest of the sample (Dewaele, 2004a).

In terms of the number of languages spoken by each individual, the sample consists of 144 bilinguals (14%), 269 trilinguals (26%), 289 speakers of four languages (28%), and 337 speakers of five or more languages (32%), with 157 people bilingual and 19 people trilingual from birth. Seventy-five L1s are represented in the sample, with the number of speakers of each L1 language as follows: English = 303; Spanish = 123; French = 101; German = 97; Dutch = 76; Italian = 52; Catalan = 32; Russian = 29; Finnish = 28; Portuguese = 20; Greek = 15; Swedish = 15; Japanese = 11; Welsh = 10; 61 other languages had fewer than 10 speakers, among them Arabic, ASL, Basque, Bengali, Bosnian, Breton, Burmese, Cantonese, Danish, Duri, Farsi, Hebrew, Hindi, Hungarian, Indonesian, Latin, Latvian, Malay, Mandarin, Navajo, Norwegian, Nugunu, Oriya, Polish, Romanian, Serbo-Croatian, Sindhi, Slovak, Slovene, Tamil, Turkish, Ukrainian, and Vietnamese. More than half of the participants declared themselves to be dominant in L1 (n = 561), a smaller proportion reported dominance in two or more languages including the L1 (n = 373), and about 10% reported dominance in a language or languages other than the L1 (n = 105).

Throughout this book, the participants' answers to close- and open-ended questions about their patterns of language use and their perceptions of their bi- and multilingual selves allow me to challenge easy generalizations about the relationship between emotions and multilingualism, be it the view of L1 as the language of emotions, or the view of anxiety as the main emotion involved in second language learning and use.

2.7. The structure of this book

I have tried to show that while some approaches to the study of multilingualism, second language learning, and emotions have been relatively fruitful, none led to a comprehensive understanding of this relationship, because they focused on single emotions, such as anomie or anxiety, or on singular aspects of the relationship between languages and emotions, such as language attitudes. None considered a full range of human emotions, nor examined the multiple ties that link emotions to languages. In order to understand multilinguals' emotional lives and affect performances, we need an approach that does not view either multilingualism or emotions as unitary phenomena. In Chapter 1, I aimed to raise the reader's awareness of the diversity of multilingual trajectories and linguistic constellations that result in very different relationships between languages and affective attitudes toward them. In this chapter I have demonstrated that the notions of 'emotions,' 'feelings,' and 'affect' can also be considered from a variety of angles in relation to language.

The main premise of this book is that there is no single coherent story to be told about the relationship between emotions and multilingualism: This relationship plays out in different ways on different levels in the human mind and its sociocultural environment. Like our childhood kaleidoscopes that offer us a different picture with every turn, the change in our conceptual lens – from the vocal or neurophysiological level, to semantic and conceptual levels, to the levels of discourse and social cognition – brings with it a change in the questions we can ask and the answers we derive. Consequently, I do not offer a single definition of 'language' or 'emotion' in the beginning of the book, but rather reconsider these two phenomena and the relationship between them anew in each chapter. As a result, emotions will appear in some chapters as states, in others as representations, and yet in others as processes or relationships. At the same time, because this book deals with the relationship between language, concepts, and emotions – rather than with emotions per se – the discussion that follows will not explore the full variety of theoretical positions on 'what emotions are.' These positions can be found in abundance in the literature on emotions (Cacioppo & Gardner, 1999; Ekman & Davidson, 1994; Harré, 1986; Harré & Parrott, 1996; Mayne & Bonanno, 2001; Oatley, 1992; Strongman, 1996). This text, on the other hand, will only highlight the work of those who made explicit connections between emotions, language, memory, and cognition.

Throughout, I will differentiate between the study of *languages of emotions* and *languages and emotions*. Chapters 3, 4, and 5 deal with the former and examine how emotions are performed and perceived in multilinguals' languages on three different levels. Chapter 3 focuses on the most immediate, vocal level of emotional expression, and considers cross-linguistic similarities and differences in this area and their implications for vocal communication of emotions across linguistic boundaries. Chapter 4 shifts the focus to semantic and conceptual levels and examines representation of emotion terms in the bilingual lexicon. I will show how bilinguals themselves view the similarities and differences between emotion terms of their respective languages, and examine similarities and differences between monolinguals' and bilinguals' emotion concepts. Chapter 5 moves the discussion to the level of discourse and examines how bilinguals express affect in their respective languages and how their distinct affective repertoires may contribute to the perception of distinct 'bilingual selves.'

The next two chapters shift the focus from languages *of* emotions to languages *and* emotions and consider this relationship from two different angles. Chapter 6 takes an embodied perspective on language, examining why bilinguals may have different perceptions of and reactions to their respective languages. Chapter 7 moves this discussion to the level of social cognition and offers the notion of emotional investment as a more sophisticated way of understanding language-related affections, desires, and hatreds. Chapter 8 concludes the discussion by bringing together its various strands to offer an integrated perspective on emotions and multilingualism and to show how a multilingual perspective can contribute to research on language and emotions, what insights emotion research can bring to the study of bilingualism and SLA, and how bi- and multilingual participants can be incorporated into cross-linguistic emotions research.

Readers who will take the time to read all of the chapters, rather than the ones that concern their areas of interest and expertise, will also notice that this is a somewhat unorthodox text. At times I will make an argument and offer an account of a particular phenomenon, only to challenge it in the next chapter as I approach the issue from a different angle. My aim in doing so is not to confuse readers but to alert them to the limitations of any single conceptual lens, to the differences in conclusions drawn at different levels of analysis, and to the multiplicity of ways in which multilinguals feel about their languages and express emotions in them.

3

Vocal level: Is the lady angry?

[We] argue in L3 English also but I can get upset and shout in Swedish even though he does not understand me. Most important thing is to shout.
(Marianne, 33, L1 Swedish, L2 German, L3 English, partner is L1 speaker of English)

It is a sunny Saturday afternoon in Philadelphia's busy Chinatown. Outside of a little grocery store, a group of middle-aged Chinese women is absorbed in a lively discussion. Their high-pitched loud voices and staccato rhythm attract the attention of a blond five-year-old kid passing by with his mother. "Mommy, why are the ladies arguing?" inquires the child. I do not hear her answer and can only hope she will explain that the ladies may not be arguing at all and that in other languages loud voices and high pitch do not necessarily signal anger. But is this in fact common knowledge? What do we really know about ways in which vocal cues signal affective meanings across languages and cultures? Some respondents to our webquestionnaire, like Marianne, believe that at least some cues are universal and all you need to do to get your anger across is to shout. So is it possible that the ladies are arguing after all?

The purpose of this chapter is to triangulate evidence from different fields of inquiry on how vocal cues function to signal emotions and on how people interpret affective meanings of vocal cues in a second or unfamiliar language. I begin by identifying suprasegmental features involved in affect performance and by pointing to cross-linguistic differences in social and linguistic meanings of these features. Then I examine findings from cross-linguistic studies of identification of emotions in vocal expression and from studies of intercultural communication. The chapter will end with a discussion of factors that may impact interpretation of vocal expression of emotions and with desiderata for future research in the area.

3.1. Vocal cues to emotional expression

Vocal cues are often seen as the most important type of cues to other people's emotions (Planalp, DeFrancisco & Rutherford, 1996). We all engage, more or less successfully, in interpretation of these cues on a daily basis ("How are you? Is everything OK? You sound a little down today . . . "). We also appeal to them to let others know how we feel. Marianne, for instance, has no doubt that her shouting in L1 Swedish will get her feelings across to her partner even though he does not understand the language. But can we always rely on the L1 patterns of vocal expression in intercultural communication?

At present, we do not yet have an adequate theory of vocal expression of emotions, but there exist two main approaches to this issue. In psychology, Scherer and associates (1979, 1986; Banse & Scherer, 1996; Pittam & Scherer, 1993; Scherer, Banse & Wallbott, 2001) contend that emotions are expressed through emotion-specific vocal profiles and that the ability to decode these profiles is based on a psychobiologically determined emotion mechanism, modified by cultural factors. Evidence for this position comes from encoding studies that show systematicity in emotion-specific vocal profiles across speakers (Banse & Scherer, 1996; Cosmides, 1983; Fairbanks & Hoaglin, 1941; Fairbanks & Pronovost, 1939; Mullenix et al., 2002; Scherer et al., 1991; van Bezooijen, 1984; Wallbott & Scherer, 1986; Williams & Stevens, 1972, 1981) and from decoding studies that show that people identify emotions correctly in content-free speech or in an unfamiliar language at a rate greater than chance (Beier & Zautra, 1972; Graham, Hamblin, & Feldstein, 2001; Kramer, 1964; McCluskey et al., 1975; Scherer et al., 2001; van Bezooijen, Otto & Heenan, 1983). These laboratory studies, which will be discussed later in the chapter, show convincing correlations between vocal cues and particular emotions, but so far they have failed to produce definitive vocal profiles for but a few emotions (cf. Banse & Scherer, 1996) or a systematic theory of encoding and decoding of vocal expression of emotions. (For comprehensive reviews of work in this area, see Frick, 1985; Murray & Arnott, 1993; Pittam & Scherer, 1993; Scherer, 1986; van Bezooijen, 1984.)

Table 3.1 offers a summary of current knowledge about emotion-specific vocal profiles in English and German, two languages in which most of the work has been conducted to date. (Because differences between the two languages have not been emphasized in previous work, I will not discuss them here either.) This table serves to illustrate the difficulties inherent in creation of such profiles. First of all, similar vocal profiles may signal a variety of affective meanings. For instance, higher pitch, increased loudness, and fast rate of speech are commonly associated with such diverse emotions as anger, happiness, joy, and fear. On the other hand, the same emotions may be conveyed by a variety of different cues, depending on the

TABLE 3.1. *Prototypical vocal cues of selected emotions and affective stances in English and German*

	Pitch Level	Pitch Range	Intonation	Loudness	Rate	Stress	Paralinguistic Features
Affection	high or low	expanded	rising	soft	fast or slow		'smiley' voice, cooing
Amusement	high		rise-falls		fast		laughter, 'smiley' voice
Anger	high	expanded, abrupt pitch changes	falling	loud	fast	strong stress, high unstressed syllables	controlled enunciation
Anxiety	high			soft			sighing
Boredom, indifference	moderate to low	narrow	flat, level	moderate to soft	slow or fast		sighing
Cheerfulness	high	expanded	rise-falls, melodious singing tone	moderate to loud	fast		'smiley' voice, audible inhalation
Complaint	low		semi-tone rises		fast		nasal voice, whiny voice
Confidence	high			loud	fast		
Contempt	low	expanded		loud	slow		precise articulation
Coquetry, flirtatiousness	high			soft		soft tertial upglide on last stressed syllable	whisper, breathy voice
Displeasure, disgust	high or low	slightly expanded	rise-fall and falling	soft or loud	slow		grumbled, chest tone
Excitement	high	expanded	rising	loud	fast		audible inhalation
Fear	high but lower than for anger	expanded, with occasional high peaks		loud	fast		falsetto, irregular voicing, precise articulation
Happiness, joy	high	expanded	rising at irregular intervals, upward inflections	loud	fast	irregular stress distribution, syllable extension	laughter, giggles, 'smiley' voice

	Pitch level	Pitch range	Contour	Loudness	Tempo	Articulation	Voice quality
Intimacy	high or low	narrow or expanded					whisper, breathy or husky voice
Longing		narrow			slow		sighing
Pleasure	high		rise-fall				'smiley' voice
Sadness, sorrow, grief	low	narrow	falling or flat, lack of melodiousness	soft	slow	little emphasis on separate syllables	whisper, crying, sobs, sighs, pauses, slurring articulation
Shame, embarrassment	low	narrow	falling	soft	slow	syllable extension	stuttering, stammering, mumbling, whisper, laughter, audible inhalation, pauses
Surprise	high global pitch	expanded, with high peaks	rise-fall, with sharp fall	loud			
Tenderness	high	narrow		soft		audible off-glide in long unstressed syllables	
Timidity	low			soft	slow		stuttering, stammering, mumbling, pauses, whisper, mumbling

Key sources: Banse & Scherer (1996), Bloch (1996), Couper-Kuhlen (1986), Davitz (1964), Fairbanks & Hoaglin (1941), Fairbanks & Pronovost (1939), Murray & Arnot (1993), Scherer (1986), Scherer et al. (1991), Selting (1996), and Williams and Stevens (1972).

47

speaker, the situation they are in, and their communicative intentions. In anger, one individual may yell (Get OUT of here!!!) and another may speak softly and slowly, enunciating clearly (I will say this only once, so listen carefully . . .). In fear, one may scream (HELP!!!) and another whisper in a trembling voice (Please, don't harm me . . .). Some states, such as anxiety, may be characterized exclusively by the divergence from the usual pattern, but the direction of such divergence in terms of pitch, loudness, or rate of articulation will vary from speaker to speaker (Frick, 1985).

In other words, while there is no doubt that some vocal cues to affective meanings are more prototypical than others, their inherent ambiguity and context-dependence are a major obstacle in creating systematic vocal profiles of emotions. The relativity of linguistic strategies, including vocal cues, both within and across languages is commonly assumed in linguistics, in particular in interactional sociolinguistics and discourse analysis (Tannen, 1993). Gumperz (1982a,b), Couper-Kuhlen (1986), Tannen (1989), Bloch (1996) and others argue that conventionalized affective meanings of prosodic cues may differ across speech communities, across speakers, and across situations; they cannot be preassigned and are negotiated in interaction.

If emotionality is reflected in changes in discursive style, then what counts as emotionality will differ across individuals and groups of speakers, because their discursive styles are different. An increase in pitch and volume may signify anger for speakers who always speak softly, yet the same acoustic criteria may characterize everyday speech of those who get very quiet in anger. As a result, intercultural communication is fraught with misunderstanding: Native American children in mainstream classrooms, for instance, see their teachers as angry because they speak in a louder voice than that common in the children's home community (Albas, McCluskey & Albas, 1976). Evidence of variability of contextualization cues to emotion comes from studies of everyday emotional communication (Arndt & Janney, 1991; Bloch, 1996; Caffi & Janney, 1994; Günthner, 1997; Selting, 1994, 1996; Tannen, 1989) and studies of intercultural miscommunication (Gumperz, 1982a,b). While sensitivity to context is a major strength of this perspective, it is simultaneously its weakness, as the focus on particular interactions has not so far resulted in a systematic explanation of how humans interpret vocal cues to emotion, what the role of conventionalized cues is in this process, and what the conventionalized cues may be.

Linguists also object to the use of 'emotions' as an umbrella term in research on affective prosody (cf. Couper-Kuhlen, 1986: 185). Take, for instance, the labels in Table 3.1. We can see that some of these labels can be interpreted as personality traits (timidity), states (confidence), affective stances and communicative intentions toward interlocutors (affection, flirtatiousness, intimacy, tenderness), or even speech acts (complaints), rather than emotions per se. Janney and associates (Arndt & Janney, 1991; Caffi &

Janney, 1994) address this inconsistency by differentiating between emotional (spontaneous bursting out) and emotive communication (strategic signaling of affective information that may or may not be related to the speaker's affective states). Thus, in emotional communication, interjections "wow!" or "really?" are uttered in genuine surprise, while in emotive communication the same interjections are uttered in a ritualized manner, to express conversational engagement and support (Günthner, 1997).

Linguists also argue that the search for vocal correlates of singular emotions may be misguided, because humans commonly communicate several, oftentimes conflicting, emotions within a single speech event or even utterance, and because these displays are almost always subject to display rules. Clearly, more research is needed before one or the other position is validated or, preferably, a compromise is reached whereby both empirical and naturalistic methods of inquiry are employed to understand how conventionalized and ambiguous vocal cues are negotiated in interaction among monolingual speakers. To judge whether the interpretation task is the same or even more challenging when more than one language is involved, let us examine what is known to date about cross-linguistic similarities and differences in affective meanings of particular vocal cues.

Vocal cues to affect are commonly discussed in terms of two types of *suprasegmental* features, that is, aspects of speech that involve more than single segments: (a) *paralinguistic* features, such as voice quality and vocal gestures, and (b) *prosodic* features, such as pitch, loudness, or rate of articulation. The three terms, prosodic, suprasegmental, and paralinguistic, are used in a variety of ways in the literature, often in an overlapping manner. I have adopted the most common usage, where the term *suprasegmental* refers to all features above the segmental level, the term *prosodic* refers to features that continuously co-occur with sequences of segmental phonemes or words, and the term *paralinguistic* refers to effects only sporadically present in the speech signal, such as temporary voice modifications, vocal gestures, or vocalizations (Couper-Kuhlen, 1986: 2–4; Cruttenden, 1997: 172).

The main paralinguistic feature, *voice quality*, or timbre of the voice, is often called "the key to the vocal differentiation of discrete emotions" (Scherer, 1986: 145). Acoustically determined by the pattern of energy distribution in the spectrum, voice quality results from voice setting, that is the overall posture of the vocal organs for speech, tenseness, the degree to which the lips are used in pronunciation, and so forth. Variations in these features produce differences in the overall voice quality both among and within speakers, because a single speaker of a particular language can also assume different voice qualities in different situations. Some of those deployed strategically to convey affect in English include whisper, nasal voice, breathy voice, whiny voice, husky voice, creaky voice, 'smiley' voice, and falsetto. Breathy or husky voice is often appropriated to signal or mock-signal (sexual) intimacy, while 'smiley' voice, giggles, and laughter are conventionally linked to joy and happiness. At the same time, 'nervous' giggles may signal apprehension, anxiety, shame, or embarrassment, and 'derisive' laughter may serve as a marker of irony, frustration, anger, or contempt. (See Chafe, 2003, for an in-depth discussion of laughter and emotion.) Paralinguistic features also include vocal gestures, such as sobs or snickers, and language-specific vocalizations, such as [pɸ:] for contempt in English or [ɸu:] for disgust in Russian.

To date, little systematic research has been conducted on voice quality and affect (see however Scherer, 1986), and even less is known about cross-linguistic differences in meanings of paralinguistic features. It is known that voice settings – and thus voice quality – differ across languages (Esling, 1994; Esling & Wong, 1983), with breathiness, for instance, used contrastively in some languages, such as Gujarati (Henton & Bladon, 1985). Vocalizations, such as "yuk," also function in a language-specific manner, while vocal gestures, such as crying or laughing, are commonly assumed to be universal, even though their appropriateness may differ across cultural contexts (Cruttenden, 1997). Impressionistic observations suggest that FL and L2 learners may transfer voice quality features into the target language, at times sounding husky or breathy and thus inappropriately 'suggestive,' while bicultural bilinguals shift voice quality when shifting languages (Esling, 1994; Pennington & Richards, 1986). "I've been told that in Spanish my voice takes on a softer, pleasant, more subservient timbre," states a Spanish–English bilingual Nelly Rosario (2000: 163). And because different muscles are involved in different voice settings, some bilinguals may feel like the Chinese student who observed: "It feels like I have an English-speaking face and a Chinese-speaking face – and they even look different on the video!" (Esling, 1994: 62).

The second set of suprasegmental features involves prosody, commonly discussed in terms of three acoustic dimensions, each associated with a cluster of features: (a) *frequency*: pitch, tone, intonation; (b) *intensity*: loudness and stress, and (c) *duration*: rhythm and rate of articulation. The first set of vocal cues revolves around *pitch*, or fundamental frequency, which depends on how fast the vocal cords vibrate – the faster they vibrate, the higher the pitch. In English and German, high pitch is commonly associated with anger, fear, and joy, and low pitch with sadness. Williams and Stevens (1972) emphasize that relative pitch (that is, pitch in relation to the speaker's normal range) is a better cue for emotional expression than is absolute pitch.

Their observation is particularly important for cross-linguistic inquiry, because mean pitch values differ across languages, for both male and female speakers (Graddol & Swann, 1989; Majewski, Hollien, & Zalewski, 1972; Ohara, 2001; van Bezooijen, 1995, 1996; Yuasa, 2002), and thus judgments based on absolute pitch values may be misleading. Cross-linguistic studies also point to variation in social meanings attached to pitch levels. For instance, Japanese listeners perceive low-pitched female speakers as more arrogant, insensitive, rational, and detached, and high-pitched ones as more modest, sensitive, and emotional; in contrast, speakers of American English favor lower pitch for both men and women and may associate high pitch in women with 'affected' or 'fake' femininity (Ohara, 2001; Valentine & Saint Damian, 1988; van Bezooijen, 1995, 1996).

In addition to pitch height, affective meanings may also be signaled by shifts in pitch. The norm for intonation phrases is to be positioned roughly in the lower third of a speaker's voice range (Cruttenden, 1997). Marked uses occur when the whole range of pitch configuration moves to a higher or lower position in the speaker's voice range. In English and German, raised pitch and expanded range may indicate anger, fear, and surprise; lowered pitch might signal intimacy or contempt; and narrowed range might indicate displeasure, sadness, or indifference. Speech communities may differ in the range typically used by the speakers. For instance, speakers of Scandinavian languages commonly use a narrower pitch range than speakers of English – as a result, they may sound 'bored' to their English-speaking interlocutors (Fant, 1973; Swan & Smith, 2001). In contrast, Japanese-speaking men have been shown to appeal to a wider pitch range than English-speaking men – as a result they may sound 'overly emotional' or even 'effeminate' to English-speaking interlocutors (Yuasa, 2002).

Languages are typically divided into two groups with regard to the function of pitch. In Cantonese, Mandarin, and Vietnamese, as well as in many African languages, a change in pitch corresponds to a change in word meaning. These languages are commonly called *tone* languages, where tones are set pitch patterns for the pronunciation of individual words. Attitudinal meanings in these languages are often conveyed through alternative linguistic means, such as adverbials or particles. In other languages, such as English, German, or Russian, pitch conveys utterance, rather than word, meanings. These languages are called *intonation* languages, where intonation refers to the contour of pitches (high/low) that occur over an utterance turn and, in combination with other cues, signal emotions and their degrees of intensity (Bolinger, 1985; Ladefoged, 1993; see also Brazil, 1997, who argues against attribution of meaning to intonation alone).

Differences in the function of pitch lead to cross-linguistic differences in intonation contours: English, an intonation language, allows for more freedom in varying the contours locally for affective signalling, while tone languages require preservation of local pitch contrasts (Ross, Edmondson, & Seibert, 1986). As will be shown later in the chapter, these cross-linguistic differences may result in miscommunication between speakers of tone and intonation languages and create difficulties for learners who attempt to master a language from a different group. An American missionary in Taiwan, Linda Petrucelli, recalls:

My major difficulty was the way I processed emotion through vocal variety. I am second-generation Italian-American and I am acccustomed to STRESS-ing certain words to add COL-or and EMPH-asis. Unfortunately, this habit of mine unintentionally altered [Taiwanese] tones and consequently changed what I said.

(Petrucelli, 2000: 162)

Speech communities may also differ in prototypical meanings assigned to intonation contours. The typical rising intonation of English questions is reserved in most South Asian languages for expressions of surprise, while questions in these languages are marked by a rise-fall intonation. As a result, a speaker of American English asking questions would sound continuously surprised to his Punjabi-speaking interlocutors, while polite questions from a Hindi speaker may be perceived as rude assertions by speakers of British English (Gumperz, 1982a; Swan & Smith, 2001). Speakers of Russian may prosodically misinterpret English politeness for enthusiasm, and enthusiasm for impatience and skepticism (Gibson, 1997). In turn, speakers of English are shown to negatively evaluate English utterances pronounced with Russian intonation patterns (Holden & Hogan, 1993).

The next cluster of factors involves stress and loudness. While overall loudness is an individual characteristic, it is also influenced by the context – in particular, by the distance between the interlocutors. Shifts in loudness may signal joy or surprise (Look who's HERE!), while a more permanent increase in loudness is characteristic of anger (DON'T YOU RAISE YOUR VOICE AT ME, missy!). *Stress*, or prominence, refers to a point in a stretch of speech that is more prominent than the surrounding context. The stressed unit, be it a syllable, part of a word, a word, or a phrase, is uttered with a greater amount of energy than the unstressed unit. It may be marked by pitch, amplitude, or duration, or by all of the above. Emotionality may be signaled by increases or decreases in overall loudness, by stress, or by emphatic stress, that is extra stress marked by more dramatic pitch changes and loudness (That's shocking! That's lovely!). Across languages, stress may be marked in different ways and there may be different affective meanings attached to particular volume levels or types of stress. For instance, speakers of Spanish, where emphatic stress is expressed through extra length rather than extra pitch variation, may appear unenthusiastic or 'bored' to speakers of English, where emphatic stress is marked by changes in pitch, length, and volume (Swan & Smith, 2001). In turn, speakers of Russian, a language with a more intense and dynamic stress system than English, may appear 'angry' or 'critical' to English speakers (Holden & Hogan, 1993).

The third important cluster of factors involves duration, and thus stress, rhythm, and *rate of articulation*, that is, the overall tempo of speech. In English and German, faster rate is commonly associated with anger and joy, and a slower rate with sadness; neutral utterances or utterances expressing indifference are typically spoken at a faster rate than sad ones (Fairbanks & Hoaglin, 1941; Scherer et al., 1991; Williams & Stevens, 1972). Increases in speed may indicate emotional intensification. Thus, among the Wolof of Senegal, the speech of the poet–singer class, deemed to be expressive, can be six times faster than the speech of the nobles, deemed to be inept and inexpressive (Irvine, 1990). Speech communities may differ in baseline rates of articulation, and in particular in strategic uses of pauses and silence, which can cause significant intercultural misunderstandings (Besnier, 1990; Scollon & Wong-Scollon, 2001).

The *rhythm* of an utterance is made up of a pattern of stresses. The unit timing that is relevant for the rhythm of languages varies from small units comprising individual segments, as in Japanese, to larger units comprising individual syllables, as in Spanish, to even larger units consisting of one stressed syllable and its accompanying unstressed syllables, as in English. In a larger sense, then, rhythm refers to a regular beat that establishes itself in talk through the even placement of accented syllables in time (Couper-Kuhlen, 2001). The distance between two accented syllables creates a temporal interval. When two or more successive intervals are perceived as equal in duration the speaker is said to be speaking rhythmically. Rhythmic synchrony is often seen as a marker of intimacy (Tannen, 1989). Shifts in rhythm and tempo function to mark information saliency, but may also signal attitudinal and affective meanings, for instance surprise or displeasure (No way!). Rhythm, emphatic stress, rapid delivery rate, and singsong intonation are common for teasing utterances (Nya nya nya nya!).

Languages fall into two large groups with regard to rhythm. The majority are seen as *syllable-timed*, where more or less equal weights are assigned to all syllables (as in Cantonese or Polish). Some, like English or Portuguese, are seen as *stress-timed*, where stressed syllables occur at more or less regular intervals and are assigned more weight than unstressed ones (Avery & Ehrlich, 1992; Swan & Smith, 2001; see however Cruttenden, 1997, and McCarthy, 1991, for a discussion of weaknesses in this classification). Because the number of tone-bearing syllables in an utterance in a syllable-timed language is greater than the number of stressed syllables in an utterance of similar length in a stress-timed language, syllable-timed languages display more numerous and rapid fluctuations in pitch than stress-timed languages (Eady, 1982). As a result of these differences, speakers of syllable-timed languages often have problems recognizing and adopting intonation patterns of stress-timed languages, and vice versa. For instance, Italian learners of English may have problems recognizing how English intonation signals affective meanings; they may also sound

'arrogant' or 'aggressive' when making requests; Italian and Polish learners may also be resistant to adopting English intonation patterns that to
them sound "exaggerated, affected, or overdone" (Swan & Smith, 2001:
166). In turn, speakers of stress-timed languages often perceive the staccato rhythm of syllable-timed languages as indicating anger, as did the
little boy I described in the beginning of this chapter.

Together, results from studies in this area point to some correspondences
between particular vocal cues, or rather bundles of cues, and affective
meanings. Clearly, most of the time we do not have to rely exclusively
on vocal cues: We can assess them in conjunction with lexical content,
facial expression, body language, and, most importantly, context. At times,
however – most often during phone conversations – we find ourselves in
need of interpreting vocal cues in the absence of visual ones. An example of how such interpretation takes place comes from a transcript of the
Radio Picadilly phone-in quiz show in England, where listeners call in with
answers to a riddle (M: moderator; C: caller):

```
1    M:   then we go to Hardwick. (.)
          and there we get -
          (.) h sexy Sharon.
          ↓hi!
5    C:   (0.4) °hello°-
     M:   {1} °hello° -
          - how are you Sharon -
     C:   °all right [thanks°
     M:             [oh: ↑cheer up dear,
10   C:   he hh
     M:   Cheer up;
          for goodness sake;
          don't- don't put me in a bad mood;
          at (.) one o'clock;
```
     (Couper-Kuhlen, 2001: 24; see transcription conventions in
     Appendix B)

Here we see that the caller misses the timing cues in the moderator's first
turn. He set up a well-defined rhythm with accents on *sexy, Sharon,* and
hi, but she comes in too late, after a significant (for this type of interaction)
pause. Moreover, it is not just her transitional timing that is off – her pitch
is also lower than expected by the moderator. He signals it with the shift in
his own register, from line 3 to line 6, in order to approximate and perhaps
mimic the low pitch of Sharon's voice. When this implicit strategy fails
and Sharon continues with the low pitch in line 8, the moderator explicitly
signals that he perceives her low pitch and timing problems as indicators
of 'bad mood' and admonishes her to cheer up.

This example serves to show how, in the absence of visual cues, speakers decode affective meanings from a combination of changes in pitch, loudness, and rate of articulation. The outcomes of this guessing game are not always successful, because the same contours may be used in a variety of affective utterances and in those without any emotive implications. Compare, for instance, examples in (a) with those in (b) and (c):

(a) /**JOHN**\/ HOW nice to **SEE**\ you! (high fall: surprise)
/he's **CO**ming on **FRI**day↗\/ **IS**n't that **GOOD**↗\! (rise-fall: excitement)

(b) A: /**CAN** i invite my **SIS**ter?\↗/
B: /**YES!**\/**BRING** her a**LONG**\! (high fall: enthusiasm? friendly acceptance?)

(c) /the **CHILD** is **BRILL**iant↗\/**BEST** in the **CLASS**\/(rise-fall: purely informative? enthusiastic? sarcastic?) (McCarthy, 1991: 107)

These examples demonstrate that without lexical or contextual cues we cannot reliably label a tone contour as conveying a particular affective meaning. Linguists agree that while in each speech community there exist conventionalized patterns of prosodic usages, the match between a particular contour and meaning is never absolute – either within or across languages – and the ultimate interpretation is always carried out in context (Brazil, 1997; Gumperz, 1982a; Halliday, 1985; McCarthy, 1991). The most we can say is that emotional intensification tends to be accompanied by wider pitch contrasts (McCarthy, 1991). As any partner in a long-term relationship knows, we are not always on firm ground even with a thoroughly familiar interlocutor. At times we find ourselves asking: "You sound different, is everything all right?" The change in our partner's voice quality or pitch may be an indicator of a negative mood, yet we need more clues to interpret whether our interlocutor is sad, angry, frustrated, simply tired, or perhaps sick.

This overview highlighted a number of cross-linguistic differences in mean values and social meanings of conventionalized vocal cues to emotion that are further complicated by individual and contextual variation. Considering the potential implications of these differences for intercultural communication, we can now ask: *Are vocal cues sufficient to decode the intended affective meaning of a speaker's utterance in a second or foreign language?*

3.2. Identification of emotions in vocal expression in another language

Cross-linguistic studies of emotion identification rely on a common design, pioneered in the first decoding studies by Fairbanks and associates (Fairbanks & Hoaglin, 1941; Fairbanks & Pronovost, 1939). The stimuli

consist of tape-recordings, made by untrained native speakers of a particular language or by professional actors and actresses. In some cases only
male or female speakers are recorded and in others both males and females
are recorded. These speakers produce speech samples in their native language, varying in length and expressing particular emotions (most often,
happiness, anger, sadness, love, and fear). Some samples are supplemented
by words or utterances with no particular emotional expression (neutral
voice).

Sample length may range from one word to several sentences to sub-
stantial monologues and dialogues. The content also varies: In some cases,
random phrases or texts are chosen and speakers are asked to produce
different emotional realizations of the same utterances (that is, to read the
texts as if they were angry, happy, and so forth). In other cases, the speakers
are provided with short scenarios describing emotion-eliciting situations
and are asked to act them out. Afterwards, the utterances may be rendered
unintelligible (content-filtered) by means of a lowpass filter in order not
to let the content interfere with the identification task. To avoid possible
confusion, care is taken to ensure that each sample expresses a single emotional state. Samples may also come from databases of emotional speech,
taken from movies, television, and radio programs (Greasley, Sherrard &
Waterman, 2000; Nakamichi et al., 2002; Williams & Stevens, 1972).

The study participants are commonly native speakers of the language(s)
in question and speakers of another language who may or may not be familiar with the language in question. If they are familiar with the language,
they may be divided into groups based on the levels of L2 proficiency
and acculturation. The participants are asked to participate in a forced-
judgment task, where they choose among emotion labels given to them
in their native language. The instructions are typically worded as follows:
"In a few minutes you will be listening to a series of recorded voices and
making some judgments based upon what you hear. Each voice that you
hear will be a person, speaking a standard passage, expressing one of eight
emotions: (1) anger, (2) fear, (3) joy, (4) sadness, (5) depression, (6) hate, (7)
nervousness, (8) neutral emotion. You are to circle the one emotion that you
think the voice is expressing. For example, if you think the voice expresses
anger, you would circle #1 above." (Graham et al., 2001: 26). Alternatively,
participants may be asked to rate every utterance they hear for each emotion on a scale from 0 (not at all) to 6 (intense). In addition, participants
may be asked to identify how confident they are in their choices, how
clearly the emotion was expressed in the voice, or how natural the recording sounded in their opinion. All instructions are presented to participants
in their native language. To ensure comparability, the original instruction
text is translated into the other language and then back-translated. Then
the instructions are pilot-tested with a few participants. Forced-choice task,
however, is not the only possibility in this research. Greasley et al. (2000)
advocate the use of a free-choice task, where participants are asked to use

words of their own choice. (See Abelin & Allwood, 2000, 2002, for the use of such tasks in cross-linguistic research.)

During the administration procedure, the participants are first given time to familiarize themselves with the instructions. Then a brief speech sample is played to ensure that they can hear it clearly. After that, they are given time to respond to practice items (tapes that are not used in the actual study) and to ask clarification questions, and then they proceed to the actual task. The results are analyzed through the means of descriptive statistics (accuracy rates) and multivariate analyses (chi-square, repeated measures ANOVA, multidimensional scaling) to determine the effect of language/culture, emotion type, language proficiency, and possibly gender of the speaker and listener. Additional item analysis helps to separate well-recognized utterances/samples from the less typical ones.

Table 3.2. summarizes cross-linguistic decoding studies. The first well-known decoding study that included a recording in another language was conducted by Kramer (1964), who asked 27 native speakers of American English to identify five emotions portrayed in different renderings of the same set of phrases in English and Japanese, with English offered in filtered and unfiltered versions. He found that in unfiltered English recordings, listeners identified emotions with 70% accuracy, with the highest identification rating for contempt (85%) and the lowest for love (56%). In filtered recordings, the overall accuracy was 61%, with the highest rating for anger (77%) and the lowest for love and contempt (48%). In unfiltered Japanese recordings, listeners identified emotions with 58% accuracy, with the highest rating for grief (90%) and the lowest for love (38%) and contempt (20%). Japanese speakers acknowledged that grief was the easiest emotion to portray, as its expression is culturally condoned, while love and contempt were the most difficult. One actor raised his pitch when portraying contempt, as would be appropriate in Japanese, but this cue was not recognized by English speakers, who commonly associate contempt with low pitch. These findings pointed both to cross-linguistic similarities (grief) and differences (love and contempt) in vocal expression of emotions.

Beier and Zautra (1972) played English-language tape-recordings of six emotions of four different lengths to 52 speakers of English, and then to 55 speakers of Polish and 54 speakers of Japanese who were unfamiliar with English. They found that Polish participants' identification rates were 53% and Japanese participants' 48%, as compared to the 60–80% rate displayed by the English speakers. Anger and indifference were the easiest emotions to decode for Polish speakers, sadness and indifference for Japanese speakers, and happiness and anger for speakers of English. Flirtatiousness and happiness were the most difficult to decode for both Polish and Japanese speakers. The accuracy of identification ratings of both Polish and Japanese speakers improved as the length of the utterances increased.

Van Bezooijen, Otto, and Heenan (1983) investigated recognition of Dutch vocal expression of emotions by Dutch, Taiwanese, and Japanese

TABLE 3.2. *Cross-linguistic studies of identification of emotions in vocal expression*

Study	Stimuli	Expression(s)	Languages	Emotions	Results
Kramer (1964)	content-filtered and unfiltered recordings by 7 male English speakers and 3 Japanese speakers	"There is no other answer. You've asked me that before. My reply has always been the same, and it will always be the same."	*Stimulus*: English, Japanese, *Listeners*: English	anger, love, contempt, indifference, grief	same language (unfiltered) 70% same language (filtered) 61% foreign language 58%
Beier & Zautra (1972)	unfiltered recordings	(1) "Hello" (2) "Good morning" (3) "How are you?" (4) Random sentence	*Stimulus*: English *Listeners*: English, Polish, Japanese	anger, fear, happiness, sadness, indifference, flirtatiousness	same language 60–80% foreign language Polish 53% Japanese 48%
Solomon & Ali (1975)	unfiltered recordings in English made by one amateur actress	teacher's verbal evaluations in three categories: (1) positive (e.g., ("Excellent"); (2) neutral (e.g., "I see"); (3) negative (e.g., "Pretty bad")	*Stimulus*: English *Listeners*: English, Urdu, Hindi, Telugu, Punjabi	positive affect, indifference, negative affect	L1 speakers of English relied more on intonation for affective judgment L2 speakers of English relied more on verbal content
McCluskey, Albas, Niemi, Cuevas & Ferrer (1975)	content-filtered recordings by 3 Canadian and 3 Mexican actresses	two sentences that came first to the speaker's mind to illustrate a particular emotion state	*Stimulus*: English, Spanish *Listeners*: English, Spanish	happiness, sadness, love, anger	Mexican boys did better than Canadian ones in identifying emotions both in Spanish and in English

Albas, McCluskey & Albas (1976)	content-filtered recordings by 6 men in each language	two sentences that came first to the speaker's mind to illustrate a particular emotion state	*Stimulus*: English, Cree *Listeners*: English, Cree	happiness, sadness, anger, love	each group did better in their own language than in the other language (p < .01)
McCluskey & Albas (1981)	content-filtered recordings by 3 women in each language	two sentences that came first to the speaker's mind to illustrate a particular emotion state	*Stimulus*: English, Spanish *Listeners*: English, Spanish	happiness, sadness, anger, love	both groups identified emotions better in Spanish; Spanish-speaking participants were better at identification of emotion in both languages
van Bezooijen, Otto & Heenan (1983) van Bezooijen (1984)	unfiltered recordings by 4 males and 4 females	utterance "two months pregnant" in Dutch	*Stimulus*: Dutch *Listeners*: Dutch, Japanese, Chinese	anger, shame, sadness, fear, disgust, joy, surprise, interest, contempt, neutral voice	same language 66% foreign language: Chinese speakers 37% Japanese speakers 33%
Rintell (1984)	unfiltered recordings	11 conversations where speakers attempted to communicate particular emotions	*Stimulus*: English *Listeners*: Arabic, Chinese, Spanish	pleasure, anger, guilt, anxiety, depression, disgust	same language 76% foreign language 33%

(continued)

TABLE 3.2 (*continued*)

Study	Stimuli	Expression(s)	Languages	Emotions	Results
Roseberry-McKibbin & Brice (1998)	unfiltered recordings by 2 native speakers of English (male and female) and 2 native speakers of Spanish (male and female)	"Will you bring me the ball?"	*Stimulus:* English, Spanish *Listeners:* L1 Spanish, L2 English	happiness, sadness, anger	more correct responses in Spanish than in English ($F_{(1,8)}$ = 6.96, p < .05)
Erickson & Maekawa (2001)	unfiltered recordings	"That's wonderful"	*Stimulus:* English *Listeners:* English, Japanese	admiration, suspicion, anger, disappointment	same language 90–100% foreign language 64–92%
Scherer, Banse & Wallbott (2001)	recordings by 2 male and 2 female professional German actors	meaningless sentences containing syllables from the six European languages in the study	*Stimulus:* language-neutral *Listeners:* German, French, English, Dutch, Italian, Spanish, Indonesian	anger, fear, sadness, joy/happiness, neutral voice (disgust dropped from final analysis due to confusions with anger and sadness)	same language 74% foreign language: Swiss French speakers 69% British and US English speakers 68% Dutch speakers 68% Italian speakers 67% French speakers 66% Spanish speakers 62% Indonesian speakers 52%

Study	Material	Stimulus text	Languages	Emotions	Results
Graham, Hamblin & Feldstein (2001)	unfiltered recordings by 2 male and 2 female professional American actors	116 word monologue	*Stimulus*: English *Listeners*: English, Japanese, Spanish	anger, fear, joy, sadness, depression, hate, nervousness, neutral voice	same language 59% foreign language: Spanish speakers 42% Japanese speakers 38%
Abelin & Allwood (2000, 2002)	unfiltered recording by one male speaker	utterance "Salted herring, mashed potatoes, and pancakes" in Swedish	*Stimulus*: Swedish *Listeners*: Swedish, Spanish, Finnish, English	anger, fear, joy, sadness, surprise, disgust, dominance, shyness	same language: 73% second language: English 59% Finnish 52% Spanish 42%
Nakamichi, Jogan, Usami & Erickson (2002)	unfiltered recordings from two versions of one movie	sentences from "Harry Potter and the Sorcerer's Stone"	*Stimuli*: English, Japanese *Listeners*: English, Japanese	anger, doubt, surprise, sarcasm, anxiety	same language 91% foreign language 72%

adults. There were 129 subjects in their study: 48 native speakers of Dutch, 40 native speakers of Chinese, and 41 native speakers of Japanese. Neither Chinese nor Japanese speakers had any prior contacts with the speakers of Dutch. The native Dutch listeners achieved a 66% correct identification rate and significantly differed from the other two groups, which achieved 37% (Chinese) and 33% (Japanese) accuracy rates. Sadness and anger were the easiest emotions to identify for non-native speakers of Dutch, contempt and joy were the hardest for Chinese speakers, and shame and fear for the Japanese.

A somewhat different methodology was employed in Rintell's (1984) study, in which eleven conversations illustrating six emotions were played to 19 native speakers of English and 127 non-native speakers, among them 66 speakers of Spanish, 20 speakers of Arabic, and 17 speakers of Chinese. In each conversation one speaker was telling another about an experience that caused him or her to feel a particular emotion, without ever naming the emotion expressed. It was found that the assistance from the verbal content did not improve the performance of L2 learners. Native speakers performed significantly better than non-native speakers (76% versus 33%), with Chinese L2 learners of English having the most difficulty with the task.

More recently, Scherer et al. (2001) examined identification of five types of emotional expression by speakers of seven languages. The stimuli in the study consisted of meaningless sentences recorded with different emotional expressions by professional German actors. The results of the study show that despite the fact that the sentences were meaningless and included syllables from all six European languages in the study (but not Indonesian), the vocal portrayals of emotions by German actors were best recognized by German participants (74%). The second best were the French Swiss participants, all of whom had different degrees of bilingualism in German (69%). Indonesian participants exhibited the lowest recognition rate (52%).

Graham et al. (2001) investigated identification of eight types of emotional expression by 85 native speakers of English, 54 Japanese L2 users of English, and 38 Spanish L2 users of English. The researchers found that English speakers' judgments ranged between 76% and 39% accuracy, with an average correct identification rate of 59%. Spanish and Japanese L2 users of English achieved overall correct identification rates of 42% and 38%, respectively. For all three groups, anger was the easiest to identify, while sadness was the most difficult for English speakers, nervousness for Japanese speakers, and fear for Spanish speakers. The authors also identified systematic differences in confusion patterns between Japanese and Spanish speakers. In six out of eight cases, English and Spanish speakers confused the same emotions (anger/hate, fear/nervousness). Japanese speakers exhibited a different confusion pattern (anger/nervousness), suggesting that there may be greater difference in prosodic and paralinguistic cues to vocal expression between typologically distinct languages.

Finally, Abelin and Allwood (2000, 2002) examined identification of eight types of emotional expression by 35 native speakers of Swedish and 23 Spanish, 23 Finnish, and 12 English L2 users of Swedish, all of them immigrants with varying degrees of proficiency in Swedish. Unlike in the other studies, the participants were offered a free choice of responses, and some even responded in their native language. (Those responses were then translated into Swedish.) After deleting the results for two emotion types – shyness and disgust, which were not well recognized by any of the participants – the authors found that native speakers of Swedish exhibited a mean accuracy rate of 73%, and L2 users exhibited mean accuracy rates of 59% (L1 English), 52% (L1 Finnish), and 42% (L1 Spanish). Anger and sadness were the easiest to identify for most participants. Joy, on the other hand, was confused for sadness by 35% of Spanish and 17% of Finnish listeners. It is also noteworthy that in several cases L2 users were more effective in identification of emotion intended by the speaker: All three groups recognized sadness better than the native speakers, many of whom interpreted the portrayal as disappointment. Finnish and Spanish L2 users of Swedish were also more accurate in recognition of anger, which many Swedish and English speakers interpreted as domination. These results suggest that L2 learners may target the most prototypical emotion portrayed by particular cues, while native speakers and advanced L2 users try to differentiate between emotional nuances.

While the majority of the studies discussed here were conducted with adults, there are also some that involved children and teenagers (McCluskey et al., 1975; Solomon & Ali, 1975). Of these only one known to this researcher considered the role of L2 proficiency. Roseberry-McKibbin and Brice (1998) asked nine Mexican–American children, between the ages of five and seven, to judge emotions conveyed by tape-recorded sentences in L1 Spanish and L2 English, in which they had only limited proficiency. The researchers found that the children performed better in L1 Spanish than in L2 English. Unfortunately, it is unclear whether these results are attributable to differences in proficiency or to the fact that the male speaker of English was not as effective as the female speaker, whose expressions the children decoded as well as those of Spanish speakers.

As seen in Table 3.2, cross-linguistic decoding studies convincingly demonstrate that native speakers of various languages, including English, Dutch, German, Cree, Japanese, Spanish, and Swedish, are quite accurate at identifying emotions conveyed vocally by other speakers of the same language, even when utterance content is neutral or unintelligible: Their accuracy rates vary between 59% and 91%. The variation suggests, however, that vocal cues are not always easy to interpret even for native speakers of a particular language. The task is even more challenging for non-native speakers and speakers unfamiliar with the language: Their rates vary between 33% and 72%. The fact that their identification patterns are often better than chance points to some overlap among languages in the meanings of vocal cues, while the difference between native and non-native speakers points to linguistic and cultural specificity of some of the cues.

3.3. Interpretation of emotions in intercultural communication

If identification of emotions in L2 in a laboratory setting is a difficult task, how does it proceed in natural contexts, where several affective meanings may be communicated at once? And what about performing affect in a second language? L2 learners' testimonies show that attempts to communicate affect in L2 may also be fraught with problems, brought on by the transfer of L1 pitch levels, intonation contours, rhythm, or word and sentence level stress. Take, for example, Linda Petrucelli, an American missionary in Taiwan, who had trouble signalling affect in Taiwanese. With time, Petrucelli began to feel that she had learned the basics of the language. One Sunday she mustered enough courage to deliver a sermon in Taiwanese:

> It had been my intention to say, "Jesus went about teaching all the people" (*Ia-so' ka-si lang*). Not an inappropriate message to hear in church on Sunday morning. But I didn't realize that my pitch went one way when it should have gone another (*Ia-so ka-si lang~*). And that one deceptively simple tone lead me to proclaim with firm conviction that "Jesus went about biting all the people to death!"
>
> (Petrucelli, 2000: 162)

In this case the speaker became aware – albeit after the fact – that her pitch patterns altered the meaning of what she intended to say. In other cases, L2 users may be completely unaware that their communicative intentions are misinterpreted by the interlocutors. At times even linguists find themselves confused by unfamiliar prosodic patterns. Well-known scholar of second language acquisition Evelyn Hatch (1992) tells a story of a Chinese student from Singapore who enrolled in one of her classes. He talked little in the beginning of the semester, but as the class progressed he began to talk more and invariably got into confrontations with his fellow students. He also sounded angry in his student–teacher conference and Hatch, bewildered, asked him why he was so angry. Equally surprised, the student replied that he wasn't angry at all.

This exchange prompted the professor to start observing his speech behavior more closely. She noticed that the student spoke in a very staccato style, common for syllable-timed languages, with large pitch fluctuations between syllables. This timing gave all words equal importance and made him sound arrogant to native speakers of English, as if all of the information he was presenting was new for his interlocutors. The student also used a higher pitch than that expected of a male English speaker, with highest pitch points in the beginnings of utterances and a gradual fall at the end. This pitch pattern made him sound angry and accusatory to his English-speaking classmates. In addition, he often used non-English fillers and backchannel signals and an in-breath /h/ that made him sound impatient. In the next student–teacher conference, he complained that he wasn't making any friends and that Americans who talked to him always seemed to get angry. By that time, Hatch was able to come up with some answers and suggestions for working on his intonation patterns.

In this case the conflict between the student and his classmates was, if not resolved, then at least clarified. In many other settings intercultural communication problems persist and vocal cues are misinterpreted as indexing particular personality characteristics or attitudes, such as rudeness or arrogance. Studies of prosody in cross-cultural communication are typically conducted in the framework of interactional sociolinguistics, pioneered by Gumperz (1982a, b), where analysts examine prosody as sequentially embedded in interaction and base their claims on how interactants respond to each other's turns. Many also ask native speakers of the languages in question to listen to and comment on the tape-recordings.

Gumperz's (1982a) most famous example of affective miscommunication comes from a study of interaction between staff and customers in a British airport cafeteria. The supervisor and the customers continually complained that the newly hired Indian and Pakistani women were surly and uncooperative, while the women – like the Chinese student in class – did not know what they were doing wrong. Upon listening to the tape-recordings of some service exchanges, linguists realized that the misunderstanding was caused by the women's intonation contours. For instance, when asking customers whether they wanted some gravy on their meat, the Indian or Pakistani assistant would use a falling intonation, appropriate for questions in many South Asian languages: "Gravy $\searrow$". The customers interpreted the statement as a rude imposition, rather than a polite offer, which in British English involves a rising intonation: "Gravy $\nearrow$?"

Another miscommunication example comes from a transcript of an interaction between a male Indian speaker (A) and a female speaker of British English (B). In the sequence below B is trying to get A to state the problem that he came to see her about:

> B: um, (high pitch)... well...[I I Miss C.
> A: [first of all
> B: hasn't said anything to me you see
>   (pause, about 2 seconds)
> A: I am very sorry if [she hasn't spoken anything
> B: (softly)   [doesn't matter
> A: on the telephone at least,
> B: doesn't matter
> A: but ah...it was very important uh thing for me
> B: ye:s. Tell, tell me what it is you want
> (Gumperz, 1982a: 175)

In this segment, B uses the statement "I...I...Miss C. hasn't said anything to me" as an indirect request for information from the visitor, followed by an unusually long pause. A's response after the pause is marked by a slow rhythm and highly contoured intonation, with stress both on 'very sorry' and 'very important.' Indian English speakers asked to listen to the interaction readily identified this pattern as a preamble conveying a serious concern, which A wanted the listener to understand (and perhaps acknowledge) before they go any further. B, however, appears to interpret A's statement as a formulaic excuse and interrupts him twice with "doesn't matter." Eventually, she appeals to an explicit direct request, "Tell, tell me what it is you want," which conveys some irritation. Other speakers of British English also missed the prosodic cues in A's speech or dismissed them as a minor and displaced indication of affect. In Gumperz's (1982a: 175–179) view, the miscommunication is caused not by A's inability to 'get to the point' but by B's ignorance of the fact that in Indian English, a shift to a slowed rhythm and contoured, rather than flattened, intonation indicates personal concern that needs to be recognized.

A similar emotional and attitudinal confusion stemming from the imposition of different affective meanings on particular contours is documented by Holden and Hogan (1993). In the study, 20 native speakers of English, interviewed in Edmonton, Canada, and 20 native speakers of Russian, interviewed in Moscow, Russia, were asked to judge a set of prerecorded sentences. English speakers heard 16 English sentences, recorded by the same native speaker, once with the intonation appropriate to English and once with a Russian intonation. Russian speakers listened to 16 Russian sentences recorded with a Russian and with an English intonation. For each of the sentences, the participants were asked to evaluate the recorded speaker for a particular emotion (angry, bored, relaxed, sad, surprised) or attitude (arrogant, critical, pleasant, polite, understanding) on a scale from 1 (not) to 7 (very). The ANOVAs performed on the participants' judgments demonstrated that the interaction between language, intonation, and sentence type was significant for almost all of the emotions and attitudes.

Several of these results are interesting for the present discussion. To begin with, English-speaking participants turned out to be much more sensitive to intonation differences than Russian participants and much more negative with regard to L2 intonation. In yes–no questions, they rated sentences with English intonation patterns significantly higher on the positive attitudes (pleasant, polite, understanding) than those with the Russian intonation. They also rated Russian intonation significantly more negatively for all syntactic types, except declaratives, on the dimensions 'angry' and 'critical.' English speakers were also much more sensitive to increased intensity in the stimulus sentences. Russian speakers, on the other hand, exhibited fewer differences in rating patterns and were not particularly sensitive to increased intensity. The authors explain their findings by the fact that Russian has a more intense and dynamic stress system than

English and they point to the danger of Russian speakers being misjudged and misunderstood if they were to maintain the L1 intonation contours in their L2 English.

Yet L2 learners, perennially concerned about pronunciation of vowels and consonants, are rarely aware of suprasegmental differences. When the differences are noticed, they elicit attitudinal judgments, such as the speakers being perceived as overly 'emotional,' unnecessarily 'angry,' or unduly 'critical.' The social meanings attributed to different acoustic characteristics, in particular pitch and intensity, may even affect the L2 learning process. Some learners are inspired to learn the new language in order to acquire a new and more authoritative voice, and others refuse to adjust their pitch or intonation contours in fear of losing their femininity or masculinity. Thus American philosopher Richard Watson (1995) explained his reluctance to speak French, which he reads fluently, by stating tongue-in-cheek that "for American men at least, French sounds syrupy and effeminate" (p. 52). In Ohara's (2001) study, some American women in Japan refused to heighten their pitch because of their critical perception of how it is used by Japanese women: "They sound too unnatural, fake, because their tone is too high. I just use my natural voice" (p. 244). Other women adjusted their pitch, to the point that friends and relatives did not recognize them on the phone when they answered in Japanese.

Not all bilinguals, however, display distinct pitch patterns or voice qualities in their two languages. Those who live in the L2 environment may experience the influence of their L2 on L1. The possibility of L2 influence in the area of affective prosody has been raised by Latomaa (1998), whose informants, Americans living in Finland, reported that under the influence of Finnish their English 'faded' and became 'flat' and 'unemotional.' The adjustability of pitch is well-illustrated in the autobiography of a Japanese–English bilingual Kyoko Mori (1997), who came back to Japan, the country she left at the age of twenty, as a well-known American writer who disapproved of "the high squeaky voice a nice woman is expected to use in public" (p. 16). One day, lost at a subway station in Osaka, she flagged down a station attendant:

"Ano, sumimasen," I started immediately with an apology ("Well, I'm so sorry to be bothering you"). Then I asked where I could catch the right train. Halfway through my inquiry, I realized that I was squeezing the air through my tightly constricted throat, making my voice thin and wavering. *I have to get out of here,* I thought. *It's a good thing I'm leaving in just a few days.* (Mori, 1997: 16)

Cross-linguistic differences in social meanings of vocal cues and cross-linguistic influence in prosody are not the only issues to be considered in thinking about vocal expression of emotions in multilingual contexts. Another interesting perspective is offered in the clinical work by Marcos and associates, discussed in detail in Chapter 6. Marcos et al. (1973a) videotaped two sets of interviews, one in Spanish and one in English, with ten bilingual schizophrenic patients, and had four psychiatrists rate these interviews on the Brief Psychiatric Rating Scale. It was found that the patients demonstrated more pathology – in this case, appeared more detached – when interviewed in L2 English. The scales significantly affected by the language of the interview included emotional withdrawal, anxiety, tension, hostility, depressed mood, and somatic concerns. Marcos et al. (1973b) examined these findings more closely, with two bilingual psychiatrists comparing the verbal and vocal content of the English and Spanish interviews. The analysis suggested that the initial ratings may have been affected by the confusion between depression effects and difficulties in speaking a second language. Depressed English-speakers often exhibit marked increases in pause times and duration of articulations. These characteristics are also common for speech in a less proficient language. Another common indicator of pathology are speech disturbances, which function as a verbal indicator of anxiety. Yet, as demonstrated in Chapter 2, in Western contexts a higher level of anxiety and speech disturbances are also common for L2 speech.

Because patients' capacity to communicate emotions is a key aspect of a psychiatric evaluation, the fact that L2 speech production difficulties can be misperceived as a lack of affective involvement are of major concern to the medical profession (Marcos, 1976a). Marcos et al. (1973a) recommended that in clinical contexts extra attention be paid to disambiguation of L2 effects from the symptoms of depression and anxiety in the interpretation of vocal cues. From the perspective assumed in this chapter, it seems equally important to consider cross-linguistic differences. Vocal correlates of depression in English include narrow or reduced pitch range, monotonous speech, and incongruent contours. As seen earlier, all of these vocal cues may also stem from L1 transfer.

Together, the studies and personal reflections discussed so far suggest that cross-linguistic differences in affective meanings conventionally attributed to vocal cues, combined with the effects of language transfer, anxiety, and difficulties experienced by L2 users, may lead to intercultural miscommunication: L2 users may unwittingly appear rude, angry, overanxious, or unemotional, and their communicative intentions may be misperceived and misinterpreted.

3.4. Factors affecting interpretation of vocal expression of emotions

Based on the studies and testimonies discussed in this chapter, what factors may influence recognition and vocal performance of affect in a second language? At present, it is difficult to reach definitive conclusions, because there is little consistency among various decoding studies in terms of methodology and the types of emotion studied, and because there is little information about vocal profiles of emotions across languages and vocal performance of affect in L2. In what follows, then, I outline ten factors that so far appear to be influential and should be considered in future work. The first set of factors is comprised of speaker and listener characteristics: (a) linguistic and cultural background; (b) degree of attention to suprasegmental cues; (c) level of L2 proficiency; (d) familiarity with the L2 culture, (e) level of anxiety, and (f) gender. The second set involves speech characteristics: (g) type of emotions to be conveyed; (h) task requirements; (i) type of elicitation stimuli, and (j) utterance length.

As seen in Table 3.2 and concomitant discussion, listeners who share linguistic and cultural backgrounds with speakers perform better on emotion identification tasks than non-native speakers of the language or speakers unfamiliar with the language. The accuracy of native speakers' interpretation is much greater than chance and varies between 59% and 91%, while the accuracy of non-native speakers' identification ranges from 33% to 72%. This is not surprising if we think of vocal cues as being relative, rather than absolute. Native speakers and advanced L2 users are familiar with baseline prosodic values of the language, such as mean pitch or mean rate of articulation, and are thus better able to judge the meaning of deviation in such values.

It is logical to posit, then, that the first factor to influence the identification and performance of affect in L2 is the speaker's and/or listener's *linguistic and cultural background*. To date, systematic differences in emotion identification in L2 and, in some cases, in confusion patterns were found between speakers of Japanese and Polish (Beier & Zautra, 1972), Japanese and Spanish (Graham et al., 2001), Chinese, Spanish, and Arabic (Rintell, 1984), French, English, Dutch, Italian, Spanish, and Indonesian (Scherer et al., 2001), and English, Finnish, and Spanish (Abelin & Allwood, 2000, 2002). These decoding studies, together with the studies of differences in social and affective meanings attributed to particular prosodic cues by speakers of Chinese and English (Hatch, 1992), Russian and English (Holden & Hogan, 1993), and Japanese and English (Erickson & Maekawa, 2001; Nakamichi et al., 2002; Ohara, 2001), suggest that speakers of typologically different languages (syllable- versus stress-timed or intonation versus tone) may rely on somewhat different prosodic and paralinguistic cues in vocal expression of emotions.

Structural differences between languages are not the only factor that can contribute to interpretation differences; interpretation difficulties may also stem from differences in the degree of *attention to suprasegmental cues* paid by particular speech communities. This possibility is suggested by Kitayama and Ishii (2002), who offered English-speaking and Japanesespeaking participants a Stroop-type interference task in which the vocal cues were incongruous with the verbal content of the utterance. They found that in the vocal-expression judgment, interference was greater among speakers of American English, while in the word-meaning judgment, interference was greater for Japanese speakers. These findings suggest that Japanese speakers may habitually pay more attention to paralinguistic and prosodic cues.

Interesting evidence also comes from studies by McCluskey, Albas, and associates (McCluskey & Albas, 1981; McCluskey et al., 1975) that compared identification of emotion in vocal expression by Canadian and Mexican children and adults. Mexican children and adults were found to be significantly more accurate than their Canadian counterparts on the identification task in both the Spanish and English samples. In addition, emotional expressions recorded by Spanish-speaking women were better identified by Mexican and Canadian participants than those of English-speaking women. The authors explain their results through differences in affective socialization in the two communities, suggesting that Mexican culture places more emphasis on effective emotional expression and its accurate interpretation.

Solomon and Ali (1975) argue that the degree of attention to verbal versus vocal cues to emotion may vary not only among speech communities but also between L1 and L2. They suggest that the verbal interpretation of affect in L2 may rely more on the verbal content, at least in the beginning stages. This somewhat counterintuitive possibility found empirical support in their study, where 60 American and 40 Indian students between the ages of 14 and 18 were asked to judge affective meanings of tape-recorded utterances in English (L1 for the first group and L2 for the second). The utterances, made to resemble teacher's comments (such as, "Very good," "Take your time"), combined three types of content (positive, neutral, negative) and three types of intonation (pleased, indifferent, displeased). Each statement was repeated once with each of the three different intonations. The analysis of the students' responses demonstrated that in their judgments American students relied more on the intonation, and Indian students on the content of the utterances.

The next factor to consider in any work with L2 users is the *level of L2 proficiency*. To date, the only two decoding studies that have considered this factor came up with contradictory results. Both Rintell (1984) and Graham et al. (2001) examined the influence of proficiency levels on identification of emotions in English by students enrolled in intensive English programs in U.S. universities. Proficiency was determined in Rintell's study by the scores on the Michigan test and in Graham et al.'s study by the scores on the in-house listening placement test. Rintell examined responses of 30 beginner, 70 intermediate, and 27 advanced learners and found a significant effect for language proficiency: The scores of the beginner group were significantly different from the scores of the intermediate and advanced students. In contrast, Graham et al. examined responses of 17 low- and 18 high-proficiency students and found no significant differences between the high- and low-proficiency group.

This contradiction suggests the need for more careful selection and grouping procedures, in particular where advanced learners are concerned. In both studies, even the most advanced learners were enrolled in intensive English programs and were effectively advanced beginners. To ensure proper comparisons, future studies need to include speakers with more advanced levels of proficiency and acculturation. Production-wise, the few existing studies and impressionistic observations suggest that beginning L2 learners may exhibit L1 transfer in affective prosody (Hatch, 1992; Ohara, 2001), while advanced L2 users may adopt the L2 prosody (Ohara, 2001) and either appeal to somewhat different prosodic and paralinguistic cues in their two languages (Esling, 1994; Rosario, 2000) or exhibit L2 influence on L1 (Latomaa, 1998; Mori, 1997).

A related factor here is the *familiarity with the L2 culture* and the degree of acculturation, which may or may not be linked to language proficiency. Due to the widespread availability of U.S. media, including Hollywood productions, Anglo expressions of anger, contempt, disappointment, or approval may be familiar to viewers around the world and thus easier to decode even for speakers who do not speak any English. This familiarity, as well as congruency, with North American culture may explain the superior performance of Spanish speakers in the study by Graham and associates (2001)[1]. Acculturation may also be an important factor in performance of affect as seen in testimonies of L2 users who talk about adjusting their pitch levels in L1 and L2 in response to social pressure (Mori, 1997; Ohara, 2001).

Another important factor related to individual differences, context, and L2 proficiency is the *level of anxiety* experienced by the L2 speaker. Studies by Marcos and associates (1973a, b) suggest that dysfluencies, hesitations, and pauses in the speech of L2 users may be caused by anxiety about communicating in the less proficient language, as well as by on-going lexical searches, and should not be taken as evidence of depression or a lack of affective involvement, in particular in clinical interviews.

The last factor in this cluster is the *gender* of the speaker and the listener. The attention to gender in this research is not accidental: Women are commonly believed to be more emotional than men and thus more attuned to the tasks of performing affect and interpreting others' feelings. A few studies indicate that women as a group may interpret vocal cues to emotion better than men. Scherer et al. (2001) found that female participants performed slightly better than the males on the identification task (67% versus 65%, $p < .04$.). Rintell (1984) also found that women slightly outperformed men, yet her findings failed to reach any level of significance. Solomon and Ali (1975) suggested that gender sensitivity may be mediated by culture: In their study, American girls were more sensitive to prosody than American boys, but Indian boys were more sensitive than

---

[1] In view of potential problems with English–language samples, it is noteworthy that several studies were conducted with German, Dutch, and Swedish speech samples.

Indian girls. Other studies suggest that female speakers may be more effective than males in portraying emotions (cf. Roseberry-McKibbin & Brice,
1998). Once again, however, these results are influenced by language and
culture: Spanish-speaking women were found to be more effective than
English-speaking ones (McCluskey et al., 1975; McCluskey & Albas, 1981).

The fact that language and culture mediate gender effects in both production and perception challenges any simplistic assumptions of universal gender differences in verbal communication. Lutz (1990) argues that
what needs to be attended to in future research is not ways in which men
and women talk differently about emotions or interpret them, but ways
in which language, gender, and emotionality are linked in everyday discourse, informing judgments made about particular speakers. Her arguments find support in cross-linguistic studies showing that male speakers
of French or Japanese may be judged as overly emotional or effeminate by
speakers of English, simply because they appeal to a wider pitch range than
English-speaking men (Watson, 1995; Yuasa, 2002), while English-speaking
women may be perceived as rude, arrogant, insensitive, or unfeminine by
their Japanese interlocutors when their pitch is lower than that of Japanese
women (Ohara, 2001; van Bezooijen, 1995, 1996).

While the factors just discussed involve characteristics of speakers and
listeners, the remaining factors involve characteristics of the speech or stimuli, starting with *the type of emotions* involved. Several studies show that
across linguistic boundaries, anger and sadness may be the easiest and joy
may be the hardest to identify through vocal cues (Abelin & Allwood, 2000,
2002; Beier & Zautra, 1972; Graham et al., 2001; Kramer, 1964; Nakamichi
et al., 2002; Scherer et al., 2001; van Bezooijen, 1984; van Bezooijen et al.,
1983). These results suggest that L2 user identification and performance
of emotions may be influenced by emotion type. Some emotions, such as
grief or sorrow, may be easier to encode and decode because they rely on
conventionalized and easily recognizable vocal cues, such as low pitch, narrow pitch range, slow rate of articulation, and sobbing. Anger appears to
be particularly easy to recognize and communicate, especially with familiar interlocutors. Several respondents to the webquestionnaire, married to
speakers of another language, reported that in emotional arguments they
switch to their own first language and convey their anger vocally, rather
than verbally:

He talks Swedish but not German. Mostly I argue in Swedish but sometimes when
I'm really angry and words run out or when I can't find the right words quickly
enough I just talk German even if he doesn't understand. It's the melody (German
feels rather useful to argue in) or what you call emphasis which is important here.
          (Lisa, 45, L1 German, L2 English, L3 Swedish, married to L1 speaker
          of Swedish; here and elsewhere the original spelling is preserved)

In contrast, vocal cues to joy and happiness – high pitch, expanded
range, fast rate, and so forth – are more ambiguous and are shared by a

number of distinct emotions. Consequently, it is possible that recognition of joy and happiness relies more on a combination of vocal, verbal, and visual cues. This possibility is born out in Rintell's (1984) study that shows that when both vocal and verbal cues are involved, pleasure becomes the easiest emotion to identify (59%). In fact, in one of the conversations involving pleasure, native speakers and L2 learners performed, respectively, with 94.7% and 93.7% accuracy. Consequently, it is possible that vocal, visual, and verbal cues are weighed differently in identification of different emotions, with recognition of joy more dependent on visual and verbal cues and recognition of anger on the vocal ones.

Another important factor likely to affect the outcomes of laboratory experiments are *task requirements*. Greasley et al. (2000) show that the forced-choice task, which requires participants to choose only one label from a small range of 'basic emotions,' does not allow for an adequate level of discrimination in identifying the speaker's emotional state. On the one hand, the 'basic emotions' labels are too broad and thus do not allow for more nuanced judgments of emotional quality and intensity – for example, 'sadness' does not differentiate between the grief of a young widow who has just lost her husband and the feelings of a gardener upset about his pumpkins wilting. On the other hand, the forced-choice task precludes attribution of more than one emotional state, which commonly happens in natural interaction. The authors show that when given an opportunity to select more than one 'basic emotion' label, in 46% of the cases native speakers of English did not agree as to what label was the most appropriate and offered 'mixed' responses. One such confusion occurred in judging the interview with a mother of a murdered child:

Mother: . . . after ten months Lesley was buried on the moors – I had to identify what was left after ten months so you can imagine – and I also had to listen to horrible tapes and look at pedophile photographs they'd taken of my little girl of ten – so innocent – I could *never* ever forgive them – *never* – and never will.

(Greasley et al., 2000: 359)

The lack of consensus in judging this segment resulted in the following split among the participants: sadness (43%), disgust (31%), and anger (26%). This outcome is surprising because these labels are normally regarded as representing discrete emotions. The authors explain that, as often happens in natural communication, the participants had a difficult time disentangling their perceptions of the speaker's emotional state with regard to the events she experienced (upset, sad, devastated, distraught, distressed, despair, grief) and her attitude toward the agents who caused the distress (disgust, anger, hate). They argue that labeling naturally occurring emotional states may involve separate references to emotions evoked by particular events, agents, and objects.

The next factor that affects the outcomes of laboratory experiments is the *type of stimuli* involved. The problems commonly cited with regard to decoding studies involve the disparity in the types of stimuli used: actors versus student speakers, elicited versus naturalistic, content-filtered versus random content versus emotional content, and, finally, monologues versus role plays and scenarios. Item analysis in Scherer et al.'s (2001) study showed that within each emotion category there was considerable variation of recognition accuracy for specific utterances, suggesting that some utterances were more prototypical than others. At the same time, the authors argue for continuous inclusion of less typical items to ensure sensitivity in detection of differences and difficulties in intercultural communication. While inclusion of a variety of items seems reasonable, what is important for future studies is inclusion of the encoding information, that is, the vocal cues used to portray particular emotions. Both encoding and decoding studies identify not only similarities but also differences in speakers' portrayals of emotions, with some speakers being more effective than others (Erickson & Maekawa, 2001; Fairbanks & Pronovost, 1939; Kramer, 1964; McCluskey & Albas, 1981; McCluskey et al., 1975; Roseberry-McKibbin & Brice, 1998; Scherer et al., 1991; Wallbott & Scherer, 1986). To understand how the identification task is performed across – or for that matter within – linguistic boundaries, it seems critical to include information on which vocal profiles elicited more agreement than others. (For an example of one such study see Banse & Scherer, 1996.)

The final factor is the *length of the speech sample*. Beier and Zautra (1972) found that as the length of samples in their study increased, Polish and Japanese participants were able to identify emotions in English-language samples more accurately, until their scores were comparable to those of American English speakers. This finding is not surprising, as longer speech samples offer more information about the speaker's baseline values and thus allow for judgments of relative rather than absolute values.

3.5. Conclusions and implications for future research

Two sets of findings can be culled from the studies discussed in this chapter. To begin with, in the absence of visual and contextual cues, native speakers of a particular language are typically more accurate than non-native speakers in interpreting emotional content of the speech of other native speakers. At the same time, the native-speaker advantage is not an across-the-board phenomenon. Research shows that L2 users improve their performance over time, and in some cases may be as good as or even more accurate than native speakers in emotion identification, at least in experimental conditions (Abelin & Allwood, 2000, 2002; Graham et al., 2001; Rintell, 1984; Scherer et al., 2001).

The differences in performance between native and non-native speakers are attributed here to cross-linguistic differences in baseline prosodic values and in prototypical affective meanings attached to particular vocal cues. The greater-than-chance performance of speakers unfamiliar with the language in question is attributed to cross-linguistic similarities in vocal cues to certain emotions, such as anger or sadness. The studies by McCluskey and Albas (1981; McCluskey et al., 1975) also suggest that differences in affective socialization may allow speakers relatively unfamiliar with the language but sensitive to emotional expression to perform as well as, or even better than, native speakers of the language on the emotion identification task. L2 users' performance also benefits from the familiarity with the baseline values of the target language and with affective meanings attached to the changes in these values.

The second set of preliminary findings concerns production. It appears that, at least in the beginning and intermediate stages, L2 users tend to exhibit L1 transfer of prosodic patterns that may lead to misinterpretation of the affective, and sometimes even linguistic, content of their utterances (Avery & Ehrlich, 1992; Gibson, 1997; Gumperz, 1982a; Hatch, 1992; Holden & Hogan, 1993; Petrucelli, 2000; Swan & Smith, 2001). Some learners may perceive the prosodic patterns of the second or foreign language as exaggerated and unnatural and refuse to imitate them (Ohara, 2001; Swan & Smith, 2001; Watson, 1995). Less proficient L2 users may also appear more detached in the L2, due to the increased pauses or hesitations common in L2 speech (Marcos et al., 1973a, b). In turn, more advanced L2 users may experience L2 influence on L1 in their affective prosody (Latomaa, 1998; Mori, 1997).

Together with studies that show language-specific confusion patterns in emotion identification, these findings suggest that linguistic background affects interpretation and expression of emotion through vocal cues in intercultural communication. The accuracy increases with the length of exposure to the target language community, as L2 users become more familiar with its discourse styles and thus better able to judge deviations from those. These findings have important implications for FL and L2 classrooms, where neither verbal nor vocal aspects of emotional expression have been getting much attention. Pronunciation instruction commonly focuses on the segmental level (for example, contrastive sounds); even when suprasegmental level is addressed, the information is commonly limited to intonation contours associated with particular syntactic structures (for example, questions) or pragmatic categories (for example, greetings). FL and L2 learners could benefit tremendously from learning more about the role of suprasegmental factors in communication, and in particular from role plays, discussions of video clips, and other exercises targeting interpretation of affective meanings, such as the conversations used in Rintell (1984).

Studies to date also have little to offer either classroom teachers or other scholars by way of information about particular languages. To learn more about affect performance and interpretation of vocal cues in specific multilingual contexts, we need to address the shortcomings of current research. To begin with, little systematic information is available on cross-linguistic similarities and differences in conventionalized affective meanings of particular combinations of vocal cues. This scarcity is understandable: Attention to affective meanings of prosody is a relatively recent development in applied linguistics (Avery & Ehrlich, 1992; Gibson, 1997; Holden & Hogan, 1993; Yuasa, 2002), the progress of which has been hampered by theoretical and methodological difficulties inherent in deciding what meanings should be attributed to particular contours, in particular when research is conducted in a second language (Cruttenden, 1997: 139). Brazil (1997) and McCarthy (1991) argue that the whole enterprise of matching intonation contours with particular meanings may in fact be futile.

The recency of this type of investigation also explains the second shortcoming – the lack of discussion of encoding cues in cross-linguistic decoding studies. In discussing their findings, scholars say that participants are 'interpreting emotions,' when in reality the participants are interpreting recordings of more or less adequate expressions of emotions. Only when the profiles of particular stimuli are disclosed will we be able to move forward, to judge how much overlap exists between vocal profiles of various emotions in particular languages and how much variation is contributed by cross-linguistic differences. Collaboration between linguists and psychologists could elucidate both universals and cross-linguistic differences in vocal expression of emotions and thus enhance our understanding of communication in multilingual contexts.

Such collaboration, or at least triangulation of the data from different paradigms, is also necessary to address the third shortcoming of the current work, the overreliance on studies conducted in laboratory contexts. At best, this work makes use of emotion portrayals by experienced actors; oftentimes, however, the portrayals are by random speakers who may be quite inefficient (cf. Kramer, 1964; Roseberry-McKibbin & Brice, 1998). Greasley et al. (2000) argue that to avoid the danger of studying exclusively stylized portrayals of conventionalized emotion cues, the field needs to begin examining the cues used by speakers in natural contexts. Several recent studies that combine conversational and acoustic analyses of emotion talk, treating suprasegmental phenomena as contextualization cues, offer a promising direction for such inquiry (Bloch, 1996; Günthner, 1997; Kyratzis, 2001; Selting, 1994, 1996). And as to the Chinese women in Philadelphia, were they arguing? Not knowing Chinese or these women, I simply do not know. I guess I should have asked.

4

Semantic and conceptual levels: The bilingual mental lexicon

> 'Frustration' is such an amazing word, the lack of it in a language is so
> amazing because it carries with it the word 'frustrate' to stop to block ... so
> the outside force is carried in that word, it's not just what you feel it's the
> way you feel because an outside force that is blocking you and you don't
> have that in Greek...
>
> (Leonidas, a Greek–English bilingual, in Panayiotou, 2004a: 13)

For Leonidas – and many other bi- and multilinguals around the world,
including the respondents to our webquestionnaire – emotion terms of one
language do not neatly map onto the emotion lexicon of another. Greek,
in Leonidas's view, does not have a counterpart of 'frustration,' which he
'learned' to feel as he acquired English; on the other hand, it does have
a feeling of *stenahoria* (discomfort/sadness/suffocation), which he experiences only in Greek-speaking surroundings (Panayiotou, 2004a).

I can relate to his experience of having somewhat distinct emotional lives
in two languages. My own daily life is lived through the means of English
and Russian, whose emotion terms and scripts at times collide and clash,
leading to misunderstandings, tears, and apologies. Take, for instance,
two verbs that are indispensable in Russian emotional life – *serdit'sia* (to
get actively angry, mad, or cross at someone, to be upset with them) and
obizhat'sia (to feel hurt by someone, offended or upset by them). Both are
relational verbs whose meanings presuppose an existing and ongoing close
relationship with another person and an impending reconciliation. These
meanings are not adequately rendered by the English terms 'mad,' 'angry,'
'upset,' or 'offended,' all of which miss the intrinsic links between inner
states and social relationships and have a much higher emotional intensity than *serdit'sia* or *obizhat'sia*. The utterances 'don't be mad/angry' and
'don't be upset/offended' have an accusatory ring to them and lack the
pragmatic intent of *ne serdis'* (don't be mad at me) and *ne obizhaisia* (don't
be upset with me), which is to smooth over an unpleasant incident and to

77

restore good feelings. (See also Wierzbicka, 1994 and 2004, for an in-depth analysis of similar Polish verbs.) Not having the Russian verbs available to me in my relationship with my English-speaking partner and my English-dominant son deprives me of an important means of relationship-building and emotion management. The fact that I can't use the words does not mean, however, that I don't continue acting out the emotional scripts of *serdit'sia* and *obizhat'sia* I learned early on in life. My partner and son are often mystified by these emotional reactions. Rather than understanding them as a legitimate means of maintaining a loving relationship, they interpret my behaviors as 'pouting' and 'overreacting' and see me as being overly sensitive or downright unreasonable.

But enough with personal examples – how much credence should we give to such subjective accounts of bilingual individuals, really? Maybe I am indeed overly sensitive and downright unreasonable (as the reader is no doubt thinking right now). Is there any way we can investigate bilinguals' emotional lives and emotion concepts in a scientific manner? The present chapter takes up this challenge and sets the following aims: (a) to introduce the reader who is unfamiliar with research on language and emotions to a variety of cross-linguistic differences in emotion terms; (b) to introduce the reader unfamiliar with bilingualism research to an array of empirical approaches to the study of the bilingual mental lexicon; (c) to show what bicultural bilinguals' judgments could offer to debates about emotion terms; and (d) to highlight the dynamic nature of the bilingual mental lexicon, where emotion categories are not always represented in the same way they are in the monolingual lexicon.

I begin the chapter with a brief overview of three competing paradigms that offer distinct conceptualizations of the relationship between emotion terms, concepts, and bodily experiences. Then I present a prototype-based definition of emotion concepts adopted in the present work, and argue that one of the key weaknesses of current studies of emotion terms is the conflation of semantic and conceptual levels of representation. Subsequently, I summarize what is known about cross-linguistic differences in emotion terms and discuss the few studies to date that have examined the bilingual emotion lexicon. I conclude with a summary of factors that affect the structure of emotion concepts in the bilingual lexicon and discuss directions for future inquiry.

4.1. Emotion words and concepts

At present, no consensus exists in emotion research on the relationship between bodily experiences, words, and concepts, on the structure and nature of emotion concepts, on the structure of the emotion lexicon, and on methods of selection and analysis of emotion terms. Three perspectives can be distinguished in this debate: nativist, universalist, and relativist.

These perspectives converge in recognizing that speakers of different languages may differ in ways they talk about and act on various emotions. They diverge, however, in their treatment of the trifecta of interest, bodily experiences/mental representations/lexical items, in the degree of importance assigned to cross-linguistic differences, in the links posited between these differences and underlying mental representations, and in the way they conceptualize the relationship between language and culture.

In the *nativist* paradigm, both language (as Universal Grammar) and concepts are seen as innate and universal, while words are considered to be mere reflections of the mental concepts, and cross-linguistic differences in meanings are nothing more than cultural 'noise' and usage conventions. Nativism privileges mental representations and posits the existence of *mentalese*, or the innate language of thought, which is prior to and independent of language (Fodor, 1975, 1998; Pinker, 1994, 1997). In this view, all emotion concepts are primary, basic, and pancultural, whether particular languages have words for them or not. Cross-linguistic differences in emotion lexicons are superfluous because they say "nothing about what . . . people feel" (Pinker, 1997: 365). Ironically, having said that, Pinker immediately contradicts himself and links the emotions he discusses not to 'feelings' (however defined), but to cognitive scenarios, such as taking pleasure in another's misfortunes (*Schadenfreude*), or behaviors, such as carefully planned and executed rampage preceded by lengthy brooding over failure (*amok*). If all possible evidence is discounted *a priori* as irrelevant or used only when convenient, it is hard to see how such a view could be tested or falsified, and how one could learn 'how people feel.' It is not surprising, then, that this approach does not have many supporters in the field of emotion research (a development that parallels the general waning of interest in the Fodorian view of concepts).

The second paradigm, sometimes referred to as *universalist*, is much more common in language and emotion research. This paradigm privileges bodily experiences and views emotions as "biologically determined processes, depending on innately set brain devices, laid down by a long evolutionary history" (Damasio, 1999: 51). These processes share common experiential qualities and are expressed through universally understood facial expressions (Ekman, 1980, 1992, 2003; Izard, 1977; Le Doux, 1996). In this view, both concepts and language are secondary. Conceptual categories are formed as the situations we experience are linked with the brain apparatus used for the triggering of emotions (Damasio, 2003: 146), and words function as "representations of emotions" (Ekman, 2003: 13) – hence, the rootedness of many emotion metaphors in bodily experiences (Kövecses, 2000). Similarly to Pinker (1997), Ekman (2003) argues that we experience emotions regardless of whether they are named by our language, and he appeals to Italian, Yiddish, and German words to illustrate emotions that are unnamed in English yet experienced by English speakers.

Other scholars who assume the existence of basic emotions acknowledge that mental representations of 'secondary' emotions may differ across cultures, and see cross-linguistic differences in the emotion lexicon as a reflection of this cultural variation (Boucher, 1979; Johnson-Laird & Oatley, 1989; Kövecses, 2000; Levy, 1984; Myhill, 1997; Russell, 1991a; Scherer, 1994; Shaver et al., 1987). While agreeing on the main premises, these scholars disagree as to (a) the range of basic emotions (how many there are and what are they, – cf. Ortony & Turner, 1990); (b) the structure of emotion concepts; and (c) the nature of universal and culture-specific in emotion concepts. With regard to the last, they debate, for instance, whether the universal level is represented by psychobiological emotion patterns (Scherer & Wallbott, 1994), basic image schemas (Kövecses, 2000), concept foci (Levy, 1984), atomistic concepts (Johnson-Laird & Oatley, 1989), concept dimensions (Myhill, 1997; Russell, 1991a), or process dimensions (Mesquita & Frijda, 1992).

The third paradigm, also known as *relativist* or *social constructionist*, questions the existence of basic emotions (Ortony & Turner, 1990; Schachter & Singer, 1962) and the universality of 'emotion,' arguing that it is a Western cultural construct and as such is a problematic category around which to organize multiple ways in which members of different cultures talk about feelings, reactions, attitudes, internal states, and external phenomena (Abu-Lughod & Lutz, 1990; Bamberg, 1997; Edwards, 1997; Heelas, 1986; Lutz, 1988; Myers, 1979; Rosaldo, 1980, 1984; Shweder, 1993, 1994; Wierzbicka, 1986, 1992, 1999). Consequently, while in the other two paradigms bodily experiences and emotion concepts preexist corresponding lexical items (which function simply as labels), in the relativist framework language guides the acquisition of concepts, and concepts influence the interpretation of bodily states. In this view, affective socialization is an intrinsic part of the language socialization process, with language focusing children's attention on phenomena linked to 'anger,' *grust'* (sadness/melancholy; Russian), or *fago* (compassion/love/sadness; Ifaluk). As corresponding conceptual categories are formed and modified, children learn how to interpret physical experiences and external events in terms of these culture-specific emotion categories, and to judge whether someone is justifiably angry, *grustnyi*, or *fago*, and when and how to respond to or with anger, *grust'*, or *fago*.

The purpose of the present chapter is to foreground cross-linguistic differences, agreed upon in all three paradigms, and to avoid taking a stance in the basic emotions debate, which is outside the scope of this book. Consequently, I will continuously refer to 'emotions' as universalists do, at the same time recognizing the linguistic and cultural specificity of this notion and its potential inapplicability to certain contexts, as relativists would. I will also abstain from offering a definition of emotions per se, acknowledging simply that I take a componential or process view of emotions, seeing them both as inner states and as relational phenomena. Instead, I will focus on *emotion concepts*, seen here as prototypical scripts that are formed as a result of repeated experiences and that involve causal antecedents, appraisals, physiological reactions, consequences, and means of regulation and display (Fehr & Russell, 1984; Kövecses, 1986, 1990, 2000; Lakoff, 1987; Mesquita & Frijda, 1992; Russell, 1991a, b; Shaver et al., 1987).

This definition differs from other script- and prototype-based definitions in that it views concepts as more than just constellations of meanings encoded in semantic memory. In the view adopted here, concepts involve the ability to categorize events and phenomena in language- and culture-specific ways, to appraise these events and phenomena as negative, positive, and personally relevant or irrelevant, and to respond to these phenomena in linguistically and culturally appropriate ways, comprehensible to other members of the speech community in question. As such, concepts include: (a) experientially learned and thus culture- and language-appropriate event and emotion categories and the autobiographic memories linked to them, encoded in episodic memory; (b) connections between these categories and somatic states associated with them, encoded in the limbic system, in particular the amygdala and the anterior cingulate gyrus (Damasio, 1994, 2003); (c) action patterns and display rules encoded in procedural memory.

This view is compatible with a universalist approach, because it can accommodate concepts that derive from shared human experiences and does not preclude the ability to experience emotions not encoded in single lexical items. It also recognizes the experiential and script-like nature of emotion concepts, emphasized in relativist approaches, which see emotions as cultural scripts (Wierzbicka, 1994) or as complex narrative structures or story-like interpretive schemes that impose meaning on somatic experiences (Shweder, 1994). From a nativist viewpoint, however, such an approach is a cop-out: Pinker (1997) contends that it is much easier to learn, observe, and analyze causes or consequences of particular emotion states than to capture the feeling itself. (See also Johnson-Laird & Oatley, 1989.) In contrast, Fehr and Russell (1984) argue that any definition of emotion in strictly mental, behavioral, or physiological terms would be oversimplified and easily met with counterexamples. Whether there exist specific physiological 'emotion states' that are interpreted in the same way by members of all cultures remains an empirical question that will be resolved elsewhere. What is of interest in the present chapter is not somatic states or sensations per se, but rather emotion categorization from a linguistic, cognitive, and cultural viewpoint.

I adopt this approach for two reasons. First of all, it is possible that there is no direct correspondence between particular physiological states and their interpretations and that biological states are an important but not a determining component of emotion scripts. Thus, the same heaviness, sleepiness, and low level of arousal may be variably interpreted as depression, sadness, illness, or tiredness, depending on the preceding chain of events and on linguistic and conceptual options available to the individual. Secondly, from the perspectives of the study of language and emotions and of bilingualism, what is important is to determine whether individuals know 'how to do' emotions and how to interpret emotion displays and emotional expression in languages learned later in life; what they experience in the process represents only one piece of the overall puzzle.

Four further caveats need to be noted with regard to the nature and structure of emotion concepts as defined above. First, to say that emotion concepts are encoded as scripts is not tantamount to claiming that people experiencing emotions act out roles from culturally shared, predetermined scenarios (Fehr & Russell, 1984). The inclusion of the autobiographic component entails individual variation of conceptual representations. It means that, as a result of distinct personal experiences, native speakers of the same language may arrive at somewhat different views of the Polish *tęsknota* (longing/melancholy/nostalgia) (see Hoffman, 1989; Kolenda, 1987; Wierzbicka, 1986), or the Japanese *ijirashii* (a feeling of empathy and pity associated with seeing someone weak but praiseworthy overcome an obstacle or do a good deed) (Araki, 1994).

Second, while conceptual cores, that is, prototypical emotion scripts, may be distinct, the boundaries of emotion categories are not discrete; rather, they are fuzzy and overlapping, so that some events, displays, or scripts fit into more than one category. This overlap is evident both in laboratory tasks (see confusions in emotion categorization discussed in Chapter 3) and in real-life contexts, whereby speakers may use several terms to describe their own or someone else's emotions (Greasley et al., 2000). This usage may signify that a person is experiencing more than one emotion simultaneously, but it also suggests that emotion displays are not necessarily subject to categorical perception. We may need several types of cues and some interactional cooperation to decide if our interlocutor is sad, upset, tired, tense, or all of the above.

Furthermore, conceptual representations are not stable and immutable entities; rather, they function in a context-dependent manner, whereby their boundaries are flexibly created and recreated by the demands of different tasks and in response to local negotiations of meaning. This means that different aspects and dimensions of a concept are activated, modified, and adapted in different settings and with different interlocutors (Barsalou & Medin, 1986; Damasio, 1989). In other words, even within a more or less homogeneous speech community, anger scripts activated in a particular setting will vary with the triggering event, and the means of anger management and display will depend on the power relationship between the interlocutors (whether we are talking to a superior or an employee, for instance), the degree of familiarity (a stranger or a friend), and the context of the interaction (home, workplace, or other). This variation highlights the links between emotion concepts and other conceptual domains, in particular those involving local systems of moral order and power relations, in which emotion categories are often embedded.

Finally, the view adopted here has important methodological implications, in particular the acknowledgment that semantic representations are just a part, rather than the equivalent, of conceptual or cognitive representations. In what follows, the term *semantic* will refer to research that explores connotative and denotative meanings of and relationships between words in a particular language or across languages. This research is often carried out with the help of linguistic approaches that involve analysts' intuitions about particular sets of linguistic data, among them the Natural Semantic Metalanguage (Wierzbicka, 1999), lexical and metaphor analysis (Kövecses, 1986, 1990, 2000; Lakoff, 1987), propositional analysis (Johnson-Laird & Oatley, 1989), and context-based comparative semantic analysis (Myhill, 1997). It can also be conducted with the help of psychological approaches, such as word recall and lexical decision tasks (Altarriba & Bauer, 2004), network mapping and cluster analysis (Brandt & Boucher, 1986; Church et al., 1998; Heider, 1991) and multidimensional scaling (Fontaine et al., 2002; Moore et al., 1999), that require study participants to recall words or make judgments about them. These studies offer rich information about cross-linguistic differences in lexical semantics, the intricacies of the semantic structure of emotion words, and semantic processing. They offer only limited information, however, on scripts activated by emotion terms in concrete speakers and do not allow us to study the multimodal, experiential, and embodied nature of these scripts.

Authentic *conceptual* analyses of emotion terms entail comprehensive empirical investigations of causal antecedents of emotions (and thus of event categorization), appraisals of such events, reports of somatic states accompanying particular emotions, emotion consequences, and means of emotional regulation and display. Understanding of these mental representations in the mind, in talk, and in action requires triangulation of methods such as interviews, questionnaires, diaries, ethnographies, and script categorization tasks, which takes us beyond representations in the mind of a single analyst and toward both group consensus and individual variation (Averill, 1982; Gerber, 1985; Lutz, 1988; Morsbach & Tyler, 1986; Scherer, 1988; Scherer & Wallbott, 1994; Schmidt-Atzert & Park, 1999). Excellent example of triangulation is offered in Heider's (1991) work on three Indonesian cultures, where the researcher combined the results of naturalistic observation of children's and adult's emotion behavior with analysis of emotion scripts in novels and films and with data from several cognitive and linguistic tasks, including definition, translation, sentence completion, and prototypicality rating.

Throughout the discussion, emotion scripts elicited by such studies will be referred to as conceptual. I fully agree, however, with Lakoff (1987) and with Ungerer and Schmid (1996: 50), who argue that cognitive and cultural models are two sides of the same coin: The terms *cognitive* or *conceptual* stress the psychological nature of these representations and allow for consideration of interindividual differences, whereas the term *cultural* stresses their sociocultural and sociohistoric nature and allows for consideration of intergroup differences. As the focus of this chapter is on the conceptual level of representation, this is the term that will be used, with the understanding that concepts have linguistic, cultural, and perceptual bases.

Conflation of the terms *semantic* and *conceptual* in scholarly discussions on the nature of meanings is not accidental – most linguists and psychologists work with healthy monolingual speakers whose concepts neatly map onto words, and thus one level appears sufficient to describe their mental representations. When researchers engage bilingual participants or translators, they assume a similarly unproblematic relationship between their respective terms and concepts (cf. Church et al., 1998). At a closer look, however, the mapping between words and concepts in the mental lexicons of various bi- and multilinguals is not as straightforward, and their representations are not necessarily equivalent to those of monolingual speakers of the languages in question.

For example, English-speaking learners of Spanish learn early on that the meanings of the English verb 'to be' are split between two verbs, *ser* and *estar*, the first of which refers to inherent or permanent characteristics or a location of an event, and the second to a physical or mental state of being. Once they learn and understand these definitions, they may perform adequately on various classroom assignments, such as fill-in-the-blank tests. Yet in spontaneous interaction they commonly exhibit L1 transfer, failing to pay attention to the distinction encoded in the two verbs, either using them interchangeably or favoring one in all contexts, even after several years of instruction (cf. Geeslin, 2003).

This happens time and again because linguistic constraints of a particular language and conceptual representations are not necessarily aligned in the mind of bi- and multilingual speakers. In the case of cross-linguistic differences between two languages, L2 words are – at least initially – linked to their memorized definitions stored in explicit memory, and to L1 translation equivalents (however inexact), which in turn are linked to the multimodal conceptual representations in implicit memory (Paradis, 1994). In classroom tasks, which allow sufficient time for engaging the metalinguistic awareness, the definitions are easily retrievable and allow for more or less correct performance. In contrast, spontaneous language production and processing – or in Slobin's (1996) terms, 'thinking for speaking'– are driven by conceptual representations in implicit memory. Consequently, in on-line performance, L2 learners sidestep definitions stored in explicit memory and link L2 words – by way of L1 translation equivalents – to L1-based concepts. And because the English concept encodes a uniform notion of 'being,' English-speaking learners of Spanish fail to differentiate systematically between *ser* and *estar*. Convincing evidence that in the lexicons of beginning and intermediate L2 learners, L2 words are strongly associated to L1 translation equivalents – and thus L1-based conceptual representations – can be found in the work of Kroll and associates on the Revised Hierarchical Model of the bilingual lexicon (Kroll & Dussias, 2004; Kroll & Stewart, 1994; Kroll et al., 2002).

Here one can ask whether this view is applicable to the emotion lexicon. In fact, Pinker (1997) claims that he has "never heard a foreign emotion word whose meaning was not instantly recognizable" (p. 367). Yet his armchair linguistics perspective runs contrary to the perceptions of linguistic anthropologists working in the field for whom the referents of emotion terms are often "genuinely unfamiliar" (Gerber, 1985: 145) and require lengthy investigations before they can be approximated in another language. It appears that Pinker does not recognize the provisional nature of translation: It is the approximations, that is, the English words, that are immediately recognizable to him, not the foreign words themselves (see also Wierzbicka, in press).

From the perspective assumed here, Pinker's 'recognition' is semantic, not conceptual. There is no doubt in my mind that speakers of English 'understand' the translation of the Spanish *susto* as 'fright,' 'fear,' or 'scare,' and the definition of the Japanese *amae* as a feeling of dependence on someone. What they do not have is a corresponding experientially acquired concept that would allow them to categorize events, situations, and phenomena in terms of *susto* or *amae*. Guided by the representation of 'fright,' they will miss many important aspects of *susto*, including its links to the folk illness of *susto* or 'magical fright' (O'Nell, 1975; Weller et al., 2002). And guided by the definition of *amae* they won't be able to differentiate between the situations in which one feels *amae* versus *itoshii* (longing for a loved one) (Doi, 1973). One also wonders to what degree they would be able to inhibit the appraisal dimensions of particular concepts acquired in the native language, and see the dependence encoded in *amae* as desirable, rather than a type of relationship that, in the Western view, adults should grow out of (Morsbach & Tyler, 1986).

Research in second language acquisition and bilingualism convincingly demonstrates that to recognize and understand the basic meaning of a particular word or expression is not the same as having an authentic conceptual representation of the linguistic item in question and acting on it (cf. Pavlenko, 2003a). Only through a prolonged process of L2 socialization can L2 users form L2-based conceptual representations that, among other things, force them to pay attention to distinctions not encoded in their

L1 and allow them to determine the prototypicality of particular events or displays of emotion. Lutz (1988) offers an excellent definition of what this representation of an emotion term would be like:

> To understand the meaning of an emotion word is to be able to envisage (and perhaps to find oneself able to participate in) a complicated scene with actors, actions, interpersonal relationships in a particular state of repair, moral points of view, facial expressions, personal and social goals, and sequences of events. (p. 10)

From this perspective, bicultural bilinguals – members of social networks in both speech communities – emerge as invaluable informants about the similarities and differences between respective emotion terms and scripts.

4.2. Cross-linguistic studies of emotion lexicons

Before we move on to bilinguals, however, let us examine first what we actually know about cross-linguistic similarities and differences between emotion terms. The intricacies of the emotion lexicon have received unprecedented attention in the study of language and emotions. Linguists, anthropologists, and psychologists have approached the lexicon from a variety of angles, attempting to determine whether there exist basic emotion terms found in all languages, whether translation equivalents of emotion terms have shared meanings, and whether some emotion concepts are language- and culture-specific. As Lutz and White (1986) perceptively noted, color-terms research initiated by Berlin and Kay (1969) offered a seductive model for the study of the emotion lexicon, in particular for those who hypothesized that "emotion lexicons will be shaped in systematic ways by the biological constraints of universal core affects" (Lutz & White, 1986: 416). Three directions can be distinguished in cross-linguistic studies of the emotion lexicon: (a) explorations of lexicalization and conceptualization of superordinate terms such as 'emotions'; (b) analyses of emotion domains of various languages; and (c) comparative analyses of translation equivalents.

To date, several findings appear to be more or less conclusive. To begin with, languages differ in lexicalization of inner states. In many Western languages, 'emotions' and 'feelings' are lexicalized semantic categories[1]. Some languages, such as Ommura of Papua, appear not to have any terms to label inner states (Heelas, 1986). Others, including Tahitian (Levy, 1973), Biminkuskusmin of Papua New Guinea (Poole, 1985), Ifaluk of Micronesia (Lutz, 1986, 1988), Chewong of Malaysia (Howell, 1981), and Gidjinggali, an aboriginal language in Australia (Hiatt, 1978), may have terms for inner

---

[1] Note however difficulties encountered by those who attempt to establish conceptual structure of these terms even within English (cf. Fehr & Russell, 1984).

states but lack superordinate terms for emotions. The absence of such superordinate terms may be interpreted differently in different paradigms. Nativists and universalists posit that emotions as basic concepts exist regardless of the presence or absence of such terms, while relativists claim that the lack of superordinate terms reflects the lack of unified concepts of emotions, and point out that talk about emotions is replaced in these speech communities by talk about normative rules and obligations (Howell, 1981).

Relativists also argue that even when non-Western languages have emotion categories, the categories may involve somewhat different sensations and perceptions, attributed to different causes, placed in different body parts (for instance, the liver), and classified and evaluated in different ways than those encoded in Western languages (Heelas, 1986; Lutz, 1988; Russell, 1991a). Most notably, while in Western languages emotions are conceptualized as individual phenomena, arising in the individual, in many non-Western languages, including Balinese (Wikan, 1990), Fula (Riesman, 1977), Ilongot (Rosaldo, 1980), Kaluli (Schieffelin, 1985), Pintupi (Myers, 1986), and Samoan (Gerber, 1985), they are seen as relational phenomena, embedded in social situations and taking place between people rather than within their bodies and minds. Consequently, emotion words in such cultures function as "statements about the relationship between a person and an event (particularly those involving another person), rather than as statements about introspection on one's internal states" (Lutz, 1986: 267).

Semin and associates (2002) made similar arguments about differences in dominant lexical categories between Dutch and Hindustani, spoken in Surinam. The researchers found that the working emotion lexicon of Hindustani speakers contained a significantly higher proportion of emotion verbs than the Dutch lexicon, which in turn contained a higher proportion of emotion nouns. They linked these differences to distinct conceptualizations of emotions in the two cultures and argued that in the Hindustani culture, which privileges relationships and interdependence, emotion verbs function as relationship-markers, while in Dutch, emotion nouns function as self-markers consistent with the individualistic view of emotions as inner states.

Importantly, differences in lexicalization and conceptualization of emotions can be found not only between broadly conceived Western and non-Western languages but also within these groups (Wierzbicka, 1995, 1999). For instance, both Russian and English have the notions of *emotsii/* emotions and *chuvstva*/feelings. However, these notions are lexicalized differently in the two languages (Pavlenko, 2002c; Wierzbicka, 1992). In English, they are most commonly expressed through copular constructions with adjectives and pseudo-participles that present emotions as passive inner states (to be upset, happy, excited). Only a few emotions are expressed primarily through intransitive verbs (to rejoice, to worry). In contrast, in Russian, emotions are commonly expressed through intransitive, oftentimes reflexive, verbs that construct feelings as actions and processes (*grustit'*/to be (actively) sad, *radovat'sia*/to be (actively) happy, *stydit'sia*/to be (actively) remorseful, ashamed) and as interpersonal relationships (for example, *serdit'sia* and *obizhat'sia* discussed in the beginning of this chapter). Some emotions can also be described as states, either through prepositional constructions (*pogruzit'sia v otchaianie*/to plunge into despair) or through adjectives (*grustnyi*/sad, *radostnyi*/joyful, *vozmushchennyi*/indignant), yet most of these nouns and adjectives also have corresponding verbs.

Considering these patterns, nativists and universalists would point to the fact that both Russian and English, or for that matter Dutch and Hindustani, have emotion words, while relativists would emphasize the significance of having different dominant lexicalization patterns in working emotion vocabularies, because they require Russian and Hindustani speakers to pay more attention to social relationships, actions, and body language related to emotional experience than would speakers of English or Dutch. Studies show that Russian indeed does have a richer vocabulary of emotional expressions and collocations linked to body language (Wierzbicka, 1998, 1999) and that its speakers are more attentive, or at least more willing to verbalize, actions that accompany the process of experiencing emotions (Pavlenko, 2002c). These arguments are similar to ones currently made with regard to Hopi time in debates about linguistic relativity. While earlier debates interpreted Whorf as saying that Standard Average European has the concept of time and Hopi does not, his real argument was that the two espouse profoundly different concepts of time (Lucy, 1992). Similarly, relativists do not argue that speakers of some languages do not have physical sensations that constitute an important element of feelings in the Western world. Rather, they suggest that these sensations feed into very different notions of inner states and their meanings, origins, and consequences.

The second line of inquiry in the field attempts to identify the number and meanings of emotion words in a particular language. Cross-linguistic studies show that languages differ widely in the size of their emotion lexicons. Some languages, such as Chewong in Malaysia, have but seven emotion words (Howell, 1981); others, such as Malay, Indonesian, Filipino, and German, contain about 230–250 (Boucher, 1979; Church et al., 1998; Gehm & Scherer, 1988; Heider, 1991). Dutch emotion lexicon was shown to have 1,500 emotion words (Heelas, 1986) and English more than 2,000, with 1,000–1,200 words regularly used by its speakers (Wallace & Carson, 1973). Some scholars take these numbers to correspond to the salience of the emotion domain. At present, it is hard to assess this claim, as it is not always clear what counted as emotion words in particular studies, how emotion words were elicited or selected, and whether some numbers represent the working emotion vocabularies of particular speakers and others the total emotion lexicons as defined through a dictonary.

Consequently, the main arguments in the field are based not on the size of emotion lexicons or the presence or absence of superordinate terms, but on the relationship between English emotion terms and their translation equivalents in other languages. While this is undoubtedly an ethnocentric approach, it is currently unavoidable due to the dominance of English in this area of research. In what follows then, *translation equivalents* will be seen as word pairs in two or more languages that have similar denotation in a range of contexts. Oftentimes, scholars perceive these words as linguistic and conceptual equivalents, yet the term 'translation equivalents' is more exact than we think: These words are equivalents for translation purposes only, and only in some contexts, while in other contexts they may require other translations. They are not necessarily full linguistic and conceptual equivalents.

Semantic or *linguistic non-equivalence* of particular word pairs may stem from differences in form, frequency of use, physical or interpersonal perspective embodied in the words, modal intensity, cultural connotations, and, most often, the range of encoded meanings (polysemy). For instance, Myhill's (1997) analysis of various English translations of the Bible shows that Biblical Hebrew emotion terms do not closely correspond to the English words 'anger,' 'fear,' or 'sadness,' and thus different translations of the same word appear in different contexts and in different versions of the Bible. *Conceptual non-equivalence*, following the definition of concepts adopted here, stems from differences in causal antecedents, appraisals, somatic states, consequences, and means of regulation and display, encoded in particular emotion concepts.

Comparative analyses of emotion categorization systems and of scripts and experiences associated with particular terms suggest that the domain of emotions is 'carved up' differently in different languages. As was pointed out earlier, this does not necessarily imply that speakers of these languages have different physiological experiences, but rather that they have somewhat different vantage points from which to interpret these experiences. Taking English as a point of depature, we can see that:

(1) Some languages lack lexical and conceptual equivalents of the English superordinate term 'emotion' (Hiatt, 1978; Howell, 1981; Levy, 1973; Lutz, 1988; Poole, 1985).
(2) Languages differ in the dominant grammatical categories encoding emotions, which has important implications for their semantic and conceptual structure: Some languages favor verbs, which encode emotions as processes and relationships; others favor adjectives and nouns, which encode emotions as inner states (Pavlenko, 2002c; Semin et al., 2002; Wierzbicka, 1992).
(3) Some languages do not have lexical and conceptual equivalents of English basic emotion terms, such as 'anger,' 'happiness/joy,'

'fear,' 'surprise,' 'sadness,' and 'disgust' (Briggs, 1970; Levy, 1973; Wierzbicka, 1992, 1999), or secondary terms, such as 'depression' or 'anxiety' (Marsella, 1980; Russell, 1991a).

(4) Emotions referred to with a single term in English are lexically differentiated in other languages: Samoan offers two terms that roughly connote 'anger' (Gerber, 1985), German and the Yankunytjatjara language of Central Australia offer three (Durst, 2001; Goddard, 1991), Mandarin Chinese uses five (Kornacki, 2001), and Biblical Hebrew has seven such terms (Myhill, 1997).

(5) Emotions lexically differentiated in English may be subsumed into one word in other languages; for instance, Ilongot and Ifaluk use the same term to refer to 'anger' and 'sadness' (Lutz, 1988; Rosaldo, 1980), while Ifaluk, Indonesian, and Pintupi appear to collapse 'shame' and 'embarrassment' (Lutz, 1988; Myers, 1979; Russell, 1991a).

(6) Cultures also differ in which emotions are elaborated as key or focal, and which are muted and less recognized: The Ilongot privilege 'passion' (Rosaldo, 1980), the Utku Eskimo 'gentleness' and 'mildness' (Briggs, 1970), the Kaluli 'anger,' 'grief,' and 'shame' (Feld, 1990; Schieffelin, 1976, 1985), and speakers of contemporary American English 'love' and 'guilt' (Hochschild, 1983). In turn, 'anger' among the Utku Eskimo (Briggs, 1970) and 'sadness' among the Tahitians (Levy, 1973) are less recognized and talked about.

(7) Some languages have emotion terms that are absent in English, such as German *Angst* and *Schadenfreude*, Samoan *lotomamā* (socially approved feeling of happy passivity and willingness to agree with the desires of others) (Gerber, 1985), or Korean *uulhada* (sadness/ loneliness/depression) (Schmidt-Atzert & Park, 1999)[2].

(8) Medical anthropologists have also identified a number of historically and socioculturally specific emotion-based somatic illnesses or pathological states, such as *susto* among rural Spanish speakers (O'Nell, 1975; Weller et al., 2002), *hwabyung* among Korean elderly (Pang, 1990), or *nevra* among Greek immigrant women in Canada (Lock, 1990), suggesting that members of different cultures may respond differently to changes in somatic states, exhibiting autonomic response specificity (Hinton & Hinton, 2002).

(9) Salience and meaning of various emotion words as well as rules of emotion display and management also vary in different sociohistoric periods: For instance, accidie and melancholy, which once had great importance in the English-speaking world, are now becoming

[2] What is particularly interesting here is that the German *Angst* and *Schadenfreude* were eventually borrowed by English, no such borrowing took place with non-Western emotion terms which reflect a different viewpoint on desirable and legitimate emotions.

obsolete while depression, anxiety, stress, and burnout are effort-
lessly discussed, even though these hardly registered even a century
ago (Harré, 1986; Stearns, 1993; Stearns & Stearns, 1986).

(10) Finally and most importantly, cross-cultural differences have been
identified in the components of emotion concepts. (For a comprehensive discussion, see also Mesquita & Frijda, 1992; Scherer, Wallbott,
& Summerfield, 1988.)

- *Causal antecedents of emotions*: In some cultures, emotions are seen
  as being generated by external events and mental perceptions of
  these events, while in others they are believed to be generated by
  gods, other people, or internal organs (Heelas, 1986; Myhill, 1997).
  Cultures also differ in antecedents of specific emotions: Japanese,
  for example, are rarely saddened by the world news in the same
  way Europeans are, nor do they fear strangers with the intensity
  Americans and Europeans do (Scherer et al., 1988);
- *Categorization of events*: Events and behaviors that signal one's
  dependence may be perceived in terms of *amae* by the Japanese
  and 'shame' by the Bedouins of the Western Desert (Abu-Lughod,
  1986); being in a presence of an unknown man may be perceived
  as a neutral event by contemporary American women, but cause
  smushchenie (embarrassment/shyness) in certain Russian women
  (Pavlenko, 2003a);
- *Appraisal*: Here, differences exist in the evaluation of emotion-
  causing events and their consequences; for instance, exhibiting
  signs of one's dependence may be seen as positive and desirable
  among the Japanese but as shameful and childish among Westerners or Bedouins (Abu-Lughod, 1986; Morsbach & Tyler, 1986).
  Among the Ifaluk, individuals who are submissive and passive in
  metagu/fear are commended, and those who display an aggressive
  stance are condemned, while an opposite attitude is assumed in
  many Western cultures (Harré, 1986; Lutz, 1988);
- *Somatic states*: The Greek emotion *stenahoria* (discomfort/sadness/
  suffocation) is typically accompanied by a feeling of suffocation,
  not being able to breathe, not having enough space, which is not
  necessarily experienced by those feeling 'frustrated' (Panayiotou,
  2004a);
- *Consequences and means of emotion regulation*: Cultures have been
  shown to differ in regulation of emotion responses, with Utku
  inhibiting expressions of anger toward other people (Briggs, 1970),
  Bedouins expressions of dependence (Abu-Lughod, 1986), and
  Fulani admissions of shame (Riesman, 1977);
- *Means of emotion display*: Members of different speech communities may appeal to distinct means of vocal (Chapter 3), verbal
  (Chapter 5), and non-verbal expression of emotions. They may also

differently categorize physical displays: For instance, in Samoa, a father's beating of a child is commonly seen as an appropriate display of *alofa* (love between parents and children) (Gerber, 1985).

The meanings of these cross-linguistic and cross-cultural differences are subject to different interpretations within different frameworks, as we have discussed. Nativists discard them as insignificant, universalists view them as cultural variations of otherwise basic emotions, and relativists see them as evidence of profound differences in the understanding of inner states, social relationships, and ongoing events. What is important for this chapter is not the theoretical interpretations per se, but the fact that cross-linguistic differences exist and may play out in interesting ways in the mental lexicon and emotional lives of bi- and multilingual speakers.

At present, investigation of the bi- and multilingual emotion lexicon is in the infancy stage. Nevertheless, the few studies conducted to date – unfortunately, only with bilingual and not multilingual speakers – offer intriguing glimpses into the functioning of the bilingual emotion lexicon, with regard to two questions: *Given cross-linguistic and cross-cultural differences in the emotion lexicons, are L1 and L2 emotion words and concepts represented similarly or differently? How do levels of language proficiency and acculturation affect semantic and conceptual representations of emotion terms?*

4.3. Emotion words: Representation, processing, and semantic networks

The studies of the emotion lexicon of bilingual speakers have approached the issue from several distinct angles and considered both *emotion words*, that is words that refer to emotions, such as 'fright' or 'grief', and *emotion-laden* and *emotion-related* words, that is words with a strong emotional connotation, such as 'rape,' 'cancer,' or 'baby.' (For a summary of emotion lexicon studies see Table 4.1).

To see if the affective dimension impacts recall, Anooshian and Hertel (1994) examined recall of emotion and emotion-laden words in 36 bilingual participants, half of whom were Spanish–English bilinguals and half English–Spanish bilinguals. In each group, fluency in a second language was acquired in late childhood or adulthood, with the mean age of acquisition being 16.3 years for the first group and 18.4 for the second. Their proficiency was assessed through self-ratings and word-naming and word-association tests. These tests indicated that although all participants were fluent in both languages, English speakers were not as fluent in Spanish as Spanish speakers were in English.

To test word recall, the authors constructed two lists of 36 words that included emotion words, emotion-laden words, and neutral words, comparable in Spanish and English in terms of concreteness, frequency, and

TABLE 4.1. *Studies of the bilingual emotion lexicon*

Study	Participants	Procedure	Results
Heider (1991)	100 Minangkabau–Indonesian bilinguals	naturalistic observation and questionnaire	L1 and L2 emotion word clusters exhibit both similarities and differences
Anooshian & Hertel (1994)	18 Spanish–English bilinguals 18 English–Spanish bilinguals	L1 and L2 word list recall	L1 emotion words recalled better than neutral words
Toya & Kodis (1996)	10 native speakers of English 10 Japanese L2 users of English	interviews about responses to 5 anger-eliciting scenarios	cross-cultural similarities and differences in causal antecedents and means of anger display
Moore, Romney, Hsia & Rusch (1999)	33 English monolinguals 32 Japanese monolinguals 32 Chinese–English bilinguals 17 Japanese L2 users of English	similarity judgment of 15 emotion terms in L1 and L2	L1 and L2 terms judged differently, with L2 terms occupying a semantic space between the L1 and L2 semantic domains
Grabois (1999)	32 Spanish monolinguals 32 English monolinguals 32 L2 users of Spanish 32 L2 learners of Spanish 32 FL learners of Spanish	free word association	L2 users' lexical networks were closest to those of Spanish monolinguals; no differences were found between L2 and FL learners
Pavlenko (2002d)	31 Russian–English bilinguals	elicited film recall	in English narratives, participants invoked L2-specific scripts, and in Russian, scripts shared by the two languages; L1-specific scripts were not invoked in recall

(*continued*)

TABLE 4.1 *(continued)*

Study	Participants	Procedure	Results
Stepanova & Coley (2002)	22 Russian monolinguals 22 English monolinguals 22 Russian–English bilinguals	categorization, triad sorting, free sorting	bilinguals performed in language-specific ways but showed some L2 influence on L1 concepts
Altarriba (2003)	63 Spanish–English bilinguals divided into three groups	word rating for concreteness, imageability and context-availability	L1 Spanish emotion words were more easily contextualized by Spanish–English bilinguals than L1 English emotion words by English monolinguals
Altarriba & Canary (2004)	45 English monolinguals 45 Spanish–English bilinguals	lexical decision task	bilinguals were slower than monolinguals in processing emotion-laden words
Panayiotou (2004a)	5 Greek–English bilinguals 3 English–Greek bilinguals 2 multilingual L2 users of Greek	semi-structured interviews, translation	'untranslatable terms' were described as different in terms of causal antecedents, appraisal, and somatic states

word length, with 18 words in each language. The word selection was based on emotional ratings given to words by bilingual participants in a pilot study. Emotion words included word pairs such as anger/*ira*. Emotion-laden words included pairs such as laugh/*risa*, mother/ *madre*, and death/*muerte*. Neutral words included pairs such as box/*caja*, street/*calle*, and table/*mesa*. The participants were first asked to rate the words in terms of ease of pronunciation, implied activity, and emotionality on a 7-point Likert scale. Then they were asked to recall as many words as possible. The proportions of words from each category and each language were subjected to a multivariate analysis, with emotion and emotion-laden words grouped together.

The analysis showed that, when presented in the native language, emotion and emotion-laden words were recalled more frequently than neutral words. In contrast, in the second language, they were recalled similarly to neutral words. These results were unrelated to whether the native language was English or Spanish. To explain their findings, the authors suggested that in the first learned language emotion and emotion-laden words may be more elaborately encoded in memory than neutral words and have a richer network of associated instances and episodes.

More recently, a series of studies by Altarriba and associates initiated a systematic investigation of representation and processing of emotion words in the bilingual mental lexicon. To begin with, Altarriba, Bauer, and Benvenuto (1999) attempted to establish normative ratings and word associations in English. The researchers asked 78 English-speaking participants to rate *a priori* identified abstract ('charity'), concrete ('desk'), and emotion ('fear') words on concreteness, context-availability, and imagery scales. *Context-availability* referred to "the ease with which a context or circumstance can be recalled for a particular word" (p. 578). The results of the study indicated that the three word types are reliably different from each other. On the context-availability and concreteness scales, emotion words were rated as significantly lower than both concrete and abstract words. On the imageability scale, they were rated lower than concrete but higher than abstract words.

Next, Altarriba et al. (1999) gave 55 English-speaking undergraduates a list with 372 abstract, concrete, and emotion words and asked them to provide the first word, meaningfully related to the stimulus, that came to mind in response to each word on the list. The analysis of these word associations demonstrated that emotion words had the highest mean number of associations, followed by abstract and then by concrete words. Together, the results demonstrated that emotion words differ from abstract and concrete words both in terms of a mean number of associations and in concreteness, imageability, and context-availability. (These conclusions were also borne out in the study conducted by Altarriba and Bauer (2004) with monolingual speakers.) The study also replicated the results of Anooshian and Hertel (1994), demonstrating higher recall of emotion words in the native language as compared to concrete and abstract words.

In a follow-up study, Altarriba (2003) examined bilinguals' ratings of the three types of words. Sixty-three Spanish–English bilinguals participated in the study; 40% of them were born in the United States and others arrived as children, with a mean time in the United States of approximately 17 years. The participants rated their abilities highly in both languages, yet all considered themselves to be native speakers of Spanish. They were randomly divided into three groups that rated a list of 315 Spanish words on either concreteness, imageability, or context-availability. The words were based on the wordlist generated in Altarriba's previous study, with the proviso that only Spanish words with a single English translation equivalent were included. The findings of the study parallel those reported by Altarriba et al. (1999), in that emotion and emotion-laden words were rated as less concrete but more easily pictured than abstract words. Contrary to the previous findings, however, bilinguals provided equal ratings for Spanish emotion and abstract words in terms of context-availability. These ratings suggest that concrete, abstract, and emotion words are represented similarly in the English and Spanish lexicons in terms of concreteness and imageability, and that for Spanish–English bilinguals, Spanish emotion words are more readily contextualized than corresponding English words for English speakers. These intriguing findings point to a possible language socialization effect, although one still awaits to see how Spanish–English bilinguals perform on the English lists and how other types of bilinguals perform on this task.

Altarriba and Canary (2004) shifted attention to emotion-laden words and examined representations of these words in the English of 45 English monolinguals and 45 Spanish–English bilinguals. The bilinguals were similar to the previous group, with a mean time in the United States of approximately 14.4 years. The researchers first asked a different group of monolingual participants to rate a set of emotion-laden English words on valence and perceived arousal. Based on these ratings, the words were divided into high arousal, moderate arousal, and unrelated conditions. Both groups of participants had to perform lexical decision tasks, that is to decide if the sequences of letters (targets) presented to them on the computer screen were English words or non-words. First, however, they were exposed to real English words (primes), which were either similar (prisoner-jail, criminal-jail) or dissimilar to the targets in terms of arousal (guitar-jail). The results revealed that when the prime and the target were congruent in arousal, the responses were faster in both groups of participants (affective priming effect). The effects were less pronounced in the bilingual group, however, suggesting that the lexical search may be taking place in two languages.

A somewhat different approach to the study of the bilingual mental lexicon is taken in linguistic anthropology, where the focus is on the organization of the semantic domain. Among the most common methods of analysis of the emotion domain are multidimensional scaling, hierarchical cluster analysis, and network mapping. (For a discussion, see Heider, 1991.) Network representations of particular clusters of emotion words were used by Heider (1991) to compare emotion lexicons of Javanese speakers of Indonesian with those of Minangkabau speakers of Indonesian, elicited in their L1 Minangkabau and L2 Indonesian. Several of Heider's findings are of interest to the present discussion. To begin with, he found that Indonesian is generally viewed by his participants as a more appropriate language for expression of strong emotions. Minangkabau speakers of L2 Indonesian also showed a much greater cultural consensus about the relationships between various Indonesian emotion words than did Javanese speakers of L2 Indonesian. In the researcher's view, the reason for this is the Javanese reticence in emotion talk and the possibility that the Minangkabau talk more about emotions than the Javanese do, and even more so when they appeal to their L2 Indonesian. His analysis also identified script differences in the meanings of translation equivalents. For instance in Minangkabau, words similar to 'happiness' refer to the result of luck and presents from others, while in Indonesian these words refer to the results of personal achievement. Differences were also identified in display rules: In Minangkabau the speakers mask their happiness, while in Indonesian they display it more.

Moore and associates (1999) examined organization of semantic domains of emotions in Japanese–English and Chinese–English bilinguals in terms of similarity. The researchers created a list of 15 emotion terms that, in their view, had translation equivalents in three languages – English, Japanese, and Chinese. Four groups of subjects performed similarity judgments of the emotion terms: (a) 33 monolingual speakers of English; (b) 32 monolingual speakers of Japanese; (c) 17 Japanese L2 users of English residing in Japan (responding in English); (d) 32 Chinese–English bilinguals residing in the United States. (Members of this last group participated in the study twice, once in English and once in Chinese.)

The participants were given 105 consecutive triads consisting of different combinations of the 15 terms. In each triad they had to pick out the term most different in meaning from the other two. The data for each participant were coded in 15 × 15 symmetric matrices with the rows and columns labelled by the 15 terms in question. For each triad, one point was entered in the cell representing the pair of words remaining after one word was removed (for example, if in the triad happy/love/bored, 'bored' was removed, one point was entered for the intersection of 'happy' and 'love'). Because each pair of terms occurred three times in the questionnaire, the cell entries had values between 0 and 3. Subsequently, the data were stacked into language-specific matrices and into a shared matrix, and analyses were performed comparing the four matrices (English, Chinese, Japanese, and Shared).

The results demonstrated both similarities and differences in the structure of the semantic space: Global configurations of the three language groups were quite similar, but there were also statistically significant differences between them. For instance, a Chinese term comparable to English 'envy,' *xian mu*, was judged as much more pleasant and favorable than its English counterpart (as in admiration for someone who has something you want). The analysis also showed that the judgments of Japanese L2 users of English and Chinese–English bilinguals elicited in English were located somewhere between those offered by English speakers and Japanese and Chinese speakers, respectively, in their native languages. These statistically significant differences indicated that bilinguals' L2 semantic domains of emotion are distinct from those of monolingual speakers of both L1 and L2 (in the case of the Japanese L2 users of English) and that bilinguals have distinct semantic spaces for L1 and L2 emotion domains (in the case of Chinese–English bilinguals).

To look closer at cross-linguistic differences in semantic networks of emotion and emotion-laden words, Grabois (1999) undertook an examination of word associations to three emotion words, 'love,' 'happiness,' and 'fear,' and one emotion-laden word, 'death.' Five groups of subjects participated in the study: (1) 32 native speakers of Spanish; (2) 32 American L2 users of Spanish who had lived in Spain for at least three years or longer; (3) 32 American L2 learners of Spanish, students in an American university enrolled in a year long study-abroad program in Spanish; (4) 32 American FL learners of Spanish, enrolled in Spanish courses in an American university; (5) 32 native speakers of English, who had no knowledge of Spanish.

Groups (1)–(4) provided associations in Spanish and group (5) in English. The participants were asked to respond verbally to prime words (love/*amor*, happiness/*felicidad*, fear/*miedo*, death/*muerte*) and then to continue to free associate, with the associations themselves subsequently becoming primes. In other words, if a participant responded to 'love' with 'family,' 'passion,' and 'emotion,' these three responses were used as the next set of primes, and so on. If the same word recurred as a prime, responses given previously were used again. Overall, in this procedure, given one initial prime, subjects generated up to 83 associations.

The qualitative analysis of the data pointed to interesting differences in lexical networks of native speakers of English and Spanish. In the domain of 'love,' native speakers of English favored indirect, that is, metaphoric and symbolic, associations (for example, 'heart,' 'red,' 'roses'), while native speakers of Spanish showed preference for sensory and referential associations. Spanish speakers also offered responses like *ternura* (tenderness, affection) and *cariño* (affection, liking, tenderness), which do not have exact translation equivalents in English. 'Family' appeared more frequently in responses from native speakers of English, while *amigos* (friends) ranked higher in lexical networks of native speakers of Spanish. In the domain of 'happiness,' 'money' appeared more frequently in the English speakers' responses and *paz* (peace) in the Spanish ones. In the domain of 'fear,' native speakers of English offered a larger number of responses related to the effects and displays of fear (for instance, 'anxiety,' 'nervous,' 'stress,' 'sweat,' 'scream,' 'shaking'). In contrast, the central association for native speakers of Spanish was *soledad* (solitude, aloneness, loneliness). Finally, in the domain of 'death,' native English speakers favored responses that had to do with ceremonies and related objects (for example, 'funeral,' 'coffin,' 'cemetery,' 'grave'), while Spanish speakers favored affective responses, such as *dolor* (pain), *tristeza* (sadness), *soledad* (solitude, aloneness, loneliness), *pena* (sufferance), and *angústia* (anguish).

Subsequent correlational analyses showed that among participants in groups (2)–(4), L2 users of Spanish achieved consistently higher correlations with the native speakers of Spanish than L2 and FL learners of Spanish. For instance, they were the only ones to use *soledad* as a response to *miedo*. Differences were also found among domains: For *amor* there was a tighter clustering among groups (1)–(4), while for *felicidad* the differences between the native speakers and non-native speakers were greater.

Together, the studies above suggest that emotion and emotion-laden words may be represented differently from abstract and concrete words in the mental lexicon in terms of concreteness, imageability, and context-availability and that they may be linked to a richer semantic network (hence, slower processing) (Altarriba, 2003; Altarriba et al., 1999; Altarriba & Bauer, 2004; Altarriba & Canary, 2004). They also show that L1 emotion and emotion-laden words may be linked to more autobiographic memories and thus are more elaborately encoded and readily contextualized (hence, better recall) than L1 concrete and abstract words (Altarriba & Bauer, 2004) or emotion and emotion-laden words in a later learned L2 (Anooshian & Hertel, 1994). The studies by Heider (1991), Moore et al. (1999), and Grabois (1999) also point to cross-linguistic variation in semantic networks of emotion and emotion-laden words and suggest that variation may be greater in some domains (for instance, happiness) than others (such as love). Heider (1991) points to differences in L2 emotion domain between speakers of different L1s (although he does not treat this issue in-depth). Moore et al.'s (1999) study suggests that bilinguals have distinct semantic networks in L1 and L2, with L2 networks somewhat different from those of monolingual speakers of both L1 and L2. Grabois' (1999) study shows that in the case of pronounced differences, L2 speakers require a prolonged period of L2 socialization to approximate the lexical networks of native speakers of the target language.

These studies also exhibit some shortcomings. Anooshian and Hertel (1994) and Grabois (1999) offer detailed descriptions of the bilingualism of their participants, yet collapse emotion and emotion-laden words together without considering possible differences between the two categories, such as the possibility that emotion words per se ('fear' or 'sadness') may not be as easily contextualizable and may not elicit as many personal associations as emotion-laden words ('cancer' or 'death'). On the other hand, Heider (1991) and Moore et al. (1999) are careful about including exclusively emotion words but they do not report sufficient information about the bilingualism of their participants (whether the Chinese–English bilinguals in Moore et al.'s study are immigrants or U.S.-born and whether they are dominant in English or Chinese, for instance).

4.4. Emotion concepts: Identification and categorization

Another new and promising direction in the study of the bilingual emotion lexicon targets bilinguals' emotion scripts and thus conceptual categories.

In one such study, Stepanova and Coley (2002) examined two pairs of translation equivalents in Russian and English, jealousy/*revnost'* and envy/*zavist'*. These pairs were chosen because of subtle differences in the scripts involved, or more precisely, in causal antecedents. In Russian, *revnost'* has a fairly narrow scope, referring to either romantic jealousy or jealousy provoked by sibling rivalry. The English 'jealousy' can be elicited by a much wider range of antecedents: ones that elicit romantic jealousy ("Stop flirting with this guy, your boyfriend already looks jealous!") and ones that elicit envy ("Your vacation in the Caribbean sounds great – I am so jealous!"). In Russian, the first situation would be interpreted in terms of *revnost'* and the second in terms of *zavist'* (often described as *belaia zavist'*/white [good] envy).

The researchers tested three groups of participants: (1) 22 monolingual speakers of Russian, recruited from Moscow public libraries; (2) 22 monolingual speakers of American English, recruited in an introductory psychology class at Northeastern University in Boston; (3) 22 Russian–English bilinguals, recruited in Moscow (n = 18) and in Boston (n = 4). Bilinguals recruited in Moscow either studied English on a college level, worked in an English-speaking workplace, or spent a considerable amount of time in the United States. Bilinguals recruited in Boston grew up speaking Russian and learned English later in life when their families moved to the United States. While it is possible that the two groups differed in their degrees of L2 socialization, they did not differ in the number of years they had been speaking English or in self-assessed proficiency.

In the first experiment, the participants were presented with five stories describing prototypically jealousy-arousing (n = 2) or envy-arousing (n = 3) situations. The stories were written and pilot-tested in English and then were translated into Russian and back-translated into English with the final English version virtually identical to the original one. Monolingual speakers of Russian and English were tested in their respective languages, while bilinguals were randomly divided into two groups: 11 were tested in Russian and 11 in English. The participants were tested individually in a quiet room. After reading each story, they were presented with 10 words describing various emotions ('happy,' 'jealous, 'upset,' 'satisfied,' 'glad,' 'proud,' 'surprised,' 'envious,' 'sad,' 'content') and asked to rate on a scale from 1 to 7 the appropriateness of each word as a description of the protagonist's feelings in the story.

The *t*-test analysis of mean appropriateness ratings demonstrated that Russian speakers made a sharp distinction between *revnost'* and *zavist'*, using only the latter term to refer to the envy stories. English speakers, on the other hand, rated both 'envy' and 'jealousy' as equally appropriate in this case. Bilinguals responded according to the language they were tested in: In Russian they differentiated between *zavist'* and *revnost'*, while in English they showed no such distinction. These results suggest that the concepts of *revnost'* and 'jealousy,' as well as *zavist'* and 'envy,' differ in the two respective speech communities. For Russian speakers, *revnost'* and *zavist'* are separate categories with distinct antecedents and thus discrete boundaries. In contrast, for English speakers, 'jealousy' and 'envy' have overlapping antecedents and fuzzy boundaries.

In the second study, Stepanova and Coley (2002) used 27 one-sentence-long situations of three kinds: jealousy-evoking ("Your girlfriend dances with someone else at a dance"), envy-evoking ("Your boyfriend buys something that you want but cannot afford"), and controls aiming to evoke general negative feelings ("Your boyfriend lost your dog"). Once again, all sentences were pretested and subjected to translation into Russian and back-translation into English. In the triad-sorting task, the subjects were offered a random set of 4 triads (out of 12), each including two situations of one kind and one of the other (2 jealousy/1 envy). The subjects were asked to pick out any two situations that go together and provide an explanation for each of their selections. In the free-sorting task they were given all 27 cards and asked to sort them into as many groups as they liked according to the kind of emotion they would be likely to experience in such situations.

The analysis examined the proportion of times the participants separated envy situations and jealousy situations. In the triad-sorting task, separate ANOVAs for each type of triad showed no differences between groups. On average, all participants separated envy and jealousy situations 78% of the time, showing reliable differentiation between the two. Differences between Russian monolinguals and other participants were identified only on one triad, which combined three kinds of situations – envy, jealousy, and control. Russian monolinguals saw the three as different, while English monolinguals and Russian–English bilinguals grouped together envy and jealousy situations. In this case, bilinguals, whether tested in English or in Russian, performed like English monolinguals and differently from Russian speakers.

The analysis of the free-sorting task demonstrated that all participants sorted envy, jealousy, and control situations in similar ways and did not differ significantly in the number of groups they formed. There were, however, striking differences in how the groups were labeled. Native Russian speakers, whether mono- or bilingual, never described an envy group with the term *revnost'* nor did they ever use both words for a single group. In contrast, English monolinguals used the term 'jealousy' to describe envy groups 36% of the time, and on some occasions applied both terms to one group.

Together, the results of the two studies show that both Russian and English speakers reliably differentiate between romantic jealousy (jealousy/*revnost'*) and feelings aroused by other people's posessions, good luck, and fortune (envy, jealousy/*zavist'*). However, the boundaries of 'envy' and 'jealousy' are fuzzy in English, due to overlap in causal antecedents. In contrast, in Russian they are more or less categorical, because the causal antecedents are distinct – and so is the range of situations and behaviors commonly associated with each emotion. Bilinguals for the most part exhibited language-specific response patterns, which suggest that they had internalized the categories encoded in English and have both L1- and L2-based conceptual representations. At the same time, bilinguals were shown to perform differently from Russian monolinguals on similarity judgments. These differences suggest that the process of socialization into English may have led to some blurring of conceptual category boundaries. It is particularly interesting that these results were achieved with participants the majority of whom have been only somewhat socialized into English. It is quite possible that the effect of L2 exposure would have been even more pronounced in L2 users residing in the United States rather than in Russia.

Another study with Russian–English bilinguals was conducted by Pavlenko (2002d) to examine both language-specific terms and translation equivalents. In this study, which will be discussed in detail in Chapter 5, 31 Russian–English bilinguals were asked to recall two short films based on the same script, one made in the former USSR and one in the United States, specifically for that study. Half of the recalls were performed in English and half in Russian. The results were compared to recalls of the same films by monolingual speakers of Russian and English (Pavlenko, 2002c). All narratives described the reason why the woman in the film became upset (*rasstroennaia*) and what she did afterwards.

The analysis revealed that in English narratives, bilinguals performed similarly to American monolinguals both on identification of the causal antecedent of the main protagonist's emotions (invasion of privacy) and in the negative appraisal of this antecedent. In contrast, in the Russian language and culture, the notion of privacy is absent and events grouped together in English under the umbrella of 'invasion of privacy' are not categorized together, nor necessarily perceived as a cause for concern (Pavlenko, 1997, 2003a). Consequently, in the Russian narratives, bilinguals opted for scripts shared by the two cultures, such as the need to be alone when one is upset. They did not invoke the salient Russian verb *perezhivat'* (to give in to one's feelings, to suffer things through) that appeared frequently in narratives by Russian monolinguals as a common behavioral consequence of being upset. These results show that in the process of L2 socialization, the Russian–English bilinguals in the study have acquired new culture-specific scripts, such as invasion of privacy (see also Pavlenko, 2003a, c) and adjusted the typicality and salience of the components of their existing emotion scripts, favoring ones shared by the two cultures and avoiding ones that are unique to the Russian culture, such as *perezhivat'*.

While language- and culture-specific concepts emerged in Pavlenko's (2002d) study, they were not the centerpoint of the research design. In contrast, Panayiotou's (2004a) research focused on language-specific emotion concepts in the lexicons of Greek–English and English–Greek bilinguals recruited in the United States and in Cyprus. The author conducted semi-structured interviews with each participant, one in Greek and one in English, to create a list of emotion terms the participants deemed untranslatable. The participants were then given two lists of such terms, one in Greek and one in English, and asked to translate the words to the nearest possible meaning in the other language and then to explain where in their body they felt this emotion. The analysis of the participants' responses identified a number of terms perceived to be untranslatable, among them the English 'frustration' and the Greek *stenahoria* (discomfort/sadness/suffocation). Julia, an American in her forties who had lived in Greece for ten years and in Cyprus for three, stated in her interview:

> JULIA: I don't think I ever felt at a loss in Greek when I was living there [in Greece] . . . for words or expressions to express myself emotionally . . . there's some well known words that can't be expressed though. . . .
> INTERVIEWER: Like what?
> JULIA: Well, I know one . . . because we were talking about that the other night . . . frustration . . . there's no word for that in Greek and there isn't an adequate way to say it. . . .
> INTERVIEWER: What would you say then in Greek?
> JULIA: Um . . . we were talking about this the other night . . . I suggested . . . you couldn't say one word . . . you would say . . . I think I always used to say . . . something like *apogoiteftika kai tsantistika* [disappointed and upset]. Because you can't say *mplokaristika, empodistika* [blocked, hindered] . . . there's nothing that you can say that would have the actual original meaning of frustrate . . . (pause). I know that most Greeks in Greece would translate it as *apogoiteftika* [disappointed] but I know that that's not enough because you don't have the frustration, frustration has this tension and that's not expressed in *apogoiteftika* but you get that in *tsantistika* but then in that it's almost like you are leaving the problem, I think, isn't it? So you can't get too close to it. . . .
> (Panayiotou, 2004a: 8–9)

In fact, 'frustration' is commonly translated into Greek as *apogoitefsi* (disappointment), *empodizo* (to hinder or to present an obstacle) or *mateosi* (to cancel). Yet for Julia and others, including the author of the paper, herself a Greek–English bilingual, this translation is inexact in terms of several conceptual components, including somatic states and their interpretations. Tongue-in-cheek, Panayiotou (2004a) explained that in trying to find translations for these terms she felt very frustrated, but not disappointed nor hindered in her attempts. She also noted that when describing a frustrating experience in Greek, Greek–English bilinguals living in Cyprus code-switch to English specifically to use the word 'frustrated,' as in *"Imoun polla* frustrated *me tin katastasi"* (I was very *frustrated* with the situation) (Panayiotou, 2004a: 8). An even more interesting case is that of *stenahoria* which literally means 'constricted space' (*stenos + horos*) and is often translated as 'lack of space', 'depression', 'vexation', 'worry.' In the interviews, L2 users of Greek discussed the term as one they often hear but do not necessarily use. Sofia, a Spanish-English-Greek trilingual who has been living in Cyprus for the last seven years, questioned her own knowledge of the meaning of the term *"frustrated me tin katastasi"* (I was very frustrated with the situation) (Panayiotou, 2004a: 8):

> SOFIA: *Stenahorieme,* what does it mean? I've heard it so many times, but, yeah its something that you are um worried yeah like you're sad, and you worry and it's something that doesn't have a translation in English, not even in Spanish I think but people in Cyprus you know you worry like things you worry I mean you are . . . you are sad and you feel sort of hopeless and you cant really help somebody . . . I thought it's something that old people use though like my mother-in-law, but erh that's something that older people use all the time . . . I heard the word many times but as I said I don't . . . because I don't hear it in my house, you know, you see this is not . . . I don't even think Andreas has ever used that word. Yeah, yeah yeah. He would only use *ntropi* a lot, but not this other one, I don't know why. So I understand it has to do with sadness and erh depression – yeah but it's not it's not worried . . . I mean . . . (pause) yeah it's also part of worry like um you could say um *stenahorieme* because you know my husband has an interview and I'm sort of worried that . . . but it's also like I'm feeling kind of hopeless because I can't really help . . . help him . . . um but, there's no equivalent in Spanish or English . . . Well you know certainly we have a word that that that means you know that when you want to say that you worry or you're . . . it's the same as as worried. No, no worry, no it's not like concerned, like you're concerned you're . . . but it's not even that no yeah I would say, I wouldn't say it's worry. You know that you have you you have this . . . this concern . . .
>
> INTERVIEWER: What context do you see it in then?
>
> SOFIA: You use it say you are worried about someone, you know ok someone's health? About someone's health, about someone's condition, someone's eh situation, maybe financial problems . . . you use it, I'm concerned about you know . . . but also worrying. . . .
>
> (Panayiotou, 2004a: 11–12)

Looking closely at the transcript we can see that for the multilingual Sofia the meaning of the term is not immediately 'recognizable' – after many years of living in the Greek-speaking context, she is still somewhat confused about its precise meaning, and spends a lot of time trying to pinpoint it. Interestingly, she can indicate a number of situations where the word would be appropriately used but cannot describe precisely what is actually felt by the experiencer, which suggests an incomplete acquisition of the concept. Greek–English bilinguals are more forthcoming in this regard. Lydia identified *stenahoria* as sadness or depression and described it as an external force pressing on the chest. Leonidas used the term in his Greek interview but not in the English one where he did otherwise code-switch. When asked why he avoided the use of this term, he replied that he cannot feel *stenahoria* in English "not just because the word doesn't exist but because that kind of situation would never arise" (Panayiotou, 2004b: 133).

These intriguing findings reveal that for the bilinguals the two concepts, 'frustration' and *stenahoria*, differ in terms of causal antecedents, appraisals, and somatic states. 'Frustration' for them is an individualistic feeling, which stems from a challenge to the pervasive Anglo–American belief that one can be in control of the situation by taking action. In contrast, *stenahoria* is a social emotion, which stems from an internalized feeling of doom, passivity, and hopelessness. It is accompanied by a feeling of suffocation, of not being able to breathe, not having enough space, which is not necessarily experienced by those feeling frustrated. These feelings are also differently linked to linguistic contexts – 'frustration' is generalized from English- to Greek-speaking contexts, while *stenahoria* is constrained to Greek-speaking ones. This difference raises interesting questions about possible globalization of Anglo emotion categories, discourses, displays, and emotion management styles.

Causal antecedents of emotions were examined in a pilot study by Toya and Kodis (1996), who compared the responses of 10 native speakers of English and 10 Japanese L2 users of English to five situations that could potentially elicit anger. The researchers found both similarities and differences in the participants' responses. In a scenario where a vending machine 'ate' the person's lunch money, for example, native speakers of English said that they would react verbally (curse) and physically (perhaps kick or punch the machine). Japanese speakers stated that they would either express their anger verbally or would not be angry at all at an inanimate object. On the other hand, in a scenario where they were required to wait in a restaurant for 30 minutes, more Japanese speakers stated that they would be angry and would feel justified in expressing their anger verbally. These preliminary findings point to cross-cultural differences in causal antecedents and resulting means of anger display. The responses of L2 users of English also showed that these speakers do not always know how to express their anger adequately in English nor feel comfortable doing so.

The four studies discussed here made the first foray into the examination of bilinguals' emotion concepts as scripts. They demonstrated that cross-linguistic differences in emotion scripts can be identified in verbal performance, elicitation, and categorization tasks (Pavlenko, 2002d; Stepanova & Coley, 2002; Toya & Kodis, 1996; see also Heider, 1991, discussed in Section 4.3) and in bicultural bilinguals' reflections (Panayiotou, 2004a). These studies have also begun identifying cross-linguistic and cross-cultural differences in components of emotion concepts underlying translation equivalents, including causal antecedents (Heider, 1991; Panayiotou, 2004a;

Pavlenko, 2002d; Stepanova & Coley, 2002; Toya & Kodis, 1996), appraisals (Panayiotou, 2004a; Pavlenko, 2002d), somatic states (Panayiotou, 2004a), consequences (Pavlenko, 2002d), and means of emotion display (Heider, 1991; Toya & Kodis, 1996).

What do these results mean for the larger field of language and emotions? To begin with, we can see that, contrary to Pinker's (1997) view, beginning L2 learners, and even bicultural bilinguals, like Sofia, may experience difficulties understanding the meaning of language-specific emotion terms and mapping words to concepts (Panayiotou, 2004a). This does not mean, however, that the new emotion categories are impossible to acquire. The prolonged process of L2 socialization allows L2 users, like Leonidas, to form new emotion concepts, down to somatic states that come with them (Panayiotou, 2004a). As a result, bicultural bilinguals perform categorization and naming tasks in language-appropriate ways, similarly to monolingual speakers of the languages in question (Pavlenko, 2002d; Stepanova & Coley, 2002). At the same time, emotion concepts in the bilingual mental lexicon do not appear to be identical to those in the monolingual lexicons – the process of L2 socialization may lead to L2 influence on L1 and consequently to conceptual restructuring, visible in the studies discussed in the rearrangements of causal antecedents (Pavlenko, 2002d; Stepanova & Coley, 2002). As discussed in Chapter 1, L2 influence may also lead to the loss of conceptual distinctions in emotion terms, as we saw in the performance of Xhosa–English bilinguals in the study by Drennan and associates (1991).

4.5. Factors affecting the structure of the bilingual emotion lexicon

The few studies conducted to date on the semantic and conceptual representations of bilingual speakers concur that representations of L1 and L2 emotion words may be distinct from each other due to cross-linguistic differences in the emotion lexicons and to language learning trajectories. Two key effects have been identified in this domain: the L1 primacy effect and the L2 socialization effect.

The L1 primacy effect in the emotion lexicon means that L1 emotion and emotion-laden words may be more elaborately encoded and contextualized than L2 words (Altarriba, 2003; Anooshian & Hertel, 1994). In the case of cross-linguistic differences between L1 and L2, this elaborate encoding and contextualization may lead to the transfer of L1 emotion scripts. The possibility of L1 transfer in verbal and non-verbal performance in L2 always needs to be considered in working with bilingual informants, especially if they have low L2 proficiency or have not been socialized in the L2 culture.

The L2 socialization effect is particularly visible in performance differences between two groups of speakers. Proficient L2 speakers with low degrees of acculturation exhibit L1 transfer effects in representation of L2 emotion and emotion-laden words (Grabois, 1999; see also Pavlenko, 2003a), while speakers socialized in the L2 culture have distinct L1 and L2 representations (Heider, 1991), which may pattern in-between those of monolingual native speakers of the two languages (Moore et al., 1999) or approximate those of the target language speakers (Grabois, 1999; Panayiotou, 2004a; Pavlenko, 2002d; Stepanova & Coley, 2002). Some may even exhibit L2 effects on L1 and thus evidence of conceptual restructuring (Drennan et al., 1991; Pavlenko, 2002d, 2003a; Stepanova & Coley, 2002). A question is often raised whether these effects are cultural rather than linguistic. The answer undoubtedly depends on one's view of language and culture. In the view adopted here, the effect is not purely cultural; rather, it stems from prolonged participation in discursive practices of the L2 speech community, where interaction in the L2 directs speakers' attention to similarities in the range of phenomena encoded by the L2 term that are non-existent in L1, or to similarities and differences between L1 and L2 translation equivalents.

4.6. Conclusions and implications for future research

The studies discussed here allow me to suggest that emotion and emotion-laden words are represented in the mental lexicon differently from concrete and abstract words and that they may be contextualized, recalled, and processed in a different manner (Altarriba, 2003; Altarriba & Bauer, 2004; Altarriba et al., 1999; Anooshian & Hertel, 1994). They also suggest that there exist at least three main types of bilingual emotion lexicons – or perhaps three main types of interactions between L1 and L2 emotion words and concepts. These include:

(a) *L1-influenced emotion lexicon*, where L2 words are linked to L1 concepts, leading to L1 transfer in L2 use and to L1-based emotion categorization. This type of lexicon is common for speakers with low levels of proficiency and acculturation who have not been socialized into the L2 culture (Grabois, 1999; Toya & Kodis, 1996). At the same time, representations of L1 emotion and emotion-laden words may also be more elaborate and better contextualized in speakers with higher levels of L2 proficiency (Altarriba, 2003; Anooshian & Hertel, 1994).

(b) *L2-influenced emotion lexicon*, where L2 concepts influence L1 concepts, leading to L2 transfer in L1 use and to L2-based emotion categorization. This type of lexicon is common for speakers who have experienced prolonged L2 socialization and live or work in the L2 environment and thus constantly interact with L2 speakers (Drennan et al., 1991; Pavlenko, 2002d; Stepanova & Coley, 2002).

(c) *Transcultural emotion lexicon,* where representations of emotion words correspond more or less to those of monolingual native speakers of the respective languages or are easily modified depending on the context and interlocutors. This type of lexicon is more typical for transcultural bilinguals who travel back and forth between two speech communities and thus consistently interact with L1 and L2 speakers and with other bilinguals (Heider, 1991; Panayiotou, 2004a). Panayiotou's (2004a) study also suggests that in this lexicon some language-specific concepts, such as 'frustration,' are generalized to other linguistic contexts, while others, such as *stenahoria,* are constrained to one linguistic context. Future inquiry needs to determine whether more generalizable terms come exclusively from global languages, such as English, in an invisible process of globalization of semantic space.

Clearly, the lexicons above are just approximations – it is most likely that in the lexicon of a single speaker one can find both L1- and L2-specific emotion concepts and instances of both L1 and L2 transfer (Pavlenko, 2002d; Pavlenko & Jarvis, 2002). Moreover, these lexicons are situated with regard to two languages, while the lexicons of multilingual speakers still await exploration. Yet even these preliminary findings are quite important for the cross-linguistic study of language and emotions, as they indicate the possibility of bidirectional transfer in the performance of bilingual informants who may not be monolingual-like either in L1 or L2.

The findings of these studies, combined with the knowledge accumulated in the field of language and emotions on cross-linguistic differences, also allow us to refine the questions to ask in future studies with bi- and multilingual participants. Here are some questions that can be asked in comparative studies of emotion terms and in studies of the multilingual emotion lexicon:

(1) *Salience of the emotion domain and particular emotions:* Is there an identifiable emotion domain and an emotion lexicon in each of the languages in question? Is the domain of emotions similarly salient in the speakers' respective languages? Are emotions frequently referred to in everyday talk? Is this salience adequately reflected in the speakers' performance? Which, if any, emotions are salient in the languages in question? Do emotions focal in the language and culture in question appear in the speakers' emotion talk or is there transfer of key emotion concepts from one lexicon to another?

(2) *Structure of the emotion domain:* Is the emotion domain lexicalized and structured similarly or differently in the languages in question? What systems of meaning define an experience as an emotional experience (Shweder, 1993)? How are these structures and meaning systems

reflected in multilingual speakers' emotion lexicons, and is there evidence of transfer or blending of two or more structures? For instance, do speakers who define emotions as predominantly social phenomena impose these definitions on emotion terms of a language like English, which conceives of emotions as individual inner states?

(3) *Structure and universality/specificity of emotion concepts:* Are emotion words in the multilingual lexicon connected across languages, and if so, how? Which emotion concepts appear to be completely language- and culture-specific and which ones are shared fully or partially? What are the similarities and differences between the shared concepts at the level of somatic experiences, antecedents, consequences, means of display, and so forth? In other words, what are the prototypical events that may cause particular emotions; how are these events categorized and evaluated; what somatic states do informants experience in reaction to these events; how do they behave as a consequence of these events and experiences; and how do they regulate their emotional behavior?

Once we have studies that carefully compare performance of particular types of bi- and multilinguals to that of monolingual speakers of respective languages, we will know more about similarities and differences between monolingual and multilingual emotion lexicons. This knowledge will allow us to make more informed judgments in a variety of domains, from clinical and legal contexts to our own academic backyard, where the status of bilingual translators and informants remains uncertain and unclear.

Additional implications and directions for future research stem from the shortcomings shared by the studies of the monolingual and bilingual emotion lexicons. To begin with, these investigations continue to exhibit a lack of clarity on what counts as an emotion word and how emotion words are selected in particular languages. (See also Heelas, 1986; Russell, 1991a.) Differences in elicitation methods and selection criteria are most visible in assessments of English emotion vocabulary that vary from 400 (Davitz, 1969) to 590 (Johnson-Laird & Oatley, 1989) to 2,000 words (Wallace & Carson, 1973). To ensure reliability and replicability, it is pivotal for future studies to include explicit discussion of selection criteria – in other words, what counted as an emotion word. While this approach will not resolve all interpretive problems, it will allow for replication and comparative analyses. One productive direction is offered by propositional analysis, devised by Clore, Ortony, and Foss (1987), which posits that in order to be considered an affective term, a word has to express emotions in two contexts, "feeling X" and "being X." Consequently, 'sadness' is considered to be an emotion word, because "feeling sad" and "being sad" are both rated as expressions of emotion, as opposed to "feeling ignored" (emotion) and "being ignored" (state of events).

Second, as pointed out earlier, there may also exist differences between emotion words that function in a more or less abstract manner denoting emotions (such as 'anger' or 'happiness'), emotion words that serve to describe and express emotions (such as 'irritated' or 'pissed off'), and emotion-laden words that express or elicit emotions but do not describe them (such as 'death' or 'fraud'). The words in the first subgroup may function more like abstract words, and those in the latter two more like concrete words. Future research also needs to pay close attention to the fact that emotion-laden terms come from all three domains – abstract, concrete, and emotion – and offer more specific definition and selection procedures for emotion-laden words. There may in fact exist significant individual differences in processing and representation in this domain. For instance, older speakers and speakers with a family history of the illness may exhibit more arousal upon hearing or seeing the terms 'cancer' or 'Alzheimer's', while younger healthy individuals may treat them as more or less abstract terms. In certain sociopolitical contexts, some abstract words such as 'Islam' or 'democracy' may also function as emotion-laden words and elicit a large spectrum of affective reactions.

The third issue to address is the relationship between semantic (that is, verbal, linguistic) and conceptual (individual, psychological) levels of representation. As Scherer (1994: 31) noted perceptively, a verbal label cannot be used as an explanans (as it often is in psychology of emotions); rather it is an explanandum. Consequently, more empirical investigations are needed to examine the relationship between words or expressions and the content of conceptual categories. At present, many studies using semantic approaches claim to shed light on the structure of concepts and cognitive domains of emotion (for example, Brandt & Boucher, 1986; Church et al., 1998; Fontaine et al., 2002; Moore et al., 1999; Rusch, 2004). Fontaine and associates (2002) state that "the cognitive structure of emotions can be conceptualized as the cognitive representation of differences and similarities between emotion terms" (Fontaine et al., 2002: 62).

In reality, however, these analyses examine the relationship between words and other words, without touching upon the nature of conceptual categories. The similarities in the core meanings of decontextualized emotion words, revealed in these studies, may be indicative of the relationship between the terms in the semantic network (although this still needs to be tested through the means of lexical decision tasks), but offer little or no information on the meanings themselves and thus on the structure of the actual domain or particular concepts within it. Even though sophisticated quantitative analyses by definition elicit trust and respect in North American academia, I am apprehensive about establishing cognitive equivalence through elaborate geometric representations (cf. Fontaine et al., 2002) and remain in the dark as to what a 54% overlap in the meanings of English, Japanese, and Chinese emotion terms (Moore et al., 1999:

539) could possibly entail. In the view adopted here, conceptual categories are best elucidated through naturalistic methods such as diaries, interviews, questionnaires, and ethnographies. These methods also allow us to address the inherent polysemy of many emotion words, an issue oftentimes neglected in emotion lexicon research.

The fourth issue, critical for this book as a whole, is the status of bilingual informants in future research on language and emotions. Wierzbicka (2003, 2004, in press) has repeatedly argued that experiences and opinions of bilingual individuals need to be taken into consideration in research on language and emotions. Yet we continue seeing studies where the judgments of monolingual speakers of English and Japanese are used to draw conclusions about similarity of the English shame and embarrassment to the Japanese *hazukashii* (Rusch, 2004). We also continue seeing ethnocentric arguments that privilege English emotion terms and discount the significance of cross-linguistic and cross-cultural differences (Pinker, 1997). Wierzbicka's (2003) response to Martha Nussbaum perfectly summarizes the position taken in this book on the necessity of using bilingual participants and informants:

If many bilingual and bicultural people say that the existence of distinct words for emotions *has* made a difference to the texture of their emotional life, can a person who has *not* lived his or her life through two languages establish *by means of argument* that such people are wrong? (p. 579)

Lastly, a major shortcoming of current research on emotion words and concepts is the limited ecological and phenomenological validity of approaches that emphasize referential meaning and focus on single emotion words taken out of context or used in made-up contexts (Abu-Lughod & Lutz, 1990; Edwards, 1997). These studies tell us a lot about prototypical cultural scenarios but very little about ways in which the interpretive process unfolds and understandings emerge on-line, in the context of local concerns, rights, obligations, and power relations. To respond to these concerns, the next chapter will shift the focus of attention from semantics and conceptual structure to pragmatics, or the study of what people actually do with words.

5

Discursive level: I feel *zhalko tebia bednogo*

I'm much nicer and quieter and more serious in French; much more loud and foul mouthed and slangy in English. In Welsh I hardly have a personality at all except that I tend to agree with everyone because it's easier than having to formulate my own ideas!

(Rebecca, 32, L1 English, L2 French, L3 Welsh)

It is a rainy and chilly fall afternoon and my son comes home from school all soaked and miserable. He had an awful day: The teachers were "totally unreasonable" in the amount of work they assigned, the lunch break was cut short, his favorite pants got stained, and someone screamed something really hurtful from a car window as he was walking back home in the rain. I hug him, stroke his wet hair, and whisper: "I feel *zhalko tebia bednogo* (sorry/pity for you poor [soul])." And then I immediately begin to ponder upon this code-switch 'across the feeling boundaries,' which violated subcategorization constraints of the Russian equivalent of 'I feel' (*Ia chuvstvuiu*). Since our conversation until that moment was in English, I must have started out saying, "I feel so sorry for you," and then changed my mind because in this context the polysemous 'sorry,' with its many connotations, may have sounded like a polite acknowledgment of his problems, and thus distancing and condescending. Switching to the Russian *zhalko*, which is used in expressions of sorrow, pity, sadness, and compassion but not in apologies (where 'I am sorry' is translated as *prostite* or *izvinite*), allowed me to convey that I am indeed feeling bad about his dreadful day. Yet I have also violated Russian subcategorization constraints that require that *Ia chuvstvuiu* be followed by a noun and that an adverb *zhalko* be preceded by a pronoun in a Dative case (*mne zhalko*/to me it is a pity).

Realistically speaking, these cross-linguistic differences and constraint violations are more important to me than to my son, who has only limited proficiency in Russian and is not always aware of such subtle distinctions. Rather, he reacts to the change in language – in our family, as in many other immigrant families around the world, first language communicates, among other things, more intense affect, positive and negative. And thus the other reason for my code-switching is the need to communicate affect in a language perceived as 'more emotional.'

Having said that, I do not intend to argue that some languages are 'better' for expressing emotions than others, or more 'sincere sounding,' as this would be a naive and essentialist argument. Rather, I am interested in affective repertoires available to bi- and multilingual speakers and in factors that influence their choices. I begin with a discussion of ways in which emotions are expressed in discourse and an overview of cross-linguistic differences in means of affect expression that make the adequate performance of affect in L2 a challenging task. Then I examine multilingual emotion talk from three distinct angles. First, I inquire if bi- and multilinguals express emotions differently in their respective languages and if so, when such differences occur, why, and whether they might contribute to the perception of 'double selves', acknowledged by many bi- and multilinguals, including Rebecca cited in the beginning of the chapter. Second, I consider factors that influence language choice for emotional expression in the presence of bi- and multilingual interlocutors. My brief utterance, "I feel *zhalko tebia bednogo,*" highlights the impact of two such factors: perceived language emotionality and cross-linguistic differences in the meaning of emotion terms. Third, I take a look at the impact of proficiency on comprehension and production of L2 emotion talk. I end with a summary of factors that impact multilinguals' affective styles and discuss implications of these findings for future inquiry in the area.

5.1. Emotions in discourse

The emotive function of language has long fascinated linguists, psychologists, and anthropologists (Henry, 1936; Jakobson, 1960; Sapir, 1921, 1927; Stankiewicz, 1964). The fascination rarely inspired systematic investigation, though, because the topic has been so difficult to conceive of in 'objective' terms. For many years, emotions in language have been examined only through the lens of vocal communication, concepts, or metaphors. It is only in the past decades that we have begun seeing theoretical proposals for a unified pragmatics of emotive communication (Arndt & Janney, 1991; Caffi & Janney, 1994; Fiehler, 1990; Ochs & Schieffelin, 1989; Wierzbicka, 1991) and systematic investigations of emotion talk in a variety of paradigms (Bucci, 1982; Edwards, 1997; Fussell, 2002; Lutz, 1988; Lutz & Abu-Lughod, 1990; Rosaldo, 1980; Wierzbicka, 1999).

Despite the fact that the field is still relatively new, we can already distinguish two key paradigms, which stem from distinct views of the relationship between language and emotions. Some of the research on vocal expression of emotions and on emotion concepts, discussed in earlier chapters, offers a perfect illustration of the first paradigm, *communication of emotions*. This paradigm views language and emotions as largely separate phenomena and posits a one-to-one correspondence between emotions as inner states and their perception, interpretation, and expression (blood 'boiling' – feel 'anger' – scream loudly). Scholars working in this framework are commonly engaged in a search for verbal and non-verbal cues to preexisting emotions and in an attempt to integrate them in a more or less coherent manner (Planalp, 1999; Planalp, De Francisco & Rutherford, 1996; Planalp & Knie, 2002; Scherer, 1986; Scherer & Wallbott, 1994).

Research on *discursive construction of emotions* throws these links into doubt and focuses attention on rhetoric alternatives available to speakers, both within and across languages, and on speakers' communicative intentions (Abu-Lughod & Lutz, 1990; Arndt & Janney, 1991; Bamberg, 1997; Besnier, 1990; Caffi & Janney, 1994; Edwards, 1997; Irvine, 1990; Lutz, 1990; Ochs & Schieffelin, 1989; White, 1990). In this view, emotion terms and scripts are implicated in the ongoing negotiation of meaning in the context of emotional, social, and power relations. Edwards (1997) makes a convincing argument in favor of decoupling event descriptions from events themselves:

The application of one description rather than another, or one scenario rather than another, is systematically oriented to the performance of local discursive business, rather than simply standing as the document of how a speaker 'saw' things, or of cultural differences. (p. 186)

In this view, even the simplest 'emotion statements,' such as "I feel angry" or "I am sad," are not taken literally as faithful descriptions of people's inner states (although they might be), but are considered as speech acts in the light of rhetorical goals the speakers may be trying to achieve (for example, to complain, prompt others to take a particular course of action, position themselves in a particular way with regard to certain events, and so on). Children, at least in our culture, master this art of affect performance very early in the process. Little Carrie may whimper "Ca-wie is ve-wy sad" and start pouting and making sad faces, but what she feels in reality is not sadness, melancholy, or nostalgia, but an overwhelming desire TO HAVE THAT TOY.

Clearly, the two paradigms are not fully incompatible. Many scholars working on communication of emotions acknowledge that speakers use emotion categories to accomplish social goals (cf. Planalp & Knie, 2002). Similarly, the work on discursive construction of emotions recognizes the embodied nature of emotional experience (Abu-Lughod & Lutz, 1990) and the role of conventionality in affective displays (Arndt & Janney, 1991; Irvine, 1990). At the same time, these frameworks are sufficiently distinct in their assumptions, research foci, and methodological approaches to warrant an explicit acknowledgment of these differences. Research agendas set for the study of body language in the two approaches offer one excellent example. Planalp and Knie (2002: 59) underscore the need to study gestures and body movement, orientation, and agitation as important nonverbal cues to particular emotion states. In turn, Abu-Lughod and Lutz (1990: 12–13) emphasize the need to understand bodily postures as symbolic vehicles of social relations (an angry glare indexing a challenge to an imposed moral obligation) and as practices that reveal the effects of power (gestures of respect or shame).

Another, more subtle split runs across these paradigms with regard to the focal phenomena worthy of attention. Building on more than a century of tradition, linguists continue to differentiate between referential, social, and affective functions of discourse. The *referential* (also known as descriptive or denotative) meaning refers to propositional or logical content of the utterances. *Social* meaning refers to ways in which speakers position themselves and are positioned as members of particular social categories such as gender, race, class, ethnicity, sexuality, or generation. *Affective* meaning refers to ways in which speakers signal their feelings, moods, and attitudes toward the referential content of communication. Besnier (1990) argues that this tripartite distinction is the key reason for which "affect has been consistently set aside as an essentially unexplorable aspect of linguistic behavior, a residual category to which aspects of language that cannot be handled conveniently with extant linguistic models were relegated to be forgotten" (p. 420). At present, some scholars still subscribe to the tripartite distinction and view emotive communication as a strategic use of nonpropositional verbal, prosodic, and kinesic signals (Arndt & Janney, 1991). Others are increasingly apprehensive about the referential/affective dichotomy and consider both verbal and non-verbal aspects of discursive construction of emotions (Bamberg, 1997; Besnier, 1990; Edwards, 1997; Irvine, 1990; Lutz, 1990).

The present discussion disregards the tripartite distinction and assumes that affect performance accomplishes all three functions in question: It informs, it positions, and it expresses. Thus I will adopt the discursive approach to the study of affect performance – its emphasis on availability of alternative emotion discourses for the same eliciting event makes it imminently more suitable for the inquiry into multilingual emotion talk. Once again, I would like to emphasize here that the issue of 'basic emotions,' or emotions as physical states, remains outside the scope of this discussion. It is possible that regardless of whether I say, "I am sorry," "*Mne zhalko*," or "I feel *zhalko*," I am referring to the same emotional experience. It is also possible that the interpretive means made available by the respective languages influence the actual emotional experience of bi- and multilingual speakers. At present, we have insufficient evidence to decide this issue one way or the other; therefore, the discussion to come focuses on ways in which speakers 'perform affect,' rather than 'communicate emotions.' Thus the terms 'affect' and 'emotions,' as well as the terms 'performing,' 'signalling,' 'indexing,' and 'expressing,' will be used interchangeably.

Undoubtedly, such an approach takes away from the primary focus of emotions research – emotions per se – and blurs the distinction between 'sincere' and 'ritualized' emotion displays or, in Arndt and Janney's (1991) view, between emotional and emotive communication. For the purposes of the present inquiry, however, such an approach is preferable because the boundary between emotional and emotive is not always clear-cut and the importance of the distinction varies from culture to culture based on the local theory of emotionality (Besnier, 1990; Ochs & Schieffelin, 1989). Even in Western contexts the dichotomy does not always allow for easy categorization. Where should we place, for instance, the quasi-emotions of fear or suspense that people experience and display when watching a thriller or reading crime fiction? The vicarious fear is not real, yet it is also not completely fake or deceitful.

Consequently, I will discuss *affective repertoires* as an integral feature of situated language use, where emotion categories function not only to inform the interlocutors about the speaker's internal states, but also to perform interactional functions, to assign causes and motives to actions, to blame, to excuse, to legitimize, to account for events and phenomena, and to explicate the intricacies of social relations (Edwards, 1997). This approach is compatible with the view of emotion concepts outlined in Chapter 4, because the discursive perspective offers a way out of the deterministic understanding of prototypes as guiding people's actions, and it allows us to see how speakers strategically adopt, challenge, and transform emotion scripts to perform a variety of interactional goals in everyday discourse.

Edwards (1997) underscores the need for both types of analysis in the study of emotion discourse. Semantic and conceptual analyses of emotion terms and metaphors are necessary because they clarify the meanings of the linguistic resources that permit discursive uses. Discursive analyses of situated talk and texts are equally necessary to challenge the artificial coherence of cognitive models, to reveal the flexibility of human concepts – commonly underestimated in semantic and conceptual analyses – and to examine how concepts function as rhetorical affordances that speakers use to accomplish different goals on different occasions. This approach allows us to move beyond the representational function of language (I am very angry at you) and to consider multiple ways in which languages index affect without naming or pointing to particular emotions (ARRGH! You IDIOT!), and a variety of discursive goals speakers aim to achieve in performing affect.

5.2. Cross-linguistic differences in affective repertoires

As Chapter 4 discussed, scholars working in different frameworks agree on the existence of cross-linguistic differences in the means of emotional expression. In turn, the approach taken here reminds us that each language offers several alternative affective repertoires and styles to its speakers. In different contexts we present ourselves as different affective personae who may express anger through soft-spoken understatement here and uncontrollable loud swearing there. These personae are constructed and negotiated at three levels: linguistic, group, and individual.

At the linguistic level, differences are often observed – or perhaps constructed – among speakers of different languages. Several respondents to our webquestionnaire discussed linguistic and cultural differences they perceive in the conventionalized emotion display and the management styles of their respective speech communities. Kumiko, a native speaker of Japanese, stated that English allows her to express her emotions directly, while in the Japanese culture emotions are commonly expressed in subtle and indirect ways, often nonverbally. Consequently, it is easier for her to say what she feels in English:

It is easier for me to express things emotionally in English since culturally open expression is condoned. In Japanese culture people are less open with their feelings and expression is not as open. You learn to read subtle signs and signals which may not be verbal. For example it is easier to scold someone in English because the expressions are more direct. In Japanese scolding may be done through distance-creating acts rather than verbal scolding. (Kumiko, 40, L1 Japanese, L2 English)

Systematic intergroup differences in affective styles and their perception also exist among speakers of different varieties of the same language. For instance, the African–American community in the United States favors a high level of emotional engagement in both private and public contexts, including sermons and church services. As a result, African–Americans are at times perceived as more emotionally engaged, dynamic, and demonstrative than European–Americans, and at other times are judged to be overbearing or impolite (Kochman, 1981). Speakers of British and American English differ in expressions of evidentiality and affect: The British commonly use evidential adverbs (absolutely, obviously, of course) to signal solidarity and involvement, while to American listeners these uses may sound superior or presumptuous (Precht, 2003).

Even individuals with a shared linguistic and cultural background may differ in affective styles (Bucci, 1982) and in the values they attribute to particular styles: Highly expressive people may judge less expressive people as cold and haughty, and less expressive people may see the highly expressive ones as rude, overbearing, and volatile (Tannen, 1984). Miscommunication may occur even among members of the same family who share conversational history yet differ in their interpretations of what a particular utterance 'meant.' What contributes to this confusion is the fact that on different occasions individuals appeal to distinct affective repertoires. Their choices are influenced by a variety of factors, among them the setting, the interlocutor, individual stylistic variation and creativity, the speaker's professional and social roles, the type of emotion expressed, and desired communicative effect.

The present chapter acknowledges intergroup differences in affective styles, yet it is mostly concerned with linguistic and individual levels, or in other words with cross-linguistic differences in affective repertoires and with ways in which these repertoires are selected, appropriated, and interpreted by multilingual speakers. Studies in the fields of anthropology and intercultural communication suggest that despite their multiplicity, affective repertoires offered by different languages and cultures do not completely overlap. Rather, they exhibit differences on a variety of levels, from the lexicon to oral and written genres (Besnier, 1990; Heelas, 1986; Middleton, 1989). As a result, affective personae created by speakers of different languages may be misinterpreted in a systematic manner in intercultural communication (Arndt & Janney, 1985a,b). Let us examine, then, what is known to date about cross-linguistic differences in affective repertoires and consider the difficulties involved in learning how to perform affect in a later learned language, and the challenges of performing affect in multiple languages.

Chapter 3 already highlighted cross-linguistic differences in vocal expression of emotions, so it is reasonable to skip them in this review while emphasizing that prosody and paralinguistic features have to be considered in any analysis of bilingual emotion talk. (Excellent examples of analyses of discursive events that incorporate prosody are offered in Bloch, 1996; Irvine, 1990.) As the focus of this chapter is on discursive construction of emotions, I also will not delve into the kinesic aspects of affect performance, such as facial expression or body language, although these aspects would be equally important for an informed analysis. (For extensive discussions of facial expressions of emotions across cultures, see Ekman, 1980, 2003; Wierzbicka, 1999.) In what follows, then, I will focus on ways in which affect is indexed through various linguistic forms and functions.

On the level of the lexicon, affect may be indexed by emotion words (upset, irritated, overjoyed), emotion-laden words with strong affective connotations (invasion, molestation, rape), kinship terms, honorifics, and forms of address (mommy, daddy, old hag), emotive interjections, exclamations, and sound clusters (uh-oh, yuk, brr, YES!!!), intensifiers (This is bloody unbelievable!), hedges (I am sort of... like... not sure what this is all about), curses and taboo words (Go to HELL!), and figurative language, including similes and metaphors (She is jumping for joy; He is crushed).

In Chapter 4 we saw that cross-linguistic differences in this area may arise in category boundaries and the semantic scope of particular translation equivalents. Languages also possess unique affective resources, such as culture-specific uses of particular terms (such as the Spanish *mamita/* little mother, an affectionate reference to one's daughter), language-specific terms referring to particular emotions (Ilongot *liget*, Japanese *amae*) or syndromes (Spanish *susto*, Korean *hwabyung*), and language- and culture-specific metaphors ('my liver was tiny' to mean 'I was very ashamed'/Chewong; I am feeling down today/English) and interjections (Polish and Russian *t'fu* to express contempt). (For in-depth overviews see Heelas, 1986; Kövecses, 2000; Wierzbicka, 1991.)

These differences imply that bicultural bilinguals, like the Cypriot Greeks discussed in Chapter 4, may find themselves in a situation where the base language of the conversation does not encode the affective meanings they would like to express and they have to code-switch to convey their message precisely. The differences also indicate that to perform affect appropriately in another language, L2 learners have to internalize language-specific terms and expressions and also uncover similarities and differences between translation equivalents in their respective languages. They also need to master the intricacies of conventionalized indexing of affect, which in American English would allow them, for instance, to differentiate between "wow!", which signals (oftentimes positive) surprise, wonder, or approval, "Oh no!", which most often signals surprise at an unfortunate outcome, and "Well, I'll be darned...," which conveys surprise at an unexpected outcome in the speech of the older generation.

On the level of morphosyntax, affect can be expressed through a range of means from pronominal choice (*tu/vous* in French), to emphatic particles and expressive derivation (Russian diminutive suffix -*chik*), to relative clauses and tag questions that often convey involvement (... shall we?... aren't you?) (Stankiewicz, 1964). Affective meanings may also be conveyed through the choice of linguistic frames and grammatical categories, among them evidentiality, tense, aspect, mood, modality, voice, reflexivity, case marking, word order, and right-left dislocation (Arndt & Janney, 1991; Besnier, 1990; Kidron & Kuzar, 2002; McCarthy & Carter, 1997; Ochs & Schieffelin, 1989; Precht, 2003; Wierzbicka, 1991). Notably, while some of these forms also serve to express positive or negative affect, most linguistic structures function as affect intensifiers rather than affect specifiers (Ochs & Schieffelin, 1989).

Languages may also offer unique morphosyntactic means of affective expression or intensification. For instance, in Japanese, Samoan, and Tongan, different forms of first-person singular pronouns can be used to mark self-deprecation and elicit sympathy (Besnier, 1990; Ochs & Schieffelin, 1989). Russian, Polish, and Spanish offer a rich system of emotive diminutives used widely in terms of endearments and baby talk (such as *dochen'ka*, *dochurka*, *dochushka*/little daughter, Russian). And a favorite Yiddish device for expressing disparagement – repeating the word and substituting 'shm' for the initial consonant – has been applied by Yiddish speakers to many languages and has been incorporated by English (cancer-shmancer, money-shmoney).

Cross-linguistic differences may also arise in preferred means of emotional expression. Russian and English as we saw in Chapter 4 both have emotion verbs, adjectives, nouns, and adverbs (albeit in somewhat different proportions), yet in the context of the same verbal task, native speakers of English favor adjectives, which construct emotions as states, while native speakers of Russian prefer verbs, which construct emotions as actions, processes, and interpersonal relationships (Pavlenko, 2002c). Both languages, however, favor the internal perspective on emotions, whether as states or as processes. In turn, Samoan, Yiddish, and Kaluli often construct emotions as external events by encoding the experiencer as a locative modifier of the emotion-denoting verb, rather than its grammatical subject (Besnier, 1990). And Hebrew offers three alternative linguistic frames to its speakers: (a) the experiencer as the subject and agent; (b) the emotion as agent and the experiencer as patient; and (c) the body part as an estranged representation of the experiencer (Kidron & Kuzar, 2002).

In mastering the 'grammar of affect,' L2 learners have to figure out affective meanings signalled by particular morphemes or syntactic configurations and also identify conventional ways of morphosyntactic encoding of affect in particular styles and registers. In turn, bilinguals have to deal with the fact that their respective languages may offer somewhat distinct morphosyntactic resources for affect performance. Some bilinguals may favor a particular language because of its unique resources, such as emotive diminutives; others may try to import these resources into another language. Whatever they do, they have to be ready for the fact that speakers of another language do not necessarily view these resources in a similar manner. The Polish–English bilingual Anna Wierzbicka recalls:

> When I tried to soothe my children in the first weeks of their lives with anxious Polish invocations of '*Córeñko! Córeñko!*' (lit. 'little daughter! little daughter!') my husband pointed out how quaint it sounds from the point of view of a native speaker of English to solemnly address a new-born baby as 'little daughter.'
>
> (Wierzbicka, 1997:117)

Affect can also be expressed directly and indirectly on the level of speech acts. Direct expression of emotions (congratulations, complaints, apologies, insults) may also have a secondary social or psychological illocutionary function. For instance, an expression of surprise or happiness may also function as bragging (I can't BELIEVE my daughter got into Harvard!). Speech acts may also express emotions indirectly, for instance, when a direct request also indexes anger (Just LOOK at this mess! I want you to clean it RIGHT NOW!). In some utterances, such as ritual insults, referential emotional content may not match the affective meaning at all. The mismatches between content and function and multiplicity of speech act functions can create problems for L2 learners who navigate murky waters, at least initially, when selecting responses to compliments or apologies.

The difficulties are compounded by cross-linguistic differences in the salience of particular emotion speech acts, in the frequency and means with which they are performed, and in appropriate responses (Rosaldo, 1982; Wierzbicka, 1985, 1991). In Russian culture, for example, litanies and complaints constitute a very salient act and aim to impress the interlocutors and elicit their compassion and empathy. Problem-solving-oriented Americans who tend to respond with constructive advice receive nothing but silence and blank stares from their Russian interlocutors (Ries, 1997: 36, 44–46). While Russian favors ritual complaints, other languages, among them African–American English, Balinese, Cypriot Greek, Hebrew, Turkish, and Yoruba, have a salient genre of verbal dueling that includes ritual insults and serves to reinforce interpersonal bonds (Kakavá, 2001). L2 learners unfamiliar with the ritual nature of such acts could easily misinterpret these exchanges.

Henry (1936) noticed long ago that the degree of directness plays an important role in speech act performance, in particular in expression of negative emotions through face-threatening speech acts (insults, orders, contradictions, challenges, threats, warnings, expressions of disapproval, criticism, accusations, and reprimands). Interacting with the Kaingang Indians in Brazil, the anthropologist was required to discuss disagreeable things without mentioning what or who he was talking about. In this as in many other cultures, to express negative emotions or to place blame directly may constitute an imposition on the interlocutor and cause the speaker to lose face. Consequently, displays of negative emotions often require mitigation and indirectness, in particular in public spaces. Thus, to perform L2 emotion speech acts in an authentic manner, L2 learners must master not just a variety of linguistic means but also a pragmatic understanding of when, how, to whom, and to what extent a particular emotion can be expressed, and which, if any, mitigators are to be used in this speech act (Rintell, 1990).

Emotions may also be constructed on the level of narratives, as personal stories about events that elicited fear, despair, or happiness, as stories describing other people's emotions, or as more general narratives such as laments about social, political, and economic inequities. Storytelling relies on a wide range of affective devices, from character naming to reported speech or voicing to narrative structure (Bucci, 1982; Rintell, 1989, 1990). These strategies vary depending on the topic, context, and interlocutor, and also on the type of emotions involved. For instance, in American English, narratives of transgressions differ from 'happy stories' in terms of structure, elaboration, sentence length, uses of reported speech, and amount of description of the protagonist's emotions (Schutz & Baumeister, 1999). Cross-linguistic differences in this area may arise in conventionalized narrative structure, amount of evaluation offered, directness of emotion description, and framing of particular events and phenomena (McCabe & Bliss, 2003; Riessman, 1987; Tannen, 1982).

Telling a story adequately in a new language is a complex task to begin with. It becomes even more challenging when storytellers aim to describe their own emotions or to elicit a particular emotional reaction from the interlocutors. To be effective, storytellers need to be familiar with a range of conventionalized narrative structures and affective devices and be able to creatively adopt these devices to engage the audience. People often tell different stories about the same event on different occasions. It should not be surprising that a change in the language of the telling, and thus in linguistic context, would also bring with it a change in the story itself, prompted by a different audience and the linguistic means available to the narrator.

In conversation, indexing of affect involves many of the rhetorical devices just mentioned, as well as manipulation of sociolinguistic registers, where shifts in the level of formality may signal intimacy, solidarity, and inclusiveness, or may function alternatively as a distancing strategy. Affect may also be signalled through communicative and involvement strategies such as reported speech, hedges, reduplication, right-left dislocations, tag questions, and predicates of personal involvement, and conversation management strategies, such as turn-taking, overlap, or backchanneling (Connor-Linton et al., 1987; Tannen, 1989; Wierzbicka, 1991).

Cross-linguistic differences in this area can be found both in the structure and in the conventionalized meanings of particular conversational strategies. Kakavá's (2001) overview of cross-linguistic dynamics of conflict negotiation and Wierzbicka's (1991) review of strategies of self-assertion across languages highlight cross-linguistic and cross-cultural differences in the meaning of conflict and self and in the preferred strategies used by speakers of different languages to assert themselves and to negotiate disagreement. They show, for instance, that Italian, German, Hebrew, Greek, and African–American English highly value argumentation and open conflict in private and public talk and offer their speakers numerous strategies to assert themselves and to directly negotiate conflict. In contrast, Japanese and Chinese view open expression of conflict more negatively and favor more indirect means of conflict negotiation. Connor-Linton and associates (1987) identify differences in strategies preferred by speakers of Russian and American English for expression of personal involvement. They note, for instance, that Russian speakers view emotional involvement as authorization for a longer turn, until they are interrupted by another speaker. As a result, American participants in the televised Soviet–American citizens' summit viewed Russian speakers as long-winded, boring, and monopolistic in holding the floor for so long at a stretch, while Russians perceived Americans as abrupt, inarticulate, and disinterested in the responses they were given.

Even within the same speech community, the same strategies may index distinct types of affect in different contexts. Tag questions may signal intimacy and solidarity in some contexts and challenge and resistance in others. The same kind of interruption in terms of form and timing may appear as a supportive overlap in one situation and as a hostile interruption in another. In intercultural communication, negotiation of meaning becomes even more difficult. Tannen (1989) points out that shared cultural backgrounds or conversational histories lead to shared assumptions about appropriate pause length or use of overlap, and thus ensure rhythmic synchrony in conversation. In contrast, conversations between interlocutors who do not share cultural assumptions may appear 'out of sync': what is appropriate and polite for speakers of one language may appear rude and offensive to speakers of another.

To theorize the idea of shared background, scholars advanced a notion of *affective or emotion styles*, organized around emotional dimensions salient in a particular culture in a particular sociohistoric period (Besnier, 1990; Middleton, 1989; Stearns, 1994). While individual emotion styles within a particular culture incorporate many conventionalized verbal and non-verbal behaviors, they do not have to match or approximate the normative styles. Rather they are constructed with the norm in mind and evaluated against it. For instance, Utku Eskimo, Japanese, and Tahitians avoid anger and emphasize emotional control (Briggs, 1970; Doi, 1973; Levy, 1973), speakers of African–American English and Israeli Hebrew emphasize directness and self-assertion (Katriel, 1985; Wierzbicka, 1991), and the Ilongot and Samoans view anger as an important aspect of being a young male (Gerber, 1985; Middleton, 1989; Rosaldo, 1980). Consequently, what constitutes a transgression with regard to anger will differ in these societies.

The multiplicity of ways in which affect can be performed in conversation is both a blessing and a bane for L2 learners. Language transfer is commonly expected in pronunciation and morphosyntax, but not in pragmatics and conversational strategies; miscommunication in intercultural encounters is often blamed on personalities or cultural differences, rather than on mismatched assumptions about the meaning of particular linguistic strategies or normativity of particular affective styles. The possibility of miscommunication of affective intentions in intercultural communication suggests that L2 users need to pay attention to local meanings of specific strategies rather than to presuppose them based on their own linguistic history or stereotypical assumptions about their interlocutors.

Emotional expression is also at the heart of certain oral and written genres, such as poetry or political oratory, that appeal to a variety of strategies to engage the audience emotionally. For example, emotional persuasiveness and eloquence of the Reverend Jessie Jackson's speeches, quite effective with his American audiences, stem from his masterful use of repetition, imagery, dialogue, and tropes, modeled on African–American, and more generally fundamentalist, sermons (Tannen, 1989). Cross-linguistic and cross-cultural differences in this area may be observed in the means of eliciting emotional engagement and in the expectations as to when it is to be elicited and displayed. Speech communities may also have unique emotional speech genres, such as poetic dueling in North Yemen

(Besnier, 1990), *brogez* (literally 'being in anger'), a ritual insult contest among Israeli children (Katriel, 1985), lamentations performed by Georgian women (Kotthoff, 2001), or *kros* (literally 'angry talk'), a public display of anger, commonly performed by women in a Papua New Guinean village of Gapun (Kulick, 1998; Stroud, 1998). In this area, reasonable expectations for L2 learners may be limited to comprehension, as not every native speaker of a particular language is skilled at emotionally engaging an audience, be it in writing or in speech. On the other hand (as will be demonstrated later on in the discussion of bilingual writers), some L2 users do succeed in mastering the art of eliciting emotional responses in a second language.

This brief overview shows that what is at stake in the study of bilingual emotion talk and L2 learners' mastery of affect performance are not emotions themselves but ways in which speakers convey and perceive affect. If at least some emotions are universal, cross-cultural communication will still be marred by differences in their expression. And if at least some emotions are culture-specific, L2 learners have an additional challenge of figuring out the contents and boundaries of new conceptual categories and emotion scripts.

Now let us consider what is at stake in selection and use of multiple affective repertoires. At present, we know relatively little about how speakers of one language make choices among alternative emotion discourses. (See, however, White, 1990.) We know even less about the ways affective repertoires are learned, selected, and used by bi- and multilingual speakers. To understand this process better, the ensuing discussion will eschew the selection of alternatives within one language (even though this is the most common process for both mono- and multilingual speakers) and focus on unique features of multilinguals' affective repertoires: cross-linguistic differences in means of emotional expression, impact of dominance and proficiency, different contexts of language acquisition and use, and different meanings assigned to the languages in question[1]. I will try to answer the following four questions: *Do multilingual speakers exhibit different affective styles in their respective languages? Are affective repertoires subject to cross-linguistic influence? What factors influence bi- and multilinguals' language choices for emotional expression? How is affect performance in L2 influenced by language proficiency?*

5.3. Multilinguals' affective repertoires

To date, there are no studies known to this researcher that examine bi- and multilinguals' spontaneous emotion talk and allow us to see how repertoires are selected and interpretations negotiated in interaction. The only

---

[1] Undoubtedly, the last two features are not generalizable to all repertoires: Some bi- and multilinguals may have learned their languages in the same environment and assign the same or similar meanings to them.

studies that offer us a glimpse into multilinguals' affective repertoires are studies in the 'twice-told stories' paradigm, initiated by Susan Ervin-Tripp (1954, 1964, 1967). In Ervin-Tripp's studies, described in Chapter 2, French– and Japanese–English bilinguals provided different emotional interpretations of TAT pictures and completed sentences differently, depending on the language in which the responses were elicited. These results suggested that bilinguals who learned their languages in distinct environments might have distinct affective repertoires and storylines associated with these languages. Three decades later, this line of inquiry was picked up again by a new generation of researchers (Koven, 2004; Panayiotou, 2004b; Pavlenko, 2002d), all of whom employed different versions of the elicitation paradigm in which the same stories are elicited from bilingual speakers twice, once in each language.

Panayiotou (2004b) asked five Greek–English and five English–Greek bilinguals to respond to a story that involved, in its two cultural versions, Andy, an American, and Andreas, a Cypriot, who lived in the United States and Cyprus, respectively. The protagonist was a businessman who worked long hours in order to become successful but neglected his mother, girlfriend, and friends. The participants were first read the story in English and then, a month later, in Greek. After each reading, they were told to assume that Andy/Andreas was a person close to them and were asked to describe their emotional reactions to his behavior.

The analysis of the participants' responses showed that they had different reactions to the story depending on the language in which it was read to them, with greater concern expressed for Andreas and indifference or disapproval expressed for Andy. In fact, some participants mentioned that even the images of 'neglected mothers' that came to them were different for the American and Cyprus contexts. These responses indicate that in each case the story was placed within a different set of sociocultural beliefs, imagery, and scripts. At the same time, in order to express their feelings fully, some participants appealed to code-switching. As with a study conducted with the same group of participants discussed in Chapter 4 (Panayiotou, 2004a), the switches were mostly unidirectional, from Greek to English, to use the terms 'concern,' 'frustration,' 'indifference,' 'sympathy,' and 'pity.' The Greek terms, on the other hand, were treated as language- and culture-specific, with *ypohreosi* (deep sense of cultural and social obligation), for instance, being something that Andreas would feel but Andy would not, because the feeling, in the words of one participant, "could never arise in the US" (Panayiotou, 2004b: 133).

Taken together, responses to the two stories, code-switching patterns, and metalinguistic comments showed that these bicultural bilinguals interpret and relate to 'the same' events in distinct contexts in a language- and culture-specific manner. They also insist on cultural specificity of particular emotion scripts, such as *stenahoria* or *ypohreosi*. At the same time, certain

TABLE 5.1. *Studies of multilinguals' affective repertoires*

Study	Participants	Analytical Approach	Results
Rintell (1989, 1990)	6 native speakers of English; 8 ESL students	Discursive analysis of narrative strategies in narratives of personal experience told in L2 English (as compared to strategies used by native speakers of English).	ESL students' stories were less detailed and elaborated than those told by native speakers of English and thus less likely to engage listeners and elicit emotional response.
Pavlenko (2002d)	31 late Russian-English bilinguals	Quantitative and qualitative analyses of elicited narratives told in L1 Russian and L2 English (as compared to narratives told by Russian and English monolinguals).	For the most part, narratives in L1 Russian and L2 English were language- and culture-appropriate, yet they also exhibited instances of L1 and L2 transfer of affective repertoires and emotion concepts.
Koven (2004)	1 simultaneous Portuguese–French bilingual	Discursive analysis of speaker role perspectives in 12 personal narratives told in Portuguese and French.	The speaker exhibited different affective styles in her two languages due to different socialization patterns in the two.
Panayiotou (2004b)	5 Greek–English and 5 English–Greek bilinguals	Qualitative analysis of metalinguistic comments and code-switching in responses to stories told in Greek and English.	For the most part, bilinguals interpreted the twice-told stories in a language- and culture-specific emotional style yet they also appealed to code-switching.
Pavlenko (2004a)	389 bi- and multilingual parents	Quantitative and qualitative analysis of responses to a webquestionnaire.	Factors affecting parental language choice for emotional expression include perceived language emotionality and cross-linguistic differences in affective repertoires.
Dewaele (2004a,b, in press)	1,039 bi- and multilinguals	Quantitative and qualitative analysis of responses to a webquestionnaire.	L1 taboo and swearwords are perceived as stronger and more emotional and L2 words are perceived as weaker and thus less offensive and easier to use.

emotions, such as 'frustration,' are invoked even in Greek conversations that take place in Cyprus (with bilingual interlocutors). This intriguing status disparity between Greek and English emotion concepts suggests that some scripts and concepts – in particular those coming from English, a global language – may be more pervasive and appear more applicable across situations and contexts. The code-switching also suggests that while bilinguals do have language- and culture-specific affective repertoires, they do not necessarily switch them 'on' and 'off.' In interaction with other bilinguals, they may draw on the full range of their repertoires.

Similar conclusions were reached in Pavlenko's (2002d) study conducted with 31 Russian–English late bilinguals (13 males and 18 females, ages 18–26), all of whom learned English between the ages of 13 and 19 upon arrival in the United States. By the time of the study, the participants had spent between three and eight years in the United States, interacting in Russian and English on a daily basis, with the predominance of English. Each participant was shown one of two three-minute-long films with a soundtrack but no dialogue. In each film a woman received and read an apparently upsetting letter; a roommate walked into the room and read the same letter without permission; the woman grabbed the letter away from the roommate and stormed out of the room. One version of this script, *The Letter*, was shot on location in the United States and another, *Pis'mo* (The Letter), on location in the former USSR. In the case of *The Letter*, 10 recalls were elicited in English and 10 in Russian, and in the case of *Pis'mo*, 4 were elicited in English and 7 in Russian.

These narratives were compared to recalls of the same films by native speakers of Russian and English who had limited levels of exposure to foreign languages and were considered monolingual for the purposes of the study (Pavlenko, 2002c). In that study, narratives were elicited from 40 native speakers of Russian, interviewed in Russia, and 40 native speakers of English, interviewed in the United States. (In each group, 20 participants watched *The Letter* and the other 20 *Pis'mo*.) It was found that Russian narrators privileged more emotionally charged words, evoking *gore* (grief, despair) where Americans talked of sadness (*grust'*, *pechal'*), or *gnev* (wrath, ire), where Americans talked about anger (*zlost'*). Consistent with the lexical patterning in each language, American narrators favored emotion adjectives (68% of all emotion terms), while Russian narrators favored emotion verbs (39% of all terms), particularly imperfective and reflexive verbs that stressed the processual aspect of the emotional experience. The most salient term in the Russian narratives was the verb *perezhivat'* (to take something hard, to feel something keenly, to suffer things through), which has no single-word translation equivalent in English; it accounted for 9% of all emotion word tokens in the Russian corpus.

The analysis of bilinguals' narratives demonstrated that in describing the protagonist's feelings, bilinguals generally patterned with monolingual speakers in each language, using appropriate lexical resources, such as adjectives in English and verbs in Russian. Russian narratives also contained emotion words of greater intensity than the English ones. The same cultural and linguistic specificity was observed in emotion scripts invoked by the participants. English narratives, for instance, featured the notion of privacy, absent in the Russian language and culture. A closer look, however, revealed a significant amount of cross-linguistic influence in participants' descriptions of emotions. L1 transfer from Russian was visible in the fact that in both sets of narratives the participants paid more attention to external appearances and body language than did American monolinguals. Some narratives also exhibited instances of L1 transfer in the use of emotion terms, such as 'she is deep inside herself' (*ona vsia v sebe*).

Interestingly, the transfer was bidirectional: In the narratives of the same participants one could see both L1 transfer and L2 transfer (Pavlenko & Jarvis, 2002). In case of the L2 transfer, several storytellers attempted to substitute verbs for adjectives in their Russian narratives, incorporating perception and change-of-state copula verbs, such as *vygliadet'* (to appear), *chuvstvovat'* (to feel), and *stanovit'sia* (to become). In contexts where Russian monolinguals used action verbs, such as *rasserdit'sia* (to get cross, angry) or *rasstroit'sia* (to get upset), some bilinguals opted for change-of-state verbs *stat'* (perfective) and *stanovit'sia* (imperfective) (to become) with emotion adjectives, producing utterances such as "*ona stala eshche bolee rasstroennaia*" (she (NOM) became even more upset (NOM)). While in English such an utterance is fully grammatical, in Russian emotion talk the verb *stanovit'sia* is typically preceded by a pronoun in a Dative case and followed by an adverb, for example *ei stalo grustno* (literally: to her (DAT) it became sad). In a less common construction, the verb *stanovit'sia* subcategorizes for adjectives in Instrumental case, for example *ona stala grustnoi* (she (NOM) became sad (INST)). Yet the participants appropriated the English construction, Pronoun (NOM) + Verb + Adj (NOM), producing instances of morphosyntactic transfer of subcategorization constraints. In these and similar instances, narrators adopted the English adjectival pattern and violated Russian sentence structure, subcategorization constraints, and discourse pragmatics in an attempt to transfer the L2 linguistic frames into L1 and to lexicalize emotions as states rather than as processes.

It is also worth noting that while overall bilinguals relied on the scripts shared by both of their linguistic communities, in English they also appealed to the language- and culture-specific notion of privacy. At the same time, the verb *perezhivat'* that dominated Russian monolinguals' narratives and the related script appeared in only one of 17 narratives produced by bilingual participants, suggesting that this Russian emotion frame may be subject to attrition, or at least that it is falling into disuse in the U.S. context where the bilinguals were interviewed.

Together, the findings of Pavlenko's (2002d) and Panayiotou's (2004b) studies suggest that while on the surface late bilinguals' emotional expression appears culture-specific and linguistically appropriate, bidirectional cross-linguistic influence is taking place in their affective repertoires, whereby new concepts and scripts are appropriated (privacy and frustration), salience of certain concepts and notions gets higher or lower (*perezhivat'*, *stenahoria*), and linguistic framing may shift in the direction of the language that dominates everyday interaction. At the same time, both studies are limited in that they considered elicited reactions to stories, describing either one's own (Panayiotou, 2004b) or other people's feelings (Pavlenko, 2002d). The question still remains as to how bilinguals express emotions in everyday talk and in narratives of personal experience.

It is precisely this question that Koven (2004) addressed in a study of affect performance by one Portuguese–French bilingual. A twenty-year-old daughter of Portuguese migrants, Linda was born and grew up in France. Her French is indistinguishable from that of a French monolingual of her age, gender, and social background. Yet Portuguese is Linda's first language and it continues to play an important role in her life. She communicates in Portuguese with her family and relatives and with her Portuguese boyfriend. She also chose Portuguese as a college major and after graduation intends to marry her boyfriend and remain with him in Portugal. French is her dominant language and sometimes it influences her Portuguese, yet Linda works hard to sound as native as possible in Portuguese and is happy when she 'passes' in Portugal for a monolingual Portuguese speaker. In this Linda is unlike the late bilinguals described earlier, who are very clear on which language is their L1 and which is L2. In Linda's case there is no easy way to decide which language is which: Even though she started learning Portuguese somewhat earlier, she is clearly dominant in French, the language of her everyday surroundings.

In the study, Linda told twelve stories of personal experience, once in French and once in Portuguese, to two different bilingual listeners. Each story involved emotional experiences, for instance a fight with her mother on Mother's Day. Koven's (2004) analysis of these narratives focused on the formally locatable speaker-role perspectives (narrator, interlocutor, character) from which the experiences were recounted and that allow the speaker to index affective stances. The analysis demonstrated that in French Linda spoke more often as an interlocutor and in Portuguese as a neutral narrator. Reported speech (character role) was performed in more extreme styles in French than in Portuguese. There was also a higher percentage of shifts into a familiar or vulgar register in French than in Portuguese. In order to systematically link particular strategies to affective stances and personae, the researcher elicited reactions to the tape-recorded narratives from five bilingual listeners. The listeners found Linda's French performance to be more forceful and intense than her Portuguese one. They also commented that she came across as a different person in each language: angry, violent, and rebellious in French, less aggressive in Portuguese. These perceptions concurred both with the researcher's analysis of the narratives and with Linda's own perceptions of her two affective styles.

Like many other bilinguals, Linda acknowledges that she has different personae in her two languages: "It's not the same personality in French and in Portuguese... when I speak French and I switch to Portuguese, there's something that's different" (Koven, 2004). She is also perceived differently by her interlocutors, in particular her cousins, who often say to her: "That's not the same Linda... there's something when you speak, it's not the same thing... shit, it's not the same cousin" (Koven, 2004: 477). What is particularly intriguing about her case is that she appears to be more timid, calm, and reserved in Portuguese, a language learned in the family, and more intense and boisterous in French, learned outside the home. Linda actually has a harder time getting angry in Portuguese, which is quite fortunate for her boyfriend who does not speak any French. She attributes these differences to her childhood socialization in which her mother prohibited taboo and swearwords in the family, saying that only old people use profanity.

Koven (2004) explains these 'double selves' through distinct affective repertoires to which Linda has access in her linguistic environments. When speaking Portuguese, Linda presents the reserved and deferential persona of a properly brought up rural woman who does not use profanity, thus reproducing the repertoires she has appropriated from her family. In French, the language of peer socialization, she performs the assertive and irreverent identity of a young urban female who feels free to express her anger in any way she wishes. The findings of Koven's (2004) study put an interesting spin on what is commonly known as the L2 detachment effect. For Linda and other bilinguals like her it is in fact the L1 that may be the language of self-control. In Linda's case such an outcome may be partially due to the lack of pragmatic competence in certain emotion speech acts, such as anger expression, and partially to language socialization effects that prevent her from using certain swearwords even if she had knowledge of them.

Together, these studies offer intriguing responses to the first two questions asked in this chapter. In response to the first question, the studies show that bicultural bilinguals socialized in distinct contexts have somewhat distinct affective styles due to differences in affective repertoires offered by the speech communities to which they have been socialized. Some of these differences stem from cross-linguistic differences in dominant emotion scripts (Ervin-Tripp, 1954, 1964, 1967; Panayiotou, 2004b; Pavlenko, 2002d), others from differences in linguistic means of emotional expression (Panayiotou, 2004a; Pavlenko, 2002d), and yet others from the idiosyncratic socialization trajectories of particular speakers (Koven, 2004). These differences in affective styles and thus in affective personae performed by the speakers are often taken as evidence of the existence of the 'double selves' referred to by bilingual participants in the studies discussed here and by respondents to our webquestionnaire (Pavlenko, in press).

In response to the second question, the studies show that depending on the speakers' languages, learning histories, and language-use contexts, their affective repertoires may exhibit little or no overlap and no cross-linguistic influence (Koven, 2004), the influence of the second language on the first (Panayiotou, 2004b), or bidirectional influence (Pavlenko, 2002d).

The differences between bilinguals' responses in L1 and L2 deserve further exploration, as they have important implications for educational, legal, and especially medical contexts, where, as will be shown in Chapter 6, bilinguals may respond to questions and describe their conditions somewhat differently in their two languages (Marcos et al., 1973b).

5.4. Language choice in emotional expression

There is a wealth of research in the field of bilingualism that illuminates factors affecting code-switching and language choice in multilingual contexts (Auer, 1998; Heller, 1988; Milroy & Muysken, 1995). Undoubtedly, some of these factors – including topic, context, interlocutor, and the speaker's language proficiency – are also relevant in analysis of bilingual emotion talk. Until recently, however, language choice in emotional expression and the affective function of code-switching have been examined only peripherally in code-switching studies. These studies offer a somewhat oversimplified portrayal of affective functions of code-switching: Speakers are posited to switch into L1 to signal intimacy and we-ness or to express their emotions, and to the L2 to mark distance and an out-group attitude or to describe emotions in a detached way (Grosjean, 1982; Gumperz, 1982a; Schecter & Bayley, 1997; Scheu, 2000; Zentella, 1997).

The scarcity of information about the intricacies of multilingual emotion talk is understandable: Arguments, quarrels, and expressions of love and intimacy are among some of the most private speech acts and as such are close to impossible to capture for research purposes (Piller, 2002a). Nevertheless, considering the fact that identities and group boundaries are constructed in interaction and are not always straightforwardly linked to a single language or language variety (Auer, 1998; Pavlenko & Blackledge, 2004a, b), we may hypothesize that the same language may have different affective meanings in different contexts, and thus L1 would not always mean simply we-ness and intimacy, and L2 distance and detachment. Speakers may use these languages to index a variety of affective stances, and they may also mix two or more languages to convey emotional meanings. Thus closer attention has to be paid to ways in which affect is constructed in interaction and to factors that influence multilinguals' linguistic choices in affect performance. To date, only a few studies have begun to explore these issues, among them studies of communication in cross-cultural couples (De Klerk, 2001; Piller, 2002a) and studies based on Dewaele and Pavlenko's (2001–2003) webquestionnaire (Dewaele, 2004a, b, c, in press; Pavlenko, 2004a, in press). Because none of these studies examined language choice and use across a variety of emotion speech acts, in what follows I will offer a thematic analysis of the original webques-tionnaire data, supplementing the discussion with the evidence from the studies I have listed here, the media, and multilinguals' autobiographies.

Several of the webquestionnaire questions inquired directly or indirectly about respondents' linguistic preferences for expression of negative and positive affect. The former referred to language choice for expression of anger (question 21), arguing (question 32), swearing (question 22), and scolding and disciplining children (question 18). The latter referred to lan-guage choice for expression of love (questions 27 and 28), intimacy (ques-tion 28), deepest feelings (questions 24 and 29), and praise for one's chil-dren (question 19). Because most of these were open-ended questions, the responses oftentimes included rationales for particular choices.

Quantitative and qualitative analyses of these responses were conducted in order to examine language choices and preferences in the light of partic-ipants' linguistic histories (including age and context of acquisition of var-ious languages), linguistic competencies (including language dominance, attrition, and levels of proficiency in up to five languages), present con-texts (including frequency of use of various languages, the language of the environment and of the interlocutors), perceived emotionality of the languages in question, and interactional goals. (For a detailed discussion of the results of the quantitative analyses, see Dewaele, 2004a,b,c, in press.) In what follows, I will examine the influence of all of these factors on the choice and use of multilinguals' affective repertoires, beginning with the goals participants aim to accomplish. Because most of the webquestion-naire respondents were multilinguals, I will use the term LX to refer to their later learned languages.

Both quantitative and qualitative analyses of participants' responses indicate that overall individuals who remain dominant in their L1 see the L1 as the most emotional and favor it for emotional expression; it remains emotional even in individuals who are undergoing the process of L1 attri-tion (Dewaele, 2004a,c). It is not surprising, then, that L1 remains a favorite choice for expression of negative affect, in particular anger, in arguments with partners and spouses (Dewaele, 2004a, in press). Piller (2002a) points out that for partners in cross-cultural couples, arguments may be the only time the usual language choice is thrown into question. Our webques-tionnaire respondents living with a speaker of another language often talk about reverting spontaneously to the L1 in fights and arguments with their partners and spouses:

We argue in both languages (but of course we tend to use each our mother tongue when we are VERY angry and too angry to think about the appropriateness of expressions. (Maria, 33, L1 German, L2 Czech, partner is L1 speaker of Czech)

Argue? – a good question – my partner is likely to switch to her L1 for whole sequences or sometimes intra-sententially while I respond almost entirely in L1 English. (Richard, 48, L1 English, L2 Spanish, L3 Italian, L4 Greek)

A mixture: I tend to argue in English and my wife switches to German and then I switch to German until she says: "Say it in English"!!!
(Robert, 66, L1 English, L2 German, wife is L1 speaker of German)

While dominance and proficiency do play a role in these choices (as will be discussed later on), in many cases speakers revert to the L1 because it feels most satisfying and 'natural.' At times, they do so even though – or precisely because – their partner is a weak speaker of that language or does not understand it at all:

We speak in english but when i am sick or angry I have to say some words in spanish. Of course he doesn't understand.
(Adela, 23, L1 Spanish, L2 English, L3 Swedish, partner is L1 speaker of English)

We use English almost exclusively. I sometimes use American Sign Language especially when we are arguing and I want to say something that she most likely won't understand. (Michelle, 21, L1 English and ASL, L2 Spanish)

In these cases, a switch to L1 allows speakers to let their interlocutors know that they are angry without hurting their feelings or self-esteem. This intriguing pattern also suggests that while interlocutors' competence determines language choice in communication in general, it does not always play the same role in expression of anger, where – in the words of Marianne quoted in Chapter 3 – "the most important thing is to shout." The responses also highlight the importance of a factor that is rarely considered in discussions of code-switching or language choice, namely, internal satisfaction. The use of a language the interlocutor does not understand goes against the grain of linguistic theory that appeals to Gricean maxims and the Cooperative Principle (Grice, 1975) to frame argument as a cooperative activity (van Eemeren et al., 1993; Walton, 1998). Yet as many bilinguals admit, at times it is more important to them to express their feelings and ideas in a way that would satisfy themselves, rather than to be fully understood by their interlocutors; perhaps we should call that the "there, I said it" phenomenon.

L1 is also a popular choice for expression of positive affect, in particular among parents (Pavlenko, 2004a). This preference is particularly clear in cases where the LX is otherwise the language of communication. For

instance, respondents who are raising their children in the LX environment at times find themselves unable to interact with the children in a
language that is not the language of their own childhood and does not
have appropriate affective connotations:

I guess my preference is L1 again – in English it just doesn't feel right somehow.
When my daughter was born I was planning to start talking English to her as soon
as possible (to comfort her when she cried etc) but found out I couldn't – I either
didn't know the words or they didn't feel good enough to express what I felt.
(Ioanna, 37, L1 Polish, L2 English, L3 Russian, uses L1 Polish with the child
in the L2 environment)

I have a preference for French. When my children were born I wanted to use English
just so that they would be accustomed to it from an early age but I just couldn't. It
sounded untrue.
(Anne Marie, 36, L1 French, L2 Dutch, L3 English, uses L1 French with
the children in the L1 environment)

Once again, language choice here is determined not by the interlocutor's competence (or even desired competence), nor by the language of the
environment, but by the speaker's desire for internal satisfaction derived
from the use of a language that feels emotional and 'natural.' Susan Fries
(1998), an American living in France and married to a Frenchman, remem-
bers her surprise when her husband decided to adopt English as the family
language:

Despite my fluency in French, had we been living in the US I would never have
spoken French to my children initially. Since I feel closer to my emotions in English,
to this day I feel awkward cooing to babies in a language other than English. (p. 133)

Many webquestionnaire respondents concur, pointing out that trying
to create an emotional connection in a second language feels 'fake' and
'unnatural':

Welsh is the language which is the one that feels natural for expressing feelings.
Expressing endearment in English has a false 'acting' ring to it. I would inevitably
talk to babies and animals in Welsh. (Maureen, 47, L1 Welsh, L2 English)

Expressing strong emotions in a language other than my mother tongue French
seems artificial. (Stephanie, 50, L1 French, L2 Dutch, L3 English, L4 German)

These responses suggest that for some bi- and multilinguals, most often
those who have recently moved to the target language context and have not
undergone the process of second language socialization, using LX affective
repertoires feels 'artificial' – it requires 'acting' and effectively constructing
another persona. Some, like Bertha, believe that using LX for emotional
expression is tantamount to offering their partners or children "emotions
of a different person":

My children get all the 'Schatzilein' and 'Spaetzchen' 'Liebchen' and whatever from me. But to use English terms of endearment seems almost wrong to me as if I was doing something forbidden. I am not an English mother and if I were to say 'darling' a lot I would give them the emotions of a different person. In my mothering I definitely feel German.

    (Bertha, 38, L1 German, L2 English, uses mostly L1 German with children)

    Yet perceived language emotionality does not influence language choice for affect performance exclusively in the direction of the most emotional language. Some respondents state that emotionality of the L1 may deter communication, and that the shift to the LX functions as an interactional strategy that allows them to gain distance and exercise self-control. As one respondent succinctly summarized: "I want to use the language that I control, not the one that controls me." Thus, some respondents actually prefer to argue in a second language, believing that such arguments offer a great opportunity for practicing the LX:

Arguing with one's partner has the one advantage of being an excellent linguistic exercise in terms of logic quick response etc.

    (Ray, 24, L1 English, L2 French, partner is L1 speaker of French)

    Case studies in psychoanalysis and psychotherapy discussed in Chapter 6 corroborate this pattern and show that bi- and multilingual patients in therapy sometimes favor a later learned language for the expression of anger. Movahedi (1996) reveals that his Persian–English bilingual patients express their anger toward him in L2 English, rather than in the shared native language Persian, as it feels safer and more polite. Some also switch to L2 English to express anger toward family members, as if using the second language will keep these revelations a secret. Susan Fries (1998), who finds her L1 English more natural for child-rearing, also argues with her husband in her L2 French, in which she feels more assertive and less vulnerable:

... my greater theoretical competence in English is accompanied by the remnants of adolescent shyness. French is the language of my adult experience, so in some cases I discover I can express myself in it more assertively, perhaps because my French-speaking models are assertive. With my husband I often speak French when I want to avoid getting carried away by my feelings. It is interesting to note that we have had arguments in which I chose to speak French, and my husband English. (p. 132)

    Using the LX in an argument offers a double advantage: Not only do speakers place themselves at a greater emotional distance, they also wield a language that has more power to hurt the interlocutor, for whom the language is native. Some do not hesitate to use that power:

We usually argue in a English/Spanish mish mash. When either of us are boiling it is each her/his own L1. When I am arguing yet am feeling clever and wittty and relaxed I will often use my L2 (Spanish) to deliver some really poisonous barbs. (Kurt, 40, L1 English, L2 Spanish, partner is L1 speaker of Spanish)

Arguments are not the only emotion speech act where bilinguals may want to gain distance. Some also favor LX for expression of positive emotions, including flirting (Movahedi, 1996) or saying "I love you." English emerges as a popular choice in this area: Several respondents noted that in English it is much more common to express 'love' for anyone and anything, from one's children to movies to ice cream. Therefore, it is much easier for them to say "I love you" in English than it would be in their native Finnish, Chinese, or Russian, where such statements would be exceedingly rare and unusual:

Finnish emotions are rarely stated explicitly. Therefore it is easier to tell my children e.g that I love them in English. . . . I rarely tell my children that I love them in Finnish (L1); it is easier in L2.
  (Marita, 45, L1 Finnish, L2 English, L3 Swedish, lives in the US, uses L1 Finnish and L2 English with the children)

"I love you" in Chinese is a very strong phrase and we Chinese don't say it often. We use it only when we really mean it. But even when we mean it we (most of us) are still reluctant to say it. It is a very strong phrase. Many of my students say that this is a Chinese phrase we feel but not speak. Personally I feel much easy to say it in English (my L2). (Jiang, 47, L1 Chinese, L2 English)

In Russian it has more weight, it is not used as frequently and hence not as devalued. Saying "I love you" in English is somewhat easier.
  (Natasha, 33, L1 Russian, L2 English)

The makers of the Spanish-language soap opera *Te amaré en silencio* (2002), where action takes place in the Mexican–American community in Los Angeles, picked up on this pattern and used code-switching to English to index – among other things – an insincere admission of love. "*No me esperes con la cena,* (Do not wait for me with dinner)" says Arsenio, a husband with a roving eye, to his wife Angelica. "I love you!" "I love you too," whispers back the unfaithful and deceitful Angelica (episode aired on February 9, 2004).

The language learned later in life also allows speakers to use taboo and swearwords, avoiding the feelings of guilt and discomfort internalized in childhood with regard to these expressions. (This issue will be discussed more fully in Chapter 6.)

I never swear in Spanish. I simply cannot. The words are too heavy and are truly a taboo for me. (Maria, L1 Spanish, L2 English)

My parents were quite strict and I still have the phrase "I'll wash your mouth out with soap and water" in my head! I'd never swear in English but it is easier in German! (Nicole, L1 English, L2 German, L3 French, L4 Italian, L5 Spanish)

Unfortunately, the speakers' perception of emotional strength of LX swearwords is not necessarily in line with that of their interlocutors, who may be extremely offended by taboo and swearwords uttered in their native language (Dewaele, 2004a,b, in press; Piller, 2002a). The fact that many speakers favor LX for self-control and detachment in emotional expression suggests that an affective stance may indeed change with the change in language, contributing, once again, to the perception of bilinguals' 'double selves.' A fascinating example of such duality is offered by Patricia Mudgett-DeCaro (1998), a hearing child of deaf parents:

> Once when I was very angry, someone asked me (in English) what I felt. I answered with very rational, controlled words, but Jim [the narrator's husband] noticed that under the table I was signing "hate, hate." I was entirely unaware that I was giving two messages simultaneously. (Mudgett-De Caro, 1998: 279)

Undoubtedly, the dissociation between form and content may also be observed in monolingual speech, where vocal cues and facial expression may signal different affect than the referential content of the message, yet nowhere is this dissociation as clear as in the case where two languages are being used simultaneously. Not surprisingly, Mudgett-De Caro believes that only American Sign Language, a language she learned from her parents, expresses her emotions adequately, while English, her 'intellectual' language, is used to exercise self-control.

This discussion clearly shows that multilingual speakers' language choices for emotional expression are driven not solely by language dominance or by what they see as 'the language of the heart,' but also by the strategic goals they aim to achieve in interaction and by social and power relations between interlocutors. In some cases a second language may be used to control not only the speakers' emotions but also those of their interlocutors. Take for instance another segment from *Te amaré en silencio* (2002), where, after a tense conversation with her father, the teenage protagonist Mari-Luz attempts to calm him down. First she tries to do so in Spanish, and then, not having achieved the desired effect, she switches to English, the language in which she has more competence than her father and thus more authority over him:

> Mari-Luz: *Tranquilo, papi, tranquilo...* Chill out...
> [Calm down, daddy, calm down... *Chill out...*]. (episode aired on January 5, 2004)

The writers of this soap opera understand the dynamics of bilingual conversation pretty well – I can certify firsthand that the child's command to 'chill' may indeed have a chilling effect on the non-native-speaking parent, reminding him or her of the child's linguistic superiority. Yet non-native speakers may also appeal to the L2 to lend authority to their affective stance. An interesting example comes from Breitborde's (1998) analysis of Kru–English code-switching in New Krutown, Liberia. There, public arguments among males almost always involve English, even when the men have only minimal competence in the language. The researcher tells the story of a carpenter who had prepared a coffin for a deceased community member without being asked to do so by the community officials. The leaders come to him, complaining that he should have waited for their request. The carpenter argues that they should have praised him for making the coffin on his own. The elders disagree and the argument continues. Because the men involved have little proficiency in English, the argument is mostly conducted in the local language Kru. At the end however, the enraged carpenter screams in Kru that he would bury the deceased by himself and then yells at the elders in English: "Now get off my premises. These are my premises. I order you to go" (Breitborde, 1998: 90), thus indexing his affective stance not through the most 'emotional' language but through one with most power and authority.

Speakers may also switch languages because certain languages offer them unique means of affect performance. Pramila Venkateswaran, a feminist scholar born in Bombay and living in the United States, believes that one of the advantages of learning new languages is the ability to express what remained inexpressible in their first:

English enabled me to use multitudinous modes of expressing my emotions that I had not been educated to express in Tamil. (Venkateswaran, 2000: 62)

Similar opinions were voiced by Japanese women in a grassroots feminist English class in Japan facilitated by an American teacher (McMahill, 2001). The women stated that English offered them the linguistic means to express themselves "less stereotypically and more honestly, directly, and assertively" (McMahill, 2001: 333) than they would in Japanese. Of particular importance for them were subject pronouns, such as 'I' or 'you': they felt that the English requirement to specify pronouns drew their attention to the distinction between their opinions and those of others, and allowed them to clarify their thoughts and feelings. Panayiotou's (2004a,b) work offers several examples of lexical enrichment of Greek repertoires with English terms, such as 'frustration.' Russian L2 users of English also like to borrow the term 'frustration,' which is nonexistent in Russian (Koreneva, 2003: 383). Another popular lexical borrowing is the term 'excitement.' *"Oni budut ochen' eksaited!"* (They will be very excited!), exclaimed one Russian immigrant in Andrews' (1999: 100) study. Dictionaries usually gloss 'excited' as *vzvolnovannyi* (agitated, anxious), but the translation is only an approximate one, as the Russian word lacks the positive coloring of 'excitement,' containing instead a negative element of anxiety, worry, and nervous agitation. The literal meaning of 'excitement' is best rendered by the Russian expression *radostnoe vozbuzhdenie* (joyful agitation), but this expression is mainly literary and may sound out of place in everyday interaction. To compensate for the lack of a single-word equivalent, Russian–English bilinguals appeal to code-switching and lexical borrowing.

An excellent illustration of centrality of cross-linguistic differences in bilinguals' lives is offered in Wierzbicka's (2004) account of the difficulties she has in describing to Australian acquaintances her newly born grand-daughter. While she is fully fluent in English and well-familiar with the register used for talking about babies, the world-famous linguist often feels 'stuck for words,' as her L2 English lacks the counterparts of L1 Polish words, such as *rozkoszna* (gorgeous, luxurious, adorable, delightful), and does not have diminutive forms, such as *loczki* (dear little curls) or *ząbki* (dear little teeth). Rather than using the inadequate, from her Polish perspective, terms 'cute,' 'sweet,' and 'adorable,' the happy grandmother often finds herself simply mumbling that her granddaughter is well.

Some of the webquestionnaire respondents revealed that due to cross-linguistic differences in the means of emotional expression, they have distinct linguistic preferences for expression of particular emotions. For instance, several Japanese–English bilinguals commented on their prefer-ence for English as the language of anger, because in the Japanese culture, anger is at best expressed indirectly while English condones a direct expres-sion of anger:

> I tend to use English when I am angry, Japanese when I'm hurt or sad, both when I am happy or excited (...) My other bilingual friends who are all returnees like me said the same thing about using English when they're angry. I guess I like the sound of the swearing words since I heard it so many times during my stay in the U.S. This swearing doesn't happen so often in Japan. It's a cultural difference.
>
> (Ryoko, L1 Japanese, L2 English)

Members of English–German couples interviewed in Piller's (2002a) study have a similar perception of English; many couples say that English is better suited for arguments than German, because it is easier, simpler, quicker, and offers a richer array of swearwords. It appears to be less well suited for positive affect, intimacy, and praise, as other languages offer larger arrays of diminutives and terms of endearment. This is particularly evident in the statements of parents who, like Silvia and Natalia, are native speakers of English yet favor languages learned later in life when in need of endearments:

> [I] tend to use L2 and L3 terms of endearment to children – just seems to express what you fell better. no equivalent in English.
>
> (Silvia, 36, L1 English, L2 Malay, L3 Tamil, uses mostly L1 English with children)

> [I prefer terms of endearment in] Spanish, because there are more ways to refer to my son in Spanish endearingly.
>
> (Natalia, 28, L1 English, L2 Spanish, L3 French, uses mostly L1 English with children)

Analyzing the statements from the webquestionnaire respondents, we can see that a second language enables emotional expression in at least two ways. First, by offering speakers new emotion terms and affective repertoires that may best capture feelings 'unnamed' in the native language (such as the English terms 'frustration' and 'excited' and Spanish diminutives), and, second, by offering speakers a degree of emotional distance, whereby they don't feel as bad about swearing, as concerned about being angry or assertive, or even as committed when they express love. Furthermore, affect is not always expressed by the choice of one language over the other. Like Brenda, many bi- and multilinguals creatively combine their languages (Pavlenko, 2004a), engaging in what Weinreich (1953) saw as affective transfer, that is the use of morphosyntactic forms of one language in another for affective purposes:

I use Spanish terms of endearment with my daughters but I Frenchify them like 'mamita' which becomes 'maminette.'
        (Brenda, 44, L1 English, L2 Spanish, L3 Portuguese, L4 French, dominant
        in L1 English, uses L1 English and L4 French with her daughters)

Together, the studies discussed in this section suggest that bi- and multilinguals may favor a particular language for emotional expression, but most often find themselves 'doing emotions' in more than one language. The thematic analysis of the webquestionnaire responses shows that bi- and multilinguals use their affective repertoires strategically to accomplish a variety of interactional purposes, communication of emotions being only one of many. Linguistic choices are also made to experience the emotional satisfaction of using the language that feels 'natural' (mothers using L1 or partners arguing in their respective L1s), to hurt the interlocutor (partners delivering 'poisonous barbs' in the language most emotional for the interlocutor), to avoid hurting the interlocutor (partners reverting to a language the interlocutor does not speak), to exercise self-control and perhaps even practice the language (partners arguing in LX), to gain distance (expressing anger or love or swearing in LX), to perform authority (using the language that has the most prestige in a particular context), and to express a specific emotional meaning (code-switching to talk about 'frustration' or 'excitement').

What is particularly interesting about these findings is the emphasis the respondents maintain on internal satisfaction in language choice. Mainstream theories of communication and code-switching typically focus on speakers' interactional goals and needs; in contrast, the responses cited here indicate that language choices may also serve to satisfy speakers' personal needs, independent of the interlocutors' proficiency or accomplishment of any discursive business other than self-expression and self-satisfaction. These perceptions, common to individuals who moved to the target language environment as adults (Pavlenko, 2004a), also have intriguing implications for the notion of 'double selves': Some speakers may feel that their L1 selves are emotionally 'true' and 'natural,' while affective selves in LX are 'fake' and 'artificial.'

The responses also highlight several factors that influence linguistic choices, among them interactional goals, speaker's and interlocutor's linguistic competence and L1 backgrounds, context of acquisition of LX, perceived language emotionality, perceived language prestige and authority, and cross-linguistic differences in affective repertoires. A particularly intriguing factor, perceived language emotionality, influences language choice in a variety of directions. The majority of respondents with a clearly defined L1 do perceive their L1 as most emotional and favor it as the language of emotional expression. Other speakers – for whom L1 is also the most emotional – may favor languages learned later in life that allow them to control themselves or their interlocutors and to express their feelings – in particular negative emotions – in a more precise manner. Some speakers see two or more of their languages as vested with similar degrees of emotionality, and they allow external circumstances to determine language choice for affect performance. Others favor a later learned language as more emotional, or have specific linguistic preferences for negative and positive emotions or for particular emotion speech acts. And some challenge the existence of strict language boundaries and engage in creative language play, combining affective resources of two or more languages.

5.5. Proficiency and self-expression

Piller's (2002a) study of cross-cultural couples reminds us that proficiency is another important factor that, together with dominance, influences language choice for emotional expression. Because emotional communication – arguments in particular – at times proceeds at a faster pace than regular conversation, in multilingual settings speakers may feel particularly compelled to revert to their dominant or most proficient language in order to draw on the richest and most accessible set of linguistic resources. Thus, in Piller's (2002a) study speakers insufficiently proficient in the partner's language acknowledged that in arguments they revert back to their native language, even if the other language is otherwise their couple language. Similarly, some of the webquestionnaire respondents admitted that they prefer to argue in L1 because they are more competent in that language, and thus can react faster and gain ground in rapidly paced arguments:

When it comes to arguing we also use Finnish although I sometimes switch to L1 English when I feel that I'm losing ground in the argument.
(Alex, 35, L1 English, L2 Finnish, L3 Swedish, wife is L1 speaker of Finnish)

I do however prefer to argue in my L1 when the other is not an L1 native speaker (but that could be the control freak in me!). (Susan, 28, L1 English, L2 German)

Lack of what Piller (2002a) calls 'rowing proficiency' is a significant deterrent in this area, as seen in comments made by members of cross-cultural couples in both Piller's (2002a) and De Klerk's (2001) studies. In the latter study, a member of an English–Afrikaans couple recalls that in the beginning they had trouble carrying on an argument:

We couldn't have an argument, because he used to say "what does that word mean?", which was terribly frustrating. I couldn't get through to him, I thought he was being dense. (De Klerk, 2001: 202)

It is of course entirely possible that the husband was using his lack of L2 proficiency as a shield and as a way to either avoid arguments or frustrate his wife even more. Yet the frustration of people who do not understand what is said to them, or cannot express their own feelings, is quite real and is corroborated by many speakers in similar arrangements. For instance, a German–English bilingual, Hildegard, in Piller's (2002a) study says that she feels disadvantaged when she has to express herself in L2 English during a hot discussion or a fierce argument, because she cannot express her arguments and make her points equally well in that language. Similar frustration is felt by the Portuguese–French bilingual Linda, who complains about her inability to adequately express anger in her L1 Portuguese:

With my boyfriend, when I fight with him, it gets in the way and I want to tell him tons of things ... once I told him, "you're lucky that you don't understand French." He's like, "why?" I'm like, "because I'd have so many things to tell you ... " I was mad and in Portuguese it didn't come, y'know. I said a couple of little things, but it didn't come with the same force as in French ... in Portuguese, I don't have that vocabulary. (Koven, 2004: 477)

While Linda is a fluent speaker of Portuguese who sometimes 'passes' for a native speaker, her anger repertoire lacks richness and sophistication because her peer socialization – and thus arguing, fighting, and quarreling – took place mainly in French. Foreign language learners whose learning took place in the classroom face an even greater predicament when they need to stand up for themselves (cf. Polanyi, 1995), because anger expression is rarely taught in the classroom. A poignant example of the inability to adequately verbalize anger in L2 comes from Jung Euen Choi (2002), who arrived in the United States from Korea as an international student. One day Jung Euen was eating lunch in a dormitory cafeteria with a Korean friend when a group of loud football players started playing with food and throwing rice around. The rice ended up on the girl's hair. The football players laughed and Jung Euen felt insulted, not only because food had been thrown at her, but because for her rice symbolized her culture and ethnic identity. She kept looking at the boys, trying to signal her displeasure, but the giggling continued. Finally, she stood up from her seat and walked over to their table:

Standing in front of the large group of football players with my face turned red, I could not find suitable words. I wanted to show them I was very angry. I was so furious that I felt all the blood from my body was gushing up to my head. I was desperately trying to find words in my mind. English! Uh! If I had spoken fluent English! . . . I turned my back and walked away from their table. "Asshole!" I swore. This word was a word I could say with clear pronunciation. . . . This word meant: "I am very angry." . . . If only I had been able to deliberately articulate the unjust situation with sophisticated, polite, strong, and eloquent language . . . Instead, I was a weak-looking Asian girl with little English, who had said a swear word. . . . That day, I could not go to sleep for the bitterness, anger, sadness, and shame I still felt from the incident. Those big white boys might have just made fun of me even more when they saw me standing up for my ideas and my opinion in mumbled and broken English. Still, the outrage was right there as a huge stone in my chest, and the fact that I could only find a swear word as a medium of language to express my emotion at that time made me feel sad and ashamed of myself. This feeling of shame, from not having access to a competent language level, broke my heart.

(Choi, 2002: 32–34)

This excerpt shows that the inability to express an identifiable emotion, and in particular anger, may leave individuals feeling frustrated, power-less, vulnerable, and ashamed of themselves and their lack of sophisticated vocabulary. Similar feelings – embarrassment, shame, anger, depression – are described by an English speaker who, after a bout with the flu, found himself unable to communicate in L2 Spanish with his Mexican hosts, with whom he previously interacted quite well (Peck, 1974).

A clinical study by Marcos and associates (1973a) indicates that the interaction between proficiency, anxiety, anger, and depression needs to be taken into consideration in psychiatric assessments. Their study, discussed in Chapter 3, shows that schizophrenics speaking a second language in which they are less proficient appear more tense, hesitant, withdrawn, and uncooperative, and may in fact give up on the whole enterprise; an inex-perienced psychiatrist or counselor, meanwhile, may confuse the effects of translation difficulties with the effects of clinical depression. This argu-ment appears to be valid for regular communication as well. An increased focus on the form of the message may result in a lack of affect, while the stress brought on by speaking in a less proficient language may account for increased anxiety and nervousness.

A series of empirical studies by Rintell (1984, 1989, 1990) directly examined the relationship between proficiency and emotional expression. Rintell's (1984) study, discussed in Chapter 3, suggested that L2 learners may experience difficulties decoding emotional expression when using cues from both verbal content and prosody, with results mediated by proficiency levels and linguistic and cultural background. (Speakers of Spanish performed better than speakers of Chinese and Arabic.) To find out how L2 learners express emotions in their less proficient language, Rin-tell (1989, 1990) collected personal experience narratives from six native speakers and eight L2 learners of English. The L2 learners were ESL stu-dents at the relatively early stages of English acquisition (with intermediate proficiency as measured by Michigan test scores ranging from 41 to 83). Narratives were elicited with the help of index cards, each naming one emotion. The participants were asked to talk about the time in their lives when they experienced this emotion; their responses were tape-recorded, transcribed, and analyzed.

The analysis showed that most of the stories collected in the study had a similar narrative structure, described by Labov and Waletzky (1967) in terms of abstract, orientation, evaluations, narrative clauses, result, and a coda. L2 learners sometimes departed from this structure, or failed to deliver an account that would be recognizable as a 'story' to native speakers of English. Stories told by native speakers of English exhibited much more elaboration, providing listeners with information not only about what happened but also how it happened and what effects it had on their mental and physical state. These storytellers appealed to epithets ("a real jerk"), figurative language ("I died! I couldn't believe it!"), and references to the body ("I felt nauseated," "My heart was pounding") to emphasize the emotional intensity of their experiences. They were also much more skillful in their use of mitigators ("So there is a little anxiety there") and depersonalization ("and you want to run out and play") to minimize the intensity of emotional expression. In contrast, L2 learners did not appeal to figurative language at all and favored direct expression of emotions ("I feel sad, depressed, sad, sad"), although a few were beginning to incorporate mitigators ("That's made me anger a little bit").

Of particular importance in emotional engagement is the ability of the speaker to use imagery and details that evoke culturally and personally recognizable scenes (Tannen, 1989). In this, native speakers were also different from L2 learners with low proficiency levels. The amount of detail provided by native speakers of English allowed listeners to form a mental image of the event in question and to imagine their own emotional reactions, while the sketchy stories told by L2 learners for the most part did not offer enough detail for the interlocutor to empathize with the speaker's experience. The detailed and elaborate stories by native speakers were found to be much more compelling and likely to elicit an emotional response, even though their own emotions may have been described indirectly. In turn, L2 learners' stories, which referred to emotions directly but lacked detail and imagery, were found to be significantly less compelling and likely to involve the interlocutors.

Despite the growing awareness of the importance of emotional expression, foreign language classrooms rarely teach learners how to perform affect. Several webquestionnaire respondents mentioned that foreign language instruction left them unprepared for the real world:

In school we learn how to use French in a polite and friendly way but when I am calling the Customer Service of a French company to complain about something and want to sound a bit more severe irritated angry ... then it is difficult to find that severe irritated angry tone because you are concentrating on French grammar and vocabulary ... I wouldn't have to do that in Dutch.

(Bart, L1 Dutch, L2 French, L3 English)

Luckily, not all classrooms operate in a decontextualized mode of instruction. McMahill (2001) introduces the readers to a typical grassroots feminist English class in Japan where Japanese women come together to talk about themselves and their lives and where personal disclosure is the dominant mode of interaction. As a result, these L2 users of English are very skilled in using a variety of rhetorical devices to enhance the listeners' emotional engagement. Their dramatic narratives of rebellion against traditional patriarchal ideologies display artful uses of repetition, detail, imagery, reported speech, and parallel structures. Unlike Jung Euen Choi (2002), who did not know how to express her anger in English, these women praise their consciousness-raising class for letting them get in touch with their repressed anger against rigid gendered norms of traditional Japanese society.

In sum, dominance and proficiency influence both language choice for emotional expression and affect performance. When able to choose, speakers tend to appeal to the language in which they are dominant, or at least more skilled and proficient. When forced to perform affect in a less proficient language, they may appear more detached and less expressive because they lack either adequate means of self-expression or the confidence to use them (Choi, 2002; Koven, 2004; Marcos et al., 1973a; Rintell, 1989, 1990). Lack of details, imagery, reported speech, and figurative language, as well as increased attention to form, all contribute to this detachment effect. Importantly, as seen in the case of Linda (Koven, 2004), proficiency in emotional expression is not necessarily equivalent to overall language proficiency. Rather, it is mediated by the context of acquisition. Instructed learners may have difficulties in expressing or understanding emotions in their second language, particularly anger (Choi, 2002; Dewaele, 2004a,b, in press; Rintell, 1984, 1989, 1990; Toya & Kodis, 1996), but so can speakers who had limited socialization experiences (Koven, 2004). These issues can be addressed in language classrooms by focusing attention on the learners and on issues relevant to their lives, and by encouraging them to discuss these issues in their second language (McMahill, 2001).

5.6. Factors influencing bilinguals' affective styles

The thematic analysis of the webquestionnaire responses, together with the other studies reviewed here, show that bi- and multilingual speakers use their multiple affective repertoires in a strategic manner. The discussion highlights three clusters of factors that affect language choice and use in emotional expression: individual, contextual, and linguistic. Typically, speakers' choices are influenced by more than one factor (as in my own example that opens this chapter), and the same factor may have different effects on different speakers or in different contexts.

Individual factors involve individual linguistic trajectories and resulting characteristics of the speakers' multicompetence: (a) language dominance and attrition; (b) levels of proficiency in the languages in question; (c) age and context of their acquisition; and (d) their perceived emotionality. *Language dominance* emerged as a particularly important factor in language choice for emotional expression. This is not surprising considering that most of our webquestionnaire respondents are L1-dominant, see their L1 as their most emotional language, and use it – at least some of the time – for everyday purposes. In contrast, L1 attriters prefer to express their emotions in a later learned and now dominant LX or in both languages (Dewaele, 2004c; Pavlenko, 2004a). Dominance appears to be particularly important in the expression of anger (Dewaele, 2004a, in press). Because extreme situations, such as an argument or a fight, require a quick rate of linguistic exchange and allow little time for lexical searches, many speakers favor languages in which they can express themselves more fluently in these situations.

A closely related factor is *language proficiency*. Rintell's (1984, 1989, 1990) studies clearly show that speakers with low levels of proficiency experience difficulties both expressing their own emotions and interpreting those of others. In turn, Koven's (2004) study underscores that competence in emotional expression may be divorced from the overall language proficiency and depend more on the context of language acquisition.

Dewaele's (in press) analysis of language choice for anger expression among webquestionnaire respondents shows a clear relationship between *context of acquisition* and language choice: Learners who learned the language in a naturalistic or mixed context are more likely to express anger in that language than those who learned it in an instructed setting; they are also more comfortable doing so. This is not surprising, as classroom learning often ignores emotional expression as a superfluous aspect of language, leaving learners unable to express their own feelings (Polanyi, 1995; Rintell, 1989, 1990; Toya & Kodis, 1996) and unsure about interpreting those of others (Rintell, 1984). The distinction is more subtle, however, than simply 'instructed' versus 'naturalistic' contexts. Attention to the intricacies of emotional expression in the classroom may result in excellent narrative construction skills (McMahill, 2001). In turn, socialization in a limited context may leave speakers unprepared to express their emotions in any but a bland and unsatisfactory manner (Choi, 2002; Koven, 2004; Toya & Kodis, 1996).

Different contexts of language acquisition also lead to differences in *perceived language emotionality*, another important factor in language choice and use for emotional expression. The overwhelming majority of bi- and multilinguals see their first language or languages as the most emotional, yet this emotionality steers speakers in different directions. Some choose the more 'emotional' language, particularly in arguments and fights or when speaking to children. These speakers state that expressing emotions in a language learned later in life feels 'fake' and 'artificial.' Others favor the language that offers more distance and detachment and thus an opportunity to control the conversation. Using a language learned later in life also allows speakers to avoid feelings of guilt and shame when using swearwords and feelings of anxiety when using terms of endearment rarely used in the first language.

Contextual factors involve: (a) interlocutor's linguistic competence; (b) individual and interactional goals; (c) perceived emotionality of the interlocutor's languages; and (d) perceived language prestige and authority. In everyday communication (a lot of which is undoubtedly emotional), interlocutors' linguistic competence plays an important role: Speakers typically choose a language that can be best understood by their interlocutors or is common for a particular type of interaction. I have aimed to show, however, that interlocutors' competence does not determine language choice in particular contexts. Even when the speakers do share a common language, one of them may switch into the language unfamiliar to the interlocutor to satisfy a variety of interactional and personal goals. For instance, in the context of fights and arguments, one speaker may switch into an L1, a language the interlocutor understands poorly or not at all, in order to derive emotional satisfaction from 'venting' personal feelings or to avoid hurting the partner. They may also do the opposite and switch to *the language most emotional for the interlocutor*, to deliver 'poisonous barbs.' Another reason speakers switch languages is to appeal to the language with the most prestige, thus lending more *authority* to their affective stance.

The last set of factors involves *cross-linguistic differences* in emotion terms and affective repertoires. In conversation, argument, or baby talk, speakers may shift to a language that offers them the richest set of linguistic resources for performing a particular type of affect – be they swearwords for expressions of anger or terms of endearment and diminutives for expression of love and intimacy. They may also appeal to code-switching or lexical borrowing to name a particular emotion precisely.

5.7. Conclusions and implications for future research

The aims of this chapter were to see whether bi- and multilinguals have distinct affective styles in their respective languages, to inquire whether these styles are subject to cross-linguistic influence, and to examine factors including language proficiency that influence bi- and multilinguals' language choice for emotional expression.

The findings to date suggest that many bilinguals do indeed display distinct affective styles in their respective languages. These distinct styles stem from cross-linguistic differences in affective repertoires (Ervin-Tripp, 1954, 1964, 1967; Panayiotou, 2004b; Pavlenko, 2002d) and from differences in language proficiency and contexts of language acquisition and socialization (Koven, 2004; Marcos et al., 1973a; Rintell, 1989, 1990; Toya & Kodis, 1996). The differences were shown to contribute to the perception of 'double selves,' both by the speakers themselves and by their interlocutors (Ervin-Tripp, 1954, 1964, 1967; Koven, 2004; McMahill, 2001; Pavlenko, in press).

Further analysis demonstrated that while most of the time bicultural bilinguals use language- and culture-appropriate lexical resources when expressing emotions in their different languages, their affective repertoires are not fully distinct and separate. As discussed in Chapter 4 with regard to the bilingual mental lexicon, some repertoires show almost no overlap (Koven, 2004), others exhibit the influence of one language on another (Panayiotou, 2004b), and others display bidirectional influence (Pavlenko, 2002d). The instances of code-switching and lexical borrowing, particularly evident in the case of 'untranslatable' emotions (Andrews, 1999; Panayiotou, 2004b), together with instances of L2 influence on L1 (Pavlenko, 2002d), point to the possibility of enrichment, transformation, and attrition in affective repertoires under the influence of a new language. With the exception of studies by Pavlenko (2002d) and Tomiyama (1999), attrition in emotional expression and the affective repertoire has not been explored to date. Yet comments offered by attriters in our database suggest that this is a phenomenon that deserves further exploration, both in the native and in later learned languages:

I cannot understand why I have lost the ability to express most of feelings in French but it has happened. Somehow it seems easier in L2 [English]; doing it in French requires more effort, concentration and involvment.
      (Helene, 32, L1 French, L2 English, L3 German, dominant in L2 English)

The analysis of webquestionnaire responses also identified three sets of factors that influence language choice and use in emotional expression: (a) *individual*: speaker's multicompetence, in particular language dominance and levels of proficiency in respective languages; age and context of acquisition of particular languages; and perceived emotionality of respective languages; (b) *contextual*: individual and interactional goals; interlocutor's linguistic competence; emotionality of the languages as perceived by the interlocutor; perceived language prestige and authority; and

(c) *linguistic*: cross-linguistic differences in emotion terms and affective repertoires offered by respective languages.

L2 proficiency was singled out as a particularly important factor in emotional expression, because L2 users speaking a less proficient language may sound more detached and less expressive (Koven, 2004; Marcos et al., 1973a; Rintell, 1989, 1990; Toya & Kodis, 1996). It was also shown that in the context of an argument, bi- and multilinguals may switch to their first language, in which their interlocutors may have little or no proficiency. This finding deserves to be explored further in the study of argument pragmatics as it challenges the view of argument as a cooperative activity (van Eemeren et al., 1993; Walton, 1998). Finally, it was shown that L2 learners and users may appropriate affective repertoires quite distinct from the ones they use in L1. For instance, some people may be much more likely to use taboo and swearwords or the expression "I love you" in their second language. These learners underscore the freedom of self-expression offered to them by languages learned later in life (McMahill, 2001; Pavlenko, 2004a, in press).

In the beginning of her book, Piller (2002a: 1) reminds the reader that "in the context of private relationships, questions of language use are rarely just that. Often they are made to stand for other relationship issues," such as emotional distance and involvement, attraction and disappointment, belonging and estrangement. She also acknowledges the exasperating difficulties in the study of private communication – be it mono-, bi-, or multilingual – and raises readers' awareness about a variety of creative research approaches that can be taken in this inquiry (Piller, 2001, 2002a). Her ideas are particularly important if research on multilingual emotion talk is to be expanded from psycholinguistic inquiry and self-reports to examinations of spontaneous talk. The importance of examining what multilinguals actually do with words when they are angry, upset, or elated is hard to underestimate. This knowledge is crucial in the increasingly globalized world, where speakers of different languages routinely find themselves at the same negotiation table, get emotional when things don't go the way they were expected to, and misinterpret each other's reactions in terms of personality characteristics (cf. Connor-Linton et al., 1987; Scollon & Wong-Scollon, 2001). This inquiry will also directly benefit foreign language curricula, as emotion talk is an area where FL and L2 learners may be most vulnerable. As shown earlier, they may be at a loss for words when in dire need to express their feelings. In highly charged interactions they also may be spoken to more rapidly and less coherently than under regular circumstances, and thus have problems with comprehension.

Throughout, I have argued that the most important direction for future inquiry is the study of spontaneous talk in natural settings, which would reveal how understanding unfolds and emerges on-line, in the course of a specific interaction, and in the context of local concerns, rights, obligations, and power relations, and not only remote cultural rules. Besides offering us information about what multilingual speakers do with words, this study would allow us to examine the nature of interpretation in emotional communication, which is as important to understand as is expression and performance. It would also allow us to paint a diachronic picture of emotion concept and script negotiation and development that will go beyond a synchronic snapshot of an emotion lexicon at a single moment in time. This diachronic investigation would also enhance our understanding of how cross-linguistic influence and attrition operate in multilingual affective repertoires. Excellent models for such investigations are offered in studies of emotion talk in discursive psychology and anthropology (Edwards, 1997; White, 1990) and in studies of childhood affective socialization (Eisenberg, 1999; Kyratzis, 2001).

At the same time, studies of multilingual emotion talk will need to incorporate aspects unique to multilingual contexts, including ways in which language choice and code-switching function as contextualization cues. The discussion here pointed to one issue that is particularly influential in the selection of affective repertoires – perceived language emotionality that may differ in bilingual's languages. What do bi- and multilinguals mean by perceived emotionality and where does it come from? To answer this question, in Chapter 6 I will shift focus from the language of emotions to the relationship between language and emotions and examine the origins of language emotionality and the commonly held perception that L1 is the language of emotions and L2 the language of detachment.

6

Neurophysiological level: His *coeur* is where his feelings dwell

It was a great surprise to me, one of many surprises of my life, that when I began speaking English, I felt freer to express myself, not just my views but my personal history, my quite private drives, all the thoughts that I would have found difficult to reveal in my mother tongue. It seemed that the languages of my childhood and adolescence – Polish and Russian – carried a sort of mental suppression. By the time I was 25, an American, my infancy in English had ended and I discovered that English, my stepmother tongue, offered me a sense of revelation, of fulfillment, of abandonment – everything contrary to the anxiety my mother tongue evoked.

(Jerzy Kosinski, in Teicholz, 1993: 125)

The first non-native speaker to win the most prestigious US literary prize, the National Book Award, Jerzy Kosinski was born in 1933 in a family of Russian Jews in Poland. In 1939, two months after the German invasion, the six-year-old Jerzy got separated from his family. He spent the next six years wandering through the Polish countryside, believing that he was either a Gypsy or a Jew and afraid of being discovered by the German authorities. Three years into the journey, the constant fear, flight, and hunger, as well as the death and atrocities witnessed by the boy, rendered him mute. When in 1945 his parents found him in an orphanage, Jerzy was a half-mad, terrified, speechless child; it took him two years to regain speech (Teicholz, 1993).

As a young man, Kosinski studied first at the University of Lodz and then at Moscow State University, the latter giving him an opportunity to witness Soviet totalitarianism in its undiluted form. In 1957 the 24-year-old left Poland for the United States, receiving a visa as a "highly skilled alien." His ascent toward the American Dream began straightaway. Within a year Kosinski was a Ford Fellow at Columbia University. In the next decade he published two novels that propelled him toward literary stardom: *The Painted Bird* (1965), the winner of *Le Prix du Meilleur Livre Étranger*, and *Steps* (1968), the winner of the 1969 National Book Award. Both were written in

English. *The Painted Bird*, Kosinski's masterpiece, is a graphic and violent account of a mute boy's odyssey in war-ravaged Poland. The new language, used as a shield, allowed the writer to draw on the memories of his tormented childhood without being silenced by the pain and anguish brought on by Polish words. In the preface to the book, Kosinski acknowledged this protective role of the second language:

My purpose in writing a novel was to examine "this new language" of brutality and its consequent new counter-language of anguish and despair. . . . as English was still new to me, I could write dispassionately, free from the emotional connotation one's native language always contains. (Kosinski, 1976: xii)

At the same time, unexpectedly for many of his readers and literary critics Kosinski disagreed that it was the connection with the war that made Polish so painful to use. Rather, he argued, it is the first learned language, the language of childhood, that has a unique power to evoke, to overpower, and to wound:

English helped me sever myself from my childhood, from my adolescence. In English I don't make involuntary associations with my childhood. I think it is childhood that is often traumatic, not this or that war.
(Kosinski, in Teicholz, 1993: 27)

One is traumatized by the language when one is growing up. . . . I think had I come to the United States at the age of nine I would have become affected by this traumatizing power of language. At the age of seventeen it would have been too late. When I came to the United States I was twenty-four. Hence, I am not traumatized by my English – no part of my English affects me more or less than any other one. (Kosinski, in Teicholz, 1993: 46)

The primeval, visceral emotionality of the first language has also been commented upon by other bilingual writers who learned their second language in late childhood or early adulthood:

Spanish certainly was the language of storytelling, the language of the body and of the senses and of the emotional wiring of the child, so that still, when someone addresses me as "Hoolia" (Spanish pronunciation of Julia), I feel my emotional self come to the fore. I answer Sí, and lean forward to kiss a cheek rather than answer Yes, and extend my hand for a handshake. Some deeper or first Julia is being summoned. (Julia Alvarez, in Novakovich & Shapard, 2000: 218)

Today, when someone addresses me as "Luke" I respond without a second thought; when I hear "lük" I jump as if I'd gotten an electric shock. Even though I know better, I feel as if someone had just looked down into my naked soul.
(Luc Sante, in Kellman, 2003: 160)

As we saw in Chapter 5, many bi- and multilinguals share this perception of the first language as the most emotional (Dewaele, 2004a; Heinz, 2001). But what does it really mean for a language to have an emotional resonance? Is it simply an elegant turn of phrase, an acknowledgment of ethnic or national allegiance, or is there a neurophysiological basis to these perceptions? In other words, do bi- and multilinguals actually perceive their respective languages differently on a physical level? And if they do, how important are these differences?

Let us start with the last question and consider the case of a White House intern Chandra Levy, who vanished without a trace in April 2001. On May 22, 2002, her remains were found in a Washington, DC, park, not far from the place where two other women were attacked around the same time. At the time the remains were discovered, the attacker of the two women, a 20-year-old Salvadoran national named Ingmar Guandique, was serving a 10-year term in prison. He was questioned about Levy's disappearance and subjected to a polygraph test – through an interpreter, due to his low English proficiency. Only a year later did authorities begin to wonder if the procedure itself rendered the results invalid and start searching for a bilingual technician to readminister the test. In this case, as in many other legal, medical, and educational contexts, the issue of whether bilingual speakers are differently affected by their languages became of crucial importance.

Unfortunately, this aspect of bilingualism is not covered in standard introductions to neurolinguistics, psycholinguistics, or psychology of bilingualism, and the evidence that speaks to the issue has until now been scattered over several research areas. The goal of this chapter is to bring this evidence together and to present an embodied perspective on multilingualism that argues that, depending on their linguistic trajectories, bi- and multilinguals may have different neurophysiological responses to their respective languages, or at least to emotion-related words. I begin by presenting a theory of language embodiment that aims to explain possible neurophysiological underpinnings of these differences. Then I consider four types of evidence that bear on the issue. Case studies in psychoanalysis will allow me to show how levels of anxiety mediate language choice and code-switching in therapy sessions. Research with taboo words will let me compare bilinguals' physiological reactions to and perceptions of swearwords in their respective languages. Research on bilingual autobiographic memory will illuminate the links between language, memory, and emotions in bi- and multilingual speakers. And the first-person narratives of bilingual writers will allow me to return to Jerzy Kosinski and similar cases and show how the embodied perception of language influences writers' language choices. I conclude by listing factors that impact language emotionality in bi- and multilingual speakers, summarizing the findings to date and making suggestions for future research in the area.

6.1. Language embodiment

Like code-switching or language choice, language emotionality is an issue that is best studied with bi- and multilingual speakers through comparison of their verbal behaviors in and reactions to different languages. Over the years, a number of scholars and writers have pondered the reasons for differences in perceived language emotionality of bilinguals' languages: Psychoanalysts contemplated the vagaries of the ego and superego, psychologists considered neurophysiological correlates, and all pointed to distinct L1 and L2 socialization trajectories of immigrants and expatriates, yet no comprehensive theory of language emotionality has ever been proposed. The present chapter offers a *theory of language embodiment* that draws on current advances in the neuroscience of emotions (Damasio, 1994, 2003; LaBar & Phelps, 1998; LeDoux, 1996; Ochsner & Feldman Barrett, 2001), on studies of classic conditioning, in particular fear conditioning (LeDoux, 2002; Manning & Melchiori, 1974; Mathews, Richards & Eysenck, 1989), on psycholinguistic studies of emotional language, in particular taboo words (Jay, 1992, 2000, 2003), and on neurolinguists' insights about differences between the processes of primary and secondary language acquisition (Lamendella, 1977a,b; Paradis, 1994).

Neuroscientists have identified several brain structures that participate in the triggering and execution of emotions, among them the amygdala, the anterior cingulate gyrus, and the prefrontal and somatosensory cortices. The amygdala and the anterior cingulate gyrus are located in what is commonly known as the limbic system, or the emotional (visceral) brain. This system receives an ongoing stream of sensory information and is centrally involved in sensory and memory processing and in relating the organism to its environment. In primates, the limbic system is also the center of the communicative functions network, and it continues to play an important role in human communication, in particular in spontaneous emotional speech. Of particular importance to emotion-mediated learning is the amygdala, located deep in the temporal lobe. The amygdala constitutes the interface between arousing visual and auditory stimuli, in particular threatening and negative ones, and the triggering of emotions, in particular fear and anger (Damasio, 2003; LeDoux, 1996, 2002), and thus is centrally involved in the processing of taboo and swearwords. The amygdala also facilitates the consolidation of episodic memories for emotionally significant events and thus contributes to the development of conceptual representations (LaBar & Phelps, 1998; Ochsner & Feldman Barrett, 2001).

Lamendella (1977a,b) and Paradis (1994) argue that primary and secondary language acquisition differ in the involvement of the limbic system and other brain structures engaged in the generation of emotions, drives, and motivation. In primary language acquisition, these structures are fully involved in both production and perception, when children "are strongly motivated to say what they say and to understand what is said to them" (Paradis, 1994: 406), while in secondary language acquisition the structures are involved to a lesser degree and sometimes not at all.

In the view adopted here, two interrelated processes take place in the mental lexicon during primary language acquisition. In the process of *conceptual development*, words and phrases acquire denotative meanings. Their multiple uses in distinct contexts aid in the formation of conceptual categories, linked to each other through elaborate semantic and conceptual networks. These conceptual representations include information received from all sensory modalities – visual, auditory, olfactory, tactile, kinesthetic, and visceral – and are subject to ongoing subtle modification that takes place in the language socialization process.

In the parallel process of *affective linguistic conditioning*, words and phrases acquire affective connotations and personal meanings through association and integration with emotionally charged memories and experiences. Some words become linked to personal fears (clown, spider) or to positive memories (Citizen Kane's 'Rosebud' or Prouste's 'madeleine'), while taboo words, such as 'piss,' 'shit,' or 'cock,' become associated with experiences of prohibition, punishment, and social stigmatization. In terms of the classic conditioning paradigm, these emotion-related words represent a *conditioned stimulus*, punishment or reward an *unconditioned stimulus*, and the reaction elicited by the words becomes a *conditioned response*. These responses will vary from individual to individual, depending on personal experiences.

Both processes contribute to the perception of *language embodiment*, whereby words invoke both sensory images and physiological reactions. Foreign languages learned in educational contexts are almost never perceived as embodied, because language learning in the classroom takes place without significant involvement of the limbic system or the majority of the sensory modalities. Two reasons explain this dissociation between declarative and emotional memory in FL learning, representation, and production. First, in the decontextualized classroom context, development of word meanings takes place through definition, translation, and memorization – and thus through declarative or explicit memory – rather than through consolidation of personal experiences channeled through multiple sensory modalities to implicit and emotional memory. Consequently, emotion or emotion-related FL words are not integrated with non-verbal sensory representations or autobiographic memories and do not activate brain structures involved in the generation of emotions. Second, to involve the limbic system in production, a speaker must have a need or a desire to produce a particular message (Paradis, 1994). But in many foreign language classrooms, utterances are elicited from learners who, on top of being unwilling interlocutors, focus on the structure rather than the meaning of the messages. The only feeling that accompanies such production is language learning anxiety.

The difference between embodied words of the first learned language and disembodied words of the second is beautifully described by the Belgian-born American writer Luc Sante:

In order to speak of my childhood I have to translate. It is as if I were writing about someone else. The words don't fit, because they are in English, and languages are not equivalent one to another. If I say, "I am a boy; I am lying in my bed; I am sitting in my room; I am lonely and afraid," attributing these thoughts to my eight-year-old self, I am being literally correct but emotionally untrue... If the boy thought the phrase "I am a boy," he would picture Dick or Zeke from the schoolbooks, or maybe his friends Mike or Joe. The word "boy" could not refer to him; he is *un garçon*. You may think this is trivial, that "*garçon*" simply means "boy", but that is missing the point. Similarly, *maman* and *papa* are people; "mother" and "father" are notions. *La nuit* is dark and filled with fear, while "the night" is a pretty picture of a starry field. The boy lives in *une maison*, with "a house" on either side. His *coeur* is where his feelings dwell, and his "heart" is a blood-pumping muscle.

(Sante, 1998: 261)

The framework advanced here differentiates between embodied and disembodied languages of bi- and multilingual individuals; it does not, however, make a dichotomous distinction between primary and secondary language acquisition, common for earlier proposals (cf. Bond & Lai, 1986). Rather, it posits a language learning continuum where on the one end we have primary language acquisition – always an emotional and contextualized process – and on the other FL learning, typically a decontextualized process. In the middle, there is a grey area of L2 learning in a natural environment, where L2 users experience different levels of socialization and degrees of affective linguistic conditioning at different points in life. Immigrant children who come to the target language country and are socialized in the L2 context eventually develop an embodied perception of their L2. In contrast, adult immigrants who are surrounded by L1-speaking family members and friends may not develop elaborate and integrated representations of L2 emotion-related words; rather, these words may piggyback on their L1 counterparts and elicit little if any autonomic arousal. On the other hand, individuals who 'marry into,' raise their children, and work in the L2 integrate the meanings of L2 words with multisensory representations and personal memories acquired in a variety of social contexts. For them, L2 words are vested with personal meanings and emotional associations and may elicit strong visceral responses (Pavlenko, 2004a). Most commonly, however, L2 users escape the strict socialization common for primary language acqusition. As a result, the level of arousal elicited by L2 words may be lower, and it may be easier to swear or tell a painful memory in the L2.

I do not want to claim, though, that strong affective linguistic conditioning cannot take place in a second language in adulthood. The fact that it can and does is poignantly illustrated in the dramatic story of Susan Brison (2002), an American scholar of French feminism who over the years made numerous extended trips to France and achieved a reasonable fluency in the language. During one such trip, in the summer of 1990, Brison became the victim of a violent, near-fatal rape-turned-murder assault. After her trachea, fractured during the suffocation attempt, healed, she still experienced trouble speaking. And even after she regained her ability to speak more or less reliably in English, she was still unable to speak without debilitating difficulty and anxiety in French. In her memoir, written more than a decade after the attack, Brison (2002) acknowledged that she still almost never speaks French, even in Francophone company. Her case suggests that, just like other emotion-mediated memory processes, affective linguistic conditioning is a life-long enterprise. This conclusion is supported by evidence from classic conditioning studies with adults in which words initially paired with unpleasant noises or electric shocks become conditioned stimuli eliciting greater skin conductance response (SCR), negative affect, and avoidance reaction. (For a review, see Jay, 2003.) In monolingual speakers, these responses are then generated to semantically related words and sentences. But are they also generated to related words in another language?

A study conducted by Javier and Marcos (1989) has addressed this question. The researchers examined SCRs to linguistic conditioning in 38 coordinate Spanish–English bilinguals. The participants were randomly assigned to a stress condition where the level of intensity of a buzzer sound (mild or strong) was hypothesized to induce lower or higher stress. Within each stress condition, the participants were randomly subdivided into two language conditions, Spanish and English. In each condition the participants were given a word list with four Spanish and four English words. In the Spanish condition, for instance, the word *bote* (boat) functioned as a conditioned stimulus (CS) word (it was paired with the buzzer sound), the words *barco* (boat) and 'ship' were semantically related to the CS word, 'butter' and *dote* (drawer) were phonologically related to the CS word, and *mesa* (table) and 'candy' were unrelated words. First, participants were presented with the assigned list and their SCR was obtained as baseline information. In the experiment, they were presented with one of the two CS words, *bote* or 'house,' accompanied by a buzzer sound, and with neutral words, 'window' and *toro* (bull), not followed by buzzer sounds. Then participants were re-exposed to the original lists. The results demonstrated that the mean SCR response to semantically or phonologically related words of the same language was always greater than to unrelated words. This response was not generalized to the words of the other language, however, explaining why translation equivalents of L1 taboo words remain affectively neutral, unless learned and used in context.

There is no doubt that the metaphors of language and emotions guiding research on language emotionality offer a limited understanding of both phenomena. Emotions are often reduced in this approach to physiological reactions, signalling levels of positive or negative arousal and anxiety, while language is often reduced to single word items. The relationship between language and emotions is viewed through the lens of neurophysiological and behavioral reactions elicited by particular languages and resulting in particular word and language choices. However reductive, this approach is unavoidable if we are to explicate the embodied and emotional nature of language that is taken for granted by monolingual speakers and continues to puzzle and delight bi- and multilinguals.

It is also clear that much more research in different paradigms is necessary to understand the nature of and constraints on language embodiment. At the same time, studies discussed in Chapter 5 suggest that late or sequential bilinguals with different L1 and L2 socialization experiences differ in perceptions of emotionality of their respective languages. To probe these perceptions a little further we can now ask: *Do late bilinguals exhibit different behavioral and neurophysiological responses to their respective languages? Do they differ in perceptions of L1 and L2 emotion words, such as taboo and swearwords? How do these responses mediate their language choice and use? And what factors contribute to perceptions of language emotionality and, in the terms proposed above, language embodiment?*

6.2. Language choice and code-switching in psychoanalysis and psychotherapy

In the middle of the twentieth century three seminal psychoanalytic case studies, Buxbaum (1949), Greenson (1950), and Krapf (1955), discussed in Chapter 2, attracted attention to the fact that bi- and multilingual patients may choose to undergo analysis in the L2 – even with therapists who speak the same L1 – in order to avoid L1-related memories and anxieties. The interest in this area was renewed in the 1970s when Luis Marcos, a Spanish analyst trained in the United States, and his associates published several clinical reports and experimental studies that confirmed the previous findings and expanded the early work in three areas of inquiry: (a) anxiety and facilitative effects of L2 as the language of therapy; (b) recall and facilitative effects of L1 as the language of therapy; and (c) linguistic, social, and neurophysiological underpinnings of the 'L2 detachment effect.' These and other key studies on language and emotionality in bi- and multilinguals in psychoanalysis and psychotherapy are summarized in Table 6.1

As Schrauf (2000) insightfully points out, both early and later clinical case studies "are not full clinical case histories in the technical sense but rather illustrative summaries and examples excerpted by therapists from their experience with bilingual clients" (p. 400). They may include a short description of the patient's language learning history and current circumstances, a few words about the diagnosis, a description of the treatment, a discussion of the patient's notable verbal and non-verbal behaviors, and, in the best case, a short transcript of the interaction between the therapist and the patient (cf. Rozensky & Gomez, 1983). However, many important details are often omitted, proficiency is not formally tested, and sometimes

TABLE 6.1. *Studies of bi- and multilinguals in psychoanalysis and psychotherapy*

Study	Participants	Languages	Procedure	Findings
Buxbaum (1949)	two bilingual women	L1 German L2 English	Analysis initially conducted in L2 with some L1	L1 facilitated recall of traumatic childhood memories
Greenson (1950)	bilingual woman	L1 German L2 English	Initial analysis in L1 and L2, then refusal to use L1, then bilingual analysis	L1 use was a technique that allowed the therapist to break through the patient's emotional defenses
Krapf (1955)	bilingual man	L1 English L2 Spanish	Analysis in L1	L2 for taboo words and topics, e.g., sex
	bilingual man	L1 Portuguese L2 Spanish	Analysis in L2	L1 for swearwords
	trilingual woman	L1 Spanish L2 German L3 English	Analysis in L3 with some L1 and L2	L3 for taboo topics; detached in L2 and L3, aggressive in L1
	bilingual woman	L1 German L2 Spanish	Analysis in L1 and later in L2	Shift to L2 improved family relationship & lessened symptoms
	trilingual man	L1 German L2 English L3 Spanish	Analysis in L1	L2 for swearwords and intimate relationships
Del Castillo (1970)	five bilingual patients: 4 men and 1 woman	L1 Spanish or Italian L2 English	Pretrial clinical interviews in both languages	Psychopathology exhibited in L1 but not in L2 interviews
Marcos (1972)	bilingual woman	L1 Spanish L2 English	Clinical interviews in both languages	L1 use led to increased anxiety

(continued)

TABLE 6.1 (*continued*)

Study	Participants	Languages	Procedure	Findings
Marcos et al. (1973,a,b)	schizophrenic patients: 6 bilingual men 4 bilingual women	L1 Spanish L2 English	Psychiatric evaluation interviews in both languages	Psychopathology exhibited in L2 more than in L1: 'detachment effect'
Gonzalez-Reigosa (1976)	bilingual woman bilingual man	L1 Spanish L2 English	Bilingual therapy	L1 speech emotional L2 speech detached
Rozensky & Gomez (1983)	bilingual woman bilingual woman bilingual woman bilingual woman	L1 Spanish L2 English L1 Spanish L2 English L1 Spanish L2 English L1 German L2 English	Analysis in L2 with some L1 Analysis in L2 and L1 Analysis in L2 with some L1 Analysis in L2 with some L1	In all cases L2 speech was detached and the use of L1 allowed patients to recognize their fears and feelings L1 word triggered early memories
Guttfreund (1990)	80 bilinguals (60 men and 20 women)	Group 1: L1 Spanish L2 English Group 2: L1 English L2 Spanish	Three types of self-report assessment measures in two languages	Both groups expressed more affect in Spanish either as L1 or L2
Foster (1992)	bilingual woman	L1 Spanish L2 English	Analysis in L2	L2 allowed creating a stronger persona
Zac de Filc (1992)	multilingual man multilingual analyst	L1 Yiddish for both	Analysis in L1	Patient offered clear and elaborate recalls in L1; analyst was initially distressed conducting analysis in L1 Yiddish
Amati-Mehler, Argentieri & Canestri (1993)	five bilingual women	L1 English L1 English L1 Spanish L1 Spanish L1 Czech L2 Italian	In all cases: analysis in L2 and eventually some use of L1	Initial rejection of L1; in all cases, L1 use led to increased symptomatology

Study	Participants	Languages	Procedure	Findings
Javier (1995)	bilingual woman	L1 Spanish L2 English	Bilingual analysis	Bilingual analysis was the best mode to bring back and recount the memories
Javier (1996)	bilingual man	Not reported	Analysis in L2 with some L1	L1 use triggered feelings and memories; L2 speech detached
Foster (1996a)	bilingual man	L1 a Scandinavian language L2 English	Analysis in L2 with some L1	L1 use raised anxiety and arousal, L2 detached
Foster (1996b)	bilingual woman	L1 Spanish L2 English	Analysis in L1 and L2	L1 use allowed release of more affect-laden memories
Aragno & Schlachet (1996)	bilingual woman two bilingual men	L1 German L2 English L1 Spanish L2 English	Bilingual analysis	L1 use triggered feelings and memories, L2 speech detached
Movahedi (1996)	two bilingual men, one suffering from schizophrenia	L1 Persian L2 English	Bilingual analysis	Switching to L2 to discuss taboo topics, express anger, and manage anxiety

even the actual languages of the patient are not mentioned (cf. Foster, 1996a; Javier, 1996). Consequently, rather than a full-fledged methodological approach, clinical case studies will be viewed here as more or less detailed descriptions of language choice and code-switching in therapy sessions.

Several behaviors are seen as evidence of language-related anxiety and emotionality in these case studies: (a) marked (that is, unexpected) language choice, such as the decision to conduct analysis in L2 when both the patient and the analyst share the same L1; (b) topic-related code-switching during a therapy session, such as switching to L2 to discuss sex or to L1 to swear; (c) crying or increasing pitch variation and range only in one of the languages used in therapy; (d) a speaker's explicit acknowledgment that the language is linked to emotional, or in some cases traumatic, events;

and (e) triggering of emotional, and possibly painful, memories prompted by the language switch. Notably, some or perhaps even all of these behaviors may be influenced by factors other than emotionality. For instance, the choice of L2 as the language of therapy could also be influenced by the desire to establish a more equitable power relationship (Movahedi, 1996). In combination, however, these behaviors function as contextualization cues to increased or decreased emotionality in the context where individuals are invited to reveal their most private inner thoughts, memories, feelings, and experiences.

The first claim in the original psychoanalytic inquiry was that, due to different socialization trajectories, late bilinguals may experience different levels of anxiety in their respective languages, with a higher level of arousal and anxiety associated with the L1 and a lower level with the L2. Krapf (1955), for instance, described the case of a German–Spanish bilingual woman who arrived in Argentina at the age of four and grew up speaking both German and Spanish. During the first stage of her therapy, which began in L1 German, the woman was resistant and uncooperative. Only when she switched to L2 Spanish, her preferred language, did she begin to talk freely about childhood memories and exhibit signs of progress.

The studies conducted in the past three decades have confirmed that some late bilinguals experience higher levels of arousal and anxiety in L1, in which case L2 can facilitate discussion of anxiety-provoking memories (Amati-Mehler et al. 1993; Aragno & Schlachet, 1996; Foster, 1996a; Gonzalez-Reigosa, 1976; Javier, 1995, 1996; Marcos, 1972; Movahedi, 1996; Rozensky & Gomez, 1983). Zac de Filc (1992), another Argentinian analyst, also offers a personal perspective on the issue. One of her patients, an Eastern European Holocaust survivor, requested that they use their common L1 Yiddish in therapy sessions. The emotional effects of using Yiddish turned out to be stronger for the analyst than for the patient. While the patient was able to articulate his memories clearly in that language, the therapist was initially distressed and disoriented, as she had not used Yiddish since the death of her parents many years earlier.

Javier (1996) presents the case of a multilingual man who chose to undergo therapy in the L2. His description of important memories in L2 was both detailed and dispassionate. When the analyst by mistake addressed him in his native language, the man was overcome with emotions and for a while continued therapy in that language. The switch enabled him to create a very complex and ambivalent portrait of his father, whom he both admired and resented. At the same time, the patient became more moody and depressed in his everyday interactions. After a few sessions he stated that he did not feel comfortable speaking in the first language and that it was not appropriate. It is possible, suggests the analyst, that switching to L1 let the patient get in touch with his rage against his father and that he desperately needed to gain some distance in order to preserve a positive image of him.

Foster (1996a) tells the story of a Scandinavian man living in the United States for whom L1 was linked to the intense and traumatic relationship with his mother, and L2 English (in which he lived and worked at the time) to social status and achievement. A successful researcher, married to a native speaker of English, the patient spoke fluent and polished English, in which he exhibited a lot of emotional restraint. In contrast, when conducting business negotiations with investment partners in L1, he behaved with much more spontaneity and less verbal caution; he also flew into verbal rages and resorted to bullying when he did not get his way. In the analyst's view, these rages were closely linked to the traumatic experiences of his childhood, when he felt abandoned by his father and exploited and "sissified" by his mother. It had taken him years to utter the words of his L1 in session, but eventually he began to retell his dreams and early memories first in the original language and then in translation. The L1 retellings were marked by a high level of anxiety and emotionality, to the point that he would stop abruptly, saying "It's too much like this – too powerful" (p. 260), and go back to English.

The increased level of anxiety linked to L1 use may even worsen the patient's moods and symptoms, at least temporarily, as some of these cases show. A dramatic example appears in the work of European analysts Amati-Mehler, Argentieri, and Canestri (1993). The authors present the cases of five foreign women who had married Italian men, settled in Italy, and learned to speak fluent Italian. They were comfortable in undergoing analysis in L2, yet eventually they began spontaneously to use words and phrases from their native languages. Sometimes they translated them and sometimes they left them untranslated. The authors remark that it was not clear whether the translation that did occur took place for the benefit of the analyst or the analysand. For some of the patients, unfortunately, the regression to L1 coincided with the return of their symptomatology or psychotic crises. For instance, the Czech patient began talking about the Czech storybooks that until then were kept in a trunk in a cellar. Simultaneously, she experienced a return of her psychosomatic symptoms. The Chilean patient expressed the desire to write to her childhood friends in L1 Spanish. She also began to suffer from an acute agoraphobia and disorientation that continued for many months. The Australian patient rediscovered the joys of using L1 English, only to develop shortly an acute delusional state. The authors link these acute states to the high levels of anxiety and traumatic emotional experiences the patients underwent in their native languages and countries, from which they attempted to escape by adopting L2 Italian as their main language.

The second claim made in the early psychoanalytic work was that L1 words may function as triggers for painful, traumatic, and previously repressed memories and unacknowledged feelings. Buxbaum (1949), for instance, described a case of a German–English bilingual woman who emigrated to the United States from Germany as an adolescent and understood German perfectly, yet refused to speak it. As a result, she began her therapy in L2 English. Eventually, an introduction of one taboo word in L1 German led to a recollection of a childhood jargon she used with her sister and released a flood of previously repressed childhood memories. Acknowledging and dealing with the past allowed the woman not only to recover from the problems that plagued her but also to reclaim her mastery of German. This claim was also borne out in numerous later studies, where L1 was shown to facilitate recall of previously repressed memories and feelings (Altarriba et al., 2004; Aragno & Schlachet, 1996; Chiarandini, 1999; Foster, 1992, 1996a,b; Gonzalez-Reigosa, 1976; Javier, 1995, 1996; Rozensky & Gomez, 1983; Zac de Filc, 1992).

Aragno and Schlachet's (1996) study is particularly interesting here because all three of their patients were able to recount the traumatic events of their early lives in their second language, English. These recalls proceeded with little or no emotional involvement, however. Returning to the same memories in the original language released the accompanying feelings, allowing the patients to relive the events, to recount them with the full force of attendant pain, misery, and guilt, and to work through these feelings. In one case, a German–English bilingual woman recalled how at age nine she was supposed to watch over her little brothers, but instead hid for a moment behind a shack to taste delicious cream she was bringing home. As she did so, her brother Max was struck by a car and died. After she recounted the incident in German, she was finally able to mourn for her brother and to work through her guilt and the rage she felt toward her mother who imposed the babysitting duties on her. Interestingly, as she worked on these issues, the affective vitality began to appear in her English recalls, although not to the same degree as in her native Swiss German.

The transcript below illustrates how a language switch from L2 to L1 during a therapy session leads the patient to become significantly more emotional and to acknowledge feelings that she previously labelled as unclear:

P: I don't want to do it. I really don't want to go into the hospital. I've already been in the hospital so many times for tests and everything else.

T: It sounds like your doctor thinks it's important.

P: I know. I know. I suppose I should do it and get it over with but I don't know . . .

T: Do you have any idea why you are so against the idea?

P: (Silence.) I am not sure. I don't know how to describe it.

P: Can you try?

P: It's hard, it's so hard.
T: Can you try in Spanish?
P: (Tears starting.) *No quiero. Tengo, tengo miedo.* (Silence.)
   [I don't want to. I'm, I'm afraid.]
T: *Miedo de que?*
   [Afraid of what?]
P: (Crying hard.) *Que no voy a salir.*
   [That I'll never come out.]

                                                    (Rozensky & Gomez, 1983: 156)

In this excerpt, the therapist tries to convince 56-year-old Señora AB to undergo an ulcer surgery recommended by her physician. This Mexican-born patient had lived in the United States for half of her life and speaks L2 English as fluently as her L1 Spanish. We can see that her use of L2 tenses is appropriate and the lexicon colloquial ("get it over with"). She is comfortable with conducting her therapy sessions in L2, yet she speaks with a marked detachment and appears unable to explain her fears. Only after the session switches to Spanish is she able to formulate her fears of the hospital, of death, of losing contact with and being rejected by her children and her therapist. At the same time, she becomes much more emotional and begins to cry, similar to other patients described by Rozensky and Gomez (1983), who speak with a flat affect in L2 but become teary and emotional when switching to L1.

In these and in many other cases, the patients performed distinct affective personae in their respective languages, oftentimes appearing more emotional and anxious in their L1 and more restrained in the later learned L2 (Aragno & Schlachet, 1996; Buxbaum, 1949; Foster, 1992, 1996a; Gonzalez-Reigosa, 1976; Greenson, 1950; Javier, 1995, 1996; Krapf, 1955; Marcos, 1972; Rozensky & Gomez, 1983). The patients often acknowledged the differences and discussed them in relation to different language selves: In the native language they perceived themselves as frightened, dependent children, and in the second language as independent, strong, refined individuals (Aragno & Schlachet, 1996; Foster, 1992; Greenson, 1950).

This difference in verbal and non-verbal behaviors in the two languages intrigued Marcos, who was no longer satisfied with confirming that the L1, learned in childhood, provokes more anxiety or makes memories more accessible than the L2, learned later in life. His work began to examine the psychological, linguistic, and interactional underpinnings of the 'L2 detachment effect.' The ground-breaking studies with ten schizophrenic Spanish–English bilinguals conducted by Marcos and associates (1973a,b) demonstrated that the patients were consistently rated as showing more pathology when interviewed in L2 English. A comparative analysis of the Spanish and English interviews demonstrated that in L2 English the patients often answered the questions with a short sentence, a word, or even silence. At times they misunderstood the questions; consequently, in many cases they offered different answers to the same questions asked in Spanish and English. Their L2 answers were also marked by language mixing, slow speech rate, hesitations, long pauses, and excessive use of the present tense where past tense would be used in Spanish.

The researchers argued that while all of these verbal and non-verbal behaviors are common for non-fluent L2 speech, English-speaking psychiatrists may misperceive them as signs of distress, depression, and incoherence, in particular in the case of language mixing. The use of the present tense may be interpreted as a sign that the symptoms are current, rather than as a lack of L2 proficiency. They also suggested that L2 users' increased concerns about the wording, pronunciation, and morphosyntax may lead to diminished attention to the affective component of the message and create an inconsistency between what is being said and how it is being communicated. This inconsistency and lack of visible affect may also contribute to an impression of emotional withdrawal and a misinterpretation of the patients' responses.

Further studies identified a difference between L1 and L2 non-verbal behaviors in healthy bilingual speakers. Marcos (1976b) demonstrated that the L2 speech of normal Spanish–English and English–Spanish bilinguals was accompanied by speech-related gestures that illustrate and emphasize the content (gestural qualifiers) and that reflect active encoding work (beats, light pounding). In contrast, when using L1 to discuss the same topic the speakers produced more gestures unrelated to speech but linked to their emotional states (touching, soothing, stroking). Marcos concluded that it is the communicative demands that accompany interaction in the less proficient L2 that prevent satisfactory integration of content and affect.

A dramatic difference between L1 and L2 verbal and non-verbal behaviors was found in Spanish– and Italian–English bilinguals examined in the forensic unit of the New Jersey State Hospital by Del Castillo (1970). These patients were observed and interviewed in an attempt to decide their legal competence and ability to stand trial. Four out of five appeared obviously psychotic in L1 interviews, but seemed much less so, or even without any psychotic symptoms at all, when interviewed in L2 English. As a result, one of these patients, a 30-year old Puerto Rican man, was found "sane enough" to stand trial, even though he exhibited numerous delusional symptoms and pathological anxiety when interacting in L1 Spanish.

Del Castillo's (1970) findings were also borne out in the study by Price and Cuellar (1981), who compared evaluations of interviews conducted in English and Spanish with 32 schizophrenic Mexican–American patients. The researchers found that the patients exhibited significantly more symptomatology in L1 Spanish, and that they also tended to disclose more personal information in their Spanish interviews. The findings of these studies differ from those of Marcos et al. (1973a,b) with regard to the actual evaluation results. (For a discussion of possible reasons, see Vázquez, 1982a,b.) What unites the studies for the purposes of the present discussion is the fact that in all cases the patients presented themselves as more emotional in L1 Spanish and as more distant in L2 English. In Del Castillo's (1970) study the more emotional appeared as 'psychotic' and the more distant as 'normal,' whereas in the studies by Marcos and associates (1973a,b), the more emotional appeared as the norm and the more detached as outside of the norm. In addition, in both Price and Cuellar's (1981) and Marcos et al.'s (1973b) studies, more information was revealed in L1 Spanish than in the L2 English interviews.

A different spin on these findings was put by Guttfreund's (1990) study, which examined how 80 Spanish–English and English–Spanish bilinguals responded to three self-report questionnaires: the State-Trait Anxiety Inventory, the Depression Adjective Check List, and the Marlowe-Crowne Social Desirability Scale. Within each bilingual group half of the participants were administered the self-report measures in Spanish and half in English. The results of this study pointed to a language rather than a mother tongue effect: Both groups exhibited higher levels of anxiety and depression in Spanish, which was L1 for the first group and L2 for the second. Thus, Guttfreund (1990) suggests, what may have appeared as the L1 effect in the previous work with Spanish–English bilinguals may in reality be a language effect, whereby the unrestrained performance of affect condoned in Spanish may appear less acceptable in English.

The 'distancing effect' was also examined outside of the clinical context. Bond and Lai (1986) asked 48 female Chinese undergraduates in a Hong Kong university to interview each other in either L1 Cantonese or L2 English on four topics: (a) the pegging of the Hong Kong dollar to the United States dollar; (b) the differences in the education system at The Chinese University compared to Hong Kong University; (c) sexual attitudes of Chinese and Westerners; and (d) a personally embarrassing episode that the interviewee recently experienced. The first two topics were considered neutral and the last two potentially embarrassing. The authors found that interviewees answered questions on embarrassing topics at greater length in their L2 English than in their L1 Cantonese. Bond and Lai interpreted these results as suggesting that embarrassing topics are easier to discuss in the L2. The results of this study are often cited in support of the L2 detachment effect. Notably, however, while six interviewees in the study reported anxiety when discussing at least one of the embarrassing topics in Cantonese, three reported anxiety when speaking English. Ultimately, it is not clear whether embarrassing topics are easier to discuss in a more 'distant' L2 and thus are expanded upon, or whether they are more difficult to discuss in a less proficient language and thus require more time.

Together, the studies suggest that bilingual patients (most of whom appeared to be late bilinguals) exhibit different behavioral responses to the use of their languages in therapy. The use of L1 may facilitate retrieval of less accessible memories and allow patients to express previously unacknowledged feelings. Patients using the L1 may also experience higher levels of anxiety and arousal, which in some cases leads to increased symptomatology or even acute states. In contrast, patients using the L2 appear more calm and able to discuss painful memories dispassionately and in detail if they possess a sufficient level of linguistic proficiency. These findings corroborate bi- and multilinguals' perception of the 'L2 detachment effect,' or emotional distance granted by the L2 learned later in life, and hint that this effect may be particularly pronounced in speakers who had learned their L2 mainly through declarative memory, with minimal involvement of emotional memory. Unfortunately, these studies provide limited information about linguistic trajectories and interactional contexts of their participants, telling us only that they were immigrants and expatriates. This research does not allow us to explore the influence of age and context of second language acquisition and use on language embodiment and, more specifically, perceived emotionality.

6.3. Emotionality of taboo words in different languages

The case studies in psychoanalysis and psychotherapy discussed so far point to visible differences between levels of emotionality, and in particular anxiety, elicited by L1 and L2 in late bilinguals. From the perspective of the present inquiry, however, this work has three important limitations. First of all, with the exception of a few studies, the conclusions are limited to a selected group of bilinguals – patients in therapy – some of whom may in fact have been motivated to leave their L1 contexts by traumatic events experienced there. Second, the indices of language emotionality adopted in these case studies (code-switching, for instance) are primarily behavioral and thus indirect. And finally, the factors impacting particular verbal behaviors, including age and context of acquisition, language proficiency, and current patterns of language use, are insufficiently documented in the majority of the descriptions (which in itself should not be surprising, as these were clinical case studies and not empirical investigations).

To see if healthy late bilinguals experience the same differences in levels of autonomic arousal elicited by L1 and later learned languages, experimental psychologists turned to the emotionally charged domain of taboo words. Lamendella (1977b), and later Jay (2000, 2003), have argued that taboo words constitute a nexus where language and emotions come together in an unprecedented manner. When processed, these words activate not only the semantic network but also the amygdala, eliciting autonomic arousal. This arousal can be detected through a variety of physiological measures, including sweating of palms and fingertips, a signal that can be quantified by measuring the transient increase in electrical conductivity of the skin. This increase, otherwise known as skin conductance response (SCR), typically occurs within 1 to 1.5 seconds following appearance of the aversive stimulus, and may last for 2 to 6 seconds (Harris, 2004).

Studies show that in monolingual speakers, reading or hearing taboo words elicits a larger SCR than reading or hearing neutral words (Manning & Melchiori, 1974). Patients with anxiety disorders are also shown to exhibit larger SCRs in reaction to words related to their fears (Mathews, Richards, & Eysenck, 1989). Interpreted as negative affect (anxiety or fear), these autonomic arousal symptoms may elicit a variety of reactions, including avoidance. The intrinsic links between taboo words, feelings (such as anxiety), and behaviors (such as avoidance) contribute to our perception of language as embodied and physically experienced. Thus, taboo words are not an eccentric and quirky way to look at the interaction between language and emotions – rather, these words represent a unique intersection between the two realms, evoking a complex chain of feelings, affective associations, autobiographic memories, vivid imagery, and olfactory sensations.

Early psychoanalysts had noted that their bilingual patients were often reluctant to utter taboo words in the native language, but did not experience the same anxiety when using L2 taboo words (Ferenczi, 1916). A German–English bilingual, Anna, had difficulties saying out loud L1 German childish terms for defecating, urinating, and the genitals, and the terms of endearment used by herself and her parents (Buxbaum, 1949). The patient in Greenson's (1950) study was similarly afraid of obscene German words, such as *Nachttopf* (chamberpot) or *Onanie* (masturbation). She stated: "A chamberpot becomes alive if you say 'Nachttopf'. It is ugly and disgusting and smells bad. In English a chamberpot is much cleaner" (Greenson, 1950: 19). And an English–Spanish bilingual man in Krapf's (1955) study always switched to L2 Spanish when talking about his sexual activities "because speaking of sex in Spanish was less embarrassing for him" (p. 346). This unique status of L1 taboo words was attributed to their ability to force the listener to imagine the thing referred to in a concrete and realistic way (Greenson, 1950). The difference in emotional force between native and foreign language swearwords has been frequently exploited by writers and playwrights. For instance, in Edward Albee's celebrated play "Who's Afraid of Virginia Woolf?" (1962), the main protagonists, George and Martha, begin their brawl by exchanging ritualistic and lighthearted insults in French – *Monstre! Cochon! Bête! Canaille!* – yet when the argument escalates they switch back to English.

To better understand the relationship between language and emotionality in this lexical domain, three approaches are currently used. The first approach, already exemplified in the studies mentioned, considers the use and perception of taboo and swearwords in the framework of therapy sessions, where more recent investigations confirm the results of the earlier studies suggesting that some patients switch to L1 swearwords in moments of greatest distress, while others prefer to use L2 taboo and swearwords to diminish the accompanying anxiety. For instance, in Movahedi's (1996) case study a young Iranian man switched to L2 English when talking about hemorrhoids, because the L1 translation equivalent is commonly used by adolescent boys to refer to anal sex. The second approach (discussed in more detail later) examines multilinguals' own perceptions of the emotional force of taboo words in their languages. The third approach (also discussed in detail later) asks whether L1 words and expressions elicit stronger physiological responses than L2 words and expressions. Table 6.2 offers a chronological summary of the studies conducted on the perception and use of emotion-related words by bi- and multilingual individuals.

One of the first studies of the anxiety-arousing effect of taboo words in bilinguals was conducted by Gonzalez-Reigosa (1976). In the study, 80 Spanish–English bilinguals were divided into high ($n = 40$) and low ($n = 40$) L2 English proficiency groups. All participants were offered a list of 30 stimulus words: 10 neutral Spanish (*casa*/house, *luz*/light), 10 taboo English (bitch, penis), and 10 taboo Spanish (*bruja*/bitch, *pene*/penis) words. The words were presented visually and measures of state anxiety were obtained immediately after each word list. The results showed that L1 Spanish taboo words evoked higher anxiety than either L2 English taboo words or neutral Spanish words, regardless of the participants' level of proficiency.

More recently, Dewaele (2004a,b,c) examined multilinguals' perceptions of the emotional force and frequency of use of swearwords in their respective languages, based on responses to two close-ended questions in our webquestionnaire. Dewaele (2004a) examined responses to question 23: "Do swear and taboo words in your different languages have the same emotional weight for you?" This question asked participants to rate their perceptions of words in each language (up to L5) on the 5-point Likert scale: 1 = does not feel strong, 2 = little, 3 = fairly, 4 = strong, 5 = very strong. Dewaele (2004b) examined responses to question 22: "If you swear in general, what language do you typically swear in?" This question asked participants to rate their swearword use in up to five languages on the 5-point Likert scale: 1 = never, 2 = rarely, 3 = sometimes, 4 = frequently, 5 = all the time. Dewaele (2004c) examined responses to these questions with the focus on the L1 attriter population, that is, speakers for whom L1 is no longer the dominant language. In his statistical analyses of the data, Dewaele used paired t-tests to examine differences in perceived emotional force and frequency of language choice among the five languages; ANOVA, MANOVA, and Scheffé post-hoc tests to examine the influence of nominal independent variables (education level, language dominance, context of acquisition); and Pearson correlation analyses and multiple linear regression analyses to examine the influence of ordinal independent variables (age, age of onset of acquisition, self-rated proficiency, frequency of language use).

TABLE 6.2. *Studies of emotionality of taboo and other emotion-related words*

Study	Participants	Languages	Procedure	Results
Gonzalez-Reigosa (1976)	80 bilinguals	L1 Spanish L2 English	Measurement of reaction times and state anxiety	L1 taboo words elicit greater anxiety than L1 neutral words and L2 taboo words
Javier & Marcos (1989)	38 bilinguals	L1 Spanish L2 English	Measurement of SCR during experimentally induced stress	Stress generalized to the words in the same language but not to equivalents
Harris, Aiçiçegi & Gleason (2003)	32 bilinguals	L1 Turkish L2 English	Measurement of SCR to five types of verbal stimuli	L1 taboo words and reprimands elicit greater SCRs
Harris (2004)	36 bilinguals	L1 Spanish L2 English	Measurement of SCR to four types of verbal stimuli	L1 reprimands elicit greater SCRs in late bilinguals; L2 taboo words elicit high SCRs in both groups
Pavlenko (2004a)	389 bi- and multilingual parents	see discussion of Dewaele and Pavlenko's web-questionnaire in Chapter 2	Statistical and thematic analysis of responses to a web-questionnaire	L1 is favored by many parents, especially for terms of endearment, yet some parents also appeal to LX terms
Dewaele (2004a,b)	1,039 multilinguals	see discussion of Dewaele and Pavlenko's web-questionnaire in Chapter 2	Statistical analysis of responses to a web-questionnaire	L1 taboo and swearwords are perceived as more emotional and used more frequently

The statistical analyses revealed that participants rated L1 taboo and swearwords as most emotional and forceful, with perceived emotionality declining gradually with age and order of acquisition (Dewaele, 2004a). They also reported using L1 for swearing more frequently, with the use of later learned languages declining in chronological order (Dewaele, 2004b). Both the perceptions and the preferences were mediated by the context of acquisition: Participants who learned their subsequent languages (LX) in a naturalistic or mixed context rated the emotional force of LX swearwords higher than those who learned the language in an instructed context; they were also more likely to use the LX swearwords. The perceived emotional force of L1 swearwords was lower in self-reported L1 attriters (Dewaele, 2004c).

Dewaele (2004a,b) has also established that perceived language emotionality influenced but did not determine language choice for swearwords. In some cases, in moments of anger, pain, or frustration, L1 swearwords may 'pop out' uncontrollably, regardless of linguistic competence of the interlocutors:

If I would happen to hit myself with a hammer the words coming out of my mouth would definitely be in Finnish.
(Kevin, L1 Finnish, L2 English, L3 Swedish, L4 German)

We speak English and we argue in English because he doesn't speak Spanish. However, many times I find myself swearing at him in Spanish.
(Erica, L1 Spanish, L2 English, L3 Italian, L4 Portuguese)

Other speakers are inhibited by the greater emotionality of the L1 taboo and swearwords and feel compelled to use their L2 equivalents (Dewaele, 2004b; Koven, 2004; Piller, 2002a):

I have noticed is that I can swear much more easily in English than in Greek. I sometimes use quite strong swear words in English but as I can't really 'hear' or 'sense' how strong they are. (Melissa, L1 Greek, L2 English)

I prefer to express anger in my L2 Italian because I do not hear the weight of my words so everything comes out quite easily. Which unfortunately means that I probably hurt people more than I intend to! (Maureen, L1 English, L2 Italian)

I find it more difficult to swear in Cantonese than in English. Swearing in Cantonese is a big taboo for people of my educational level however swearing in English doesn't sound vulgar . . . When the subject involves cultural taboos such as sex or swear words I prefer to use English . . . I feel less inhibited using L2 about cultural taboos probably because I don't feel the emotional intensity so strongly in L2. (Li, L1 Cantonese, L2 English, L3 French, L4 Putonghua, L5 Japanese)

Dewaele (2004a,b,c) established that perceived language emotionality decreases with the increase in age of acquisition and is low for languages learned in formal contexts:

I do not feel the emotional load of words in foreign lnaguages. I've only learned them in an "instructed" environment.

(Pierre, L1 French, L2 Dutch, L3 English, L4 German)

These findings offer evidence in support of the theory of language embodiment, which posits that languages learned in natural contexts will be judged as more emotional than those learned in formal contexts, regardless of age of acquisition or proficiency level.

While Dewaele's (2004a,b,c) work explored implications of perceived emotionality for verbal behaviors, Harris and associates (2004; Harris, Aiçiçegi & Gleason, 2003; Harris, Gleason & Aiçiçegi, in press) examined bilinguals' physiological responses to emotion-related words. Harris et al. (2003) conducted a study with 32 Turkish–English bilinguals who had begun studying English after the age of 12 and had arrived in the United States for work or study when they were in their 20s. The participants were exposed to five categories of verbal stimuli in the two languages in either auditory or visual modality: neutral (door), positive (joy), aversive (disease), taboo (asshole), and reprimands (Go to your room!). It was found that taboo words elicited the greatest SCRs in both languages, with L1 taboo words eliciting a slightly stronger reaction, especially in the auditory modality. Overall, SCRs were stronger to L1 emotional expression than to L2, with the largest difference occurring for reprimands. Interestingly, in the debriefing session several participants said that they could hear, in their mind, family members addressing Turkish reprimands to them. These comments confirmed that the effect indeed stems from affective linguistic conditioning in childhood. At the same time, L2 taboo words elicited same-size SCRs as L1 reprimands, pointing to effects of ongoing peer socialization.

To see whether these effects were mediated by age of acquisition, Harris (2004) repeated the procedure with 36 Spanish–English bilinguals. Early bilinguals (n = 15) either grew up in the United States or arrived there by the age of 7; middle-childhood bilinguals (n = 21) began studying English in middle childhood in Latin America, and arrived in the US in their mid-teens or early 20s. Early bilinguals learned Spanish as their L1 but rated their proficiency at best as near-native; their dominant language was English. Middle-childhood bilinguals were highly fluent in English but rated their L1 Spanish as superior to L2 English. Four categories of words were used in the study: taboo words, reprimands, endearments, and insults, with 8 English and 8 Spanish items in each category. Statistical analyses, which included pairwise comparisons, ANOVA, and correlation analyses, demonstrated that taboo words elicited the highest SCRs in both languages and in both groups of participants. To explain the difference between these results and those in previous studies the researcher pointed to the fact that both groups of participants live in the United

States and interact in English on a daily basis, and to the fact that, in their own view, in Spanish invectives are more common and less harsh than in English.

Differences were also identified between early and middle-childhood bilinguals. The latter group performed similarly to Turkish–English bilinguals in that L1 emotional expressions elicited larger SCRs than L2 expressions; no such difference was obtained for early bilinguals. Middle-childhood bilinguals also showed greater responses to reprimands in L1 Spanish than in L2 English; no such effect was found in early bilinguals. Early bilinguals showed similar reactions to words in both languages. Interestingly, reprimands did not elicit high SCRs in English monolinguals either, which suggests that word-type effects may be influenced by culture-specific approaches to childhood socialization. Cross-linguistic studies of affect socialization suggest that reprimands and imperatives are much more central in Spanish-speaking than in English-speaking families (Bhimji, 1997; Eisenberg, 1999); consequently, they may elicit more emotional reactions from those who grew up in such families. Overall, these findings reveal the effects of age and context of acquisition on language emotionality and point to an ongoing peer language socialization effect with regard to taboo words, whereby both L1 and L2 taboo words elicit heightened SCRs in bilingual speakers.

The ground-breaking studies by Harris and associates (2004; Harris et al., 2003, in press) established correlations between perceived language emotionality and SCRs, and showed the interaction between age of acquisition and perceived language emotionality. It is worth noting, however, that all of the studies included learners who acquired their L2, at least at some point, in a natural context. It would be worthwhile to examine the effects in proficient learners who never used their foreign language outside of the classroom.

Together, the studies reviewed here extend to healthy bi- and multilingual speakers the claims made in the psychoanalytic literature; at the same time, they narrow these claims down to specific categories of words. The studies confirm that late bilinguals exhibit different behavioral and psychophysiological responses to and perceptions of emotion-related words of their respective languages. To begin with, they show that taboo words elicit greater autonomic arousal and anxiety in bilingual speakers than do neutral words and that in late bilinguals, L1 taboo words typically elicit greater arousal and anxiety than L2 words, in particular in the auditory modality (Gonzalez-Reigosa, 1976; Harris et al., 2003; but see Harris, 2004). These results corroborate Pavlenko's (2004a) findings (discussed in Chapter 5), that L1 endearments are commonly perceived as more emotional and meaningful than the corresponding terms in languages speakers have not been socialized into. It is not surprising, then, that L1 taboo and swearwords and terms of endearment are reported to be more frequently used than their equivalents in later learned languages (Dewaele, 2004a; Pavlenko, 2004a).

At the same time, some webquestionnaire respondents who are married to L2 speakers and raise children in the L2 see their L2 terms of endearment as highly emotional and expressive, especially in cases when direct expression of emotions is not condoned in L1 (Pavlenko, 2004a). Harris and associates (2004; Harris et al., 2003, in press) also identified an intriguing reprimand effect, whereby L1 childhood reprimands elicit heightened reactivity in middle-childhood and late bilinguals as compared to L2 reprimands.

6.4. Bilingualism, emotions, and autobiographic memory

In addition to studies of taboo words, psychoanalytic case studies also gave the impulse to empirical investigations of bilingual memory that attempted to determine whether recall of autobiographic memories is indeed tied to language and if so, how and to what degree. Central to this new development are the investigations of Schrauf and associates (Larsen et al., 2002; Schrauf, 2000, 2002, 2003; Schrauf, Pavlenko, & Dewaele, 2003; Schrauf & Rubin, 1998, 2000, 2003, 2004), which pioneered new theoretical and methodological approaches to the study of bilingual memory. Table 6.3 offers a chronological summary of studies in this field.

Two paradigms are commonly used in bilingual autobiographic memory studies: cued recall and free recall. In the free recall procedure, participants are asked to recall meaningful personal events without a specific cue. If comparative analysis of narratives is performed, these memories are elicited twice, once in each language (preferably on different days). They are examined qualitatively and quantitatively with regard to length, detail, linguistic organization, and emotional valence and intensity (as scored by independent raters).

In the more common cued recall procedure, each participant is given several cue words (30–50) and asked to associate each cue with a specific autobiographical event, writing down a few words about the event in question. (For a detailed discussion, see Schrauf & Rubin, 1998.) Instructions may be worded as follows: "The memory should be for an event that took place at some definite time and place – something that happened to you or something that you did. It can be something that happened a long time ago, or something that happened very recently. It can be important or trivial. It doesn't matter, so long as it is a definite event that happened in a particular time and place. So for instance, the word 'lake' might make you think of the time you got together with all your relatives in Cleveland for your nephew's baptism and took a boat trip on Lake Erie. That's a particular event in a particular time and place. On the other hand, for instance, just thinking of Lake Erie would <u>not</u> be a memory of an event." (Schrauf, 2003: 241). The sessions are conducted first in one language and then in the other (preferably on different days), with the order of language counterbalanced across participants.

TABLE 6.3. _Studies of bilingual autobiographic memory_

Study	Participants	Languages	Procedure	Results
Otoya (1987)	40 bilinguals ages 18–26	L1 Spanish L2 English	cued recall free recall	Memories cued by L1 earlier than those cued by L2
Javier, Barroso & Muñoz (1993)	5 bilinguals (3 females, 2 males), ages 29–66	L1 Spanish L2 English	free recall	More detail and emotional intensity when languages of encoding and retrieval match
Schrauf & Rubin (1998)	12 bilinguals (8 females, 4 males) ages 61–69	L1 Spanish L2 English	cued recall	Memories cued by L1 earlier than those cued by L2
Schrauf & Rubin (2000)	8 bilinguals (6 females, 2 males) mean age = 65.63	L1 Spanish L2 English	cued recall	Memories cued by L1 earlier than those cued by L2
Marian & Neisser (2000)	20 bilinguals (11 males, 9 females) mean age 21.8	L1 Russian L2 English	cued recall	Memories cued by L1 earlier than those cued by L2
Larsen, Schrauf, Fromholt & Rubin (2002)	20 bilinguals 1st group, mean age 51 2nd group, mean age 61	L1 Polish L2 Danish	cued recall	Memories cued by L1 earlier than those cued by L2
Carrillo & Kim (2003)	92 bilinguals	L1 Spanish L2 English	free recall	Memories in L1 higher in affective details
Marian & Kaushanskaya (2004)	47 bilinguals (23 males, 24 females) mean age 21	L1 Russian L2 English	cued recall and narrative analysis	More emotional intensity when languages of encoding and retrieval match
Schrauf & Rubin (2004)	30 bilinguals over 60 years of age	L1 Spanish L2 English	cued recall and rating of memories	More emotional intensity in recent memories

The question asked in this work is whether memories cued by L1 words are earlier than those cued by L2 words and whether they are tied to different linguistic and cultural contexts. Schrauf and Rubin (2000) also expanded the procedure by asking the participants to characterize the memories in terms of sensory content, visual detail, emotionality, and linguistic specificity (whether a memory came in a particular language, and if so which one). The results are typically analyzed through the means of descriptive statistics and t-tests (mean age at memory), Pearson r correlations (memory characteristics), and ANOVA or ANCOVA (effects of such variables as language of encoding and retrieval). In both free recall and cued recall, language proficiency and dominance is assessed through language questionnaires and self-reports (Larsen et al., 2002; Marian & Neisser, 2000; Schrauf & Rubin, 1998, 2000), independent ratings (Marian & Kaushanskaya, 2004), or the WAIS vocabulary test and the Global Word Naming Task administered in both languages (Javier, Barroso, & Muñoz, 1993).

Cued recall studies conducted with Spanish–English (Otoya, 1987; Schrauf & Rubin, 1998, 2000, 2004), Russian–English (Marian & Neisser, 2000), and Polish–Danish (Larsen et al., 2002) bilingual immigrants who learned their languages at different times and in distinct environments show that L1 cues commonly activate memories of events in the country of origin and L2 cues activate memories for events that took place after immigration. These studies reveal a *language specificity effect*, whereby the language of encoding is a stable property for linguistic memories, even though a memory can then be 'translated' into another language.

Some studies also point to the *language congruity effect*, whereby memories elicited in the language in which the event took place are more detailed and higher in emotional intensity (as in the clinical case studies already discussed). Javier, Barroso, and Muñoz (1993) asked five Spanish–English bilinguals to speak for five minutes "about any interesting or dramatic personal life experiences" (p. 325) using the language in which these experiences took place. Later in the day the participants were asked to retell the experiences in the other language. The authors found that regardless of whether it was in English or Spanish, the retelling in the language of the event evoked a higher number of idea units and a higher level of detail, imagery, and emotional texture, as seen in this excerpt:

First retelling: ... Anyway, I took a long walk through the woods and I was walking through the rocks and the trees and I was just gazing upon the beauty of what nature has ... and ah it was just like wow! you know, you just see all the different colors and, and the different types of barks on the trees, you know, the wood on it, and you just listen to all the crisp of the leaves, as you walk through. ...

Second retelling: *tambien caminé por, por la selva mirando la belleza que hay, a donde ví los diferentes colores, miré los arboles ... estaban muy crisposas las hojas que estaban*

ahí. [. . . [I] also walked through, through the woods, looking at the beauty around, I saw different colors, I looked at the trees . . . the leaves there were very crisp.]
(Javier et al., 1993: 327–328)

Schrauf (2000) points out that the results of this study need to be interpreted with caution, as there were only five participants, who were interviewed twice on the same day. Consequently, the second retelling may have been shorter because the story was produced for the second time on the same day. We can add to this that neither language history nor dominance was discussed by the authors and that these factors could have affected both language choice and performance. More recently the congruity effect was demonstrated by Marian and Kaushanskaya (2004), who conducted a cued recall procedure with 47 Russian–English bilinguals. The authors analyzed the narratives collected in Russian and English in terms of emotional intensity, which was rated by two independent judges. The results demonstrated that participants' autobiographic memories were higher in emotional intensity when the languages of encoding and retrieval matched.

The language of first recall was controlled in Carrillo and Kim's (2003) study in which 92 Spanish–English bilingual students in the United States were asked to first recall a recent sad or happy event, then a remote sad or happy event. Half of the participants performed the procedure in English and half in Spanish. After a five-minute break they were asked to switch languages and to recall extra details of the two events. The results showed that in the Spanish-first group, more affect-related and concrete items were recalled in Spanish than in English, while in the English-first group, more concrete items were recalled in English and more affect-related items in Spanish, even though Spanish was used only for recall of additional details. These results suggest that events may be somewhat differently encoded and recalled in the two languages.

Another intriguing effect was identified by Schrauf and Rubin (2004) in a study with 30 Spanish–English bilinguals. The participants rated their memories in both languages for visual, emotional, auditory, and linguistic detail. Multidimensional scaling analyses showed that visual detail and emotional intensity clustered together, suggesting that these are linked contributors to the sense of re-experiencing past events. Comparison of recalls in Spanish and English showed more intensity of imagery and emotion in L2 English than L1 Spanish memories. The authors explain their results by the *recency effect*, suggesting that English memories are more recent, more novel, and require more effort-after-meaning (Bartlett, 1932) than Spanish memories and are therefore recalled with more imagistic detail and emotional intensity than Spanish memories.

The effect of age at immigration on memory encoding, inner speech, and language preferences for emotional expression was examined by Larsen and associates (2002). They found that Polish immigrants to Denmark who emigrated earlier (mean age 24) were more likely to use Danish for expression of feelings and other inner speech behaviors than were Polish immigrants who emigrated later (mean age 34). Concomitantly, the early immigrants' retrievals cued by L1 Polish dropped off soon after immigration, while later immigrants' retrievals cued by L1 dropped off ten years later, suggesting that Polish continued to organize their thoughts and memories for a longer period of time. In other words, those who had arrived in Denmark earlier appear to have started thinking and feeling 'in Danish' earlier and were doing it more than later arrivals.

Altogether, the work in experimental psychology reveals that language, memory, and emotions interact in at least three ways in bilingual autobiographic memory: Language specificity effect suggests that linguistic memories are more likely to be elicited by the language in which the events took place. Language congruity effect suggests that memories are higher in detail and emotional intensity when told in the language in which they were encoded, while in translation they may lose some emotionality and richness of the account. Carrillo and Kim (2003) also argue that first language, or perhaps Spanish as a language, may privilege affect-related items in encoding and recall. The results of these studies confirm the intrinsic links between words and autobiographic memories and explain why in therapy L1 words may cue long-forgotten memories (language specificity effect) and why healthy late bilinguals' memories of childhood and youth events are more numerous, more detailed, and more emotionally intense when accomplished in L1 (language congruity effect).

6.5. Translingual writers: A case study in emancipatory detachment

Together, the studies just reviewed established that late bilinguals may exhibit different behavioral and neurophysiological perceptions of and responses to their respective languages, provided there are differences in the contexts of acquisition. These perceptions were shown to affect language choices in therapy, in arguments, and in interactions with infants and children. The quotations that opened this chapter suggest that the traumatizing power and primeval emotionality of the first language may also affect language choices for fiction writing, the inherently emotional written genre. I return to this issue, examining bilingual writers' reflections on language choice and emotionality. These reflections are invariably a rich source of information, because as writers these bilinguals "needed to develop knowledge about language and, as a rule, an ear for meanings that is more acute and subtler than that possessed by the rest of us" (Miller, 1996: 275).

Many bilingual writers acknowledge that the language of the childhood has remained for them the language of the heart. For instance, Minfong Ho, who grew up in a Chinese family in Thailand only to become an American writer, reveals:

> Chinese is the language with the deepest emotional resonance for me. It was the only language which mattered, and I think of it as the language of my heart. Perhaps that's why, even now, when I cry, I cry in Chinese.
>
> (Ho, in Novakovich & Shapard, 2000: 161)

"No one will ever break his heart with English," says Luc Sante about the child protagonist of his memoir, whose feelings dwell in his *coeur*, but not in his heart:

> The French language is a part of his body and his soul, and has a latent capacity for violence. (Sante, 1998: 262)

The embodied view of language – which links the primary language or languages to instinctive reactions and childhood memories, traumas, and anxieties – provides us with a cogent explanation of these writers' perceptions of emotions invoked by the first language and the deeper self, summoned by the Polish "Yezhy," the Spanish "Hoolia," or the French "Lük."

In view of the greater expressiveness, emotionality, and visceral power of the mother tongue, it is not surprising that most bi- and multilingual writers write in the first language, even when living in exile. Even those who write in two or more languages, like Iossif Brodsky or Felipe Alfau, often reserve the L1 for that most revered of the literary genres, poetry:

> The poems I wrote in my mother tongue because poetry is too close to the heart, whereas fiction is a mental activity, an invention, something foreign, distant.
>
> (Alfau, in Kellman, 2000: 28)

It is precisely because *translingual writing* (Kellman, 2000) – that is, writing in more than one language, or at least in a language that is not one's primary language – is so uncommon that writers who made this choice elicit such great interest from readers and scholars (Beaujour, 1989; Besemeres, 2002, 2004; De Courtivron, 2003; Forster, 1970; Kellman, 2000, 2003; Kinginger, 2004a; Miller, 1996; Pavlenko, 1998, 2001, 2004b; Pérez Firmat, 2003).

While translingual writing has always been a part of the world's literary landscape (Forster, 1970; Kellman, 2000, 2003), global migrations of the twentieth century led to proliferation of such writing in a few metropolitan languages. English literature can no longer be imagined without the contributions from the Polish-born Joseph Conrad. England's prestigious Booker Prize has been awarded to several translingual writers writing in English, including Salman Rushdie, whose first language is Urdu.

Among the most prominent figures of the French literary landscape are Irishman Samuel Beckett, Senegalese Léopold Sédar Senghor, anglophone

Canadian Nancy Huston, Bulgarians Julia Kristeva and Tzvetan Todorov, Romanians Tristan Tzara and Eugène Ionesco, Algerians Assia Djebar and Leïla Sebbar, Greek Vassilis Alexakis, and Russian-born Elsa Triolet, Nathalie Sarraute, and Andreï Makine. Andreï Makine, born in Siberia in 1957, emigrated to France at the age of 30. Eight years later he became the first non-Frenchman to win the most prestigious literary prize in France, *Le Prix Goncourt*. His book, *Le Testament Français* (1995), was the first to win both *Le Prix Goncourt* and *Le Prix Médicis*.

And contemporary American literature is unimaginable without a Russian, Vladimir Nabokov, a Pole, Jerzy Kosinski, and their more recent counterparts Julia Alvarez, an immigrant from the Dominican Republic, Andrei Codrescu from Romania, Ursula Hegi from Germany, Eva Hoffman from Poland, Ha Jin from China, Kyoko Mori from Japan, Bharatee Mukherjee from India, Josip Novakovich from Croatia, and Luc Sante from Belgium, to name but a few. Kosinski, who had begun learning English at the age of 24, became the first foreign-born writer to win, in 1969, the National Book Award in Fiction. In 1999, this feat was repeated by Ha Jin, a native of China, who had begun learning English at the age of 21.

Given their unusual circumstances and a counterintuitive choice of language, translingual writers are compelled to reflect upon their relationship with their languages and the reasons that prompted them to choose the second language for writing purposes. Undoubtedly, the critical issue is that of the audience. Solzhenitsyn, Milosz, or Kundera, who wrote in Czech for the first twenty years of his exile in France, chose to address first and foremost their compatriots behind the Iron Curtain, while the rest of the world could read their work in translation. This may not be a feasible choice for aspiring writers who want to address a local or a worldwide audience and who, being relatively unknown, are concerned that no one would be interested in translating their work. Yet even when established, many writers continue to write in a 'stepmother tongue' rather than revert back to the primary language, in which one could presumably be more eloquent and creative. Cited among the reasons for this choice are the desire to appropriate a postcolonial tongue, the need to impose a particular kind of discipline required by writing in a language one has not learned on mother's knees, and a wish to reach the effect of linguistic estrangement whereby words, idioms, and colloquialisms are no longer taken for granted but invented anew. Pérez Firmat (2003) also discusses the unique case of Cuban writer Calvert Casey, who switched from Spanish to English in exile not to gain an audience but to deprive himself of one.

Many writers acknowledge that their choice is also prompted by emotional estrangement and liberation granted by the 'stepmother tongue.' A Vietnamese–American writer, Andrew Lam, arrived in the United States as an 11-year-old child during the mass exodus at the end of the Vietnam war. For that child, Vietnamese came to stand for a life of poverty and misery. Spoken around him in a crowded refugee apartment, it suffocated and silenced him:

Vietnamese was spoken there and often only in whispers and occasionally in exploded exchanges when the crowded conditions became too much for us to bear. In that apartment I fell silent, became essentially a mute, overwhelmed by sadness and confusions. (Lam, in Kellman, 2003: 88)

In contrast, English offered Lam freedom and new opportunities. It had a similar effect on Josip Novakovich, a 20-year-old son of a Croatian clog-maker, who tried to shake off Croatian words, imbued with the ideologies of the Big Brother:

In my own case, English words didn't carry the political and emotional baggage of a repressive upbringing, so I could say whatever I wanted without provoking childhood demons, to which Croatian words were still chained, to tug at me and to make me cringe. (Novakovich, in Novakovich & Shapard, 2000: 16)

And to Israeli–Arab writer Anton Shammas, his second language, Hebrew, offered a safe distance from whispers and shouts, laughter and tears, arguments and opinions already encrypted in the words of his native Arabic:

You cannot write about the people whom you love in a language that they understand; you can't write freely. In order not to feel my heroes breathing down my neck all the time, I used Hebrew. (Shammas, in Kellman, 2003: 83)

For these writers, the emotional memory of the mother tongue is forever linked to childhood and wartime traumas, political oppression, dejection, and the sadness of refugee life, while the new language promises to set them free, separating them from the voices and shadows of their past. Yet languages linked to war, repressive regimes, and political turmoil are not the only ones relinquished by translingual writers. Nancy Huston, an anglophone Canadian who became a celebrated French author, offers particularly convincing evidence in support of Kosinski's arguments about the traumatizing power of the language of childhood. Huston readily acknowledges the lack of climactic events of global significance in her life: She was not driven to emigration by persecution or oppression, but had a chance to move from one country to another freely and willingly as a privileged member of the middle class. And yet she feels that her childhood, with its anguishes, pains, torments, and suffocating boredom burdens her English and stifles her voice. (For an in-depth discussion, see Kinginger, 2004a.) A native speaker of English – a global language that provides access to a world-wide literary audience – Huston chooses to write in her second language, French, because its coolness releases her creativity.

Oui, je crois que c'était là l'essentiel: la langue française (et pas seulement ses mots tabous) était, par rapport à ma langue maternelle, moins chargée d'affect et donc moins dangereuse.

Elle était froide, et je l'abordais froidement. Elle m'était égale. C'était une substance lisse et homogène, autant dire neutre. Au début, je m'en rends compte maintenant, cela me conférait une immense liberté dans l'écriture – car je ne savais pas par rapport à quoi, sur fond de quoi, j'écrivais. (Huston, 1999: 63)

[Yes, I think that was the essential thing: compared to my mother tongue, the French language (and not only its taboo words) was less burdened with emotion and therefore less dangerous. She was cold and I approached her coldly. She was uniform. It was a smooth and homogeneous substance, one might say neutral. In the beginning, I realize now, this conveyed an enormous liberty to me in writing – because I didn't know with respect to what, or against what background I was writing.] (Translated by Kinginger, 2004a: 171)

Echoing each other, translingual writers point to the freedom of using new, 'clean' words of the second language, which are not imbued with memories, anxieties, and taboos. The 'stepmother tongue' creates a distance between their writing and memories and allows them to gain control over their words, stories, and plots. These words do not spontaneously erupt in a Bakhtinian heteroglossia of voices, images, and recollections; they do not constrain the writer, they do not impose. Pliable and devoid of associations (or at least of links to one's childhood), they allow translingual writers to talk about the dear and the painful, the holy and the profane, without necessarily throwing themselves into the whirlwind of suffering and torment. They offer an exhilarating release from 'childhood demons.' The words of the second language, simply speaking, do not feel as real, as tangible, and potentially as hurtful, as those of the first. Reminiscent of debates in psychology and psychoanalysis, a literary scholar Kellman (2000) terms this L2 writing phenomenon 'emancipatory detachment.'

In Kosinski's view, emancipatory detachment gives the non-native writer an edge. In the writer's native language, creative choices are influenced by uncontrollable reflexes acquired in childhood and adolescence, in particular with regard to the vernacular, the language of reprimands, or the language of abuse. In Kosinski's own daily life, for instance, Russian bureaucratic language or Polish language of the law would elicit visceral fear, while a comparable English register would elicit only an intellectual response. A second language user, in Kosinski's view, has an advantage in that the language does not have the power to traumatize or affect the writer:

A native is less in control of the language. The language controls him.
(Kosinski, in Teicholz, 1993: 47)

Yet the non-native also has a price to pay. A Spanish–English bilingual writer, María Luisa Bombal, has remarked once that writing in English, she never experienced the "intimate pleasure" (*goce íntimo*) offered to her by Spanish (Pérez Firmat, 2003: 134).

Different emotional attachments to their languages can also be found in the work of writers who were childhood bilinguals. Pérez Firmat (2003) offers an intriguing analysis of two Spanish–English bilingual writers, Calvert Casey and Richard Rodriguez, who chose English to acknowledge their homosexuality. While Rodriguez, for whom English is now a primary language, may not have had much of a choice, Casey's situation was quite different. Born in 1924 in Baltimore of a Cuban mother and an American father, Casey spent his childhood years alternating between Cuba and the United States. His spiritual allegiance to Cuba prompted him to write in Spanish and to move to Havana. After the Castro revolution, however, Casey left for Italy where he wrote his last novel in English. This choice, in the view of Pérez Firmat (2003), is best explained by Casey's desire to dissociate himself from Spanish as the language of the heterosexual norm and to pour his feelings out in English, a language that allowed him to acknowledge and poeticize his intimate relationship with his gay lover. Not surprisingly, in Spanish he comes across as dry, restrained, and affectless, while his English prose is emotional and dynamic.

Bilingual writers' reflections suggest that in this area, too, perceptions of language emotionality and embodiment impact language choices and may, in some cases, override the superior linguistic competence late bilinguals have in their first language. Some, like Czeslaw Milosz or Isaac Bashevis Singer, cannot imagine writing outside of the intimacy of the first learned languages. Others, like Iossif Brodsky or Felipe Alfau, share their affections between two or more languages yet preserve the first language for poetry, the most intimate of all literary genres. Others, like the celebrated Nuyorican poets, appeal to the interplay of languages or, like Calvert Casey, reserve their two languages for distinct purposes. And yet others, like Nancy Huston or Jerzy Kosinski, escape the confines of their childhood and embrace the creative freedom and emotional distance offered by languages learned later in life.

6.6. Factors affecting perceived language emotionality

The case studies, empirical investigations, and personal reflections examined in this chapter suggest that languages of bi- and multilingual individuals may differ in terms of their perceived embodiment, and more specifically in physiological reactions, levels of arousal and anxiety, autobiographic memories, sensory associations, and perceptions of emotionality elicited by their emotion-related words. In extreme cases, emotion-related words of the second language may even be perceived as 'fake,' as was mentioned in Chapter 5. While studies show that for most late or sequential bilinguals the first language retains the strongest emotional resonance, they do not necessarily suggest that languages learned later in life are always characterized by complete emotional detachment. Rather, they point to a number of factors that mediate language emotionality in multilingual speakers. These factors include: (a) age of acquisition; (b) context of acquisition; (c) personal history of trauma, stress, and violence; (d) language dominance; and (e) word types. In addition, we also need to consider (f) language proficiency, a factor that impacts the speaker's performance of affect and thus its perception by interlocutors.

The first factor is the *age of acquisition*, which for many immigrants is also the age at immigration and subsequent language (re)socialization. The analysis of our webquestionnaire responses indicates that age of acquisition influences perceived language emotionality: Languages learned earlier in life are rated as the most emotional (Dewaele, 2004a). Age of acquisition also mediates the perceived emotionality of and skin conductance responses to swearwords in multilinguals' languages (Dewaele, 2004a; Harris, 2004; Harris et al., in press). The results of the study by Larsen and associates (2002) underscore these findings, pointing to a significant difference in inner speech behaviors between early (mean age 24) and later (mean age 34) immigrants from Poland to Denmark. While speakers in both groups were similar in their L2 Danish proficiency, it was found that late immigrants more often use L1 Polish for inner speech and emotional expression, while early immigrants use L2 Danish.

The second and related factor is the *context of acquisition*, which was shown to influence perceived emotionality of languages in general and of swearwords in particular (Dewaele, 2004a). Several studies showed higher emotionality of childhood reprimands, terms of endearment, and taboo and swearwords acquired in natural contexts, in particular ones acquired in the process of language socialization in the family (Dewaele, 2004a; Harris, 2004; Harris et al., 2003, in press; Koven, 2004; Pavlenko, 2004a). These studies suggest that lower levels of arousal are not simply a property of a language learned later in life, but rather a function of the context in which it had been learned. Emotion-related words in the languages learned in formal contexts were consistently judged to be least emotional (Dewaele, 2004a,b). On the other hand, L2 terms of endearment learned in the context of an intimate relationship or while raising a child in an L2 environment may become emotionally meaningful (Pavlenko, 2004a), and L2 taboo and swearwords hurtful and offensive (Harris, 2004; Harris et al., in press). There also exists a subtle link between age and context of acquisition in this area: Younger immigrants are more likely than adults to participate in extended social networks offered by educational and peer contexts, and thus to undergo a process of intense second language (re)socialization in which they develop affective meanings in a new language, including visceral reactions to L2 emotion words.

The next and related factor is the speaker's *personal history of trauma, stress, and violence*. While it is common to think of translingual writers or patients in psychoanalysis and psychotherapy as trying to distance themselves from emotional traumas experienced in the L1 in childhood, bilinguals who, like Brison (2002), experienced traumatic events in an L2 offer testimonies to the power of any language to leave an indelible imprint on one's psyche far beyond the childhood years.

The fourth important factor that affects perceived language emotionality is *language dominance*. The analysis of the webquestionnaire responses shows that speakers dominant in LX, that is, a language other than their first, tend to perceive LX as more emotional than those who remained L1-dominant. These speakers also rate the emotionality of L1 swearwords lower than L1-dominant speakers (Dewaele, 2004a). These findings underscore the importance of eliciting detailed information about the speaker's language dominance, linguistic history, and patterns and contexts of language use. Schrauf and Rubin (1998) and Larsen et al. (2002) also recommend to elicit information about the participants' choice of language for private and inner speech (the monologues and dialogues played out in one's head, notes written to self, expression of feelings, calculations, dreams, etc.).

The studies discussed here also point to variation in perceived emotionality and physiological reactions among different *types of words*. Taboo words elicited strong reactions in both languages of bilingual individuals, in both early and late bilinguals, although the reactions were judged to be stronger in L1 (Dewaele, 2004a,b; Harris, 2004; Harris et al., 2003, in press). Reprimands, on the other hand, elicited strong reactions only in the L1 of the late bilinguals (Harris, 2004; Harris et al., 2003). Terms of endearment elicit particularly strong opinions from bi- and multilingual speakers: Some view their L1 terms as the only possible option, and others complain about the 'devaluation' of L1 and prefer the sparkle offered by the language learned later in life (Pavlenko, 2004a).

Language emotionality also interacts with *proficiency*. Notably, perceived emotionality is independent of proficiency per se: Many L1 attriters still see their first language as the most emotional (Dewaele, 2004c), even though they may possess higher proficiency in LX. Bilingual writers writing in a second language may still be nostalgic for their mother tongue but no longer competent in it (Pérez Firmat, 2003). On the other hand, speakers with low L2 proficiency, socialized into the L2 community, may react quite emotionally to L2 swearwords or terms of endearment. Thus, as Chapter 5 argued, it is not perceived emotionality that is influenced by proficiency, but the speaker's performance of affect. Speakers with low or intermediate proficiency in a second language struggle with morphosyntactic and pronunciation difficulties and have to perform lengthy lexical searches to express their thoughts adequately. These challenges serve to increase L2 performance anxiety. In the view of Marcos and associates (1973a,b; Marcos & Alpert, 1976; Marcos & Urcuyo, 1979), they also contribute to the 'L2 detachment effect,' whereby the focus on form exhibited by speakers with low L2 competence detracts from the affective underpinnings of the message and makes them appear either overly or insufficiently emotional.

6.7. Conclusions and implications for future research

Over the years, Jay (1992, 2000, 2003) has repeatedly pointed to an emotion gap in psycholinguistic theory, in other words, the lack of integration between theories of language and theories of emotion. The present chapter attempted to integrate the two in theorizing late or sequential bilingualism, where contrasts in language emotionality are particulary visible. The theory of language embodiment advanced in the beginning of the chapter argues that speakers who had different socialization experiences in the first and later learned languages may perceive these languages as differentially embodied. Languages learned in the process of intense childhood socialization seem connected to the body through an intricate web of personal memories, images, sensory associations, and affective reactions, while languages learned later in life, in the classroom, or through limited socialization (for instance, the workplace) do not have the same sensual associations; they do not stir or evoke. Here is how Eva Hoffman (1989), who came to North America from Poland as a teenager, recalls the contrast between L1 and L2 words:

> the words I learn now don't stand for things in the same unquestioned way they did in my native tongue. "River" in Polish was a vital sound, energized with the essence of riverhood, of my rivers, of being immersed in rivers. "River" in English is cold – a word without an aura. It has no accumulated associations for me, and it does not give off the radiating haze of connotation. It does not evoke.
>
> (Hoffman, 1989: 106)

Even that most emotional of all words, our name, is differently perceived by late bilinguals, depending on the language it is uttered in. Julia Alvarez and Luc Sante, cited in the beginning of this chapter, comment on the 'deeper selves' summoned by the sound of their names in their first languages. Hoffman complains about the Anglicization of her name, or the 'careless baptism' she and her sister had undergone in their Canadian school:

> Nothing much has happened, except a small, seismic mental shift. The twist in our names takes them a tiny distance from us – but it's a gap into which the infinite hobgoblin of abstraction enters. Our Polish names didn't refer to us; they were as surely us as our eyes or hands. These new appellations, which we ourselves can't yet pronounce, are not us. They are identification tags, disembodied signs pointing to objects that happen to be my sister and myself. We walk to our seats, into a roomful of unknown faces, with names that make us strangers to ourselves.
>
> (Hoffman, 1989: 105)

This chapter attempted to investigate the nature of language embodiment – a phenomenon frequently commented on by bilingual writers – and pointed to its physiological and behavioral correlates. The evidence examined suggests that late bilinguals, most commonly immigrants or expatriates, undergo different socialization processes in their respective languages, and consequently different processes of conceptual development and affective linguistic conditioning. As a result, they may have (at least initially) different perceptions of and different neurophysiological reactions and verbal and behavioral responses to their respective languages.

The studies reviewed in this chapter show that bi- and multilinguals themselves perceive the emotionality of their languages differently, with L1 commonly seen as the most emotional. The taboo word studies show that these perceptions have neurophysiological correlates: The participants experience higher levels of anxiety and autonomic arousal when exposed to L1 taboo words or childhood reprimands (Gonzalez-Reigosa, 1976; Harris, 2004; Harris et al., 2003). Patients who had experienced traumatic events or childhood conflicts in the L1 may also experience high levels of anxiety when using the language in therapy or they may refuse to use it at all (Amati-Mehler et al. 1993; Buxbaum, 1949; Foster, 1996a; Greenson,1950; Javier, 1996; Krapf, 1955; Rozensky & Gomez, 1983). Some may exhibit dramatic symptomatology when using the L1, especially after a prolonged period of non-use (Amati-Mehler et al., 1993).

These studies also reveal links between words and autobiographic memories, showing that the L1 is more likely to elicit memories of events that took place in the country of origin and the L2 memories of events that took place after immigration (Larsen et al., 2002; Marian & Neisser, 2000; Otoya, 1987; Schrauf, 2000; Schrauf & Rubin, 2000). Language specificity in linguistic memory encoding explains why L1 use in therapy may facilitate access to memories and previously unacknowledged feelings (Altarriba et al., 2004; Aragno & Schlachet, 1996; Buxbaum, 1949; Chiarandini, 1999; Foster, 1996a; Gonzalez-Reigosa, 1976; Greenson, 1950; Javier, 1996; Rozensky & Gomez, 1983; Zac de Filc, 1992). The specificity also contributes to the language congruity effect, that is, the finding that memories are more numerous, detailed, and emotionally intense when told in the language in which they were encoded, while in translation they lose some emotionality and richness of the account (Javier et al., 1993; Marian & Kaushanskaya, 2004).

Psychoanalytic case studies also document differences in L1 and L2 affective personae performed by the speakers, suggesting that L1 personae may be more emotional, spontaneous, and in some cases anxious, while L2 personae appear more restrained (Buxbaum, 1949; Foster, 1996a; Greenson, 1950; Javier, 1996; Krapf, 1955; Rozensky & Gomez, 1983). Marcos and associates (1976a,b; Marcos et al., 1973a,b; Marcos & Urcuyo, 1979) also remind us that communicative demands on performance in the less proficient L2 contribute to the perception of L2 speech as more detached. In some contexts this detachment may lead to misdiagnosis of patients' psychiatric symptoms (Marcos et al., 1973a,b), but in many others it has a facilitative affect, allowing for creation of new selves and identities and for better emotional self-regulation.

In Chapter 5, the differences between L1 and L2 selves were examined from a sociolinguistic and discursive perspective, as well as from the point of view of proficiency. The theory of language embodiment deepens our understanding of these differences, suggesting that they may also stem from different perceptions of embodied selves. Speakers whose languages were acquired with the engagement of emotional memory perceive their language selves as emotional, embodied, and natural; in contrast, speakers whose later learned languages were acquired mainly through declarative memory see their L2 selves as detached and unemotional, and in some cases even 'fake' (Pavlenko, 2004a). These differences in perceptions of linguistically embodied selves are invaluable in understanding the trajectories of translingual writers who, like Jerzy Kosinski, Nancy Huston, Josip Novakovich, or Andrew Lam, choose to write in their second language in order to create a safe distance between themselves and emotional traumas of their past.

While conclusive and useful, these findings are also limited in a number of ways. The first problem, particularly pervasive in the psychoanalytic literature, is an essentialist view of a bilingual as a person with two languages, "insulated from each other" (Marcos & Alpert, 1976: 1275) and maintained as two separate codes, each with its own lexical, syntactic, phonological, and conceptual components. In this view, the second language is often learned "for survival and basic communicative purposes, not emotional expression" (Rozensky & Gomez, 1983: 153), which makes it "intellectualized and somewhat distanced from feelings" (Rozensky & Gomez, 1983: 153). These preconceived notions are problematic because: (a) they do not recognize the dynamic nature of the mental lexicon, where languages may be subject to cross-linguistic influence and attrition; (b) they do not acknowledge the contextual nature of language learning, where L2 may be learned for emotional reasons, such as communication with loved ones; and (c) they focus scholarly attention on a single group of individuals – late or post-puberty bilinguals who had learned their second language in adulthood, most often as immigrants in the target culture – while in reality late immigrant bilingualism represents only one of many existing language learning trajectories of bi- and multilingual speakers. Unfortunately, in the search of clear correlates of L1 as the language of emotions and L2 as the language of detachment, the experiences of other multilinguals were most often relegated to the background. Future research needs to expand the focus from late bilinguals to individuals with other language learning histories and incorporate experiences of those who learned two or more languages from birth, those who speak more than two languages, and those who experienced several relocations.

The findings are also limited in terms of the languages involved. The majority of the studies to date have been conducted with Spanish–English and German–English bilinguals in the United States; future studies need to expand the participant pool to other language combinations. This development is particularly important, because Guttfreund (1990), Carrillo and Kim (2003), and Harris (2004), all of whom worked with Spanish–English bilinguals, hypothesized that the language itself may mediate the results: expressions of affect, including swearwords, have different status and frequency in different speech communities. This possibility is corroborated by studies of cross-linguistic differences in affect expression discussed in the previous chapters and by studies of emotional socialization in different speech communities (Bhimji, 1997; Clancy, 1999; Eisenberg, 1999; Fung, 1999). Future studies could examine, for instance, whether self- and other-ratings for affect, anxiety, and depression are different in the two or more languages of bi- and multilingual individuals. If they were shown to be consistently different, the use of two types of participants, as in Guttfreund's (1990) study, could help to disambiguate the results and to see if they really stem from differences in chronology of acquisition or if they are influenced by cross-linguistic differences in affective styles and patterns of emotional socialization.

Assessment-wise, the studies suffer from a very narrow view of proficiency, which is commonly examined only in L2 and through a narrow array of measures. Considering what we now know about L2 influence on L1 and L1 attrition, it is critical to examine proficiency and fluency both in first learned and in subsequent languages. While self-report measures are popular in this area, they are clearly insufficient, and so are measurements of word-knowledge, such as the WAIS vocabulary subtest or The Global Word Naming Test. Another problematic measure is accent analysis, because the degree of accentness does not necessarily correlate with overall proficiency. An intriguing approach is offered by dysfluency analysis, which considers the number of hesitations, self-corrections, and so forth, in each language (Marian & Kaushanskaya, 2004), yet this approach may also confound the effects of proficiency with those of anxiety and other emotions.

Another important issue is acculturation, or degree of L2 socialization, which is not equivalent to proficiency. One can be fluent and grammatically correct speaking a language learned predominantly in educational settings without being socialized into it or acculturated to the target language environment – and thus exhibit the 'L2 detachment effect.' Conversely, one may possess a low level of proficiency in the language and yet be acculturated (cf. Schmidt, 1983) and have multiple means of expressing affect in that language and emotional reactions to it. Acculturation measures developed for different Hispanic subgroups in the United States are discussed in Altarriba and Santiago-Rivera (1994). Schrauf (2002) offers an insightful discussion of how acculturation might be examined in different domains.

This discussion would not be complete without touching upon measures of emotionality. Research with multilingual individuals typically considers the following verbal and non-verbal behaviors and responses to be evidence of emotionality: (a) refusal to use or to continue a conversation in a language in which the speaker is fluent; (b) crying, or increase in pitch variation and range, exhibited only in one language; (c) speaker's explicit acknowledgment that the language is linked to emotional, or in some cases traumatic, events; (d) recall of emotional, and possibly painful, memories unavailable through another language; (e) length and level of detail in narrative recalls; and (f) increase in levels of skin conductance response following the presentation of an emotionally charged stimulus. In the future, more caution is needed with regard to the meaning of particular linguistic strategies, as hesitations, pauses, and speech disturbances may be alternatively perceived as signs of detachment, anxiety, or dysfluency in the language in question. It is also important to reconsider the meaning of narrative length – does the increased length mean that the speaker is more comfortable in the language (and thus discloses more) or that the speaker is less fluent (and thus needs more time and resources to get to the point)? In future studies, it would also be helpful to analyze the functions of pauses, hesitations, and other linguistic phenomena in the actual transcripts.

Finally, the inquiry into the relationship between languages and emotions conducted from the perspective of embodied affective selves is reductive in nature. Emotions in this paradigm are most often seen as internal states or processes and are studied through self-reports or psychophysiological measures, while language is most often examined on the level of single decontextualized words. This approach does help us understand many instances of language choice and autobiographic recall, both in therapy and in translingual writing, but its focus is narrow and its explanatory power is limited to speakers' personal experiences. In reality, both emotions and languages are complex and multifaceted phenomena and speakers' evaluative judgments are grounded not only in autobiographic memories but also in sociohistoric realities and in ideologies of language and identity. Consequently, in Chapter 7 I will consider the issue of language choice from a social perspective, focusing on the interplay between emotions and identity options offered to speakers by particular languages.

7

Social cognition: "I no longer wanted to speak German."

> The truth was, I no longer wanted to speak German; I was repelled by the
> sound of it; for me as for other Americans it had become the language of the
> enemy. . . . I ceased speaking German altogether.
>
> (Lerner, 1997: 40)

Gerda Lerner arrived in the United States in 1939 as a nineteen-year-old
Jewish refugee from Vienna. Bent on reclaiming a life violently interrupted
by the Nazi rise to power, she wanted to master English, yet she also
felt that she had "a responsibility to uphold, treasure and keep intact
the integrity of the German language" (Lerner, 1997: 33), appropriated
and deformed by the Nazis. Unlike some of her European compatriots
who were resentful of being transplanted and nostalgic for the lost world,
Lerner embraced English with the same gratitude and fascination that
she embraced America. Two years after her arrival she was married to an
American man, had a steady job, and had made many American friends.
When the United States went to war with Germany, she found herself
repelled by the sound of German. She refused to use the language, to speak
it to her children, or to read German books; eventually she experienced a
profound language attrition.

When in 1948 Gerda met with her younger sister Nora, from whom she
was separated by emigration, neither spoke German. Nora, who settled
in England, spoke British English, Gerda spoke English with an American
accent, and neither liked the persona presented by the other. These interactional difficulties continued over the years, despite the sisters' sincere
desire to recapture their old intimacy. Once, in 1965, during Nora's visit to
New York, the two suddenly found themselves singing Austrian folksongs
and then smiling and hugging with the spontaneity that had been all but
lost. Yet English continued to be their language of communication, both
in letters and in face-to-face encounters. It was only in 1973 that the two
started using German with each other and began swapping silly jokes from

their Viennese childhood about a stick joke character, Count Bobby. It was then that "language unlocked the gates and memory took over" (Lerner, 1997: 44) for both sisters, and they recaptured the closeness and intimacy of their childhood, brought back by the sounds of their native language.

Lerner's memoir offers a beautiful and poignant illustration of the complexity of affective factors at play in language choice. An embodied view of language, outlined in Chapter 6, is well-suited to explain the explosion of memories and the return of intimacy prompted by the use of the German dialect of Gerda's and Nora's childhood. It is not sufficient, however, to explain the shift from Gerda's deep commitment to maintaining her German pure, "so that some day it might be restored" (Lerner, 1997: 33), to complete rejection of the language. To explain this and other instances of language choice, this chapter moves beyond the relationship between language and emotions on the neurophysiological level to the level of social cognition, and examines the role of emotions in speakers' decisions about what language or languages they would rather speak, study, or write in.

The chapter opens with a proposed account of links between languages, identities, and emotions, and ways in which emotions influence language-related reasoning. Subsequently, I discuss cases where identity-related emotions force speakers to reject their first languages, prompt them to fashion alternative or additional identities in later learned languages, or shape their decision to distance themselves from a particular language. I conclude with a summary of ways in which particular identities influence emotional investments in languages and discuss the implications of this line of inquiry for future research.

7.1. Identities, emotions, and linguistic decision making

Emotions often fly high in multilingual contexts, where language disputes constitute major sources of tension and instability. Elderly Russians openly cry over their inability to pass the Estonian language test and gain legitimate citizenship in the country where they had lived most of their lives. In Turkey, Kurds are arrested for trying to study their own language (Bollag, 2002). In Kosovo, a decision to end Albanian language secondary and higher education spurs a decade-long bloodshed. And in South India, since the 1930s young men have continued to fast, to die under police fire, and to burn themselves alive to protest the imposition of Hindi and to promote their native Tamil, with their deaths commemorated on the Language Martyrs' Day, January 25th (Ramaswamy, 1997: 228–229). Linguistic human beings, we get emotional about what languages we should and should not be using, when and how particular languages should be used, what values should be assigned to them, and what constitutes proper usage and linguistic purity. It is not surprising, then, that emotions influence both language policy and individual language choices. Elsewhere, I have considered the role of emotions in language policy, in particular with regard to the 'language of the enemy' (Pavlenko, 2003b). In what follows, I will examine the influence of emotions on individual reasoning and linguistic decision making.

In the past decade, Schumann (1994, 1997, 1999, 2001) made a pioneering attempt to understand the role of affect in decision making by second language learners, reconceptualizing what was previously known as the Affective Filter (Krashen, 1981). Drawing on the work in neurosciences and cognitive psychology, Schumann (1994, 1997) presented linguistic decision making as the assessment of emotional and motivational relevance of agents, events, and objects encountered by the individual on five dimensions proposed by Scherer (1984): novelty, intrinsic pleasantness, goal or need significance, coping potential, and compatibility with self- and social image. He argued that because each individual's experiences are different, so are their emotional memories, appraisals, and resulting reactions. Consequently, two individuals may appraise the same language learning situation differently or they may evaluate it in the same way but for different reasons.

To illustrate how this approach works, Schumann (1997) examined a number of second language learner diaries and memoirs in terms of stimulus appraisal, showing how positive appraisals of the language learning situation, the target language, its speakers, the teacher, the syllabus, and the text along Scherer's five dimensions enhance language learning, while negative appraisals ("I hated the method") inhibit the learning ("my reaction was to reject it and withdraw from learning"). Schumann also argued that learners may be willing to endure events they view as unpleasant if they see them as necessary steps in achieving a desirable long-term goal.

Similar to the embodied view of language presented in Chapter 6, this approach does explain the cases it set out to explain – namely, foreign and second language learning by university students. It comes up short, however, when applied to Lerner's case or to that of Tamil speakers willing to die at the altar of their language. The first problem with the stimulus appraisal approach is its reductive nature: The focus on the lower-level processes highlights only one piece of a big puzzle and obscures the higher level of cognition at which humans engage in reflection, plan sequences of events, construct and reconstruct narratives and selves, and position themselves as particular kinds of people. The second problem with the approach is its inherently Western view of individuals as rational and autonomous decision makers and of cognition and emotion as internal states and processes. This view ignores the relational nature of emotions and cognition that take place in the social context, under the influence of social, political, economic, and historical circumstances, and that may lead individuals to take actions that are not necessarily rational from an academic point of view.

Imposing his framework on the language learning memoirs of bilingual writers, Schumann said dismissively that their authors are not applied linguists and are thus "naive about psychological issues in SLA" (Schumann, 1997: 113). In reality, nothing could be farther from the truth. Many writers writing about languages and bilingualism are very aware of the literature in question, yet they are invariably disappointed by its lack of sophistication and contextual grounding (cf. Kaplan, 1994; Pérez Firmat, 2003). One of the writers discussed by Schumann, Alice Kaplan, had the following to say:

> For several years I have been working on a memoir which I refer to, in shorthand, as a "memoir about learning French".... When I began, I read as many scholarly disquisitions as I could find on second language acquisition – linguistics, sociology, education – and I found methods and statistics and the occasional anecdote, but nothing, really, about what is going on inside the head of the person who suddenly finds herself passionately engaged in new sounds and a new voice, who discovers that "*chat*" is not a cat at all, but a new creature in new surroundings.
>
> (Kaplan, 1994: 59)

Not much has changed in the decade that passed since Kaplan's statement. The literature in SLA and bilingualism still ignores such intrinsic aspects of bilinguals' lives as bilingual selves, bilingual emotions, or the incompatibility between the *chat* and the cat. It is possible, then, that it is research that remains naive about the language learning process, not bilingual writers and literary scholars, many of whom produced some of the most insightful and inspired writing there is on language, learning, and emotions, making connections that have not yet been made in the scholarly literature (Hoffman, 1989; Kellman, 2000; Pérez Firmat, 2003). In contrast, Schumann's reductionist approach strips away all of the complexity, boiling down immigrants' and expatriates' thorny journeys to chronicles of positive and negative appraisal.

For example, discussing his wife's reluctance to study Arabic in Tunisia as compared to her willingness to study Farsi in Iran, Schumann pointed to her dislike of the teaching method in the Arabic class and to her inability to "nest" comfortably in her Tunisian residence. In contrast, in Iran they lived in the hotel where she was "free of cleaning responsibilities" (Schumann, 1997: 105). Francine Schumann's (1980) own analysis of her learning of Farsi undermines this account and enables a much more contextually aware view of what transpired in Iran. To begin with, Schumann (1980) notes that as a woman she did not have the same interactional opportunities as her husband: Local women were invisible in the public sphere and the opportunities to interact with Farsi-speaking men only came in the company of Francine's husband. She also had to be continuously concerned about sexual harassment when in public. Her opportunities were additionally impacted by the fact that she was a speaker of English, a powerful language in which many Iranians were very proficient. Interactions with members of the local expatriate community also negatively affected her feelings toward Farsi.

Examining Francine Schumann's (1980) experiences in Iran and Tunisia from the perspective adopted here, we can see that her decision making was mediated by her social status, class, gender, citizenship, professional identities (her own and her husband's), and continuous emotional investment in English as the global language of power and of her own primary identity. As an upper-middle-class American woman, Francine Schumann could afford to be upset about the lack of hot water or comfortable furniture in her temporary Tunisian residence. As a wife of a visiting scholar, she had the freedom of transforming her alienation and hostility in Tunisia into language learning resistance, a stance not available to immigrants, refugees, or guestworkers. And as a speaker of the world's most powerful language, she was accommodated by her interlocutors and had no need whatsoever to fashion an alternative identity either in Arabic or Farsi. Yet even her extremely high social status did not protect her against sexual harassment and her gender identity imposed limitations on her interactional opportunities.

The reasoning that links identities to emotions, motivation, and interactional opportunities is finding more and more adherents in the fields of SLA and bilingualism. (For a review, see Pavlenko, 2000b.) These scholars do not dispute the neuroscientists' findings about the role of the amygdala in emotion-mediated learning; rather, they are simply not interested in the neurophysiological level of explanation. Instead of considering motivation in terms of stimulus appraisal, many found a compelling alternative in the socially and contextually grounded notion of *language investment* advanced by Norton (2000), who considers learners' choices, decisions, and behaviors in the light of their social identities, inequitable power relations, and multiple and often contradictory desires. Interestingly, accounts of language learning in terms of race, gender, and class also abound in Schumann's (1997) collection of learner autobiographies, yet his analysis ignores these identities in favor of such factors as novelty or pleasantness.

The goal of the present chapter is to offer an alternative, comprehensive, and context-sensitive account of the role of emotions in linguistic decision making. To be inclusive, I will examine decision making on the neuropsychological level, building on the discussion in Chapter 6 and drawing on some of the same literature as Schumann (1997). The primary focus of the discussion, however, will be on the level of social cognition, and I will examine both cognitive processes and social issues that impact these processes. I will begin by considering the question Schumann's account ignored – where do language-related emotions come from?

Social emotions, including the emotional underpinnings of linguistic decision making, are relational and as such are intrinsically tied to our identities, or subject positions, and identity narratives. These terms are often used in different ways by different scholars. Here, the terms *identities* and *subject positions* will be used interchangeably to refer to discursive categories (that is, identity options) offered by a particular society in a specific time and place and to which individuals appeal in an attempt to self-name, self-characterize, and claim social spaces and prerogatives (Pavlenko & Blackledge, 2004b). In contemporary Western society, recognizable subject positions are constructed at the axis of age, race, ethnicity, gender, sexuality, class, generation, social status, occupation, and political and religious affiliation, whereby individuals can be referred to (positioned) as a young African–American executive, a gay Republican, or a Chicana professor of women's studies. These subject positions are implicated in identity narratives or stories we exchange with others about who we are, where we are from, where we are going, and what group or groups we belong to. Constantly involved in the production of selves, individuals inherit narratives, contest them, revise them, and create new ones, valorizing new modes of being and belonging and new memberships in local or national 'imagined communities' (Anderson, 1991).

Emotions in this view are not only narratives by themselves, they are also embedded within identity narratives and experienced from particular subject positions. For instance, Armenians born half a century after the 1915 Armenian genocide inherit a set of narratives about the event that instill anger and outrage toward Turkey. In turn, Turks inherit a very different set of narratives that commemorate Turkish diplomats assassinated by Armenian terrorists and aim to elicit resentment and outrage at the unfair portrayal of Turkey in the world's eyes. (For the most recent example of the ongoing debate, see the exchange in the July 2004 issue of the *National Geographic*, prompted by an article about life in Armenia.) In a similar vein, generations of children growing up in the former Soviet Union were socialized into disliking German, associated with the Nazi invasion of Russia, Ukraine, and Belorussia, while children growing up in the neighboring Baltic republics or the countries of Eastern Europe were socialized into disliking Russian, the language of the oppressive Big Brother (Pavlenko, 2003b).

Multilingual contexts are notoriously fraught with identity politics, and most instances of language use or silence in these contexts may be interpreted as 'acts of identity' (Le Page & Tabouret-Keller, 1985). Heller's (1982, 1992, 1995) work on negotiation of language choice in Montreal in the context of francophone resistance to English domination offers but one excellent example of how identity politics play out in the linguistic arena. Undoubtedly, languages are tied not only to national and ethnic identities; they may also be linked to racial, cultural, and religious identities or to social status and class, so that, for instance, some languages or dialects are associated with low class and others with prestige and opportunities for social advancement (Constantinidou, 1994; Gal, 1978; McDonald, 1994).

The associations between languages, identities, and emotions are commonly formed through two processes, simultaneously social and cognitive: identification and misrecognition (Bourdieu, 1991; Gal & Irvine, 1995; Irvine & Gal, 2000). In the process of *identification*, also known as iconization, languages become symbolically linked to particular groups of people and emblematic of particular identities. In the process of *misrecognition*, linguistic varieties become linked with character types and cultural traits, so that the linguistic behaviors of others are seen as deriving from speakers' social, political, intellectual, or moral character rather than from historical accident. It is in the process of misrecognition that languages spoken by the dominant groups are recognized as inherently superior, while negative attitudes toward minority groups are transposed onto 'their' languages, resulting in instances of linguistic discrimination. Thus, debates about Spanish, Spanglish, and African–American Vernacular English in the United States or Russian in the Baltic countries are only superficially about language. In reality these are disputes about moral superiority, citizenship, belonging, political and social status quo, or participation in the global marketplace (Anderson, 1991; Lippi-Green, 1997; Schmidt, 2000). Similarly, individual learners' emotional investments in particular languages are investments in the learners' own desired identities and memberships in imagined communities, be it professional communities or the target language country as a whole (Norton, 2000).

When these investments, and with them the imagined future, are threatened or questioned – in other words, at junctures where there are changes in goals, plans, or likely outcomes of plans – emotions help individuals to evaluate the changes, to continue, relinquish, or modify their plans and goals, and to take action (Oatley, 1992; Oatley & Johnson-Laird, 1987). Language-related emotions are likely to influence individual decisions and choices in situations like ethnic conflict or immigration that necessitate a reappraisal or reaffirmation of one's desired identities and consequently of one's linguistic priorities and investments.

Damasio's (1994) somatic marker theory illuminates how this appraisal, reappraisal, and decision making take place on a neuropsychological level. Although both Damasio (1994) and Oatley (1992) assume the existence of basic or primary emotions, they agree that decision making is mainly influenced by secondary or social emotions. In Damasio's (1994, 2003) view, primary emotions (fear, anger, disgust, surprise, sadness, happiness) are innate and supported by the limbic system, in particular by the amygdala and the anterior cingulate gyrus. In turn, secondary or social emotions (sympathy, shame, embarrassment, guilt, pride, jealousy, envy, gratitude, admiration, indignation, contempt) are supported by the prefrontal and somatosensory cortices and are learned through systematic formation of connections between primary emotions and categories of objects and situations. In the process of associative learning, connections are also made between certain somatic states and predicted future outcomes of certain scenarios (social advancement following immigration to a more economically developed country, for example). In this way, the outcomes are marked by *somatic markers*, or visceral and nonvisceral sensations known in common parlance as 'gut feelings.' The role of somatic markers is to enable emotional appraisal of future scenarios: A negative somatic marker attached to a future outcome serves as an alarm bell, while a positive one may function as an incentive. The markers do not determine the outcomes of the decision making process. Rather, their presence increases its accuracy and efficiency, and their absence reduces them, as evident in clinical case studies of patients with frontal lobe damage and resulting impairments in affective judgments.

Together, these three perspectives explain how emotion-mediated linguistic decision making takes place on three converging levels. On the neuropsychological level, Damasio's (1994) theory illuminates the *how*, that is, the mechanisms by which languages acquire somatic affective values and the ways in which these values influence decision making outcomes. On the cognitive level, Oatley's (1992) work clarifies the *when*, that is, the times when emotions are likely to arise and influence long-term goal planning, adjustment, and evaluation. And on the social level, sociolinguists offer a compelling account of the *why*, describing ways in which languages become imbued with particular emotional values and linked to particular identities (Bourdieu, 1991; Gal & Irvine, 1995; Heller, 1982, 1992, 1995; Irvine & Gal, 2000; Norton, 2000; Pavlenko & Blackledge, 2004a,b; Schieffelin, Woolard & Kroskrity, 1998). The triangulation allows me to emphasize the ideological aspect of emotions as evaluative judgments without ignoring their embodied nature, and to pinpoint the links between social processes (for example, misrecognition of particular languages or language varieties) and individual emotional evaluations.

This socially informed perspective is much better equipped to explain the shift in Lerner's feelings about German and her subsequent actions than a stimulus appraisal theory. The picture that emerges from the pages of Lerner's autobiography is that of a young woman in love with German, whose early aspiration was to become a German linguist, and who paid a very high price for her linguistic transition – sounding childish, awkward, and incompetent in her new language. Yet she made a conscious decision not only to learn English but to live solely in English, separating herself from the comfortable German-speaking world of the expatriate community. In this she differed from her many compatriots, who transformed New York's Washington Heights into a small *Mittel-Europa* of coffeehouses, bakeries, shops, and clubs where they could maintain their ties to the German language and culture.

The key reason for this difference lies in the distinct subject positions occupied by Lerner and her compatriots and in identity narratives and imagined futures linked to these subject positions. The Washington Heights immigrants continued to see themselves as transplanted Europeans, temporary visitors on American soil. As a consequence, German in their minds was separate from the crimes of the Nazi regime and linked to the memories of prewar life and the traditions of Schiller and Goethe, to which they hoped to return one day. In contrast, Lerner ceased to see herself as a refugee to whom the German language was entrusted for safekeeping, and began to identify herself with "other Americans" (1997: 40). In this capacity, German was of no use to her and so she adopted the emotional judgments of her environment, identifying German with the Nazis and allowing her hatred of the enemy to dominate over the affection she used to feel for the language.

This framework, which emphasizes the role of identities in emotional decision making, represents a radical break from the scholarship on affective factors in SLA discussed in Chapter 2. The traditional study of motivation and language attitudes is commonly concerned with correlations between individual beliefs (elicited through questionnaires) and language learning outcomes (measured through tests or grades). In contrast, the study of identities and emotions in linguistic decision making is concerned with the sociohistoric contexts that shape individuals' subject positions, identity narratives, emotional evaluations, judgments, and subsequent actions. In other words, it is centrally concerned with the origins of individual beliefs that until now have remained unquestioned. In what follows, I will assume that neuropsychological and cognitive mechanisms of the decision-making process are shared across individuals and will not discuss them again. Instead, to remind the reader that decisions made by individuals are rarely fully autonomous and are always embedded within narratives of identity, I will discuss emotional influences on linguistic decision making within the larger historic, economic, political, social, and ideological backgrounds against which particular decisions have been made.

7.2. German Jews and the Holocaust: A case study in first language rejection

Examining Lerner's case, we face several important questions: How much can be generalized from first person narratives? Is this case representative of a larger population? How common is first language rejection? Can we find actual hard data to prove that emotions influence not only rejection of a language but also its attrition?

Discourses of language and identity commonly present mother tongue as the language of the self, of the heart, of one's ethnic, national, and cultural identity, and argue that losing one's language is tantamount to losing one's self. The powerful emotional link between the language and the self explains fierce language loyalties witnessed in contexts of ethnic strife, where individuals are willing to fight, go to jail, and even die rather than give up their mother tongue (Bollag, 2002; Ramaswamy, 1997). At the same time, other people and sometimes whole groups willingly give up their native languages, challenging an essentialist meta-narrative of self as permanently bounded to the first learned language. Zionist socialists arriving in Palestine leave their native languages behind, together with the history of oppression they symbolize, and adopt Hebrew that promises liberation and authenticity (Spolsky & Shohamy, 1999). Young Hungarian women in Austrian villages shift to German, the language that opens doors to the industrial workplaces and urban lifestyles they desire (Gal, 1978). And peasant Breton mothers refuse to transmit Breton to their children, behaving as if the language itself smelled of cow-shit while French offered affinity and sophistication moving them up the social ladder all the way to middle class (McDonald, 1994).

Sociolinguistic studies of language attrition in immigrant contexts and of language shift in the context of minority languages suggest that first language rejection is motivated by social, political, economic, and ideological reasons. Emotions have rarely taken a center place in this research, but it is becoming increasingly clear that people's feelings about their languages, identities, and futures play an important role in their linguistic choices. In what follows I will illustrate this argument through the case study of the only group whose first language rejection has been explicitly considered from the point of view of emotional memory, investment, and identity – postwar German immigrants in the English-speaking world.

Ursula Hegi (1997), an American writer and herself a German immigrant, argues that German immigrant identities – and the attitudes of their interlocutors – are invariably shaped by the legacy of the Holocaust, whether the immigrants are Jewish or German and emigrated pre- or post-World War II. The Nazi past is an issue German immigrants are forced to face even if they were born after the end of the war, like the author herself, because by virtue of living abroad they become representative of things German. Forty years after the end of the war, a new American classmate of Hegi's American-born son came over to their house and, hearing that she came from Germany, asked immediately: "Does that mean you are a Nazi?" (p. 29).

Hegi's (1997) interviews with other German immigrants in the United States show that this experience is not unique and that the war, the Holocaust, and anti-German prejudice are implicated, consciously or unconsciously, in most immigrant trajectories and linguistic choices. Hegi made numerous attempts to distance herself from the past, first by leaving Germany and then by attempting to abandon her native language and shed her accent. In her case, these attempts did not work – she could not escape the memories, the associations, and the overwhelming sense of guilt, shame, and grief. Every time someone praised her for being efficient, the image that came to her mind was that of concentration-camp efficiency.

Studies of first language rejection and attrition among German immigrants in the English-speaking world (Bossard, 1945; Schmid, 2002, 2004; Waas, 1996) and memoirs and interviews with these immigrants (Altmann, 1992; Hegi, 1997; Kluger, 1992, 2001; Laqueur, 2003; Lerner, 1997; Strauss, 1986; Uhlman, 1960) corroborate Hegi's arguments and show that linguistic choices of pre- and postwar immigrants are grounded in emotions elicited by particular interpretations of historic events.

Resentment of things German is particularly common among German Jews, even those who managed to escape Germany prior to the beginning of the war, because many, if not all, lost family, friends, and relatives in the Holocaust. Similarly to Lerner, they felt betrayed by their former motherland and extended their hatred of the Third Reich to the German language and culture with which they could no longer identify:

When the war broke out, 6 months after my arrival in England, I vowed I would not speak, write nor read German ever again. (Berta D., in Schmid, 2002: 71)

For many years I had refused to have anything to do with the language, the two countries (Austria and Germany), or their people. (Kluger, 2001: 205)

Instead, German Jews formed an emotional tie to their new homeland and with it, to their new language:

I feel that my family did a lot for Germany and for Düsseldorf, and therefore I feel that Germany betrayed me. America is my country, and English is my language.
(Gertrud U., in Schmid, 2002: 27)

Almost two-thirds of the informants in Schmid's (2002) study who were married to other native speakers of German reported that they seldom or never use German with each other. One married couple who had known each other in Germany prior to emigration stated that in more than fifty years of marriage they have never spoken German to each other, not even intimately. And like Lerner, they did not transmit the language to their children:

As an adult I had such animosity towards Germany because of its slaughter of Jews, that I would not let my children take German in high school even though they wanted to. I was insistent as a child that my parents, who did not speak English, learn English immediately. (Kläre S., in Schmid, 2002: 71)

While most respondents acknowledge that they consciously rejected the language, some claimed that they were simply unable to speak it, reminiscent of trauma survivors like Brison (2002), discussed in Chapter 6:

I was physically *unable* to speak German. . . . When I visited Germany for 3 or 4 days in 1949 – I found myself unable to utter one word of German although the

Frontiergard was a dear old man. I had to speak French in order to answer his questions! (Ruth K., in Schmid, 2002: 177)

Jewish immigrants were not the only ones to reject German. Some non-Jewish German immigrants also abandoned the language, either because they, like Ursula Hegi, felt shame and guilt over the war crimes, or because they were afraid of repercussions, like the families of some of Hegi's informants and friends:

One of my friends, who grew up in America with German parents, tells me her family used to speak German until she started school in 1943 and her teacher called her a Nazi. After that her family spoke only English at home. (Hegi, 1997: 38)

In this case a single instance of positioning led the family to assume a new linguistic identity and set of behaviors, even in the privacy of their own home, because it took place against a social background of an intense anti-German sentiment. This sentiment is reminiscent of an earlier time in American history, World War I, when an anti-German campaign prompted a rapid language shift in a previously bilingual German–American community (Pavlenko, 2003b).

An analysis of German–Americans' narratives suggests that many of them did not develop the negative feelings about their mother tongue on their own; rather they have been pushed along, internalizing the prevalent attitudes visible in public discourses. Note, for instance, the seamless transition from public sentiments to personal feelings in the narrative of John, a U.S.-born German–American informant in Bossard's (1945) study. John, who lived through both wars, recalls that during World War I, "the feeling against the Germans in this country was very strong. I was ashamed of my name, of my family and of my ancestry" (p. 707). As a result of this internalized shame, John abandoned German, changed his name, and left his home community, determined to speak "German-less" English and to live an Anglo life. The anti-German sentiment that arose during World War II served to confirm his stance: He admitted to the interviewer that it was "a great relief to live in a community which is not marked" (Bossard, 1945: 707).

Clearly, not all German immigrants in the anglophone world identified German with the Third Reich. Many, including some of the war-generation Jews, retained their affective ties to the language. For them, German was linked to childhood memories, the rhythms of Goethe's and Heine's poetry, the expressiveness of Schiller's drama, the tastes of delicious homemade meals. Some saw their native language as the last refuge of the now-scattered population. This attitude found reflection in the memoir *Muttersprache: Heimat der Heimatslosen* (Mother tongue: Home of the Homeless) by another Jewish refugee, Hans Heinz Altmann (1992), who left Germany for Bolivia and Argentina. A Jewish immigrant living in the

United States expressed similar feelings when responding to the question about his attitude toward German, underscoring his preference for German in emotional discussions:

Ich liebe meine deutsche Muttersprache und spreche und lese viel deutsch. Je emotionaler der Gegenstand des Sprechens ist, umso mehr neige ich dazu, deutsch zu sprechen.

[I love my German mother tongue, and I speak and read German a lot. The more emotional the topic, the more I tend to use German.]

(Martin R., in Schmid, 2002: 25)

In order to maintain German as an important aspect of their identity, these German Jews had to dissociate the language from its Nazi users and follow Thomas Mann in believing that Germany was where they were. Ruth Kluger (2001) goes further than many in her attempt to reappropriate the language. She ties it to her Jewish identity:

German, strange as this statement may sound, is a Jewish language. Consider that until the Holocaust, most of the world's prominent secular Jews spoke and wrote it: Kafka, Freud, Einstein, Marx, Heine, Theodor Herzl (!), and Hannah Arendt, to name the first that come to mind. (Kluger, 2001: 205)

Thomas Laqueur, a child of assimilated German Jews who immigrated to the United States prior to the Holocaust, recalls that his parents did not reflect on Hitler in relation to their past. Rather they opted for a membership in an imagined German community, reproducing its rituals in the middle of West Virginia:

Both of them remained passionately German, but without any real contact with Germany. They drank only German wines; they staged an elaborate German Christmas, complete with candles on the tree . . . they listened almost exclusively to German music . . . I lived a childhood produced by the children of 19th-century Jews, who imagined the land of Goethe and Schiller with little of its reality or recent history. (Laqueur, 2003: 39)

Non-Jewish interviewees in Hegi's (1997) book, all of them born in Germany between 1939 and 1949, adopt a similar attitude, linking the language to cultural, ethnic, and culinary traditions, rather than recent history. One of them, a woman named Eva, states explicitly that despite the witnessed apprehensions and prejudice, she does not want to shed everything German:

I cook German meals. Both my children speak German. I kept that because it had nothing to do with the war and Hitler. Lots of women who came over here did not teach their children any German at all. But I wanted them to talk to their grandparents when we go to Germany. (Hegi, 1997: 131)

Even those who refused to use the language do not deny its intimate overtones or the links it has to their own childhood and language socialization. Lerner (1997) confesses that despite her reluctance to use German otherwise, she sang lullabies to her children in German, because they were the only ones she knew. An informant in Schmid's (2002) study similarly admitted that despite her negative attitudes towards the language, she talked and sang to her children and grandchildren in German when they were small. Another informant stated:

Among Jewish refugees like myself we only talk English, since it would seem too intimate to use German. (anonymous, in Schmid, 2002: 5)

These testimonies show that neither loyalty to the first language nor absolute rejection can be unproblematically assumed across contexts, and that language attitudes cannot be easily reduced to levels of autonomic arousal or positive and negative appraisals. Rather, the longing is mixed with hatred, and the sweet intimacy of childhood remembrances with bitter memories of atrocities and deprivations suffered by survivors and their relatives and friends. How else could one explain the fact that Ruth Kluger, another Jewish immigrant in the United States, keeps going back to her native Vienna only to listen to the language she admittedly does not like:

Only the language was what it had always been, the speech of my childhood with its peculiar inflections and rhythms, a sense of humor that Germans often don't get, and a wealth of malicious half tones that would be obscene in any other tongue; also an intense lyricism that easily degenerates into kitsch. I understand this language, but I don't like it. I speak it, but I wouldn't have chosen it. I am hooked on it, and it's the reason I go back for visits. . . . (Kluger, 2001: 59)

Yet for those like Gerda Lerner who identified the language with the Third Reich, German became inseparable from the feelings of betrayal, repugnance, and hatred aroused by the Nazi atrocities. The losses afflicted by the Holocaust overpowered their childhood allegiances and led to language rejection and subsequent attrition. Voluntary abandonment of German signalled a desire to dissociate oneself and one's family from any possible connection to Hitler's Germany. Even when visiting Germany after the war, some of these immigrants would speak English, French, or English-accented German (Lerner, 1997; Schmid, 2002).

Some German immigrants and German–Americans, like John who was quoted earlier, did not abandon their mother tongue voluntarily. Rather, they were 'scared out' of language maintenance and internalized the feelings of fear, shame, and embarassment linked to the language. Others, like Eva or Ruth Kluger, chose to maintain the language despite their own ambivalence and the anti-German attitudes in their environment[1]. And yet others who may have felt affection toward German shifted to English over time and experienced first language attrition. Perhaps, then, attrition

---

[1] Kluger (2001) recalls that even in the concentration camp where she and her mother were interned, Czech Jews looked down on them because they spoke the language of the enemy.

is simply a logical outcome of language disuse? Or do emotional attitudes play a more direct role in the process? In other words, would outcomes be the same for immigrants who love their first language yet lack opportunities to use it and for immigrants who made a conscious decision to dissociate themselves from their first language and eschew such opportunities?

Schmid's (2002, 2004) ground-breaking study set out to answer these questions by examining the relationship between emotional memory and the degree of German attrition in German Jewish immigrants in the anglophone world. To examine language use and loss in these speakers, Schmid analyzed transcripts of thirty-five autobiographical interviews with former citizens of Düsseldorf, conducted in German by historians at the Düsseldorf Holocaust Memorial Center between 1995 and 1997. The fact that the interviews were collected by historians and not linguists is a definite advantage of this corpus, as this means that the interviewees were not self-conscious about their language abilities. The linguistic interest in the data was expressed only after all of the interviews had been conducted, through a letter that described the purposes of the study and asked for permission to use the interviews to study language attrition. These permissions were then followed up by questionnaires that inquired, in English and German, about the interviewees' language learning contexts and patterns of language use. All of the interviewees were assimilated middle-class German Jews, former citizens of Düsseldorf, where they lived in a monolingual German environment until they emigrated. At the time of emigration they were between eight and thirty years old.

Earlier studies of the relationship between language attitudes and attrition typically elicited attitudes through questions with quantifiable Likert scales. Schmid (2002, 2004), on the other hand, opted for a dramatically different approach, dividing the participants into three groups based on the severity of the persecution they experienced prior to immigration. The first group was comprised of people who left Germany between 1933 and 1935, within the first two-and-a-half years after the Nazi seizure of power, when concerted efforts began to exclude Jews from public life and limit their educational and professional opportunities. During this phase the emigration process was still relatively easy and people were able to take most of their money and belongings with them. Relatively few people emigrated during these years and those who did were mostly convinced that the Nazi regime would not last and they would be able to return to Germany. Thus, Schmid hypothesized, they may have still retained their positive memories and their identification with things German.

The second group left after the persecution entered a new and more radical stage, with the passing of the Nuremberg race laws in September of 1935. These laws redefined Jews as a race, rather than simply a religious minority, and essentially established two classes of citizenship on the basis of racial distinctions, prohibiting 'Aryans' from marrying or having sexual relations with 'non-Aryans' (Jews, Blacks, Gypsies, etc.). After the passage of these laws, which became the basis for legal marginalization of the Jews, the number of Jews seeking to emigrate significantly grew, while the process became much more difficult. Many countries were not interested in taking on the increasingly more impoverished German Jews, while Germany refused to extend passports to Jewish citizens, making them virtually stateless and thus ineligible for visas. Immigrants from this period would, in Schmid's hypothesis, be significantly less attached to their Germanness.

The third group emigrated after the persecution turned into genocide, beginning with two memorable events: the deportation of all Jews of Polish citizenship to Poland on October 28, 1938, and the pogrom on November 9, 1938, known as *Reichskristallnacht*. During this pogrom storm troopers and civilians killed numerous Jews and destroyed more than 1,000 synagogues and 7,500 houses, apartments, and businesses. More than 30,000 Jews were arrested and sent to the concentration camps Buchenwald, Sachsenhausen, and Dachau. This night was the turning point for German Jews – it signalled that they no longer had to be concerned about their civil freedoms; now, they had to fear for their lives. At that point nearly everyone wanted to leave, but the lists of applicants became too long and the procedures too difficult. And after the outbreak of World War II in September 1939 it became virtually impossible for Jews to leave the country.

This division into three time periods, each characterized by intensification of persecution and thus a higher likelihood of traumatic experiences, allowed Schmid to explore the influence of 'traumatization' in emotional memory on the degree of attrition. She hypothesized that the different conditions under which the participants left Germany may have impacted their reasons for leaving, their attitudes toward Germany and things German, and their initial expectations as to whether exile would be temporary or permanent. In particular, she hypothesized that while the Jews who left early may have retained some allegiances to German, those who left later would no longer consider themselves German and try to distance themselves from their past.

The interview transcripts were analyzed by two native speakers of German, the researcher and one of her three student assistants, with the focus on lexical, morphological, and syntactic errors (interference) as well as lexical richness, and lexical, morphological, and syntactic complexity (proficiency). In addition, thirteen native speakers of German were asked to listen to interview excerpts and rate each interviewee in terms of their nativeness on the scale from 1 (native-like) to 3 (non-native-like). These procedures yielded two sets of dependent variables: interference data (the amount of deviations from morphological and syntactic rules) and proficiency data (overall assessment of lexical richness, morphological and syntactic complexity, and nativeness ratings). To compare the participants' performance to that of monolingual speakers of German, the researcher and her assistants also analyzed interviews with ten speakers who remained in a monolingual German environment.

Three independent variables were considered in the study: (a) age at the time of emigration (lower or higher than 17); (b) interim use of the language (based on self-report data and on the native language of the spouse); and (c) the degree of 'traumatization' (based on the emigration period). Statistical analyses of these variables showed that age at the time of emigration was not consistently predictive of language attrition. The interim language use was not consistently predictive either: While there was a correlation between reduced language use and degree of interference, the three immigrant groups did not significantly differ in the reported amount of L1 use with parents, partners, and children, and each group contained speakers who spoke negatively about German. The only significant predictive factor for all morphological and syntactic variables (except for subordinate clauses) in terms of interference was the time at emigration. This variable did not significantly interact with other independent variables. In other words, the results revealed that even though the three groups did not significantly differ in the amount of L1 use, members of one group exhibited significantly more attrition than members of the two others. The biggest attriters were not the immigrants who left Germany earliest, not those who came to the United States as the youngest, not even those who used German least; they were immigrants who left Germany after 1938 and thus witnessed and experienced the most discrimination and persecution.

These results show that historically shaped emotional memory and adopted subject positions played a decisive role in language attrition of these immigrants: The earliest group seems to have preserved their German to a surprising degree, given the fact that they spent more than sixty years in an anglophone environment. They have a slightly smaller lexicon than monolingual speakers but are perfectly native-like in all other aspects. Those who emigrated between 1935 and 1938 have lost some linguistic complexity but are able to 'conceal' their attrition quite well. It is only those who left later, after 1938, who no longer sound like native speakers: Their linguistic repertoires are reduced, they use non-standard structures, and many speak German with an English accent. It is clear, then, that while speakers in all three groups may have felt a certain reluctance to use German, it was the speakers in the third group who made the most concerted effort to distance themselves from the language and have succeeded in doing so. Importantly, the study suggests that emotions impact not only attitudes, decisions, and choices, but actual linguistic outcomes.

All in all, postwar German immigrants offer an outstanding case study in the role of emotional memory and identity in linguistic decision making, and the ambivalences and complexities of this case are only beginning to be unraveled. The theoretical and methodological sophistication of Schmid's (2002, 2004) study offers a solid ground for future studies of the influence of socially and historically shaped emotions and identity narratives on language choices, language use, and the degree of attrition and interference in various immigrant and minority groups.

7.3. Second language learning and desire

As linguistic human beings, we cannot afford to simply reject a language without finding a replacement. Thus, first language rejection is invariably accompanied by an investment in a second language. Previous chapters cited several compelling reasons for emotional investment in a second language identity, among them the appeal of new affective repertoires that allow individuals to create not only more detached and mature selves but also more emotional and carefree ones. Yet the possibility of creating different affective selves is only part of the attraction. For immigrants, refugees, and members of linguistic minorities, languages of power also offer opportunities for upward mobility and social advancement, and thus for construction of more prestigious and powerful selves. Andrew Lam, an escapee from war-torn Vietnam who as a child associated his native Vietnamese with the anguish and sorrow of refugee existence, recalls the intense joy and happiness he derived from learning English. Looking at San Franciso, he would say to himself:

"City," I said. "My beautiful city." And the words slipped into my bloodstream and made it real and me intensely happy for the first time in a long time. For it was then that I saw that I, sad and confused and full of longing, through my new love for the new language, and through the renaming of things, could too claim my stake in the New World. (Lam, in Kellman, 2003: 88)

For Lam, the love for the new language is inextricable from the opportunity to stake a claim in the New World. A similar desire for a new, capable, and powerful identity has been documented in numerous studies with immigrants in Western contexts (cf. Norton, 2000). These studies also reveal that the learners' desires are often contradictory, their feelings ambivalent, and their investments multiple. Goldstein's (1997), Kouritzin's (2000) and Norton's (2000) studies of immigrant women in Canada show that when workplace or family demands come into conflict with women's study of English or attendance of ESL classes, the women may reconsider their investment in English. Norton's (2000) ethnography of English learning by five immigrant women is particularly successful in portraying the learning journey as a struggle, where feelings of elation brought on by communicative successes are often followed by disappointments and depression, brought on by experiences of marginalization and discrimination.

Power, prestige, and social class are implicated not only in immigrants' emotional investments, they may also underlie the emotional investments of expatriates and temporary visitors who long to construct an identity in another language. Kinginger's (2004b) study exposes this yearning in the French-learning odyssey of a young American woman, Alice, the daughter of a migrant worker. When Alice was still a child, a chance encounter with another migrant worker, a man twice her age, sparked her interest in French: The man would sometimes say or write things to her in French and refuse to translate them. While her childish crush on the man eventually dissipated, the interest in French remained and fueled her efforts to graduate from college despite hardships, failed relationships, pregnancy, transience, and homelessness. For Alice, just as for peasant women in Austria or France or for immigrant women in Canada, the emotional investment in French became a bid for a better life, a life of civilization and cultural refinement.

Prompted by her desire to conquer French and to become the sophisticated urbanite she could not be in English, Alice, then a student at a midwestern state university, applied for financial aid and departed for study abroad in France. She landed there with enthusiastic anticipation, only to discover that strangers on the street did not necessarily want to greet her or engage in conversations, and when she attempted to do so, they crossed to the other side. The impressionistic landscape of her imaginary France turned out to be the gritty, industrial, urban environment of Lille, and regular university courses in which she was placed were impossible to locate. Her financial situation prevented her from going out and traveling, and while other students did so she would stay in the campus bar and let "old, drunk French men" buy her drinks (p. 233). Eventually, the disappointments of the first semester turned into anger and frustration and then into a severe depression, prompted by what Alice saw as a complete shattering of her dream. She felt that she had nothing to live for and contemplated killing herself.

It was at this point, which Oatley (1992) views as a juncture in the planning activity, that Alice managed to reconsider her plans and to revise her behaviors in order to achieve her goal. She stopped trying to find her classes, got a job as an English language teaching assistant in a local school, and began to work her way into local student networks. By the end of the year her imagined future turned into reality – she was sitting around with fellow students, smoking, drinking coffee, and having long philosophical conversations in French. By the time she had to go back she was, in her own words, "the Queen of France" (p. 236). Undoubtedly, Alice's trajectory can be analyzed in terms of positive and negative appraisal of surrounding stimuli. What would be lost in such an analysis, however, is the driving force behind her journey – the all-consuming desire to 'jump class' and to rewrite her own identity narrative into that of someone urbane, interesting, cultivated, and glamorous, who deserves attention and respect.

While Alice made an investment in her friendships with French-speakers, other learners may invest in romantic relationships in their desire to get the language of the other. It is this language longing that suffuses romantic desire for the protagonists of Alice Kaplan's (1993) and Eva Hoffman's (1989) language memoirs. For them, attraction to male native speakers of, respectively, French and English, is inseparable from the language itself:

I wanted to breathe in French with André, I wanted to sweat French sweat. It was the rhythm and pulse of his French I wanted, the body of it.... Learning French and learning to think, learning to desire, is all mixed up in my head, until I can't tell the difference. (Kaplan, 1993: 94, 140)

When I fall in love, I am seduced by language. When I get married, I am seduced by language. My husband too is a master of the riff, and when I listen to him improvise about Whitman's poetry, or his Jewish aunts and uncles, or a Wasp Connecticut wedding, I think, maybe this bebop speech can carry me right into the heart of America... (Hoffman, 1989: 219)

This fusion of romantic and linguistic desire does not come as a surprise to literary scholars who have long been aware of romantic and sexual longings underlying linguistic allegiances. Pérez Firmat (2003), for instance, dedicates his latest work on Spanish–English bilingual writers to the exploration of logo-eroticism, or the intermingling of language and desire. Here, literary scholarship appears to be once again ahead of the fields of SLA and bilingualism that have yet to find a legitimate place for the study of language and desire.

A pioneering attempt to theorize and understand this phenomenon in relation to second language learning has been made by Piller (2002a; Piller & Takahashi, in press). Piller argues that motivation, and its more recent version, investment (Norton Peirce, 1995; Norton, 2000), traditionally have been understood as having an economic basis, while "the sheer 'sex appeal' of some languages for some people has been widely overlooked" (Piller, 2002a: 270). She proposes the term *language desire* to capture this intense intermingling of romantic and sexual desire with the desire for another linguistic identity and argues that the inquiry into the role of sexual attraction in the processes, practices, and outcomes of second language learning is a promising direction for future research.

Her first foray into the area is an inquiry into linguistic intermarriage as a case study in language desire and language choice. Piller's (2002a) study involves couples where one partner is a speaker of German and the other a speaker of English. Thus it covers the same linguistic configuration as the previous discussion of German immigrants in anglophone countries, but from a very different vantage point. This is especially important in order not to leave the reader with an impression that most English speakers continue to associate German with the Nazi regime, as it would be an incorrect and oversimplifying assumption. While that perception

may have been common during and immediately after the war, and may
have persevered in certain families (cf. Hegi, 1997), the new generation
of English speakers has clearly formed a much broader view of Germany.
Even children and grandchildren of German Jews are ready to leave the
past behind. Take for instance Ben, a participant in Piller's (2002a) study.
A child of German–Jewish parents, Ben grew up in Britain speaking only
English. His parents did not pass German on to him and used it only as a
language of secret communication. At the same time, they did not pass on
any dislike of German, and so Ben chose German as his foreign language
in secondary school. Eventually, he fell in love with and married a speaker
of German, Vera. Ben and Vera opted to use German as a family language,
even though they both live and work as translators in Brussels and speak
several European languages.

To understand the reasons behind language choice in bilingual couples,
Piller (2002a) conducted a study with 36 German–English couples. She
asked the couples, recruited by mail, to answer a language choice questionnaire she sent and to tape-record themselves while discussing their
answers. The answers showed that 18 of the 69 core participants[2] (26%)
exhibited a consistent pattern of interest in the partner's language: Ten
were English speakers who studied German in an American or British university, and 8 were German speakers who studied English in a German
university. These speakers expressed a longstanding interest in and affection for the second language and culture:

I came over because I liked England. I loved English. I love British culture. I wanted
to live here. (Maren, in Piller, 2002a: 101)

I have to say that I have been attracted to the English-speaking culture from my
earliest childhood. . . . I loved the chants of the soccer fans and the fact that 'love'
was such an easy word for these people. . . . I majored in English for my translating
and interpreting degree. . . . I can't imagine a life without English and without the
English culture. I would have moved to England after I graduated if I had not met
my husband, who substitutes England for me here, so to speak.
(anonymous, in Piller, 2002a: 99–100)

Like the German woman above, some participants made explicit links
between their emotional attachment to the language and their subsequent
actions. They legitimized the attachment by moving to the country where
the language is spoken or by marrying the speaker of the language 'as a
substitute':

NATALIE: like, I just said this jokingly but even as a kid I always wanted to
marry a cowboy. I always liked America, and the idea of America, and having
married you was NOT AT ALL coincidental, like you just happened to be
American.
STEVEN: uhmhu. [. . .]

---

[2] In three couples, only one member chose to participate in the study.

NATALIE: I like English. @ I studied English. I've always liked English. Everything that has to do with English. Old English, Middle English, American English, British English.

(Piller, 2002a: 100–101)

Interestingly, Natalie's husband, Steven, reciprocates her feelings and acknowledges that he used to have the same feelings for German, even though his relationship with the language was somewhat more complicated. A child of German immigrants in the United States, Steven refused to speak German at a very early age, and then had to relearn it and majored in German Studies. In this case (as in several others), rather than studying the second language because they accidentally got into a cross-cultural relationship, Natalie and Steven met as a result of their emotional linguistic investments and subsequent educational and professional choices.

Piller and Takahashi's (in press) study goes beyond the description of the phenomenon of language desire accomplished in Piller (2002a) and examines its discursive underpinnings and its location at the intersection of race, gender, language, and sexuality. The focus of the study is on *akogare*, a desire that some Japanese women feel for the West and Western men. The authors' analysis of Japanese women's magazines, ladies' comics, and English language websites shows how these sources use *akogare* to promote the study of English. Advertisements for English language schools and study abroad promise the fulfillment of one's dreams, a new self found overseas, and a possibility of becoming "who you want to be." Ads for English classes in Japan feature young, good-looking Western men and imply that the women will learn English better and faster with these teachers, as they will be keen to return to the classroom to see them. In some of the ads, teachers' professional bios resemble personal ads for romantic partners. The implicit romantic and sexual innuendo of these ads and the implied links between mastery of English and glamorous futures serve to sell the services of the English teaching industry as a powerful intermediary between female consumers and that precious commodity, an English-speaking identity, the key to the white world.

Having established the discursive links between *akogare* and the study of English, the authors interview five Japanese women who moved to Sydney, Australia, in search of better futures, English proficiency, and, inevitably, English-speaking boyfriends. The women arrived in Australia with joyful apprehension, similar to that experienced by Alice in France. Like Alice, they were soon to discover that to move beyond the initial greeting level and to form social relationships with Australians was close to impossible. And just like Alice, they felt that their dreams were shattered. Unlike Alice, however, who focused on entering French-speaking social networks, these Japanese women espoused a shared assumption that all they needed was an English-speaking boyfriend, the ultimate method in language improvement. But simply a native speaker won't do: The women's romantic and sexual desire is for white English-speaking men and they reject both Asian–Australians and white men who speak some Japanese. The latter group's attempts to use Japanese endearments or to speak Japanese during intercourse make them less authentic and are seen as a powerful turnoff. In turn, English endearments transport the women into a different world – one of glamor and fantasy – not contained in the corresponding Japanese terms. The analysis of these women's language learning outcomes attests that language desire is a treacherous guide: While it does turn on the women's agency, it may also lead to failure. Unable to fully realize their dreams, some women became resentful and depressed, and gave up on their attempts to master English.

A particularly intriguing phenomenon documented in Piller and Takahashi's (in press) study is the emotional attraction to the second language lexicon, in particular its terms of endearment. The researchers corroborate the findings of Pavlenko's (2004a) study, which showed that some multilinguals see the L1 emotion vocabulary as overused, tired, and 'worn out,' and favor the L2 endearment terms for their sparkle, novelty, and emotional force:

Whilst I use the English terms with my own children they are also very 'worn out'. I have had my children in Norway and the 'new terms' I have learnt and heard my husband use have a 'novelty' which is special and has emotional connections.
     (Sophia, 32, L1 English, L2 Norwegian, uses both languages with her children)

Even though we speak mostly English at home, [I prefer] the words (terms of endearment) for which my husband only uses Farsi and he uses them a lot with me and our 4-year old son. So those are the words I use and prefer as well. He also says them with such emotion and we have been living together for ten years so I got very use to the words they are my words too.
     (Aida, 33, L1 Spanish, L2 English, L3 French, L4 Farsi, uses predominantly L2 English with her children)

Volim te feels stronger in Bosnian than it does in English because the phrase "I love you" tends to be thrown around much more casually in English (especially in American English) than it does in Bosnian – my husband has never actually used the phrase with me but he has responded very emotionally (positively I might add) when I've said it in Bosnian. (Catherine, 42, L1 English, L2 Bosnian)

It is possible, then, that in the process of L2 socialization through romantic and family relationships, L2 words may become as emotionally meaningful and resonant as those of the L1, and elicit a similar or even higher emotional response.

Together, the studies reviewed here show that learners espouse multiple and at times contradictory desires, make multiple emotional investments, and revise and rewrite their identity narratives. Languages offering opportunities for social advancement, cultural refinement, cosmopolitanism, or simply identity change and escape from the old self, become vested with affective values, while their speakers may become objects of sexual desire.

7.4. Second language learning and negative emotions

The discussion so far has presented second languages in a very positive light, as languages that offer a second chance in life, an opportunity to create new, more mature, appealing, and sophisticated emotional selves and to invest in new futures. This role, however, is one of many played by languages learned later in life. In some contexts, these languages may remain emotionally neutral, offering their speakers nothing more than a tool for particular purposes. In others, where they are implicated in the processes of oppression, discrimination, and marginalization, these languages may be vested with negative emotional values. Most often, however, language learning trajectories are accompanied by ambivalent and contradictory feelings, positive in some situations, negative in others. I will now illustrate this complexity and the links between language choices, emotions, and identity narratives, drawing on SLA studies that break with the tradition of learner erasure, and portray language learners as gendered, racialized, sexual human beings who experience numerous emotions in language learning contexts as a result of being positioned in particular ways.

I begin with a subject position not yet mentioned in this chapter, that of a child. Earlier, I cited speakers who see the second language as the means to construct a credible and mature adult identity. This is not the only perception of a second language, however. Many learners, especially those in the early stages of the learning process, see themselves and are perceived by others as childish and incompetent. Here is how Gerda Lerner recalls the process of living in translation:

Lacking both an adequate vocabulary and sense of the rhythm of the language it was as though my adult knowledge had to be transposed into the vocabulary of a six-year-old. . . . More and more, as I began to move among English-speakers, I lived with an overwhelming sense of inadequacy and frustration . . . from being fast to a fault, I now appeared slow, if not slow-witted. (Lerner, 1997: 35–36, 39)

Many of our respondents have had similar experiences in their later learned languages, leading sometimes to feelings of depression and alienation from the language and its speakers:

During my year in Germany I felt for the first few months that I had completely lost my identity. I was slow to understand could not express precisely what I meant and could not shape my verbal persona nor could I make jokes or entertaining remarks as I had no shared frame of context. I felt alienated and painfully frustrated and became very depressed. (Jean, 22, L1 English, L2 French, L3 German)

Creative, intellectual, and humorous adults in their native language, L2 users often resent their new fumbling and mumbling personae and the inability to position themselves as competent and mature adults. They may also resent interlocutors who underscore their deficiencies and teachers who infantilize them in the classroom. An excellent example of *infantilization* of L2 learners in the classroom and of ensuing resistance is offered in Golden's (2001) ethnographic study of immigrants from the Soviet Union learning Hebrew in Israel. The researcher argues that the Hebrew teaching enterprise in Israel is different from regular foreign or second language learning. Its main purpose is to nurture national loyalties among the newcomers and to help them remake their identities and construct new emotional memories and collective feelings associated with their new country. Adina, the teacher in the class, used two means to achieve these goals. To help students experience and internalize the national emotional memory, she appealed to singing, storytelling, scolding, strolling, simulation, role play, and celebration of various national and religious holidays, strategies common in elementary school classrooms. To erase their prior identities, she discouraged mention of the Soviet Union or the students' past, asking them to focus on the current events in Israel.

This approach served both to socialize the students into the new emotional landscape and to desocialize them, signalling that their past is irrelevant to the Hebrew learning enterprise. Unlike many FL or ESL classes where students are explicitly encouraged to 'translate themselves' into the new language and talk about 'their country,' these immigrants were reduced to the status of 'blank slates' and forced to relive an imagined Israeli childhood. Ironically, however, by treating her students as children and denying their identity narratives, Adina inadvertently reinforced their position as Russian-speaking adults in Israel or, in the words of one former Soviet citizen, "adults in a baby state" (p. 70). Golden (2001) shows that whereas in the Soviet Union, most if not all of the study participants felt Jewish, their current circumstances diminished their emotional investment in a Hebrew-speaking identity and reinforced their emotional commitment to the Russian language and culture.

Undoubtedly, the stance taken by some of these mature immigrants cannot be generalized to the whole population. For instance, in Aronin's (2004) study of young immigrants from post-Soviet countries in Israel, the youngsters displayed emotional investments in both Russian, their mother tongue, and Hebrew, the language of their new friends, surroundings, and ethnic sensibilities. These emotional investments are also linked to imagined futures, as seen in a comment by one of the participants: "Now I speak mostly Hebrew, my future is connected with Hebrew, it is more and more my native language" (Aronin, 2004: 74). It is possible that age and generation mediate responses to infantilization: Young people, knowing that this is a temporary state, are more accepting of it, while older mature adults are more upset, because they have apprehensions about their language learning abilities, possible futures, and the identities they may be able to construct in the new culture.

Yet benign infantilization is probably one of the least harmful ways in which L2 users can be positioned. In other situations, their linguistic competence may be challenged or even denied. Important insights into the links between linguistic discrimination, language use, and language learning outcomes come from the study by Bremer and associates (1996). One emblematic instance of linguistic discrimination discussed by the researchers involves Berta, a Chilean immigrant in France, whose daughter had an accident at school and was taken into a hospital for emergency surgery. When Berta arrived at the hospital it was late and past visiting time. She tried to talk to the surgeon who operated on her daughter but he told her to leave at once, not giving her any information on her daughter's health. Berta interpreted his behavior as a refusal to see her as a legitimate speaker of French and the mother of an injured child he had just taken care of. Frustrated and emotional, she was unable to find words to protest his behavior and express her anger, and remained silent and powerless. The study highlights the consequences of such interactions using the trajectories of two Turkish workers in Germany: Cevdet, who had a good relationship with his supervisors and co-workers, continued to progress in German, while Ilhami, discriminated against in the workplace, was thrust into a cycle of misunderstanding, negative reaction to German, and, consequently, little progress in the language.

Notably, not all non-native speakers are discriminated against, or at least not in the same way. Some individuals appear to be more 'imaginable' than others as authentic and legitimate users of particular languages. Miller's (2000, 2003) study of ESL students in an Australian high school shows that white and fair-haired Bosnian students join the mainstream rapidly and without hesitation, establishing close relationships with their Australian peers. In contrast, Chinese students feel discriminated against, by both their teachers and their classmates. One of the students in the study, Nora, wrote bitterly in her diary: "I just don't know why the teachers always like fornigner, they always like white skin, gold hairs?" (Miller, 2000: 87). Another Chinese student, Tina, similarly complained about her Australian classmates:

Seems that they don't like the "black hairs." Because I have a classmate from Bosnia now in my class. If we go to [a mainstream] class together, they, they know that she is not Australian, don't speak much English, but go to talk to her not me.

(Miller, 2003: 84)

For Tina and Nora, marginalization, be it real or perceived, resulted in resentment, diminished emotional investment in English, and increased investment in Chinese language and culture. A similar situation is depicted in Kanno's (2000, 2003) study of Japanese students in the Canadian context. The study reveals that some L2 users eventually internalize the view of themselves as deficient communicators and let the feelings of shame, anxiety, and embarrassment take over, preventing them from taking advantage of speaking and learning opportunities. Being visibly different from their peers contributes to the students' self- and other-marginalization, as the interview with one of the female students, Sawako, shows:

[In a class where both English-speaking and ESL students are present] you understand the content of the class, but when you have to find a partner and do some group work together, you can't get into a group actively. You are too embarrassed to find a partner. You feel like you are going to be a burden on your partner, so you don't ask them; you wait for them to ask you. (Kanno, 2003: 35)

Minorities in English-speaking contexts are not the only ones for whom race mediates speaking opportunities and emotional investments. Caucasians are often similarly rebuffed in their attempts to use Japanese in Japan, where common ideology holds that non-Japanese cannot master the language. Susan Shrimpton, a Canadian who lived in Japan for a while, recalls several episodes where her attempts to communicate in Japanese were brushed off, and even increased fluency in the language did not lead to her acceptance as a legitimate speaker of Japanese:

Learning to cope in Japan as a white person means learning to cope with the appellation "gaijin". Literally, the word means "outside person." ... On more than one occasion I have hopped into the back of a taxi, reeled off what I thought were clear, simple directions (in Japanese) only to have the driver turn to me and say "no speak English." (Shrimpton, in Schumann, 1997: 294–295)

Shrimpton also notes that as a woman she had to put up with patronizing attitudes from her Japanese doctor and with racy jokes from the police officer and the locksmith who, hearing that someone broke into her apartment, were amused that the burglar did not steal any of her underwear. As Francine Schumann (1980) noted a long time ago, women in multilingual contexts experience unique difficulties and emotional hurdles. Immigrant and minority women as well as female expatriates and temporary visitors are in particular danger of being dismissed (like Berta), being silenced (like Tina and Nora), or being ignored, insulted, or ridiculed (like Sawako or Susan). As Susan Shrimpton's case shows, even speakers of powerful languages are not exempt from sexual harassment and gender discrimination. Studies conducted with Americans studying or living in Spain, Russia, Japan, and Costa Rica suggest that male and female speakers of English are positioned differently as L2 users and that this positioning has implications for their emotional investments and resulting language learning outcomes (Pichette, 2000; Polanyi, 1995; Siegal, 1996; Talburt & Stewart, 1999; Twombly, 1995).

A particularly clear link between emotional investments and outcomes is shown in Polanyi's (1995) study of American students in Russia. The study compares Russian Oral Proficiency Interview (OPI) test scores of male and female students prior to and upon return from the study abroad program. Intriguingly, while prior to the trip males and females achieved similar scores, upon return male students showed greater gains and outperformed female students, in particular on the listening test. The author links this diffierential achievement to a different quality of gender encounters experienced by men and women. In their travel journals and diaries, American men typically told tales of pleasure in which they met beautiful Russian women and won them over, in the process improving their Russian, which became "smooth and flexible" (Polanyi, 1995: 281). In turn, American women were trying to deflect the unwanted sexual advances of Russian men they did not consider desirable partners. The diary of one of the students, Hilda, reveals that the men's patriarchal attitudes were at least in part responsible for this negativity:

What happened was I had a meeting with a friend of mine who I had known three years ago, who I thought was a really big blackmarketeer, and this meeting didn't go very well because he decided that I was his woman immediately and he started to be extremely demanding of me and telling me who I could see, when I could see them, what my life was going to be like and everything like that. And I was feeling extremely uncomfortable during this exchange, and very disgusted, because I couldn't make myself clear to him . . . he wouldn't listen to me.

(Polanyi, 1995: 281–2)

Polanyi's (1995) analysis of the students' gendered experiences in Russia suggests that it is the inability to appropriately handle unwanted advances that led to American women's diminished emotional investment in the language and reluctance to interact with Russian speakers. On the other hand, some have acquired very important affective repertoires from their Russian female friends that allowed them to deal with sexual harassment – yet these hard-won repertoires were not tested by the OPI. What is particularly important about Polanyi's (1995) study is a clear link between emotional disinvestment and diminished language achievement. In U.S. classrooms, American women invested in the Russian language similarly to their male classmates and, as a result, got similar test scores. Negotiation of gender roles and experiences of sexual harassment in Russia changed this investment, diminished the range of speaking opportunities, and did not allow the women to make the same advances in listening ability that were made by the men, who enjoyed their power status and interactions with Russian friends and girlfriends.

Together, these studies underscore that identities can be contested and identity narratives threatened in certain language learning situations, with important implications for ensuing emotional investments in the language itself, the learning process, and, eventually, learning outcomes. The studies discussed here and in Section 7.3 also point to the importance of understanding the gender and sexual politics of language learning and intercultural communication, and in particular who is seen as an appropriate romantic partner for whom and under what circumstances. For instance, American men benefit tremendously from their liaisons with compliant Russian and Japanese women, while American women, perceived as independent and perhaps even dominating, do not elicit the same interest from Russian or Japanese men – and when they do, some, like Hilda above, may refuse to be positioned as 'little women.'

7.5. Identities, languages, and emotions

The proposed account of emotion-mediated linguistic decision making shifts the focus from the commonly accepted affective factors (attitudes, motivation, personality) to the intersections of subject positions and identity narratives. I showed that through the processes of identification and misrecognition, languages become vested with particular symbolic and emotional values and linked to preferred or dispreferred identities. These links between languages and identity narratives have the power to enhance or weaken speakers' emotional investments in particular languages, steer them away from 'languages of the enemy' and toward the languages of power and desire. Because the focus in the present chapter is on identities, this section will differ from similar sections in other chapters in that it will examine, not factors, but identities affecting emotional investments in particular languages.

Studies of language ideologies and linguistic identities conducted in sociolinguistics and linguistic and educational anthropology suggest that all aspects of identity can influence speakers' emotional investments and mediate linguistic outcomes. Central in this discussion are undoubtedly *national* or *ethnic* identities that may steer individuals toward certain languages and away from others. Thus, Zionists arriving in Palestine shunned their native languages in favor of Hebrew, which would unite them in a single ethnic and historic identity. Tamil devotees in India spearheaded one of the most intense and violent linguistic nationalism movements to revive and protect their ethnic identity wrapped around their mother tongue. And ethnic Estonians, Latvians, and Lithuanians, having proclaimed independence, immediately distanced themselves from their second language, Russian. While many, if not most, spoke Russian fluently, they associated it with the oppressive Soviet regime and thus saw it as incompatible with the pursuit of an independent national identity.

Similarly, a well-known Kenyan writer, Ngùgì wa Thiong'o, after having published four successful novels as well as numerous essays, plays, and short stories in English, publicly rejected that language in 1977. In doing so, he decried his allegiance to the language of Kenya's colonial past, in which the poorest and most oppressed citizens of the country could neither read nor communicate. Instead, to transcend the 'colonial alienation' of the African intelligentsia from its own people and to contribute to the national identity project, he began to write in the local language Gikùyù, which at the time had not developed traditions of written narrative. Tragically, that same year he was arrested for his politically controversial writings and thrown into a maximum-security prison. Soon Ngùgì wa Thiong'o found himself in exile, and once again writing in English.

These examples underscore that national and ethnic identities are tightly linked to *political identities*, whereby individuals invest not only in particular ethnicities or national belongings but also in political allegiances, rejecting languages linked to oppressive regimes, be it colonialism or totalitarianism. Jerzy Kosinski, for instance, is very clear that it was his desire to be himself and not to be ordered around that propelled him to leave Poland:

I was, like many others, willing to get out no matter what the price. We knew what was in store for us was not worth waiting for anymore. We had seen it, we detested it. It was the ultimate enemy of how we perceived ourselves. I'm asked quite often whether I left the Soviet orbit because I hated communism, and I quite honestly answer no. I hated myself in it. I felt my life was wasted, and so my duty was to get out. (Kosinski, in Teicholz, 1993: 106–107)

While Kosinski did not have much choice in terms of language after he got accepted as an immigrant by the United States, contemporary citizens of Eastern European countries do have some choices and joyfully invest in English and German, languages vested with promises of Westernization, sophistication, and upward mobility (Pavlenko, 2003b).

Political oppression is not the only reason for changing languages and communities. Ilan Stavans, a well-known American writer and professor of Latin American Studies, admits that it was the conflict between his national, ethnic, and cultural identities that propelled him to leave Mexico:

I fled Mexico (and Spanish) mainly because as a secular Jew – what Freud would have called "a psychological Jew" – I felt marginalized, a stereotype.
(Stavans, in Kellman, 2003: 120)

A desire for public success informed the decision by another Mexican, Richard Rodriguez, to abandon his native language in favor of English, a language that aided in his transformation from a poor working-class boy into an American writer and scholar:

Coming from a home in which mostly Spanish was spoken, I had to decide to forget Spanish when I began my education. To succeed in the classroom, I needed psychologically to sever my ties with Spanish. (Rodriguez, 1997: 410).

Rodriguez is not alone in his quest for social mobility and acceptance, as we have seen. *Class* and *social identity* play a central role in Alice's trajectory (Kinginger, 2004b), where French is imagined as the language that guarantees refinement, cultural consciousness, and a prestigious middle-class future. A similar emotional investment is made in French by peasant Breton women in France (McDonald, 1994), in German by peasant Hungarian women in Austria (Gal, 1978), and in English by Gaelic women in fishing villages in Scotland (Constantinidou, 1994). Majority languages promise upward mobility to these women, while adherence to the native languages will keep them in second-class roles in their communities.

The cases of women spearheading a language shift suggest that linguistic decision making is often linked to *gender identities*, where emotional attachments are prompted by gendered social opportunities and represent investments in gendered futures. Studies of Japanese women learning English point to an explicit connection many women make between English and more equitable gender relations and professional advancement (Kobayashi, 2002; McMahill, 2001; Piller & Takahashi, in press). For instance, Chizu Kanada, a Japanese learner of English, admits that by investing in English she invested in a more visible and prestigious identity and higher self-esteem and social status:

English is the foreign language of choice among many Japanese, in terms of general prestige and acceptability. This is held to be especially true for young Japanese women who aspire to a professional life. Somehow the deviation this signals from the traditional-ideal track of becoming "a good wife and wise mother" can be compensated for by the cultivation of special skills such as English. As a young woman studying English at a prestigious Tokyo college, I took advantage of this cultural expectation. I was able to justify my aspiration to obtain a skilled, full-time job by demonstrating excellence in English. (Kanada, in Schumann, 1997: 274–275).

On the other hand, women's experiences of ridicule, insults, sexual harassment, and gender discrimination elicit negative attitudes and, through the process of identification of these behaviors with a particular language, a diminished emotional investment in the language in question. For instance, women in Ocongate, Peru, are commonly ridiculed by men for their attempts to use the L2 Spanish (Harvey, 1994). The insults portray them as trying to pass themselves off as better and more educated than they are in reality and are very effective in silencing the women: Many younger women have a good passive understanding of Spanish but are afraid or ashamed to speak it in public. Studies conducted with women in study abroad contexts point to similar outcomes linked to unwanted sexual advances and limited interactional opportunities (Pichette, 2000; Polanyi, 1995; Schumann, 1980; Talburt & Stewart, 1999; Twombly, 1995).

An African–American student, Misheila, on a study abroad trip to Spain (Talburt & Stewart, 1999) felt that she was particularly singled out due to both her race and her gender:

Mi observación es muy negativa. Para mí mientras estoy en España noto que mujer africana es un símbolo de sexualidad. Cuando camino en las calles siempre recibo comentos sobre piel y comentarios sexuales, especialmente con los viejos y adolescentes entre la edad de 15 y 20. Es muy difícil para mí y no pienso que es algo de cultura, es un mente ignorante. Cuando dicen comentarios a mí me siento que taking advantage *que soy extraño y no tengo* command *de idioma. Y no me gusta.*

[My observation is very negative. For me while I've been in Spain I notice that the African woman is a symbol of sexuality. When I walk in the streets I always receive comments on my skin and sexual commentaries, especially with old men and adolescents between the age of 15 and 20. It's very difficult for me and I don't think it's something cultural, it's an ignorant mind. When they make commentaries to me I feel they're *taking advantage* of me being different (a foreigner) and not having *command* of the language. And I don't like it.] (Talburt & Stewart, 1999: 168–169)

This observation made in the context of a discussion in the Spanish class shows that Misheila feels both angry at being singled out and inadequate in her ability to express her feelings, be it in response to catcalls or in the session with her peers. To emphatically reinforce the systematic nature of the harassment she experienced and the detrimental effect it had on her, she first code-switches to use the expressions 'taking advantage' and 'command of language' and later switches to English. She describes her experiences in Spain negatively and comments on the fact that her textbooks did not prepare her for this, as they are not written with African–American students in mind.

While Misheila may decide to reject the language in which she is positioned as a racialized sexual object, in other cases *racial identities* may shape positive emotional investments in particular languages. Ibrahim (1999) shows how African immigrant students in a Canadian school make a transition from identities that make sense to them – Sudanese, Liberian, or Nigerian – to those that make sense in their environment. In doing so, they identify with the African–American and African–Canadian communities and invest in Black English, a symbol of membership in the community to which they could authentically belong.

In sum, we can see that identity options and narratives are inextricably linked to language learning choices and decisions: The languages we speak or refuse to speak have a lot to do with who we are, what subject positions we claim or contest, and what futures we invest in.

7.6. Conclusions and implications for future research

I have argued that three perspectives are necessary to fully understand emotion-mediated linguistic decision making: neuropsychological, cognitive, and sociolinguistic. Damasio's (1994) theory illuminates the formation of secondary or social emotions linked to particular languages, and of resulting somatic markers that mark future outcomes related to these languages as desirable or undesirable. Oatley's (1992) account clarifies how social emotions, in this case emotional values of particular languages and preferred identity options and imagined futures, influence ongoing planning and reasoning. Sociolinguistically oriented research (Bourdieu, 1991; Gal & Irvine, 1995; Heller, 1982, 1992, 1995; Irvine & Gal, 2000; Kanno, 2003; Miller; 2003; Norton Peirce, 1995, 2000, 2001; Pavlenko & Blackledge, 2004a) shows how emotional evaluations and judgments of particular languages, identities, and narratives develop in a social, political, economic, and historic context through two key processes – identification and misrecognition.

As the world around us alters its ever-changing shape, these sociocul- turally and sociohistorically shaped emotions may also undergo modifica- tion and development. Gerda Lerner's story, which opened up the chapter, serves to illustrate the ambivalent and contradictory emotions languages may elicit in their speakers and the ongoing twists and turns in their lin- guistic trajectories. Prompted by the burning hatred of the Nazi regime, uncompromising young Gerda rejected German, opting to fashion a new identity entirely in English. She did so with staggering success, becom- ing a world-renowned historian and a pioneer of the field of women's history. Yet the youthful inflexibility that separated her from her mother tongue also carried a price, which Lerner recognized and acknowledged only decades later:

> When you lose your language, you lose the sound, the rhythm, the forms of your unconscious. Deep memories, resonances, sounds of childhood come through the mother tongue – when these are missing the brain cuts off connections. Language communicates much more than literal meaning. It gives us timbre, tone, a rich undercurrent of resonances and shadings, multiple and ambiguous crosscurrents.
>
> (Lerner, 1997: 39)

Fifty years after her arrival in the United States, in the wake of the wars in Vietnam, Korea, and Iraq, Lerner was ready for reconciliation. "One cannot live with hatred," she stated:

> After the A-bomb and the H-bomb and the Vietnam war, I carry war guilt on my shoulders as an American, even though I always opposed those weapons and that abominable and despicable war. I am no longer on such firm ground in condemning Germany for the deeds of the Nazis. I feel more strongly than ever that to transcend

hatred bred of racism and ethnic prejudice, one must at least make an attempt to distinguish between the guilty and the others. One must strive for reconciliation.

(Lerner, 1997: 18–19)

This reconciliation began with her own language, which she started to recapture first through editing the translation of her work into German, and then through lecture tours in Germany. Altogether, five decades have passed between the time she had ceased speaking German and the time she spoke it in public again, thus beginning to heal the wounds inflicted by the war, emigration, and separation from her family and the language of her childhood.

Ruth Kluger's (2001) trajectory is similar if not as dramatic. For many years, Kluger, married and raising two sons in English, refused to have anything to do with German, its speakers, and her two countries, Austria and Germany. Yet eventually the language pulled her back. She went to graduate school and became a professor of German literature. In the late 1980s she also began writing in German, an undertaking that culminated in publication of the German version of her autobiography (Klüger, 1992). Ursula Hegi (1997) similarly admits that two decades after her arrival in the United States she is living more within the language than ever before. The trajectories of these women serve as a powerful reminder that our feelings do not stand still; they evolve just as we do. The notion of language embodiment captures but one aspect of the language/emotion interface, and perhaps the most stable one. When considering emotions as relational phenomena, we discover that a language that once elicited affection may begin to arouse anger and resentment and be repressed and rejected, only to go back full circle to evoke tenderness, love, and sadness for all the losses inflicted by the time of separation.

As humans we are constantly organizing and reorganizing our sense of who we are and how we relate to the social world. As a consequence, our feelings, desires, and emotional investments, including language investments, are complex, contradictory, and in a state of flux. The view of social emotions as deriving from subject positions and informing identity narratives offers an appealing alternative to what is known as the study of affective factors, motivation, and language attitudes in the fields of SLA and bilingualism. It is also an alternative that calls for a much more engaged and time-consuming scholarship. Questioning the value of elicited statements along the lines of "I like French-speaking people. Yes or No," it forces scholars to consider the social context in which their participants live, the futures they imagine for themselves, and linguistic choices they make on an everyday basis. What does liking French-speaking people mean and who is doing the liking? Is the speaker an anglophone Canadian referring to francophone neighbors? Or is it a North American, like Alice, for whom

French represents the only possibility of crossing the class lines and creating a more educated, more civilized, more sophisticated persona? And what if the respondent chose 'No' as an answer? Are the imaginary French speakers nothing but cartoon figures waving the white flag, popular in the post-9/11 American media? Or are they perhaps Quebec separatists? Or maybe the response indicates "Leave me alone, I am tired of this class and of your questionnaire"?

New advances in sociolinguistics force the mainstream scholarship in SLA and bilingualism to admit that no opinions exist outside of context and no answers are given from nowhere in particular. To focus on learners' identities exclusively as learners is to profoundly misunderstand and misrepresent them. To acknowledge that identities are constructed and reconstructed in language is to admit that identities, subjectivities, agency, emotions, and power are profoundly implicated in language choice, learning, and use.

8

Emotions and multilingualism: An integrated perspective

My mother says I'm becoming "English." This hurts me, because I know she means I'm becoming cold. I'm no colder than I've ever been, but I'm learning to be less demonstrative.

(Hoffman, 1989: 146)

The closing chapter of a scholarly book commonly aims to end and summarize the story told in the preceding chapters. This book is no different in that I will indeed try to close and summarize. It is different, however, in that there was no single story told on its pages. Rather, for those who never thought of emotions and multilingualism in a single sentence, I pointed to a number of important connections between the two phenomena. For those who thought there was only one lens through which the relationship could be considered, I highlighted the existence of several lenses and, with them, several stories that could be told. For those who thought there was one dominant story – that of L1 being the language of emotions – I told an alternative story, that of affective socialization into an L2. The possibility of affective (re)socialization in a new discursive community, which the opening quote vividly illustrates, is perhaps the most prominent new story to emerge from this book.

In addition to telling new stories, academic books also challenge earlier stories and accounts. In keeping with this tradition, I have tried to dismantle the myth of a simple, tangible, easily described relationship between the languages and emotions of bi- and multilingual speakers, and to show that this relationship plays out differently for different individuals, and even in the distinct language areas of a single speaker. I have also tried to show that multilingualism offers unique insights into the relationship between language and emotions through such diverse phenomena as language choice, language embodiment, and affective (re)socialization.

Unlike in fiction, closing chapters in the scholarly genre serve not only to tie up loose ends but to ask new questions along the lines of: What have we learned? Where to from here? Chapters 3 through 7 already offered directions for inquiry in specific language areas, and so here I will sketch some general directions for the integration of multilingual approaches into the study of language and emotions, and for the integration of emotions into the study of multilingualism. To come full circle, I will end by answering questions raised in the first chapter of this book with regard to bi- and multilingual participants in emotion research. And because the preceding discussion was organized in terms of language levels, it will be only fair if the coming discussion takes as its departing point alternative views of emotions.

8.1. Emotions as inner states: Insights from multilingualism

I sit by my mother's bed in a nursing home in Philadelphia. She is dying, and I am holding her hand, willing her to stay with me. I can't bear to part with her – I am her child, I can't imagine life without her, we have been through so much together, I love her, and I need her to be here to love me back. But she is leaving me – she exhales one last time and then she is gone. The nurse confirms that she is dead and leaves me alone with my mother's body, plunged into the darkest grief and despair. The English words do capture what I am feeling, and so does their Russian equivalent *gore*, as do many other words of the world's languages, but at that moment I am beyond language. I am falling into the black abyss just as I did when I lost my first boyfriend many years ago in Kiev. This time the feeling is more acute, more profound, more tinged with fear because there is no one any longer between me and eternity. But still I recognize it. The feeling did not change just because I live in a new place and in a new language.

I come to the window and wave to my son leaving for school. He smiles but does not wave back – he is feeling too grown-up for that. I watch him adjust his backpack and walk away, in a purposeful manner. I am overcome with love, tenderness, and anxiety. It is the same feeling and the same tightness in my chest I experienced for the first time sixteen years ago in a Kiev hospital, when the doctors showed me the helpless wailing newborn covered in yellow gook. Since then, he has grown into a young man and we have changed countries and languages, but the way I feel about him remains the same.

Far be it from me, then, to say that transition into a new language and culture fully transforms our feelings. My own experience of having lived as an adult in two languages and cultures tells me that if we think of emotions as inner states, some of my own most basic feelings, including love and grief, remained unchanged. I do not know, however, if they remained unchanged because they are universal, because they are still Russian, or because Russian and English speakers are similarly socialized into love and grief, with similar stories within which these feelings are embedded, and with similar triggers. The research discussed in this book does not address the issue of emotions apart from language and thus does not directly contribute to the debate on universality versus language-specificity of emotion states. It does, however, point to promising new directions for future inquiry.

Until now, in an attempt to pinpoint similarities and differences in emotional experiences across cultures, researchers have examined individuals' emotional reactions within and across a variety of cultures (cf. Scherer, 1988; Scherer et al., 1988). This approach is not the only one possible, though. Studies discussed in Chapters 4 and 5 demonstrated how we could examine emotions through the lens of bilingualism, considering similarities and differences in bicultural bilinguals' emotional experiences. Panayiotou's (2004a,b) work breaks new ground in this field in that it looks beyond linguistic and conceptual frames and into the physical domain, asking participants where and how they experience particular emotions. Her work indicates that some emotion-related physical experiences may be culture-specific. Cypriot Greek speakers in her study describe *stenahoria* (discomfort/sadness/suffocation) as a feeling of suffocation, of not being able to breathe, of not having enough space – experiences that do not accompany the feeling of the English equivalent 'frustration' and are not reported by English-speaking L2 users of Greek.

Ways in which Greek speakers appropriate the notion of 'frustration' (Panayiotou, 2004a) also point to an interesting direction for future investigations – the study of the emotion lexicon from the perspective of language contact and change. Current research typically approaches lexicons as fully separable and impermeable phenomena. In reality, however, language boundaries are permeable and researchers in the fields of bilingualism and second language acquisition are becoming increasingly aware of the worldwide adoption of Anglo concepts and notions of what represents effective communication (Block & Cameron, 2002). This spread is referred to here as *globalization of semantic space*. As Chapters 4 and 5 showed, emotion terms and expressions constitute an important part of this process, and it is not simply English words, such as 'privacy,' 'frustration,' or 'depression', that are borrowed by other languages, but also language- and culture-specific concepts and values encoded in these words. The economic and sociopolitical prestige accorded to the English language makes its emotion terms look desirable (Piller & Takahashi, in press) and universally applicable (Panayiotou, 2004a); only close attention to language contact and change will allow us to judge if the data we gather reflect universalism of basic emotions or increasing domination of Anglo discourses of emotions.

8.2. Emotions as relational processes: Insights from multilingualism

My mother is gone, and when the first wave of despair washes over me I descend back into the linguistic realm. The English words are the first to come. I realize that I am still clutching my mother's beautiful hand and that I am doing so for 'comfort' – yet for the first time in her life she cannot offer me any. She is gone and I am left 'to deal with it.' From that point on, my emotions are no longer purely physical feelings. Now they take shape through the stories and the angry, bitter words that run through my head: Why did she postpone seeing a doctor? Why did she refuse the second round of chemo? Why did she give up? As I question and accuse her, my emotions become relational – a way for me to preserve our connection: As long as I can argue with her, as long as our storyline continues, I can keep her alive. This way of relating emotionally to the dead is not common to all discourse communities; some condone nothing but acceptance of the fact that the beloved relative had passed away, and they would not easily accommodate the story of being angry with one's dead mother.

If we change our lens on emotions and consider them as relational processes, the possibility of distinct storylines increases, and so does the potential for contributions from a multilingual perspective. The first promising domain for future study involves socialization of emotions. Studies in this area commonly focus on affective socialization in general (Saarni, 1993), on socialization into particular emotions (Capps & Ochs, 1995), or on socialization of affect in a particular language community (Bhimji, 1997; Clancy, 1999; Fung, 1999; Miller & Sperry, 1988; Schieffelin & Ochs, 1986). The studies discussed in this book extend the focus to multilingual affective socialization and consider what happens when children are socialized into more than one language or when adults are socialized into a new language.

Both personal insights and empirical studies indicate that bi- and multilingual parents may assign their languages somewhat distinct affective roles, with some languages judged more convenient for scolding and others for praise and terms of endearment (Luykx, 2003; Pavlenko, 2004a). In some multilingual communities, such judgments may operate on a more general level, with certain languages used more often than others for expression of strong emotions (Heider, 1991). And in some contexts, children may simply be exposed to different repertoires by virtue of the fact that one language is learned through interaction with parents and grandparents, and another through interaction with peers. As a result, even when the two or more languages are learned from infancy or early childhood, speakers may be socialized into somewhat different affective repertoires – and thus ways of relating to others – in these languages (Koven, 2004). This point is well illustrated in the reminiscences of bilingual psychoanalyst Rosemarie Perez Foster, whose Spanish and English played distinct affective roles as she was growing up:

> I was born in urban New York to parents who migrated to the U.S. from Cuba and the Dominican Republic in the 1930s. Spanish and English were expressive, vivid, and equally used modes of communicating in our daily lives.... In the world of relationships within my family, each language included instructions about what

part of me I could express, articulate, and develop through its use within a particular relationship. I used Spanish for loving my father, English for anger with my mother, Spanish for political discourse with everyone, and English for witty sarcasm with my aunts. These were rules about domains of language use and experience in my home that were finer than the gross distinctions of Spanish for home and English for school, or Spanish for early trauma and English for defense.

(Foster, 1996c: 142–143)

As Chapter 5 showed, differences in repertoires internalized in the process of affective socialization, combined with cross-linguistic differences in emotion concepts and scripts, may result in development of distinct affective styles in the respective languages, often perceived as distinct affective and relational selves (Ervin-Tripp, 1954, 1964, 1967; Koven, 2004; Pavlenko, in press). Case studies discussed in Chapter 6 suggest that these differences may also emerge if the languages were learned at different points in life: L1 selves may be perceived as more emotional, anxious, childish, and vulnerable, while the selves constructed in later learned languages may be perceived as more independent, controlled, and mature.

This difference in perceived selves brings us to the second important direction suggested by the work reviewed here – inquiry into affective (re)socialization of children and adults. Research on language socialization commonly focuses on monolingual children and does not take into consideration linguistic transitions. (See, however, Bayley & Schecter, 2003.) In turn, research on second language socialization in adulthood typically describes the process as a social and linguistic one, with the key changes taking place in the areas of linguistic proficiency. Eva Hoffman's (1989) account of her own transformation from an immigrant Polish girl into a Canadian teenager and then into an American woman attracts our attention to a less known aspect of language socialization, where changes take place not simply on the level of proficiency but in the individual's affective styles. Challenging the conventional wisdom, Hoffman argues that she is 'becoming cold' not because she is speaking a second language, but because the Anglo affective style appropriate for a person of her age, gender, and socioeducational background is less effusive and temperamental than the one she had developed in her Polish surroundings. She links this change to distinct identity stories or stories of the self offered to her by her two discursive communities:

I've become caught between stories, between the kinds of story we tell ourselves about ourselves. In one story, circumstance plays the part of fate, in the other, character. In one, I've been poised against my surroundings at an embattled tilt because I was thrown into an alien world. In the other, the world was alien because I was prepared to make it so, and all events registered on me as dye making patterns in the grain of already woven fabric. Between the two stories and two vocabularies, there's a vast alteration in the diagram of the psyche and the relationship to inner life. When I say to myself, "I'm anxious," I draw on different faculties than when

I say, "I'm afraid." "I'm anxious because I have problems with separation," I tell myself very rationally when a boyfriend leaves for a long trip, and in that quick movement of self-analysis and explanation the trajectory of feeling is rerouted. I no longer follow it from impulse to expression; now that I understand what the problem is, I won't cry at the airport. (Hoffman, 1989: 268–269)

For Hoffman (1989), feelings are not simply physical experiences; they are implicated in the narratives of the self, and 'the rerouting of the feeling trajectory' is an unavoidable consequence of the change in the self-narrative prompted by second language socialization. Her mother, on the other hand, has maintained the emotional self condoned by Polish narratives of emotionality and femininity and thus does not see feelings as subject to restraint. One day young Eva advised her mother that she should try and control her feelings:

"What do you mean?" she asked, as if this was an idea proffered by a member of a computer species. "How can I do that? They are my feelings."
(Hoffman, 1989: 269)

Studies discussed in Chapters 4, 5, and 6 build on Hoffman's (1989) insights and show that affective (re)socialization may take place on all levels of interaction between emotions and languages: neurolinguistic, psycholinguistic, and sociolinguistic. L2 users may change the ways in which they relate to themselves and others, and the ways in which they perceive and interpret others' emotion displays. If the individuals in question are moving from a more expressive culture to a more restrained one, they may, like Eva, become more subdued. If, on the other hand, they move to a more emotional culture, they may feel the license to become more expressive and spontaneous. They also develop more native-like semantic and conceptual representations of emotion words, and if the language is used in the context of family and intimate relationships, these words begin to trigger sensory images, physical sensations, and autobiographic memories.

The possibility of conceptual change in affective (re)socialization opens up new questions for research on linguistic relativity, in particular in contexts where transitions are made from non-Western to Western languages. One could potentially ask: Do speakers whose native languages do not encode the notion of emotions begin to conceptualize the world and frame their interactions with others from this new perspective? Do those whose native languages view emotions as interpersonal processes begin seeing them as inner states, at least when using the L2? Do they now refer to emotions not encoded in their native languages? And are physical experiences accompanying these new concepts familiar or novel? Reverse questions could also be asked of speakers of Western languages learning non-Western ones, yet the difference in power and prestige is commonly such that full assimilation in this direction is extremely rare. As Chapter 5 showed, these questions are not limited to Western/non-Western transitions, and one could also consider two Western languages where emotions are differently encoded. So far, it has been shown that Russian L2 users of English may change the linguistic framing of emotions from processes to states (Pavlenko, 2002d) – but the larger implications of this change for their cognitive functioning remain to be seen.

8.3. Sociolinguistics of multilingualism: Insights from emotion research

In the wake of the U.S. presidential election of 2004, which firmly divided the country into red and blue states, I got into a conversation about the importance of voting with two Russian acquaintances. Immigrants from the former Soviet Union and by now U.S. citizens, both men espoused a very *laissez-faire* attitude toward the political turmoil in the country, stating with a typically Russian cynicism that little people cannot change the course of history and that politicians are all the same. The hot-headed idealistic American in me wanted to convince them that they should follow the events more closely, that the two dominant parties are not always identical, and that every vote counts. The Russian in me did not disagree, even though it remembered how naive and uncool it was to care about politics back in the USSR. Yet that self fell curiously silent because it did not have the appropriate vocabulary for an impassioned political argument. I was mumbling, fumbling, and stumbling, using simple Russian words and basic sentence structure instead of the ready-made, prefabricated English utterances floating freely in my head. Time and again I switched into English to present a more emotional plea, to make a more coherent point, to offer a more cogent argument, but every switch distanced my interlocutors, who did not have the same level of English proficiency and favored Russian as the language of conversation. I did not want to hurt my friends' feelings but I did want to express myself clearly. In this case, I could only do so in English.

Traditional analyses of code-switching and language choice in bilingual conversation commonly reduce affective factors to the 'us versus them' dichotomy, where L1 represents 'us' and L2 unproblematically stands for 'them.' This dichotomy captures well the way my friends position themselves with regard to their two languages – Russian is indeed their language of the self, of *po dusham* (soul-to-soul) conversations and intimacy with friends and family, while English is the language of the Other, of employers, INS, IRS, and the government. In my own case, however, the dichotomy fails – because for me, and for many others in similar circumstances, the second language has become another language of the self. It is the language in which I grieve, make love, reprimand my child, laugh at Jerry Seinfeld's jokes, get upset about the corruption of our city's government, and get angry at the mismanagement of our local schools. My words, laughter, tears, and frustration are intertwined with the here and now of my life in the United States. Only English, the language of heated political discussions with my partner, son, and American and international friends, allows me to express myself clearly on the subject of politics, especially when emotions run high and lexical choices need to be made quickly. Russian, my native language, is undergoing attrition.

These personal experiences fuel my drive to expand the understanding of ways in which emotions affect language choice, learning, and use in multilingual contexts beyond the 'us versus them' framework. Chapter 7 points to the first direction in future inquiry in this area – the study of ways in which emotions influence linguistic decision making. The approach advanced here highlights the interplay between sociohistoric, sociopolitical, and linguistic circumstances that shape individuals' investments in particular languages and shows that the languages speakers choose to learn, speak, or abandon are intrinsically linked to their social, political, gender, and national identities and imagined futures.

The second and related direction is the inquiry into the emotional underpinnings of language attrition. Personal insights and studies discussed in Chapter 7, in particular those by Schmid (2002, 2004), indicate that emotional investments and disinvestments play a prominent role in L1 attrition and maintenance. In turn, studies by Tomiyama (1999) and Waas (1996) show that emotional expression itself may be particularly vulnerable to attrition. Tomiyama's (1999) study of attrition of L2 English in an eight-year-old Japanese child demonstrated that switching to L1 began with emotion-laden utterances and interjections. Emotional expression in L2 was one of the first areas where the child lost confidence and competence. The researcher described this behavior as an on-stage (L2 English) and an off-stage (L1 Japanese) performance, where the performer relaxes off-stage, expressing his genuine feelings.

These findings are linked to the third promising area of research – inquiry into affective factors that impact code-switching and language choice. Studies reviewed in Chapters 5, 6, and 7 show that cross-linguistic differences in affective repertoires, perceived language emotionality, and emotions linked to particular languages are oftentimes central in speakers' decisions about which languages they would rather live, write, undergo therapy, argue, or whisper sweet nothings in. In some contexts, certain languages in multilinguals' repertoires may be judged better suited for emotional expression (Heider, 1991). In others, speakers may prefer to use the language they control, not the one that controls them. They may feel that a later learned and less emotional language allows for better emotional self-control and may facilitate discussion of anxiety-provoking feelings or memories. Other speakers may, in the heat of the moment, switch to their first language, even when their interlocutors are not proficient in that language, because the language 'feels right' or offers them an extra advantage in terms of communicative efficiency. In fact, some may switch to the language unfamiliar to the interlocutor simply because they derive internal satisfaction from using this language in the context of a fight or an argument. This intriguing behavior presents a challenge to linguistic theory, and in particular to theories of communication and argument that commonly assume that speakers at all times make rational language selections based on the interlocutors' competence.

In addition to pointing to new directions, this book also aims to challenge previous frameworks, such as the focus on 'us versus them' in understanding emotional dynamics of language choice, or the belief in a single language of emotions. Looking back at my own interactions, I come to a conclusion that English must be my new internal (as seen in inner speech) and external (as seen in arguments) 'language of the heart.' My relationships are negotiated in English, and when I get emotional I want to speak my second language because it is the language that most correctly and fluently represents my emotional world.

Yet incidents here and there remind me of the power Russian still has over me. One episode that took place many years ago is particularly memorable. I am standing in the departmental mailroom, sorting through my mail, when an American colleague who teaches in the Russian program walks in. He tries to use the Xerox machine, it jams, and he emits a fluent stream of filthy Russian swearwords. I am so hurt and offended that I leave the room and do not talk to him for months. In Russian culture it is inappropriate to swear in the presence of a decent woman such as myself. (I temporarily forget that the same colleague had heard me swear in English and had sworn in English himself in my presence.) Russian swearwords still have the ability to get to me and to wound me deeply – they make me jump higher than their English counterparts. Undoubtedly, it works the other way around for my colleague, who did not mean to offend me but simply wanted to show off his native-like Russian repertoire.

Interestingly, his swearwords also trigger for me the Russian emotion script of *obizhat'sia* (to feel hurt by someone, to be offended or upset by them) that prescribes and legitimizes my uncompromising behavior after the incident: I walk out without acknowledging the colleague's presence and stop talking to him, presumably until an appropriate apology is offered. The colleague is unaware of what went wrong, however, and only thinks of me as strange. Some months go by before we are able to sort this confusion out. Perhaps, then, my earlier conclusions are wrong and Russian is still my most emotional language? It is still the language of my childhood memories, conversations with my family, the movies I love, the songs by my favorite singer Vladimir Vysotsky, whose every inflection, every consonant, every trill reverberates in my whole body.

Or perhaps what is wrong is not my conclusions at all, but a pervasive belief in a single 'language of the heart'? What do we mean by the language of emotions, anyway? If all we mean is the language that evokes childhood memories or higher levels of autonomic arousal, then Russian is indeed the language of my heart, because Russian taboo words, childhood reprimands, or for that matter songs, will undoubtedly elicit higher skin conductance response. At the same time, I suspect that if I were presented with an array of political terms, L2 English words would elicit higher levels of arousal than those of L1 Russian. And if it is the language one chooses to address one's child, I do appeal to Russian for all the delicious coo-ings about dear-little-ears (*ushki*) or dear-little-feet (*nozhki*), but switch to English for emotional discussions – English allows me to make my points better, faster, and more coherently and effectively. It fits my reality and it feels right.

Throughout this book, I have argued that to think of the first language as the language of emotions or the self and the second language as the language of detachment is to oversimplify the relationship between lan-guages, emotions, and identities in bi- and multilingualism. The ques-tion about the language of the heart of bi- and multilingual individuals is misguided because it does not have a single referent and may elicit dif-ferent answers depending on its interpretation. Our favorite language is not always the one whose swearwords make us jump highest, and the language that affects us most is not always the one in which we choose to express our emotions. Similarly, different languages may index 'us' at different points in time or even in different segments of the same conver-sation. Future research needs to acknowledge this and to examine mul-tiple ways in which emotions affect what we say and what language we say it in.

8.4. Psycholinguistics of the multilingual lexicon: Insights from emotion research

Hoffman's (1989) story offers a unique portrayal of the 'rerouting of the feeling trajectory' and of changes that take place in her relationships with others and even with herself. Her insights also highlight the transformation of her emotional vocabulary, showing that L2 words learned in the con-text of intimate relationships may become embodied, and elicit physical sensations and autobiographic memories:

But now the language has entered my body, has incorporated itself in the softest tissue of my being. "Darling," I say to my lover, "my dear," and the words are filled and brimming with the motions of my desire; they curve themselves within my mouth to the complex music of tenderness. (Hoffman, 1989: 245)

Coupled with studies reviewed in Chapters 4, 5, and 6, these insights have important implications for future research in the psycholinguistics of bilingualism and for the modeling of the bi- and multilingual lexicon. These implications converge on four themes: (a) differences in representation, processing, and recall of distinct categories of words; (b) cross-linguistic differences between emotion terms of different languages; (c) differences in mental representation and perceived embodiment of emotion-related words learned in different contexts; and (d) bidirectional cross-linguistic influence.

To begin, research discussed in Chapters 4 and 6, in particular that by Altarriba and associates (Altarriba, 2003; Altarriba & Bauer, 2004; Altarriba, Bauer & Benvenuto, 1999; Altarriba & Canary, 2004), points to differences between word classes in the mental lexicon in terms of representation, processing, and recall. This work advances a convincing argument that in future studies of the mental lexicon, emotion words should be examined in their own right because they differ from both abstract and concrete words. Due to rich links to autobiographic memory and semantic networks, they are more elaborately encoded and readily contextualized than abstract words. They also differ from concrete words in that they don't have visual referents.

Second, studies examined in Chapter 4 show that regardless of whether there exists a concept of 'emotions' shared by all cultures, and independent of whether emotions are universal or culture-specific, languages offer distinct emotion lexicons and affective repertoires to their speakers. This means that bicultural bilinguals have distinct, language- and culture-appropriate semantic and conceptual representations of emotion and emotion-related words and that L2 users have to master new semantic and conceptual distinctions in this area. These findings point to the need for differentiation between translation equivalents of L1 and L2 emotion words, and to the need for studies of development of L2 emotion vocabulary and competence in emotional expression. (For an expanded version of this argument, see Dewaele & Pavlenko, 2002.) The dissociation between semantic and conceptual representations in foreign language learning also warrants differentiation between these two levels of representation in future research.

Third, studies reviewed in Chapters 4 and 6 indicate that differences in the age of acquisition and the contexts of language socialization lead to distinct mental representations of emotion and emotion-related words and to distinct perceptions of their embodiment. Languages into which speakers have been socialized in natural contexts, in particular at a young age, have been learned with the involvement of emotional memory. As a result, their words are perceived as embodied and emotional, which means that they are processed not only through cognitive channels but also through affective ones, triggering associations in autobiographic and emotional memory, bodily sensations, and physiological responses, examined through levels of autonomic arousal. These words bring back voices and memories, elicit tenderness, joy, and affection; they may also feel like blows and arrows, leaving wounds that may never heal. On the other hand, languages learned in classroom contexts do not hurt; they are learned through declarative memory and are not integrated with personal memories, sensory representations, and affective associations. As a result, their words are often perceived as empty sounds. Endearments uttered in these languages may feel meaningless and swearwords bland and inoffensive.

We have also seen that the links between emotion and emotion-related words and autobiographic memories are bidirectional in that each can trigger the other. This bidirectionality leads to three types of effects: (a) words learned in the natural context and grounded in autobiographic and emotional memories are better contextualized and thus better recalled than words learned in the classroom context; (b) words learned in the natural context early in life and grounded in personal and emotional memories elicit physiological reactions, and as a result are perceived as embodied; words learned later in life in decontextualized settings are perceived as disembodied and at times even 'fake'; (c) words grounded in autobiographic memories may also function as triggers for these memories, as clinical case studies of bilingual patients in therapy and psychoanalysis show.

Differences in representation and physiological reactions may also crosscut languages and appear as word category effects. For instance, in terms of physiological reactions, taboo and swearwords appear to be the strongest stimuli, followed by childhood reprimands (Harris et al., in press). These effects are additionally mediated by age and context of acquisition: L1 taboo and swearwords may be strongest even for those who spent most of their lives in the L2 environment. Belgian-born American writer Luc Sante thus describes the relationship between the degrees of pain and his language choice for swearwords:

If I stub my toe, I may profanely exclaim, in English, "Jesus!" But in agony, such as when I am passing a kidney stone, I might cry, "*Petit Jésus!*" with all the reverence of nursery religion. (Sante, 1998: 265)

Those who use two or more languages on a daily basis may have similar perceptions of and reactions to taboo and swearwords in these languages. Speakers who learned a second language in a natural context in late childhood or early adulthood may exhibit more subdued reactions to L2 taboo words and no reactions whatsoever to L2 reprimands (to which they were not exposed in their childhood). If they are in a relationship with L2 speakers and/or raising children in L2, they may, however, favor the L2 terms of endearment. And speakers who learned their second language in a decontextualized environment may exhibit no reaction whatsoever and feel completely at ease using L2 swear and taboo words, to the detriment of their interlocutors.

Last but not least, studies reviewed in Chapters 4 and 5 point to bidirectional cross-linguistic influence and ongoing transformation in the multilingual emotion lexicon that accompanies the processes of language acquisition and attrition. For instance, Cathy Davidson (1993), an American scholar who visited Japan several times and stayed there for extended periods, internalized the Japanese affective repertoire for expressing embarrassment. While on a trip to France, she suddenly found herself apologizing in Japanese, which came as a shock not only to her husband and the customs officials but even to herself:

And in France, I realized that my language for cultural embarrassment, for not quite knowing just how I should act, is Japanese. If I were blindfolded and tossed into absolutely any foreign country – France, Hong Kong, Zaire – I'm positive that within two minutes I'd be bowing, apologizing, and exclaiming, "*Hazukashii!*"

(Davidson, 1993: 196)

Chapters 3, 4, and 5 show that cross-linguistic influence and internalization of new emotion concepts, structures, and repertoires take place on all linguistic levels. Beginning L2 learners may exhibit L1 transfer in affective prosody, lexicon, or pragmatics, while advanced learners may adopt the L2 prosody or exhibit L2 influence on L1 in vocal cues and in word choice and use. To express notions unavailable to them in the base language of the conversation, bilinguals may appeal to code-switching and lexical borrowing, as Cathy Davidson did in France. For many bilinguals, as it is for Eva Hoffman, the process of cross-linguistic influence is dynamic, ongoing, and bidirectional:

When I speak Polish now, it is infiltrated, permeated, and inflected by the English in my head. Each language modifies the other, crossbreeds with it, fertilizes it. Each language makes the other relative. (Hoffman, 1989: 273)

In sum, the research discussed here reveals unique characteristics of emotion and emotion-related words in the mental lexicon. Until recently, though, studies of the bi- and multilingual lexicon did not consider emotion words in separation from abstract and concrete words. Psycholinguistic theory will benefit from further exploration of the following: (a) differences in representation, processing, and recall of abstract, concrete, and emotion words; (b) differences in processing and recall of emotion and emotion-related words in L1 and later learned languages; and (c) differences in representation, processing, and recall of particular categories of emotion-related words, including but not limited to taboo and swearwords and endearments. From now on, words in the bi- and multilingual lexicon can be compared not only on their semantic, conceptual, and processing dimensions, but also on their affective characteristics, including affective processing and physiological responses exhibited by different groups of bilingual speakers. It would also be interesting to use the free- and cued-recall paradigm with speakers who learned their additional language or languages in the classroom, to see what memories and associations are elicited by languages learned without major involvement of emotional memory. It is hypothesized here that because these languages are not directly linked to autobiographic memory, recall would take longer and the memories per se would be accessed by means of translation equivalence, connecting L2 words to their L1 counterparts and only then to related memories.

8.5. Multilingual participants: Data collection, reporting, and analysis

In the beginning of this book, I argued that the 'one language–one speaker' perspective in emotion research violates the notion of ecological validity, and that reliability, validity, and true interdisciplinarity in cross-linguistic research – including that in language and emotions – require insights from the field of bilingualism. Subsequently, I demonstrated that bi- and multilinguals' emotion lexicons and affective repertoires may differ in meaningful ways from those of monolingual speakers; thus one cannot always receive 'monolingual' data from bi- and multilingual participants. These arguments were made not to discourage the use of bi- and multilingual participants, but to encourage a systematic, structured, comprehensive, and, most importantly, explicit incorporation of these participants and informants. In what follows, I will discuss this incorporation in terms of data collection, reporting, and analysis.

Data collection
I begin with the data collection, considering the who, where, and how in cross-linguistic research on language and emotions. In terms of the who, I have argued for recognition of the linguistic competencies of researchers and participants and for *inclusion* of bi- and multilingual speakers in their own right, as representative of more than half the world's population. In terms of linguistic backgrounds, I have argued for going beyond Spanish–English and German–English bilingualism – or any other combination of English plus another language – and for inclusion of various other types of bi- and multilinguals, among them sign language speakers.

Any research with bi- and multilingual participants should also be sensitive to the notion of where, that is, the *context* in which the data are collected and the role of the language mode and the interlocutor. Even in the same language, bilinguals vary their lexical choices and the amount of lexical borrowing in their speech, depending on the interlocutors they are addressing (Otheguy & Garcia, 1993). Speakers' performance may change even more drastically with a change in language: Bicultural bilinguals may perform differently in their respective languages on a variety of measures, including self-esteem and self-description (Ross, Xun, & Wilson, 2002).

Discussions in this book also touched upon the how of future data collection and highlighted the need for *triangulation* of laboratory and naturalistic studies, or a combination of experimental tasks with ethnographic approaches, interviews, diaries, and questionnaires. The emphasis on the possibility of affective (re)socialization also emphasized the need for diachronic studies that would illuminate the development of emotion vocabulary and affective repertoires. In addition, the discussions revealed the need for more conversational data that would show how emotional intersubjectivity or miscommunication develop in real time.

A particularly problematic aspect of the data collection procedure is translation and interpretation. Research shows that the back-translation procedure may result in erroneous translation equivalents of emotion terms (Goddard, 2002; Drennan, Levett, & Swartz, 1991) and that untrained interpreters translating emotionally charged conversations may commit a variety of errors, including addition, substitution, omission, condensation, paraphrasing, and misinterpretation of information (Bolton, 2002; Valdés, 2003; Vasquez & Javier, 1991). In fact, omissions and paraphrasing may not even be errors – oftentimes, these are strategic decisions made by inter-preters. An excellent example of such decision making is offered in a study conducted by Valdés (2003). The study examined communicative strategies of 25 Spanish–English bilingual teenagers between the ages of 14 and 17 who often served as translators for their families and friends. All but two were first-generation immigrant children. The participants were asked to translate a scripted interaction between an English-speaking principal and a Spanish-speaking mother. The interaction was tense because the school accused the woman's daughter of stealing, the mother attempted to defend her daughter, and in turn she accused the school of racism. To emulate challenges faced by translators in real-life situations, the script contained a number of face-threatening acts, including accusations, threats, contradic-tions, challenges, and insults, as well as explicit requests by the principal for the mother to calm down. The analysis of young interpreters' renditions showed that some remarks were omitted completely (such as the mother's references to the teacher as *vieja* (old bag)), and others were softened (for instance, *mugres* (junk, shit) was translated as 'stuff'). These translations demonstrated a high level of strategic competence in decision making in terms of what information to convey, omit, or mitigate. At the same time, the translations showed that informal community interpreters commonly take an editorial role in the translation process.

In the context of an interaction with the principal, this editorializing may be appropriate and helpful, but in the context of an ethnographic study it may be downright harmful. To minimize such interference, it is important to rely not simply on bilingual speakers but on *trained transla-tors and interpreters*, or at least to ensure interpreter training that would decrease the occurrence of addition, omission, substitution, and para-phrasing. Altarriba and Morier (2004) offer useful suggestions for inter-preter training in therapy and counseling contexts from the point of view of emotional communication. Bolton (2002) and Erzinger (1991) add to these suggestions through their analysis of intercultural communication and miscommunication between doctors and patients. Useful discussions of instrument translation, including bilingual committee approach, reliability, and validity testing, are contained in Bravo and associates (1993) and Drennan and associates (1991), who also focus on emotion concepts. All of these studies approach translation as a social phenomenon and as an important epistemological issue, deserving of attention and analysis. They expose weaknesses of such commonly accepted approaches as back-translation and offer numerous examples of difficulties in attaining semantic and conceptual equivalence of emotion terms.

Reporting

The fact that the field of emotion research lacks common criteria of what constitutes semantic and conceptual equivalence has important implications for research reporting. It puts the onus on researchers *to explicitly discuss their analytic choices* in terms of: (a) what counted as emotion and emotion-related words; (b) what counted as affective functions and structures (considering that the same structures often have both affective and non-affective functions); (c) what counted as evidence of semantic and conceptual equivalence or non-equivalence; (d) how and why particular translation choices were made (single word glosses, multiple word glosses, or phrases); (e) what counted as emotions and how they were defined and assessed, and (f) whether a lexicon study examined emotion lexicon of a particular language or a working lexicon of its speakers. Beginning researchers should be particularly aware of concerns raised by several scholars with regard to single-word glosses that imply semantic and conceptual equivalence (cf. Goddard, 2002), and of alternatives such as the use of multiple word glosses or phrases in rendering particular emotion words (cf. Lutz, 1988; Panayiotou, 2004a).

When the work in question is conducted in the researcher's second language, there also needs to be *an explicit reporting of researchers'* and *research assistants' linguistic proficiencies*, which would minimally include information on their language learning trajectories, contexts of language use, levels of L2 productive and receptive skills, and degree of L2 socialization. Exemplary descriptions of researchers' language competencies are offered in Bolton (2002: 99), Harvey (1992: 75–76, 82) and Zentella (1997: 7–8); useful discussions are also offered in ethnographic studies by Briggs (1970), Heider (1991), Levy (1973), Riesman (1977), and Feld (1990). These reports need to disclose whether communication between the researcher and participants took place in the researcher's L1, L2 or both. In the case of lesser-known languages, it is also important to disclose the amount and type of primary descriptive work available to the ethnographer, including grammars and dictionaries.

Even more extensive reporting needs to take place in linguistic, ethnographic, and psycholinguistic studies with bi- and multilingual informants and participants. These reports have to minimally include: sociobiographical data (age, gender, socioeconomic background, educational level, occupation); a detailed language history (age, context, and manner of acquisition for each language); information about language proficiency (what is the speaker's dominance? which language or languages are still being acquired? which may be undergoing the process of attrition?); language use (what are the functions of the respective languages in the speaker's daily life? what are the past and present patterns of language use, that is, which languages were/are used in which context or domain, with whom, and to what extent?); and language mode (how much time do participants spend in a monolingual mode, that is, speaking one language only? how much time is spent in a bilingual mode? how much code-switching and borrowing occurs in a bilingual mode? what mode were they in during the interviews or experiments in question?). (Excellent recommendations in this area are offered in Grosjean, 1998.)

Of particular importance here is the issue of *language proficiency*. As already mentioned earlier, self-evaluation of language proficiency is not a fully reliable approach because individuals often hold disparate assessment criteria and understandings of what is meant by 'fluent' and 'native-like.' Marian and Kaushanskaya's (2004) study also discredits language preference as an index of language proficiency. Their analysis revealed the lack of any significant relationship between participants' self-reported language preference and independent raters' judgments of their proficiency, accent, or dysfluency. This dissociation stems from the fact that L2 users living in the L2 context may confuse proficiency, dominance, preference, and high level of activation. Thus they report the L2 as their dominant or preferred language because, as the language of their immediate environment, it is highly activated and is often more effective in terms of lexical searches. From a linguistic (phonology, morphosyntax, lexical richness) point of view, however, they continue to be more proficient in the L1 and may appeal to L1 patterns in evaluating and producing emotional speech. A word of caution also needs to be offered on the use of dysfluency as an index of proficiency: In the context of emotional communication in the L2, it is not always clear whether the high degree of dysfluency reflects insufficient language proficiency or anxiety stemming from the topic of the conversation.

Considering the elusive nature of proficiency, it is best to evaluate it through a combination of independent raters' judgments and standardized tests and measures, such as morphological complexity or lexical richness. Where relevant, such an evaluation should also include the L1, as it may be subject to attrition. While this approach would not necessarily offer a 'true' measure of proficiency, it would nonetheless apply the same standard to all participants. Regardless of what measures the researcher finally settles on, best results on self-reports and independent raters' judgments will be achieved with the most detailed and concrete rating scales that offer expanded descriptions of each rating, while comparability across studies will be achieved through the use of standardized approaches to proficiency measurement. In ethnographic contexts and other cases where the use of standardized tests and measures is impossible, a combination of self-reports with a detailed description by the researcher of the participants' language competence and skills will have to suffice.

Standardized self-report or can-do scales, found to be reliable in the context of citizenship language testing, are available from the website of the Association of Language Testers in Europe (www.alte.org/can_do). Standardized guidelines for assessment of oral proficiency, created by the American Council of Teachers of Foreign Languages, are available from the website of Language Testing International (www.languagetesting.com/acad_opi.htm). Young and He (1998) offer an expanded discussion of this approach and provide useful recommendations on how to assess oral proficiency in the context of intercultural communication. Exemplary uses of independent raters' judgments are found in studies by Marian and Kaushanskaya (2004) and Schmid (2002). Schmid's (2002) study also offers an excellent example of triangulation of three measures: nativeness ratings, morphological complexity, and lexical richness. Dewaele and Pavlenko (2003) discuss measurement of lexical richness, otherwise known as lexical diversity, in stories elicited from bilingual speakers.

Data analysis

In terms of data analysis, the key procedure for interpretation of the data collected in the researcher's L2 is collaborative analysis, an approach promoted by Gumperz (1982a), who commonly played tapes back to participants, eliciting their interpretation of contextualization cues. In the process of *collaborative analysis*, data and interpretations are discussed with participants, informants, and native speakers of the language in question (Duranti, 1997; Everett, 2001; McLaughlin & Sall, 2001). While this type of feedback is valuable in any kind of ethnographic interpretive work, in the work conducted in the L2 it is critical. Native speakers should assist the researcher with a low level of L2 competence both in checking the transcripts of the recordings and in offering perceptions and interpretations of their own and others' performances.

This is not to say, however, that native speakers' interpretations should replace those of the ethnographer. It is worth remembering that informants do not have at their disposal the analytical tools available to scholars and that it is scholars who are responsible for final data analyses and interpretations. To do so to the best of their ability, scholars working in their L2 should collect interpretations and perceptions from several speakers independently and check them against each other. Everett (2001) also recommends group sessions, which increase opportunities for discussion and consensus and put peer pressure on individual language consultants to provide reflective, thoughtful answers. The group sessions, as well as the checking of interpretations with several speakers, ensure that on the one hand a subjective view of one informant would not dominate the data analysis, and on the other that tensions, discontinuities, and disagreements present in the speech community with regard to a particular emotion term or affective repertoire would be identified and further explored.

In the opening chapters of this book I have argued that as the world is becoming increasingly multilingual and multicultural, it is the height of scholarly irresponsibility to continue pretending that linguistic and psychological theories based on work with monolingual subjects and focusing on monolingual minds are sufficient and satisfactory to ensure scholarly progress and to satisfy ecological validity requirements. I hope that this book has contributed to the enterprise of factoring bilingualism both as a topic and a method in language and emotions research. I similarly hope that the dismantlement of old myths and the discussion of fresh perspectives will be useful for the fields of second language acquisition and bilingualism and compel a more rigorous and systematic approach to what is currently known as 'affective factors.'

Appendix A

Bilingualism and emotions webquestionnaire

INTERNATIONAL RESEARCH PROJECT: Bilingualism and Emotions

Preferences

Please choose one of the options listed below to indicate how you would prefer us to proceed with the information you supply

☑ Give you credit if we cite you in our work.

☐ Use your responses but to keep your name and other identifying information confidential.

☐ Use your responses in our analysis but not to quote them in any work that may appear in press.

Background Information

All information will be kept confidential. If you would rather not identify yourself, please use random initials and a number, e.g., AV38.

1. Name

2. Contact address (preferably e-mail)

3. Sex

4. Age

5. Education level (highest diploma or degree)

6. Which ethnic group/community do you belong to or most identify with

7. Occupation/Profession

8. Is your occupation related to your bilingualism or languages in any way

---

Linguistic information

9. Which **languages** do you know and what order did you learn them in? Was acquisition **naturalistic** (outside of school), **instructed** (at school), or both?

	Language	Age at which you started learning the language	Context of Acquisition
1st LANGUAGE (L1)			
2nd LANGUAGE (L2)			
3rd LANGUAGE (L3)			

4th LANGUAGE (L4) [   ] [▼] [▼]

5th LANGUAGE (L5) [   ] [▼] [▼]

10. Which do you consider to be your dominant language(s)? [   ]

11. What language(s) does your partner speak? [   ]

12. On the scale from 1 (least proficient) to 5 (fully fluent) how do you rate yourself in speaking, understanding, reading, writing in all of the languages in question

	Speaking	Comprehension	Reading	Writing
L1	[▼]	[▼]	[▼]	[▼]
L2	[▼]	[▼]	[▼]	[▼]
L3	[▼]	[▼]	[▼]	[▼]
L4	[▼]	[▼]	[▼]	[▼]
L5	[▼]	[▼]	[▼]	[▼]

13. How frequently do you use each of the languages and with whom? Never=0, every year=1, every month=2, every week=3, every day=4, several hours a day=5)

	With whom		Frequency
L1	[▼]		[▼]
L2	[▼]		[▼]
L3	[▼]		[▼]
L4	[▼]		[▼]
L5	[▼]		[▼]

14. Which language (s) do you use for mental calculations/arithmetic? (Click where appropriate)

	Never	Rarely	Sometimes	Frequently	All the time	Not applicable
L1	☐	☐	☐	☐	☐	☑
L2	☐	☐	☐	☐	☐	☑
L3	☐	☐	☐	☐	☐	☑
L4	☐	☐	☐	☐	☐	☑
L5	☐	☐	☐	☐	☐	☑

15. Do you switch between languages within a conversation with certain people? (Click where appropriate)

	Never	Rarely	Sometimes	Frequently	All the time	Not applicable
When speaking with friends and family	☐	☐	☐	☐	☐	☑
When speaking with strangers	☐	☐	☐	☐	☐	☑
When speaking in public	☐	☐	☐	☐	☐	☑
At work	☐	☐	☐	☐	☐	☑

16. Do you switch between languages when talking about certain matters? (Click where appropriate)

	Never	Rarely	Sometimes	Frequently	All the time	Not applicable
When speaking about neutral matters	☐	☐	☐	☐	☐	☑
When speaking about personal matters	☐	☐	☐	☐	☐	☑
When speaking about emotional matters	☐	☐	☐	☐	☐	☑

If you have **no** children click here ☐ and go to **question 20**

17. If you have children, what language do you typically use with:

a) the oldest? (Click where appropriate)

	Never	Rarely	Sometimes	Frequently	All the time	Not applicable
L1	☐	☐	☐	☐	☐	☑
L2	☐	☐	☐	☐	☐	☑
L3	☐	☐	☐	☐	☐	☑
L4	☐	☐	☐	☐	☐	☑
L5	☐	☐	☐	☐	☐	☑

b) the youngest? (Click where appropriate)

	Never	Rarely	Sometimes	Frequently	All the time	Not applicable
L1	☐	☐	☐	☐	☐	☑
L2	☐	☐	☐	☐	☐	☑
L3	☐	☐	☐	☐	☐	☑
L4	☐	☐	☐	☐	☐	☑
L5	☐	☐	☐	☐	☐	☑

18. What language do you favor in scolding or disciplining them? (Click where appropriate)

	Never	Rarely	Sometimes	Frequently	All the time	Not applicable
L1	☐	☐	☐	☐	☐	☑
L2	☐	☐	☐	☐	☐	☑
L3	☐	☐	☐	☐	☐	☑
L4	☐	☐	☐	☐	☐	☑
L5	☐	☐	☐	☐	☐	☑

19. What language do you select for praise and/or intimate conversations with them? (Click where appropriate)

	Never	Rarely	Sometimes	Frequently	All the time	Not applicable
L1	☐	☐	☐	☐	☐	☑
L2	☐	☐	☐	☐	☐	☑
L3	☐	☐	☐	☐	☐	☑
L4	☐	☐	☐	☐	☐	☑
L5	☐	☐	☐	☐	☐	☑

Languages and Emotions

20. Here are some **subjective statements** about the languages you know. Please mark to what extent they correspond to your own perceptions. There are no right or wrong answers. (Click where appropriate)

Which is your first language? [   ]

	Not at all	somewhat	More or less	To a large extent	Absolutely	Not applicable
My L1 is useful	☐	☐	☐	☐	☐	☑
My L1 is colourful	☐	☐	☐	☐	☐	☑
My L1 is rich	☐	☐	☐	☐	☐	☑
My L1 is poetic	☐	☐	☐	☐	☐	☑
My L1 is emotional	☐	☐	☐	☐	☐	☑
My L1 is cold	☐	☐	☐	☐	☐	☑

Which is your 2nd language? [   ]

	Not at all	somewhat	More or less	To a large extent	Absolutely	Not applicable
My L2 is useful	☐	☐	☐	☐	☐	☑
My L2 is colourful	☐	☐	☐	☐	☐	☑
My L2 is rich	☐	☐	☐	☐	☐	☑
My L2 is poetic	☐	☐	☐	☐	☐	☑
My L2 is emotional	☐	☐	☐	☐	☐	☑
My L2 is cold	☐	☐	☐	☐	☐	☑

Which is your 3rd language? [   ]

	Not at all	somewhat	More or less	To a large extent	Absolutely	Not applicable
My L3 is useful	☐	☐	☐	☐	☐	☑
My L3 is colourful	☐	☐	☐	☐	☐	☑
My L3 is rich	☐	☐	☐	☐	☐	☑
My L3 is poetic	☐	☐	☐	☐	☐	☑
My L3 is emotional	☐	☐	☐	☐	☐	☑
My L3 is cold	☐	☐	☐	☐	☐	☑

Which is your 4th language? [   ]

	Not at all	somewhat	More or less	To a large extent	Absolutely	Not applicable
My L4 is useful	☐	☐	☐	☐	☐	☑
My L4 is colourful	☐	☐	☐	☐	☐	☑
My L4 is rich	☐	☐	☐	☐	☐	☑
My L4 is poetic	☐	☐	☐	☐	☐	☑

	Not at all	somewhat	More or less	To a large extent	Absolutely	Not applicable
My L4 is emotional	☐	☐	☐	☐	☐	☑
My L4 is cold	☐	☐	☐	☐	☐	☑

Which is your 5th language? [_____]

	Not at all	somewhat	More or less	To a large extent	Absolutely	Not applicable
My L5 is useful	☐	☐	☐	☐	☐	☑
My L5 is colourful	☐	☐	☐	☐	☐	☑
My L5 is rich	☐	☐	☐	☐	☐	☑
My L5 is poetic	☐	☐	☐	☐	☐	☑
My L5 is emotional	☐	☐	☐	☐	☐	☑
My L5 is cold	☐	☐	☐	☐	☐	☑

21. If you are **angry**, what language do you typically use to express your anger? (Click where appropriate)

a) When alone

	Never	Rarely	Sometimes	Frequently	All the time	Not applicable
L1	☐	☐	☐	☐	☐	☑
L2	☐	☐	☐	☐	☐	☑
L3	☐	☐	☐	☐	☐	☑
L4	☐	☐	☐	☐	☐	☑
L5	☐	☐	☐	☐	☐	☑

b) In letters and e-mail

	Never	Rarely	Sometimes	Frequently	All the time	Not applicable
L1	☐	☐	☐	☐	☐	☑
L2	☐	☐	☐	☐	☐	☑
L3	☐	☐	☐	☐	☐	☑
L4	☐	☐	☐	☐	☐	☑
L5	☐	☐	☐	☐	☐	☑

c) When talking to friends

	Never	Rarely	Sometimes	Frequently	All the time	Not applicable
L1	☐	☐	☐	☐	☐	☑
L2	☐	☐	☐	☐	☐	☑
L3	☐	☐	☐	☐	☐	☑
L4	☐	☐	☐	☐	☐	☑
L5	☐	☐	☐	☐	☐	☑

d) When talking to parents/partners

	Never	Rarely	Sometimes	Frequently	All the time	Not applicable
L1	☐	☐	☐	☐	☐	☑
L2	☐	☐	☐	☐	☐	☑

L3 ☐   ☐   ☐   ☐   ☐   ☑
L4 ☐   ☐   ☐   ☐   ☐   ☑
L5 ☐   ☐   ☐   ☐   ☐   ☑

e) When talking to strangers

	Never	Rarely	Sometimes	Frequently	All the time	Not applicable
L1	☐	☐	☐	☐	☐	☑
L2	☐	☐	☐	☐	☐	☑
L3	☐	☐	☐	☐	☐	☑
L4	☐	☐	☐	☐	☐	☑
L5	☐	☐	☐	☐	☐	☑

---

22. If you **swear** in general, what language do you typically swear in? (Click where appropriate)

	Never	Rarely	Sometimes	Frequently	All the time	Not applicable
L1	☐	☐	☐	☐	☐	☑
L2	☐	☐	☐	☐	☐	☑
L3	☐	☐	☐	☐	☐	☑
L4	☐	☐	☐	☐	☐	☑
L5	☐	☐	☐	☐	☐	☑

---

23. Do **swear** and **taboo words** in your different languages have the same **emotional weight** for you? (Click where appropriate)

	Not strong	Little	Fairly	Strong	Very strong	Not applicable
L1	☐	☐	☐	☐	☐	☑
L2	☐	☐	☐	☐	☐	☑
L3	☐	☐	☐	☐	☐	☑
L4	☐	☐	☐	☐	☐	☑
L5	☐	☐	☐	☐	☐	☑

---

24. What language do you express your **deepest feelings** in? (Click where appropriate)

a) When alone

	Never	Maybe	Probably	Certainly	Without any doubt	Not applicable
L1	☐	☐	☐	☐	☐	☑
L2	☐	☐	☐	☐	☐	☑
L3	☐	☐	☐	☐	☐	☑
L4	☐	☐	☐	☐	☐	☑
L5	☐	☐	☐	☐	☐	☑

b) In letters and e-mail

	Never	Maybe	Probably	Certainly	Without any doubt	Not applicable
L1	☐	☐	☐	☐	☐	☑
L2	☐	☐	☐	☐	☐	☑
L3	☐	☐	☐	☐	☐	☑

L4	☐	☐	☐	☐	☐	☒
L5	☐	☐	☐	☐	☐	☒

c) When talking to friends

	Never	Maybe	Probably	Certainly	Without any doubt	Not applicable
L1	☐	☐	☐	☐	☐	☒
L2	☐	☐	☐	☐	☐	☒
L3	☐	☐	☐	☐	☐	☒
L4	☐	☐	☐	☐	☐	☒
L5	☐	☐	☐	☐	☐	☒

d) When talking to parents/partners

	Never	Maybe	Probably	Certainly	Without any doubt	Not applicable
L1	☐	☐	☐	☐	☐	☒
L2	☐	☐	☐	☐	☐	☒
L3	☐	☐	☐	☐	☐	☒
L4	☐	☐	☐	☐	☐	☒
L5	☐	☐	☐	☐	☐	☒

25. How **anxious** are you when speaking your different languages with different people in different situations? (Click where appropriate)

	Not at all	A little	Quite anxious	Very anxious	Extremely anxious	Not applicable
When speaking L1 with friends	☐	☐	☐	☐	☐	☒
When speaking L1 with colleagues	☐	☐	☐	☐	☐	☒
When speaking L1 with strangers	☐	☐	☐	☐	☐	☒
When speaking L1 on the telephone	☐	☐	☐	☐	☐	☒
When speaking L1 in public	☐	☐	☐	☐	☐	☒

	Not at all	A little	Quite anxious	Very anxious	Extremely anxious	Not applicable
When speaking L2 with friends	☐	☐	☐	☐	☐	☒
When speaking L2 with colleagues	☐	☐	☐	☐	☐	☒
When speaking L2 with strangers	☐	☐	☐	☐	☐	☒
When speaking L2 on the telephone	☐	☐	☐	☐	☐	☒
When speaking L2 in public	☐	☐	☐	☐	☐	☒

	Not at all	A little	Quite anxious	Very anxious	Extremely anxious	Not applicable
When speaking L3 with friends	☐	☐	☐	☐	☐	☒
When speaking L3 with colleagues	☐	☐	☐	☐	☐	☒

	Not at all	A little	Quite anxious	Very anxious	Extremely anxious	Not applicable
When speaking L3 with strangers	☐	☐	☐	☐	☐	☐
When speaking L3 on the telephone	☐	☐	☐	☐	☐	☐
When speaking L3 in public	☐	☐	☐	☐	☐	☐

	Not at all	A little	Quite anxious	Very anxious	Extremely anxious	Not applicable
When speaking L4 with friends	☐	☐	☐	☐	☐	☐
When speaking L4 with colleagues	☐	☐	☐	☐	☐	☐
When speaking L4 with strangers	☐	☐	☐	☐	☐	☐
When speaking L4 on the telephone	☐	☐	☐	☐	☐	☐
When speaking L4 in public	☐	☐	☐	☐	☐	☐

	Not at all	A little	Quite anxious	Very anxious	Extremely anxious	Not applicable
When speaking L5 with friends	☐	☐	☐	☐	☐	☐
When speaking L5 with colleagues	☐	☐	☐	☐	☐	☐
When speaking L5 with strangers	☐	☐	☐	☐	☐	☐
When speaking L5 on the telephone	☐	☐	☐	☐	☐	☐
When speaking L5 in public	☐	☐	☐	☐	☐	☐

26. If you form sentences silently **(inner speech)**, what language do you typically use? (Click where appropriate)

	Never	Really	Sometimes	Frequently	All the time	Not applicable
L1	☐	☐	☐	☐	☐	☐
L2	☐	☐	☐	☐	☐	☐
L3	☐	☐	☐	☐	☐	☐
L4	☐	☐	☐	☐	☐	☐
L5	☐	☐	☐	☐	☐	☐

27. Does the phrase **"I love you"** have the same emotional weight for you in your different language Which language does it feel strongest in?

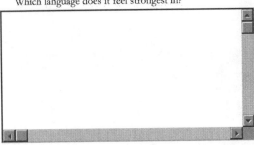

28. Do you have a **preference** for emotion terms and terms of endearment in one language over all others? Which language is it and why?

29. Do your languages have different **emotional significance** for you? if yes, then how do you see this significance for each language? Is one more appropriate as the language of your emotions than others?

30. If you do write in a **personal diary** - or were to write in one - what language(s) do you or would you use and why?

31. If you were to recall some **bad or difficult memories**, what language would you prefer to discuss them in and why?

32. If you are married to or living with a speaker of a language that is not your L1, what language do you generally use at home? What language do you **argue** in?

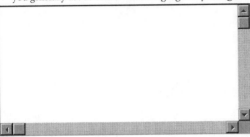

33. Do you feel like a **different person** sometimes when you use your different languages?

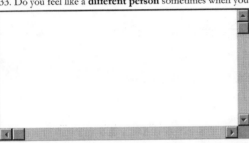

34. Is it easier or more difficult for you to **talk about emotional topics** in your second or third language? If there is a difference, could you tell us about that and perhaps provide some examples?

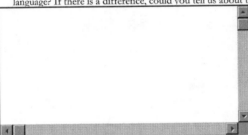

35. Do you have any other **comments** and/or suggestions for the authors of this questionnaire?

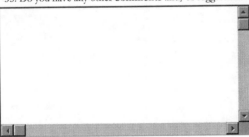

Appendix B

Transcription conventions

one line	one intonation phrase
[line	
[line	overlapped utterances
↘	falling pitch
line.	final pitch falling to low
line!	final pitch falling to low from high starting point
line;	final pitch falling slightly
line -	final level pitch
line,	final pitch rising slightly
↗	rising pitch
line?	final pitch rising to high
↘↗	fall-rise
↗↘	rise-fall
{l}	low register
{h}	high register
↑ word	noticeable step-up in pitch
↓ word	noticeable step-down in pitch
wo::rd	lengthened sound or syllable
WORD	loud volume
WORD	very loud volume
°word°	soft volume
FRIday	word stress
word	stress
<u>WORD</u>	emphatic stress
(h)	breathiness
.hhh	inbreath
hhh	outbreath
(.)	brief pause
(1.0)	measured pause

Based on Couper-Kuhlen (2001), McCarthy (1991).

References

Abelin, Å. & J. Allwood (2000) *Crosslinguistic interpretation of emotional prosody*. Proceedings of the ISCA Workshop on Speech and Emotion, Belfast, 2000. Retrieved at http://www.qub.ac.uk/en/isca/proceedings on August 3, 2004.

Abelin, Å. & J. Allwood (2002) *Crosslinguistic interpretation of emotional prosody*. Gothenburg Papers in Theoretical Linguistics 87, Department of Linguistics, University of Goteborg. Retrieved at http://www.ling.gu.se/~jens/publications/index.html on August 3, 2004.

Abu-Lughod, L. (1986) *Veiled sentiments: Honor and poetry in a Bedouin society*. Berkeley, CA: University of California Press.

Abu-Lughod, L. & C. Lutz (1990) Introduction: Emotion, discourse, and the politics of everyday life. In Lutz, C. & L. Abu-Lughod (eds.) *Language and the politics of emotion*. Cambridge: Cambridge University Press, pp. 1–23.

Albas, D., McCluskey, K. & Ch. Albas (1976) Perception of the emotional content of speech: A comparison of two Canadian groups. *Journal of Cross-Cultural Psychology*, 7, 4, 481–490.

Altarriba, J. (2003) Does *cariño* equal 'liking'? A theoretical approach to conceptual nonequivalence between languages. *International Journal of Bilingualism*, 7, 3, 305–322.

Altarriba, J. & L. Bauer (2004) The distinctiveness of emotion concepts: A comparison between emotion, abstract, and concrete words. *American Journal of Psychology*, 117, 389–410.

Altarriba, J., Bauer, L. & C. Benvenuto (1999) Concreteness, context availability, and imageability ratings and word associations for abstract, concrete, and emotion words. *Behavior Research Methods, Instruments, and Computers*, 31, 4, 578–602.

Altarriba, J. & T. Canary (2004) The influence of emotional arousal on affective priming in monolingual and bilingual speakers. *Journal of Multilingual and Multicultural Development*, 25, 2/3, 248–265.

Altarriba, J. & R. Morier (2004) Bilingualism: Language, emotion, and mental health. In Bhatia, T. & W. Ritchie (eds.) *The handbook of bilingualism*. Malden, MA: Blackwell, pp. 250–280.

Altarriba, J. & A. Santiago-Rivera (1994) Current perspectives on using linguistic and cultural factors in counseling the Hispanic client. *Professional Psychology: Research and Practice*, 25, 4, 388–397.

Altarriba, J., Santiago-Rivera, A., Poll, N. & N. Gonzalez (2004) *The development of cultural competencies: Linguistics, culture, and emotion in the counseling domain.* Invited talk presented at Columbia University.

Altmann, H. H. (1992) *Muttersprache: Heimat der Heimatslosen* (Mother tongue: Home of the Homeless). Balleschweil: Verlag Grub Nachf.

Amati-Mehler, J., Argentieri, S. & J. Canestri (1993) *The Babel of the unconscious: Mother tongue and foreign languages in the psychoanalytic dimension.* Translated from Italian by J. Whitelaw-Cucco. Madison, CT: International Universities Press.

Anastasi, A. & F. Cordova (1953) Some effects of bilingualism upon the intelligence test performance of Puerto Rican children in New York City. *Journal of Educational Psychology*, 44, 1–19.

Anderson, B. (1991) *Imagined communities.* London/New York: Verso.

Andrews, D. (1994) The Russian color categories *sinij* and *goluboj*: An experimental analysis of their interpretation in the standard and emigré languages. *Journal of Slavic Linguistics*, 2, 1, 9–28.

Andrews, D. (1999) *Sociocultural perspectives on language change in diaspora: Soviet immigrants in the United States.* Amsterdam/Philadelphia: John Benjamins.

Anooshian, L. & P. Hertel (1994) Emotionality in free recall: Specificity in bilingual memory. *Cognition and Emotion*, 8, 6, 503–514.

Aragno, A. & P. Schlachet (1996) Accessibility of early experience through the language of origin: A theoretical integration. *Psychoanalytic Psychology*, 13, 1, 23–34.

Araki, H. (1994) *Nihongo ga mieru to eigo mo mieru: shin eigo kyouiku ron* (Once you understand Japanese, you will understand English, too: A new theory for English education). Tokyo: Chuo Couron Sha.

Arndt, H. & R. Janney (1985a) Improving emotive communication. *Per Linguam*, 1, 21–30.

Arndt, H. & R. Janney (1985b) Politeness revisited. *International Review of Applied Linguistics*, 23, 281–300.

Arndt, H. & R. Janney (1991) Verbal, prosodic, and kinesic emotive contrasts in speech. *Journal of Pragmatics*, 15, 521–549.

Arnold, J. (ed.) (1999) *Affect in language learning.* Cambridge: Cambridge University Press.

Aronin, L. (2004) Multilinguality and emotions: Emotional experiences and language attitudes of trilingual immigrant students in Israel. *Estudios de Sociolingüística*, 5, 1, 59–81.

Arsenian, S. (1937) *Bilingualism and mental development: A study of the intelligence and the social background of bilingual children in New York.* New York: Teachers College, Columbia University.

Arsenian, S. (1945) Bilingualism in the post-war world. *Psychological Bulletin*, 42, 2, 65–86.

Athanasiadou, A. & E. Tabakowska (eds.) (1998) *Speaking of emotions: Conceptualization and expression.* Berlin/New York: Mouton de Gruyter.

Auer, P. (1998) *Code-switching in conversation: Language, interaction, and identity.* London/New York: Routledge.

Averill, J. (1982) *Anger and aggression: An essay on emotion.* New York/Berlin: Springer-Verlag.

Avery, P. & S. Ehrlich (1992) *Teaching American English pronunciation.* New York/Oxford: Oxford University Press.

Baetens Beardsmore, H. (1982) *Bilingualism: Basic principles.* Clevedon, UK: Multilingual Matters.

Bailey, K. (1983) Competitiveness and anxiety in adult second language learning: Looking at and through the diary studies. In H. Seliger & M. Long (eds.) *Classroom-oriented research in second language acquisition.* Rowley, MA: Newbury House, pp. 67–102.

Baker, C. (1992) *Attitudes and language.* Clevedon, UK: Multilingual Matters.

Baker, C. (2000) *A parents' and teachers' guide to bilingualism.* 2nd edition. Clevedon, UK: Multilingual Matters.

Baker, C. (2001) *Foundations of bilingual education and bilingualism.* 3rd edition. Clevedon, UK: Multilingual Matters.

Baker, C. & S. Prys Jones (1997) *Encyclopedia of bilingualism and bilingual education.* Clevedon, UK: Multilingual Matters.

Bamberg, M. (1997) Language, concepts, and emotions: The role of language in the construction of emotions. *Language Sciences,* 19, 4, 309–340.

Banse, R. & K. Scherer (1996) Acoustic profiles in vocal emotion expression. *Journal of Personality and Social Psychology,* 70, 3, 614–636.

Barsalou, L. & D. Medin (1986) Concepts: Fixed definitions or dynamic context-dependent representations? *Cahiers de Psychologie Cognitive,* 6, 187–202.

Bartlett, F. (1932; reissued in 1995) *Remembering: A study in experimental and social psychology.* Cambridge, UK: Cambridge University Press.

Bayley, R. & S. Schecter (eds.) (2003) *Language socialization in bilingual and multilingual societies.* Clevedon, UK: Multilingual Matters.

Beaujour, E. (1989) *Alien tongues: Bilingual Russian writers of the "first" emigration.* Ithaca, NY: Cornell University Press.

Beier, E. & A. Zautra (1972) Identification of vocal communication of emotions across cultures. *Journal of Consulting and Clinical Psychology,* 39, 1, 166.

Berlin, B. & P. Kay (1969) *Basic color terms: Their universality and evolution.* Berkeley, CA: University of California Press.

Besemeres, M. (2002) *Translating one's self.* Oxford/New York: Peter Lang.

Besemeres, M. (2004) Different languages, different emotions? Perspectives from autobiographical literature. *Journal of Multilingual and Multicultural Development,* 25, 2/3, 140–158.

Besnier, N. (1990) Language and affect. *Annual Review of Anthropology,* 19, 419–451.

Besnier, N. (1995) *Literacy, emotion, and authority: Reading and writing on a Polynesian atoll.* UK: Cambridge University Press.

Bhatia, T. & W. Ritchie (eds.) (2004) *The handbook of bilingualism.* Malden, MA: Blackwell.

Bhimji, F. (1997) *!Mueve la almohada! !Levante la cara!* (Move the pillow! Lift your head!): An analysis of correction talk in Mexican and Central American parent-child interaction. *Issues in Applied Linguistics,* 8, 2, 133–145.

Bialystok, E. (2001) *Bilingualism in development: Language, literacy, and cognition.* Cambridge: Cambridge University Press.

Birdsong, D. (1992) Ultimate attainment in second language acquisition. *Language,* 68, 706–755.

Birdsong, D. (ed.) (1999) *Second language acquisition and the Critical Period Hypothesis.* Mahwah, NJ: Lawrence Erlbaum.

Bloch, Ch. (1996) Emotions and discourse. *Text,* 16, 3, 323–341.

Block, D. & D. Cameron (eds.) (2002) *Globalization and language teaching.* London/New York: Routledge.

Blunkett, D. (2002) *Integration with diversity: Globalisation and the renewal of democracy and civil society.* The Foreign Policy Centre. Retrieved at http://fpc.org.uk/articles/182 on August 2, 2004.

Bolinger, D. (1985) The inherent iconism of intonation. In J. Haiman (ed.) *Iconicity in syntax.* Amsterdam: Benjamins, pp. 97–108.

Bollag, B. (2002) Silenced minority: In Turkey, Kurds are arrested for trying to study their own language. *The Chronicle of Higher Education,* July 19, p. A34.

Bolton, J. (2002) The third presence: A psychiatrist's experience of working with non-English speaking patients and interpreters. *Transcultural Psychiatry,* 39, 1, 97–114.

Bonaparte, M. (1945) Notes on the analytic discovery of a primal scene. *The Psychoanalytic Study of the Child,* 1, 119–125.

Bond, M. & T.-M. Lai (1986) Embarrassment and code-switching into a second language. *Journal of Social Psychology,* 126, 2, 179–186.

Bongaerts, T. (1999) Ultimate attainment in L2 pronunciation: The case of very advanced late L2 learners. In D. Birdsong (ed.) *Second language acquisition and the Critical Period Hypothesis.* Mahwah, NJ: Lawrence Erlbaum, pp. 133–159.

Bongaerts, T., van Summeren, C., Planken, B. & E. Schils (1997) Age and ultimate attainment in the pronunciation of a foreign language. *Studies in Second Language Acquisition,* 19, 447–465.

Bossard, J. (1945) The bilingual as a person – linguistic identification with status. *American Sociological Review,* 10, 6, 699–709.

Boucher, J. (1979) Culture and emotion. In Marsella, A., Tharp, R. & T. Ciborowski (eds.) *Perspectives on cross-cultural psychology.* San Diego, CA: Academic Press, pp. 159–178.

Bourdieu, P. (1991) *Language and symbolic power.* Cambridge: Polity Press.

Brandt, M. & J. Boucher (1986) Concepts of depression in emotion lexicon of eight cultures. *International Journal of Intercultural Relations,* 10, 321–346.

Bravo, M., Woodbury-Fariña, M., Canino, G. & M. Rubio-Stipec (1993) The Spanish translation and cultural adaptation of the diagnostic interview schedule for children (DISC) in Puerto-Rico. *Culture, Medicine, and Psychiatry,* 17, 3, 329–344.

Brazil, D. C. (1997) *The communicative value of intonation in English.* Cambridge: Cambridge University Press.

Breitborde, L. (1998) *Speaking and social identity: English in the lives of urban Africans.* Berlin/New York: Mouton de Gruyter.

Bremer, K., Roberts, C., Vasseur, M.-T., Simonot, M. & P. Broeder (1996) *Achieving understanding: Discourse in intercultural encounters.* Harlow: Longman.

Breuer, J. & S. Freud (1895/1955) Studies on hysteria. *Standard Edition,* 2. London: Hogarth Press.

Briggs, J. (1970) *Never in anger: Portrait of an Eskimo family.* Cambridge, MA: Harvard University Press.

Brison, S. (2002) *Aftermath: Violence and the remaking of a self.* Princeton/Oxford: Princeton University Press.

Brown, D. (1987) *Principles of language learning and teaching.* 2nd edition. Englewood Cliffs, NJ: Prentice Hall.

Bucci, W. (1982) The vocalization of painful affect. *Journal of Communication Disorders,* 15, 415–440.

Burling, R. (1984) *Learning a field language.* Ann Arbor: U of Michigan Press.

Buxbaum, E. (1949) The role of a second language in the formation of ego and superego. *Psychoanalytic Quarterly,* 18, 279–289.

Cacioppo, J. & W. Gardner (1999) Emotion. *Annual Review of Psychology,* 50, 191–214.

Caffi, C. & R. Janney (1994) Towards a pragmatics of emotive communication. *Journal of Pragmatics,* 22, 325–373.

Capps, L. & E. Ochs (1995) *Constructing panic: The discourse of agoraphobia.* Cambridge, MA: Harvard University Press.

Carrasquillo, A. & V. Rodríguez (2002) *Language minority students in the mainstream classroom.* 2nd edition. Clevedon, UK: Multilingual Matters.

Carrillo, M. & I. Kim (2003) *The relationship between coordinate bilingualism and the production of affect.* Poster presented at the American Psychological Society conference, May 30, 2003.

Carroll, J. (1962) The prediction of success in intensive foreign language training. In R. Glazer (ed.) *Training, research, and education.* Pittsburgh: University of Pittsburgh Press.

Caskey-Sirmons, L. & Hickerson, N. (1977) Semantic shift and bilingualism: Variation in color terms of five languages. *Anthropological Linguistics,* 19, 358–367.

Cenoz, J., Hufeisen, B. & U. Jessner (eds.) (2001) *Cross-linguistic influence in third language acquisition: Psycholinguistic perspectives.* Clevedon, UK: Multilingual Matters.

Cenoz, J., Hufeisen, B. & U. Jessner (eds.) (2003) *The multilingual lexicon.* Dordrecht: Kluwer Academic Publishers.

Chafe, W. (2003) Laughing while talking. In D. Tannen & J. Alatis (eds.) *Georgetown University Round Table on Languages and Linguistics* 2001. Washington, DC: Georgetown University Press, pp. 36–49.

Chastain, K. (1975) Affective and ability factors in second language acquisition. *Language Learning,* 25, 153–161.

Chiarandini, I. (1999) *Listen to my mother tongue: Creating an affective truth through bilingualism.* Paper presented at the 41st Congress of the International Psychoanalytical Association, Santiago de Chile, 26 July 1999. [For a summary, see Reppen, J. (2000) Development of affect in bilingual patients. *The International Journal of Psychoanalysis,* 81, 1, 153–155.]

Child, I. (1943) *Italian or American? The second generation in conflict.* New Haven: Yale University Press.

Choi, J. (2002) Blending oil into water: Making the invisible visible and giving voice to the silenced. In Tochon, F. (ed.) *The foreign self: Truth telling as educational inquiry.* Madison, WI: Atwood Publishing, pp. 31–61.

Church, T., Katigbak, M., Reyes, J. & S. Jensen (1998) Language and organization of Filipino emotion concepts: Comparing emotion concepts and dimensions across cultures. *Cognition and Emotion*, 12, 1, 63–92.

Clancy, P. (1999) The socialization of affect in Japanese mother-child conversation. *Journal of Pragmatics*, 31, 1397–1421.

Clarke, M. (1976) Second language acquisition as a clash of consciousness. *Language Learning*, 26, 2, 377–390.

Clifford, J. (1997) *Routes: Travel and translation in the twentieth century*. Cambridge: Harvard University Press.

Clore, G., Ortony, A. & M. Foss (1987) The psychological foundations of the affective lexicon. *Journal of Personality and Social Psychology*, 53, 751–766.

Connor-Linton, J., Taylor, C., Landolfi, L. & M. Seki (1987) Soviet and American expression of personal involvement: Some implications for cross-cultural and cross-gender communication. *Multilingua*, 6, 3, 257–286.

Constantinidou, E. (1994) The 'death' of East Sutherland Gaelic: Death by women? In P. Burton, K. Dyson, & Sh. Ardener (eds.) *Bilingual women: Anthropological approaches to second-language use*. Oxford/Providence: Berg, pp. 111–127.

Cook, V. (1991) The poverty of the stimulus argument and multicompetence. *Second Language Research*, 7, 2, 103–117.

Cook, V. (1992) Evidence for multicompetence. *Language Learning*, 42, 4, 557–591.

Cook, V. (1999) Going beyond the native speaker in language teaching. *TESOL Quarterly*, 33, 185–209.

Cook, V. (ed.) (2002) *Portraits of the L2 user*. Clevedon, UK: Multilingual Matters.

Cook, V. (ed.) (2003) *Effects of the second language on the first*. Clevedon, UK: Multilingual Matters.

Coppieters, R. (1987) Competence differences between native and non-native speakers. *Language*, 63, 544–573.

Cosmides, L. (1983) Invariances in the acoustic expression of emotion during speech. *Journal of Experimental Psychology: Human Perception and Performance*, 9, 6, 864–881.

Coulmas, F. (ed.) (1981) *A Festschrift for native speaker*. The Hague: Mouton.

Couper-Kuhlen, E. (1986) *An introduction to English prosody*. London: Edward Arnold.

Couper-Kuhlen, E. (2001) Intonation and discourse: Current views from within. In Schiffrin, D., Tannen, D. & H. Hamilton (eds.) *The handbook of discourse analysis*. Malden, MA: Blackwell, pp. 13–34.

Cruttenden, A. (1997) *Intonation*. Second ed. New York: Cambridge University Press.

Curran, Ch. (1976) *Counseling-learning in second languages*. Apple River, IL: Apple River Press.

Damasio, A. (1989) Concepts in the brain. *Mind and Language*, 4, 1/2, 24–28.

Damasio, A. (1994) *Descartes' error: Emotion, reason, and the human brain*. New York: Putnam.

Damasio, A. (1999) *The feeling of what happens: Body and emotion in the making of consciousness*. New York: Harcourt Brace.

Damasio, A. (2003) *Looking for Spinoza: Joy, sorrow and the feeling brain*. New York: Harcourt Brace.

Davidson, C. (1993) *36 views of Mount Fuji: On finding myself in Japan*. New York: Plume/Penguin.

Davitz, J. (1964) *The communication of emotional meaning.* New York: McGraw-Hill.

Davitz, J. (1969) *The language of emotion.* New York/London: Academic Press.

De Courtivron, I. (ed.) (2003) *Lives in translation: Bilingual writers on identity and creativity.* New York: Palgrave Macmillan.

De Klerk, V. (2001) The cross-marriage language dilemma: His language or hers? *International Journal of Bilingual Education and Bilingualism,* 4, 3, 197–216.

Del Castillo, J. (1970) The influence of language upon symptomatology in foreign-born patients. *American Journal of Psychiatry,* 127, 2, 160–162.

Dewaele, J.-M. (2002a) Psychological and sociodemographic correlates of communicative anxiety in L2 and L3 production. *International Journal of Bilingualism,* 6, 1, 23–38.

Dewaele, J.-M. (2002b) Individual differences in L2 fluency: The effect of neurobiological correlates. In V. Cook (ed.) *Portraits of the L2 user.* Clevedon, UK: Multilingual Matters, pp. 221–249.

Dewaele, J.-M. (2004a) The emotional force of swearwords and taboo words in the speech of multilinguals. *Journal of Multilingual and Multicultural Development,* 25, 2/3, 204–222.

Dewaele, J.-M. (2004b) Blistering barnacles! What language do multilinguals swear in?! *Estudios de Sociolingüística,* 5, 1, 83–105.

Dewaele, J.-M. (2004c) Perceived language dominance and language preference for emotional speech: The implications for attrition research. In M. Schmid, B. Köpke, M. Kejser & L. Weilemar (eds.) *First language attrition: Interdisciplinary perspectives on methodological issues.* Amsterdam/Philadelphia: John Benjamins, pp. 81–104.

Dewaele, J.-M. (in press) Expressing anger in multiple languages. In A. Pavlenko (ed.) *Bilingual minds: Emotional experience, expression, and representation.* Clevedon, UK: Multilingual Matters.

Dewaele, J.-M. & A. Furnham (1999) Extraversion: The unloved variable in applied linguistic research. *Language Learning,* 49, 3, 509–544.

Dewaele, J.-M. & A. Furnham (2000) Personality and speech production: A pilot study of second language learners. *Personality and Individual Differences,* 28, 355–365.

Dewaele, J.-M. & A. Pavlenko (2001–2003) Webquestionnaire *Bilingualism and emotions.* University of London. http://www.bbk.ac.uk/llc/biling+emotions/questionnaire.html

Dewaele, J.-M. & A. Pavlenko (2002) Emotion vocabulary in interlanguage. *Language Learning,* 52, 2, 265–324.

Dewaele, J.-M. & A. Pavlenko (2003) Productivity and lexical diversity in native and non-native speech: A study of cross-cultural effects. In Cook, V. (ed.) *Effects of the second language on the first.* Clevedon, UK: Multilingual Matters, pp. 120–141.

Diebold, R. (1968) The consequences of early bilingualism in cognitive development and personality formation. In E. Norbeck, D. Price-Williams & M. McCord (eds.) *The study of personality: An interdisciplinary approach.* New York: Holt, Rinehart & Winston, pp. 218–245.

Doi, T. (1973) *The anatomy of dependence.* Tokyo: Kodansha International.

Dörnyei, Z. (2001) New themes and approaches in second language motivation research. *Annual Review of Applied Linguistics,* 21, 43–59.

Drennan, G., Levett, A. & L. Swartz (1991) Hidden dimensions of power and resistance in the translation process: A South African study. *Culture, Medicine, and Psychiatry,* 15, 361–381.

Duranti, A. (1997) *Linguistic anthropology.* Cambridge: Cambridge University Press.

Durkheim, E. (1897) *Le suicide: Étude de sociologie.* Paris: Alcan.

Durst, U. (2001) Why Germans don't feel 'anger'. In Harkins, J. & A. Wierzbicka (eds.) *Emotions in crosslinguistic perspective.* Berlin/New York: Mouton De Gruyter, pp. 115–148.

Eady, S. (1982) Differences in the Fo patterns of speech: Tone language versus stress language. *Language and Speech,* 25, 1, 29–42.

Edwards, D. (1997) *Discourse and cognition.* Thousand Oaks, CA: Sage.

Eggins, S. & D. Slade (1997) *Analyzing casual conversation.* London/Washington: Cassell.

Ehrman, M. (1996) *Understanding second language learning difficulties.* Thousand Oaks, CA: Sage.

Eisenberg, A. (1999) Emotion talk among Mexican American and Anglo American mothers and children from two social classes. *Merrill-Palmer Quarterly,* 45, 2, 267–284.

Ekman, P. (1980) *The face of man: Expressions of universal emotions in a New Guinea village.* New York: Garland STMP Press.

Ekman, P. (1992) Are there basic emotions? *Psychological Review,* 99, 3, 550–553.

Ekman, P. (2003) *Emotions revealed: Recognizing faces and feelings to improve communication and emotional life.* New York: Henry Holt.

Ekman, P. & R. Davidson (eds.) (1994) *The nature of emotion: Fundamental questions.* Oxford: Oxford University Press.

Ellis, R. (1994) *The study of second language acquisition.* Oxford: Oxford University Press.

Epstein, I. (1915) *La pensée et la polyglossie: Essai psychologique et didactique.* Lausanne: Librarie Payot et Cie.

Erickson, D. & K. Maekawa (2001) *Perception of American English emotion by Japanese listeners.* Paper presented at the Spring 2001 meeting of the Acoustical Society of Japan. Retrieved at http://www.ericksonphd.org/emotion.htm on August 2, 2004.

Erikson, E. (1946) Ego development and historical change. *The Psychoanalytic Study of the Child,* 1, 359–396.

Ervin, S. (1954, reprinted in 1973). Identification and bilingualism. In A. Dil (Ed.), *Language acquisition and communicative choice. Essays by Susan M. Ervin-Tripp.* Stanford, CA: Stanford University Press, pp. 1–14.

Ervin-Tripp, S. (1964, reprinted in 1973). Language and TAT content in bilinguals. In A. Dil (Ed.), *Language acquisition and communicative choice. Essays by Susan M. Ervin-Tripp.* Stanford, CA: Stanford University Press, pp. 45–61.

Ervin-Tripp, S. (1967, reprinted in 1973). An issei learns English. In A. Dil (Ed.), *Language acquisition and communicative choice. Essays by Susan M. Ervin-Tripp.* Stanford, CA: Stanford University Press, pp. 62–77.

Erzinger, S. (1991) Communication between Spanish-speaking patients and their doctors in medical encounters. *Culture, Medicine, and Psychiatry,* 15, 91–110.

Esling, J. (1994) Some perspectives on accent: Range of voice quality variation, the periphery, and focusing. In Morley, J. (ed.) *Pronunciation pedagogy and theory: New views, new directions.* TESOL Inc., pp. 49–63.

Esling, J. & R. Wong (1983) Voice quality settings and the teaching of pronunciation. *TESOL Quarterly*, 17, 1, 89–95.

Everett, D. (2001) Monolingual field research. In P. Newman & M. Ratliff (eds.) *Linguistic fieldwork*. Cambridge: Cambridge University Press, pp. 166– 188.

Fairbanks, G. & L. Hoaglin (1941) An experimental study of the durational characteristics of the voice during the expression of emotion. *Speech Monographs*, 8, 85–90.

Fairbanks, G. & W. Pronovost (1939) An experimental study of the pitch characteristics of the voice during the expression of emotion. *Speech Monographs*, 6, 87–104.

Fant, G. (1973) *Speech sounds and features*. Cambridge, MA: MIT Press.

Fehr, B. & J. Russell (1984) Concept of emotion viewed from a prototype perspective. *Journal of Experimental Psychology: General*, 11, 3, 464–486.

Feld, S. (1990) *Sound and sentiment: Birds, weeping, poetics, and song in Kaluli expression*. Second ed. Philadelphia: University of Pennsylvania Press.

Ferenczi, S. (1916) *Contributions to psychoanalysis*. Boston: Badger.

Fiehler, R. (1990) *Kommunikation und Emotion. Theoretische und empirische Untersuchungen zur Rolle von Emotionen in der verbalen Interaktion*. Berlin: Mouton de Gruyter.

Fodor, J. (1975) *The language of thought*. Cambridge, MA: Harvard University Press.

Fodor, J. (1998) *Concepts: Where cognitive science went wrong*. Oxford, UK: Clarendon Press.

Fontaine, J., Poortinga, Y., Setiadi, B. & S. Markam (2002) Cognitive structure of emotion terms in Indonesia and The Netherlands. *Cognition and Emotion*, 16, 1, 61–86.

Forster, L. (1970) *The poet's tongues: Multilingualism in literature*. London: Cambridge University Press.

Foster, R. (1992) Psychoanalysis and the bilingual patient: Some observations on the influence of language choice on the transference. *Psychoanalytic Psychology*, 9, 1, 61–76.

Foster, R. (1996a) Assessing the psychodynamic function of language in the bilingual patient. In: Foster, R., Moskowitz, M. & R. Javier (eds.) *Reaching across boundaries of culture and class: Widening the scope of psychotherapy*. Northvale, NJ: Jason Aronson, Inc., pp. 243–263.

Foster, R. (1996b) The bilingual self: Duet in two voices. *Psychoanalytic Dialogues*, 6, 1, 99–121.

Foster, R. (1996c) The bilingual self – thoughts from a scientific positivist or pragmatic psychoanalyst? Reply to Massey. *Psychoanalytic Dialogues*, 6, 1, 141–150.

Freeman, D. (1999) *The fateful hoaxing of Margaret Mead: A historical analysis of her Samoan research*. Westview Press.

Freud, S. (1893) The psychical mechanisms of hysterical phenomena. *Standard Edition*, 2, 1–189. London: Hogarth Press.

Frick, R. (1985) Communicating emotion: The role of prosodic features. *Psychological Bulletin*, 97, 3, 412–429.

Fries, S. (1998) Different phases: A personal case study in language adjustment and children's bilingualism. *International Journal of the Sociology of Language*, 133, 129–141.

Fung, H. (1999) Becoming a moral child: The socialization of shame among young Chinese children. *Ethos*, 27, 2, 180–209.

Fussell, S. (2002) (ed.) *The verbal communication of emotions: Interdisciplinary perspectives.* Mahwah, NJ: Lawrence Erlbaum.

Gal, S. (1978) Peasant men can't get wives: Language change and sex roles in a bilingual community. *Language in Society,* 7, 1, 1–17.

Gal, S. & J. Irvine (1995) The boundaries of languages and disciplines: How ideologies construct difference. *Social Research,* 62, 4, 967–1001.

Gardner, R. (1980) On the validity of affective variables in second language acquisition: Conceptual, contextual, and statistical considerations. *Language Learning,* 30, 255–270.

Gardner, R. (1985) *Social psychology and second language learning: The role of attitudes and motivation.* London: Edward Arnold.

Gardner, R. (1988) The socio-educational model of second language learning: Assumptions, findings, and issues. *Language Learning,* 38, 101–126.

Gardner, R. & W. Lambert (1959) Motivational variables in second-language acquisition. *Canadian Journal of Psychology,* 13, 266–272.

Gardner, R. & W. Lambert (1972) *Attitudes and motivation in second language learning.* Rowley, MA: Newbury House.

Gardner, R. & P. MacIntyre (1993) On the measurement of affective variables in second language learning. *Language Learning,* 43, 157–194.

Gardner, R. & P. Smythe (1975) *Second language acquisition: A social psychological approach.* Research Bulletin No. 332. Ontario: University of Western Ontario.

Gass, S. & L. Selinker (eds.) (1992) *Language transfer in language learning.* Revised ed. Amsterdam/Philadelphia: John Benjamins.

Gass, S. & L. Selinker (1994) *Second language acquisition. An introductory course.* Hillsdale, NJ: Lawrence Erlbaum.

Geeslin, K. (2003) A comparison of copula choice: Native Spanish speakers and advanced learners. *Language Learning,* 53, 4, 703–764.

Gehm, T. & K. Scherer (1988) Factors determining the dimensions of subjunctive emotional space. In Scherer, K. (ed.) *Facets of emotion: Recent research.* Hillsdale, NJ: Lawrence Erlbaum, pp. 99–113.

Gerber, E. (1985) Rage and obligation: Samoan emotion in conflict. In White, G. & J. Kirkpatrick (eds.) *Person, self, and experience: Exploring Pacific ethnopsychologies.* Berkeley, CA: University of California Press, pp. 121–167.

Gibson, M. (1997) Non-native perception and production of English attitudinal intonation. In J. Leather and A. James (eds.) *New Sounds 97: Proceedings of the Third International Symposium on the Acquisition of Second-Language Speech.* Klagenfurt: University of Klagenfurt, pp. 96–102.

Goddard, C. (1991) Anger in the Western Desert: A case study in the cross-cultural semantics of emotion. *Man,* 26, 265–279.

Goddard, C. (2002) Explicating emotions across languages and cultures: A semantic approach. In S. Fussell (ed.) *The verbal communication of emotions: Interdisciplinary perspectives.* Mahwah, NJ: Lawrence Erlbaum, pp. 19–53.

Goldberg, M. (1941) A qualification of the Marginal Man theory. *American Sociological Review,* 6, 52–58.

Golden, D. (2001) "Now, like real Israelis, let's stand up and sing": Teaching the national language to Russian newcomers in Israel. *Anthropology and Education Quarterly,* 32, 1, 52–79.

Goldstein, T. (1997) *Two languages at work: Bilingual life on the production floor.* Berlin/New York: Mouton de Gruyter.

Gonzalez-Reigosa, F. (1976) The anxiety-arousing effect of taboo words in bilinguals. In C. Spielberger & R. Diaz-Guerrero (eds.) *Cross-cultural anxiety.* Washington, DC: Hemisphere, pp. 89–105.

Grabois, H. (1999) The convergence of sociocultural theory and cognitive linguistics: Lexical semantics and the L2 acquisition of love, fear, and happiness. In Palmer, G. & D. Occhi (eds.), *Languages of sentiment: Cultural constructions of emotional substrates.* Amsterdam/Philadelphia: John Benjamins, pp. 201–233.

Graddol, D. & J. Swann (1989) *Gender voices.* Oxford, UK: Basil Blackwell.

Graham, R., Hamblin, A. & S. Feldstein (2001) Recognition of emotion in English voices by speakers of Japanese, Spanish and English. *International Review of Applied Linguistics*, 39, 19–37.

Greasley, P., Sherrard, C. & M. Waterman (2000) Emotion in language and speech: Methodological issues in naturalistic approaches. *Language and Speech*, 43, 4, 355–375.

Greenson, R. (1950) The mother tongue and the mother. *International Journal of Psycho-Analysis*, 31, 18–23.

Grice, P. (1975) Logic and conversation. In P. Cole & J. Morgan (eds.) *Syntax and semantics. Vol. 9: Pragmatics.* New York: Academic Press, pp. 113–128.

Grosjean, F. (1982) *Life with two languages: An introduction to bilingualism.* Cambridge, MA: Harvard University Press.

Grosjean, F. (1989) Neurolinguists, beware! The bilingual is not two monolinguals in one person. *Brain and Language*, 36, 3–15.

Grosjean, F. (1992) Another view of bilingualism. In R. Harris (ed.), *Cognitive Processing in Bilinguals.* Amsterdam/New York: North Holland, pp. 51–62.

Grosjean, F. (1998) Studying bilinguals: Methodological and conceptual issues. *Bilingualism: Language and Cognition*, 1, 2, 131–149.

Guiora, A., Acton, W., Erard, R. & F. Strickland (1980) The effects of benzodiazepine (Valium) on permeability of ego boundaries. *Language Learning*, 30, 351–363.

Guiora, A., Beit-Hallami, B., Brannon, R., Dull, C. & T. Scovel (1972) The effects of experimentally induced changes in ego states on pronunciation ability in second language: An exploratory study. *Comprehensive Psychiatry*, 13.

Guiora, A., Brannon, R. & C. Dull (1972) Empathy and second language learning. *Language Learning*, 22, 111–130.

Gumperz, J. (1964) Linguistic and social interaction in two communities. *American Anthropologist*, 66, 6, 137–153.

Gumperz, J. (1982a) *Discourse strategies.* Cambridge, UK: Cambridge University Press.

Gumperz, J. (ed.) (1982b) *Language and social identity.* Cambridge, UK: Cambridge University Press.

Günthner, S. (1997) Complaint stories: Constructing emotional reciprocity among women. In H. Kotthoff & R. Wodak (eds.) *Communicating gender in context.* Amsterdam: John Benjamins, pp. 179–218.

Guttfreund, D. (1990) Effects of language usage on the emotional experience of Spanish-English and English-Spanish bilinguals. *Journal of Consulting and Clinical Psychology*, 58, 5, 604–607.

Hale, K. (1969) Some questions about anthropological linguistics: The role of native knowledge. In D. Hymes (ed.) *Reinventing anthropology.* New York: Pantheon Books, pp. 382–397.

Halliday, M. A. K. (1985) *Spoken and written language.* Oxford University Press.

Hansen, D. (1995) A study of the effect of the acculturation model on second language acquisition. In Eckman, F., Highland, D., Lee, P., Mileham, J. & R. Rutkowski Weber (eds.) *Second language acquisition theory and pedagogy.* Mahwah, NJ: Lawrence Erlbaum, pp. 305–316.

Harkins, J. & A. Wierzbicka (eds.) (2001) *Emotions in crosslinguistic perspective.* Berlin/New York: Mouton de Gruyter.

Harley, B. & W. Wang (1997) The Critical Period Hypothesis: Where are we now? In De Groot, A. & J. Kroll (eds.) *Tutorials in bilingualism: Psycholinguistic perspectives.* Mahwah, NJ: Lawrence Erlbaum, pp. 19–51.

Harré, R. (1986) (ed.) *The social construction of emotion.* Oxford: Basil Blackwell.

Harré, R. & G. Parrott (eds.) (1996) *The emotions: Social, cultural, and biological dimensions.* Thousand Oaks, CA: Sage.

Harris, C. (2004) Bilingual speakers in the lab: Psychophysiological measures of emotional reactivity. *Journal of Multilingual and Multicultural Development,* 25, 2/3, 223–247.

Harris, C., Aiçiçegi, A. & J. Gleason (2003) Taboo words and reprimands elicit greater autonomic reactivity in a first language than in a second language. *Applied Psycholinguistics,* 24, 4, 561–579.

Harris, C., Gleason, J. & A. Aiçiçegi (in press) Why is a first language more emotional? Psychophysiological evidence from bilingual speakers. In A. Pavlenko (ed.) *Bilingual minds: Emotional experience, expression, and representation.* Clevedon, UK: Multilingual Matters.

Harvey, P. (1992) Bilingualism in the Peruvian Andes. In Cameron, D., Frazer, E., Harvey, P., Rampton, M. H. B. & K. Richardson (eds.) *Researching language: Issues of power and method.* London/New York: Routledge, pp. 65–89.

Harvey, P. (1994) The presence and absence of speech in the communication of gender. In P. Burton, K. Dyson, & Sh. Ardener (eds.) *Bilingual women: Anthropological approaches to second-language use.* Oxford/Providence: Berg, pp. 44–64.

Hatch, E. (1992) *Discourse and language education.* Cambridge, UK: Cambridge University Press.

Haugen, E. (1962) Schizoglossia and the linguistic norm. *Georgetown University Monograph Series on Languages and Linguistics.* Washington, DC: Georgetown University Press, pp. 63–74.

Heelas, P. (1986) Emotion talk across cultures. In Harré, R. (ed.) *The social construction of emotions.* Oxford: Blackwell, pp. 234–266.

Hegi, U. (1997) *Tearing the silence: On being German in America.* New York: Touchstone/Simon & Shuster.

Heider, K. (1991) *Landscapes of emotion: Mapping three cultures in Indonesia.* New York: Cambridge University Press.

Heinz, B. (2001) "Fish in the river": Experiences of bicultural bilingual speakers. *Multilingua,* 20, 1, 85–108.

Heller, M. (1982) Negotiations of language choice in Montreal. In J. Gumperz (ed.) *Language and social identity.* Cambridge: Cambridge University Press, pp. 108–118.

Heller, M. (1988) (ed.) *Codeswitching: Anthropological and sociolinguistic perspectives.* Berlin: Mouton de Gruyter.

Heller, M. (1992) The politics of codeswitching and language choice. *Journal of Multilingual and Multicultural Development,* 13, 1/2, 123–142.

Heller, M. (1995) Language choice, social institutions, and symbolic domination. *Language in Society,* 24, 373–405.

Henry, J. (1936) The linguistic expression of emotion. *American Anthropologist,* 38, 250–256.

Henss, W. (1931) Zweisprachigkeit als Pädagogisches Problem. *Ethnopolitischer Almanach,* 2, 47–55.

Henton, C. & R. Bladon (1985) Breathiness in normal female speech: Inefficiency versus desirability. *Language and Communication,* 5, 3, 221–227.

Hiatt, L. (1978) *Australian aboriginal concepts.* Princeton, NJ: Humanities Press.

Hinton, D. & S. Hinton (2002) Panic disorder, somatization, and the new cross-cultural psychiatry; or the seven bodies of a medical anthropology of panic. *Culture, Medicine, and Psychiatry,* 26, 155–178.

Hochschild, A. (1983) *The managed heart.* Berkeley, CA: University of California Press.

Hoffman, E. (1989) *Lost in translation. A life in a new language.* New York: Penguin Books.

Holden, K. & J. Hogan (1993) The emotive impact of foreign intonation: An experiment in switching English and Russian intonation. *Language and Speech,* 36, 1, 67–88.

Horwitz, E. (1986) Preliminary evidence for the reliability and validity of a foreign language anxiety scale. *TESOL Quarterly,* 20, 559–562.

Horwitz, E. (2001) Language anxiety and achievement. *Annual Review of Applied Linguistics,* 21, 112–126.

Horwitz, E., Horwitz, M. & J. Cope (1986) Foreign language classroom anxiety. *Modern Language Journal,* 70, 125–132.

Howell, S. (1981) Rules not words. In Heelas, P. & A. Lock (eds.) *Indigenous psychologies: The anthropology of the self.* San Diego, CA: Academic Press, pp. 133–143.

Husband, C. & V. Saifullah-Khan (1982) The viability of ethnolinguistic vitality: Some creative doubts. *Journal of Multilingual and Multicultural Development,* 3, 195–205.

Huston, N. (1999) *Nord perdu.* Arles: Actes Sud.

Ibrahim, A. (1999) Becoming Black: Rap and hip-hop, race, gender, identity, and the politics of ESL learning. *TESOL Quarterly,* 23, 3, 349–369.

Ioup, G., Boustagui, E., El Tigi, M. & M. Mosel (1994) Reexamining the Critical Period Hypothesis: A case study of successful adult SLA in a naturalistic environment. *Studies in Second Language Acquisition,* 16, 73–98.

Irvine, J. (1990) Registering affect: Heteroglossia in the linguistic expression of emotion. In Lutz, C. & L. Abu-Lughod (eds.) *Language and the politics of emotion.* Cambridge, NY: Cambridge University Press, pp. 126–161.

Irvine, J. & S. Gal (2000) Language ideology and linguistic differentiation. In P. Kroskrity (ed.) *Regimes of language: Ideologies, politics, and identities.* Santa Fe, NM/Oxford: School of American Research Press, pp. 35–84.

Izard, C. (1977) *Human emotions.* New York: Plenum Press.

Jakobson, R. (1960) Closing statement: Linguistics and poetics. In Sebeok, T. (ed.) *Style in language*. Cambridge, MA: MIT Press, pp. 350–377.

Jarvis, S. (1998) *Conceptual transfer in the interlingual lexicon*. Bloomington, IN: Indiana University Linguistics Club Publications.

Javier, R. (1995) Vicissitudes of autobiographical memories in a bilingual analysis. *Psychoanalytic Psychology*, 12, 3, 429–438.

Javier, R. (1996) In search of repressed memories in bilingual individuals. In R. Foster, M. Moskowitz & R. Javier (eds.) *Reaching across boundaries of culture and class: Widening the scope of psychotherapy*. Northvale, NJ: Jason Aronson, Inc., pp. 225–241.

Javier, R., Barroso, F. & M. Muñoz (1993) Autobiographical memory in bilinguals. *Journal of Psycholinguistic Research*, 22, 3, 319–338.

Javier, R. & L. Marcos (1989) The role of stress on the language-independence and code-switching phenomena. *Journal of Psycholinguistic Research*, 18, 5, 449–472.

Jay, T. (1992) *Cursing in America*. Philadelphia/Amsterdam: John Benjamins.

Jay, T. (2000) *Why we curse: The neuro-psychological model of speech*. Philadelphia/Amsterdam: John Benjamins.

Jay, T. (2003) *The psychology of language*. Upper Saddle River, NJ: Prentice Hall.

Johnson, J. & E. Newport (1989) Critical period effects in second language learning: The influence of maturational state on the acquisition of English as a second language. *Cognitive Psychology*, 21, 60–99.

Johnson-Laird, P. & K. Oatley (1989) The language of emotions: An analysis of a semantic field. *Cognition and Emotion*, 3, 2, 81–123.

Kakavá, C. (2001) Discourse and conflict. In D. Schiffrin, D. Tannen, & H. Hamilton (eds.) *The handbook of discourse analysis*. Malden, MA: Blackwell, pp. 650–670.

Kanno, Y. (2000) Bilingualism and identity: The stories of Japanese returnees. *International Journal of Bilingual Education and Bilingualism*, 3, 1, 1–18.

Kanno, Y. (2003) *Negotiating bilingual and bicultural identities: Japanese returnees betwixt two worlds*. Mahwah, NJ: Lawrence Erlbaum.

Kaplan, A. (1993) *French Lessons: A memoir*. Chicago/London: University of Chicago Press.

Kaplan, A. (1994) On language memoir. In A. Bammer (ed.) *Displacements: Cultural Identities in Question*. Bloomington, IN: Indiana University Press, pp. 59–70.

Katriel, T. (1985) *Brogez*: Ritual and strategy in Israeli children's conflicts. *Language in Society*, 14, 467–490.

Kecskes, I. & T. Papp (2000) *Foreign language and mother tongue*. Mahwah, NJ: Lawrence Erlbaum.

Kellerman, E. & M. Sharwood Smith (eds.) (1986) *Crosslinguistic influence in second language acquisition*. New York/Oxford: Pergamon Press.

Kellman, S. (2000) *The translingual imagination*. Lincoln/London: University of Nebraska Press.

Kellman, S. (ed.) (2003) *Switching languages: Translingual writers reflect on their craft*. Lincoln/London: University of Nebraska Press.

Kidron, Y. & R. Kuzar (2002) My face is paling against my will: Emotion and control in English and Hebrew. *Pragmatics & Cognition*, 10, 1/2, 129–157.

Kinginger, C. (2004a) Bilingualism and emotion in the autobiographical works of Nancy Huston. *Journal of Multilingual and Multicultural Development*, 25, 2/3, 159–178.

Kinginger, C. (2004b) Alice doesn't live here anymore: Foreign language learning and identity reconstruction. In A. Pavlenko & A. Blackledge (eds.) *Negotiation of identities in multilingual contexts*. Clevedon, UK: Multilingual Matters, pp. 219–242.

Kitayama, Sh. & K. Ishii (2002) Word and voice: Spontaneous attention to emotional utterances in two languages. *Cognition and Emotion*, 16, 1, 29–59.

Kleinmann, H. (1977) Avoidance behavior in adult second language acquisition. *Language Learning*, 27, 93–107.

Klüger, R. (1992) *weiter leben: Eine Jugend* (living on: A Youth). München.

Kluger, R. (2001) *Still alive: A Holocaust girlhood remembered*. New York: The Feminist Press.

Kobayashi, Y. (2002) The role of gender in foreign language learning attitudes: Japanese female students' attitudes toward English learning. *Gender and Education*, 14, 2, 181–197.

Kochman, T. (1981) *Black and white styles in conflict*. Chicago: University of Chicago Press.

Kolenda, K. (1987) On human emotions. *American Anthropologist*, 89, 946–947.

Koreneva, E. (2003) *Idiotka: Roman-biographia* (She-idiot: An autobiography). Moscow: ACT Astrel'.

Kornacki, P. (2001) Concepts of anger in Chinese. In Harkins, J. & A. Wierzbicka (eds.) *Emotions in crosslinguistic perspective*. Berlin/New York: Mouton De Gruyter, pp. 255–289.

Kosinski, J. (1976) *The painted bird*. Second ed. New York: Grove Press.

Kotthoff, H. (2001) Gender, emotion, and poeticity in Georgian mourning rituals. In B. Baron & H. Kotthoff (eds.) *Gender in interaction*. Amsterdam/Philadelphia: John Benjamins, pp. 283–327.

Kouritzin, S. (2000) Immigrant mothers redefine access to ESL classes: Contradiction and ambivalence. *Journal of Multilingual and Multicultural Development*, 21, 1, 14–32.

Kövecses, Z. (1986) *Metaphors of anger, pride, and love: A lexical approach to the structure of concepts*. Philadelphia/Amsterdam: John Benjamins.

Kövecses, Z. (1990) *Emotion concepts*. New York/Berlin: Springer-Verlag.

Kövecses, Z. (2000) *Metaphor and emotion: Language, culture, and body in human feeling*. Cambridge, NY: Cambridge University Press.

Koven, M. (2004) Getting 'emotional' in two languages: Bilinguals' verbal performance of affect in narratives of personal experience. *Text*, 24, 4, 471–515.

Kramer, E. (1964) Elimination of verbal cues in judgments of emotion from voice. *Journal of Abnormal and Social Psychology*, 68, 4, 390–396.

Kramsch, C. (1997) The privilege of the nonnative speaker. *PMLA*, 112, 3, 359–369.

Krapf, E. (1955) The choice of language in polyglot psychoanalysis. *Psychoanalytic Quarterly*, 24, 343–357.

Krashen, S. (1977) The Monitor Model for second language performance. In M. Burt, H. Dulay & M. Finocchiaro (eds.) *Viewpoints on English as a Second Language*. New York Regents.

Krashen, S. (1981) *Second language acquisition and second language learning*. New York: Pergamon Press.

Krashen, S. (1994) The input hypothesis and its rivals. In N. Ellis (ed.) *Implicit and explicit learning of languages*. New York: Academic Press, pp. 45–77.

Kroll, J. & P. Dussias (2004) The comprehension of words and sentences in two languages. In Bhatia, T. & W. Ritchie (eds.) *The handbook of bilingualism.* Oxford: Blackwell, pp. 169–200.

Kroll, J. & E. Stewart (1994) Category interference in translation and picture naming: Evidence for asymmetric connections between bilingual memory representations. *Journal of Memory and Language,* 33, 149–174.

Kroll, J., Michael, E., Tokowicz, N. & R. Dufour (2002) The development of lexical fluency in a second language. *Second Language Research,* 18, 137–171.

Kubota, R., Austin, T. & Y. Saito-Abbott (2003) Diversity and inclusion of sociopolitical issues in foreign language classrooms: An exploratory survey. *Foreign Language Annals,* 36, 1, 12–24.

Kulick, D. (1998) Anger, gender, language shift, and the politics of revelation in a Papua New Guinean village. In Schieffelin, B., Woolard, K. & P. Kroskrity (eds.) *Language ideologies: Practice and theory.* New York/Oxford: Oxford University Press, pp. 87–102.

Kyratzis, A. (2001) Constituting the emotions: A longitudinal study of emotion talk in a preschool friendship group of boys. In B. Baron & H. Kotthoff (eds.) *Gender in interaction.* Amsterdam/Philadelphia: John Benjamins, pp. 51–74.

LaBar, K. & E. Phelps (1998) Arousal-mediated memory consolidation: Role of the medial temporal lobe in humans. *Psychological Science,* 9, 490–493.

Labov, W. & J. Waletzky (1967) Narrative analysis: Oral versions of personal experience. In Helm, J. (ed.) *Essays on the verbal and visual arts: Proceedings of the 1966 annual spring meeting of the American Ethnological Society.* Seattle: University of Washington Press, pp. 12–44. (Reprinted in *Journal of Narrative and Life History,* 7, 1–4, 3–38).

Ladefoged, P. (1993) *A course in phonetics.* 3rd edition. Harcourt Brace Jovanovich.

Lakoff, G. (1987) *Women, fire, and dangerous things: What categories reveal about the mind.* Chicago, IL: University of Chicago Press.

Lambert, W. (1967) A social psychology of bilingualism. *The Journal of Social Issues,* 23, 2, 91–109.

Lambert, W. & C. Aellen (1969) Ethnic identification and personality adjustments of Canadian adolescents of mixed English-French parentage. *Canadian Journal of Behavioral Science,* 1, 2, 69–86.

Lambert, W., Just, M. & Segalowitz, N. (1970) Some cognitive consequences of following the curricula of the early school grades in a foreign language. In Alatis, J. (ed.) *Georgetown University Monograph Series on Language and Linguistics.* Washington, DC: Georgetown University Press, pp. 229–279.

Lamendella, J. (1977a) General principles of neurofunctional organization and their manifestation in primary and nonprimary language acquisition. *Language Learning,* 27, 1, 155–196.

Lamendella, J. (1977b) The limbic system in human communication. In Whitaker, H. & H. A. Whitaker (eds.) *Studies in neurolinguistics. Volume 3.* New York: Academic Press, pp. 157–222.

Laqueur, T. (2003) Diary. *London Review of Books,* 25 (23), December 4, pp. 38–39.

Larsen, S., Schrauf, R., Fromholt, P. & D. Rubin (2002) Inner speech and bilingual autobiographical memory: A Polish-Danish cross-cultural study. *Memory,* 10, 1, 45–54.

Larsen-Freeman, D. (2001) Individual cognitive/affective learner contributions and differential success in second language acquisition. In M. Breen (ed.) *Learner contributions to language learning: New directions in research*. London: Longman, pp. 12–24.

Larsen-Freeman, D. & M. Long (1991) *An introduction to second language acquisition research*. London: Longman.

Latomaa, S. (1998) English in contact with "the most difficult language in the world": The linguistic situation of Americans living in Finland. *International Journal of the Sociology of Language*, 133, 51–71.

Laurie, S. (1899) *Lectures on language and linguistic method in the school*. 3rd revised edition. Edinburgh: Oliver and Boyd.

LeDoux, J. (1996) *The emotional brain: The mysterious underpinnings of emotional life*. New York: Simon and Schuster.

LeDoux, J. (2002) Emotion, memory, and the brain. *Scientific American*, 12, 1, 62–71.

Le Page, R. & A. Tabouret-Keller (1985) *Acts of identity: Creole-based approaches to language and ethnicity*. Cambridge/New York: Cambridge University Press.

Lerner, G. (1997) *Why history matters: Life and thought*. New York/Oxford: Oxford University Press.

Levy, R. (1973) *The Tahitians: Mind and experience in the Society Islands*. Chicago/London: University of Chicago Press.

Levy, R. (1984) Emotion, knowing, and culture. In Shweder, R. & R. LeVine (eds.) *Culture theory: Essays on mind, self, and emotion*. Cambridge: Cambridge University Press, pp. 214–237.

Lippi-Green, R. (1997) *English with an accent: Language, ideology, and discrimination in the United States*. London/New York: Routledge.

Li Wei (ed.) (2000) *The bilingualism reader*. London/New York: Routledge.

Lock, M. (1990) On being ethnic: The politics of identity breaking and making in Canada, or, *nevra* on Sunday. *Culture, Medicine, and Psychiatry*, 14, 2, 237–254.

Lowie, R. (1940) Native languages as ethnographic tools. *American Anthropologist*, 42, 81–89.

Lowie, R. (1945) A case of bilingualism. *Word*, 1, 3, 249–259.

Lozanov, G. (1979) *Suggestology and outlines of suggestopedy*. New York: Gordon and Breach.

Lucy, J. (1992) *Language diversity and thought. A reformulation of the linguistic relativity hypothesis*. Cambridge: Cambridge University Press.

Lutz, C. (1986) The domain of emotion words on Ifaluk. In Harré, R. (ed.) *The social construction of emotions*. Oxford: Blackwell, pp. 267–288.

Lutz, C. (1988) *Unnatural emotions: Everyday sentiments on a Micronesian atoll and their challenge to Western theory*. Chicago, IL: University of Chicago Press.

Lutz, C. (1990) Engendered emotion: Gender, power, and the rhetoric of emotional control in American discourse. In Lutz, C. & L. Abu-Lughod (eds.) *Language and the politics of emotion*. Cambridge: Cambridge University Press, pp. 69–91.

Lutz, C. & L. Abu-Lughod (1990) (eds.) *Language and the politics of emotion*. Cambridge: Cambridge University Press.

Lutz, C. & G. White (1986) The anthropology of emotions. *Annual Review of Anthropology*, 15, 405–436.

Luykx, A. (2003) Weaving languages together: Family language policy and gender socialization in bilingual Aymara households. In Bayley, R. & S. Schecter (eds.) *Language socialization in bilingual and multilingual societies*. Clevedon, UK: Multilingual Matters, pp. 25–43.

MacIntyre, P. & R. Gardner (1989) Anxiety and second language learning: Toward a theoretical clarification. *Language Learning*, 39, 251–275.

MacIntyre, P. & R. Gardner (1994) The subtle effects of language anxiety on cognitive processing in the second language. *Language Learning*, 44, 283–305.

MacWhinney, B. (1997) Second language acquisition and the competition model. In De Groot, A. & J. Kroll (eds.) *Tutorials in bilingualism: Psycholinguistic perspectives*. Mahwah, NJ: Lawrence Erlbaum, pp. 113–142.

Majewski, W., Hollien, H. & J. Zalewski (1972) Speaking fundamental frequency of Polish adult males. *Phonetica*, 25, 119–125.

Manning, S. & M. Melchiori (1974) Words that upset urban college students: Measures with GSRs and rating scales. *Journal of Social Psychology*, 94, 305–306.

Marcos, L. (1972) Lying: A particular defense met in psychoanalytic therapy. *American Journal of Psychoanalysis*, 32, 195–202.

Marcos, L. (1976a) Linguistic dimensions in the bilingual patient. *American Journal of Psychoanalysis*, 36, 347–354.

Marcos, L. (1976b) Bilinguals in psychotherapy: Language as an emotional barrier. *American Journal of Psychotherapy*, 30, 552–560.

Marcos, L. (1979) Effects of interpreters on the evaluation of psychopathology in non-English speaking patients. *American Journal of Psychiatry*, 136, 2, 171–174.

Marcos, L. & M. Alpert (1976) Strategies and risks in psychotherapy with bilingual patients: The phenomenon of language independence. *American Journal of Psychiatry*, 133, 11, 1275–1278.

Marcos, L., Alpert, M., Urcuyo, L. & M. Kesselman (1973a) The effect of interview language on the evaluation of psychopathology in Spanish-American schizophrenic patients. *American Journal of Psychiatry*, 130, 5, 549–553.

Marcos, L., Urcuyo, L., Kesselman, M. & M. Alpert (1973b) The language barrier in evaluating Spanish-American patients. *Archives of General Psychiatry*, 29, 655–659.

Marcos, L. & L. Urcuyo (1979) Dynamic psychotherapy with the bilingual patient. *American Journal of Psychotherapy*, 33, 3, 331–338.

Marian, V. & M. Kaushanskaya (2004) Self-construal and emotion in bicultural bilinguals. *Journal of Memory and Language*, 51, 190–201.

Marian, V. & U. Neisser (2000) Language-dependent recall of autobiographical memories. *Journal of Experimental Psychology: General*, 129, 3, 361–368.

Marinova-Todd, S., Marshall, B. & C. Snow (2000) Three misconceptions about age and L2 learning. *TESOL Quarterly*, 34, 1, 9–34.

Marsella, A. (1980) Depressive experience and disorder across cultures. In Triandis, H. & J. Draguns (eds.) *Handbook of cross-cultural psychopathology*. Boston: Allyn and Bacon, pp. 237–289.

Marx, N. (2003) Never quite a 'native speaker': Accent and identity in the L2 – and the L1. *Canadian Modern Language Review*, 59, 2, 264–281.

Mathews, A., Richards, A. & M. Eysenck (1989) Interpretation of homophones related to threat in anxiety states. *Journal of Abnormal Psychology*, 98, 31–34.

May, S. (2001) *Language and minority rights: Ethnicity, nationalism, and the politics of language*. Harlow, UK: Pearson Education.

Mayne, T. & G. Bonanno (eds.) (2001) *Emotions: Current issues and future directions*. New York/London: Guilford Press.

McCabe, A. & L. Bliss (2003) *Patterns of narrative discourse: A multicultural, life span approach*. Boston, MA: Allyn & Bacon.

McCarthy, M. (1991) *Discourse analysis for language teachers*. Cambridge, UK: Cambridge University Press.

McCarthy, M. & R. Carter (1997) Grammar, tails, and affect: Constructing expressive choices in discourse. *Text*, 17, 3, 405–429.

McCluskey, K. & D. Albas (1981) Perception of the emotional content of speech by Canadian and Mexican children, adolescents, and adults. *International Journal of Psychology*, 16, 119–132.

McCluskey, K., Albas, D., Niemi, R., Cuevas, C. & C. Ferrer (1975) Cross-cultural differences in the perception of emotional content of speech: A study of the development of sensitivity in Canadian and Mexican children. *Developmental Psychology*, 11, 5, 551–555.

McDonald, M. (1994) Women and linguistic innovation in Brittany. In P. Burton, K. Dyson & Sh. Ardener (eds.) *Bilingual Women: Anthropological Approaches to Second-Language Use*. Oxford/Providence: Berg, pp. 85–110.

McLaughlin, F. & Th. S. Sall (2001) The give and take of fieldwork: Noun classes and other concerns in Fatick, Senegal. In P. Newman & M. Ratliff (eds.) *Linguistic fieldwork*. Cambridge: Cambridge University Press, pp. 189–210.

McMahill, C. (2001) Self-expression, gender, and community: A Japanese feminist English class. In A. Pavlenko, A. Blackledge, I. Piller & M. Teutsch-Dwyer (eds.) *Multilingualism, second language learning, and gender*. New York/Berlin: Mouton De Gruyter, pp. 307–344.

Mead, M. (1939) Native languages as field-work tools. *American Anthropologist*, 41, 2, 189–205.

Mesquita, B. & N. Frijda (1992) Cultural variations in emotions: A review. *Psychological Bulletin*, 112, 2, 179–204.

Middleton, D. (1989) Emotional style: The cultural ordering of emotions. *Ethos*, 17, 2, 187–201.

Miller, J. (1996) A tongue, for sighing. In J. Maybin & N. Mercer (eds) *Using English: From conversation to canon*. London: Routledge, pp. 275–310.

Miller, J. (2000) Language use, identity, and social interaction: Migrant students in Australia. *Research on Language and Social Interaction*, 33, 69–100.

Miller, J. (2003) *Audible difference: ESL and social identity in schools*. Clevedon, UK: Multilingual Matters.

Miller, P. & L. Sperry (1988) The socialization and acquisition of emotional meanings. *Merrill-Palmer Quarterly*, 34, 217–222.

Milroy, L. & P. Muysken (1995) *One speaker, two languages: Cross-disciplinary perspectives on code-switching*. Cambridge: Cambridge University Press.

Moore, C., Romney, A., Hsia, T. & C. Rusch (1999) The universality of the semantic structure of emotion terms: Methods for study of inter- and intra-cultural variability. *American Anthropologist*, 101, 3, 529–546.

Mori, K. (1997) *Polite lies: On being a woman caught between cultures*. New York: Henry Holt.

Morsbach, H. & W. Tyler (1986) A Japanese emotion: *Amae*. In R. Harré (ed.) *The social construction of emotions*. Oxford: Blackwell, pp. 289–307.

Moskowitz, G. (1978) *Caring and sharing in the foreign language class: A sourcebook on humanistic techniques*. Boston, MA: Heinle & Heinle.

Moskowitz, G. (1999) Enhancing personal development: Humanistic activities at work. In J. Arnold (ed.) *Affect in language learning*. Cambridge: Cambridge University Press, pp. 177–193.

Movahedi, S. (1996) Metalinguistic analysis of therapeutic discourse: Flight into a second language when the analyst and the analysand are multilingual. *Journal of the American Psychoanalytic Association*, 44, 3, 837–862.

Muchnick, A. & D. Wolfe (1982) Attitudes and motivations of American students of Spanish. *Canadian Modern Language Review*, 38, 262–281.

Mudgett-De Caro, P. (1998) On being both Hearing and Deaf: My bicultural-bilingual experience. In Parasnis, I. (ed.) *Cultural and language diversity and the Deaf experience*. Cambridge: Cambridge University Press, pp. 272–288.

Mullenix, J., Bihon, T., Bricklemyer, J., Gaston, J. & J. Keener (2002) Effects of variation in emotional tone of voice in speech perception. *Language and Speech*, 45, 3, 255–283.

Müller, K. (1934) *Die Psyche des Oberschlesiers im Lichte des Zweisprachen-Problems*. Bonn.

Murray, I. & J. Arnott (1993) Toward the simulation of emotion in synthetic speech: A review of the literature on human vocal emotion. *Journal of the Acoustic Society of America*, 93, 2, 1097–1108.

Myers, F. (1979) Emotions and the self: A theory of personhood and political order among Pintupi aborigines. *Ethos*, 7, 4, 343–370.

Myers, F. (1986) *Pintupi country, Pintupi self: Sentiment, place, and politics among Western Desert aborigines*. Washington: Smithsonian Institution Press.

Myhill, J. (1997) What is universal and what is language-specific in emotion words? Evidence from Biblical Hebrew. *Pragmatics and Cognition*, 5, 1, 79–129.

Nakamichi, A., Jogan, A., Usami, M. & D. Erickson (2002) Perception by native and non-native listeners of vocal emotion in a bilingual movie. *Gifu City Women's College Research Bulletin*, 52, 87–91. Retrieved at http://www.ericksonphd.org/emotion.htm on August 2, 2004.

Newman, P. & M. Ratliff (eds.) (2001a) *Linguistic fieldwork*. Cambridge: Cambridge University Press.

Newman, P. & M. Ratliff (2001b) Introduction. In P. Newman & M. Ratliff (eds.) *Linguistic fieldwork*. Cambridge: Cambridge University Press, pp. 1–14.

Niedenthal, P., Auxiette, C., Nugier, A., Dalle, N., Bonin, P. & M. Fayol (2004) A prototype analysis of the French category 'émotion.' *Cognition and Emotion*, 18, 3, 289–312.

Norton Peirce, B. (1995) Social identity, investment, and language learning. *TESOL Quarterly*, 29, 1, 9–31.

Norton, B. (2000) *Identity and language learning: Gender, ethnicity, and educational change*. London: Longman.

Norton, B. (2001) Non-participation, imagined communities, and the language classroom. In M. Breen (ed) *Learner contributions to language learning: New directions in research*. London: Longman, pp. 159–171.

Novakovich, J. & R. Shapard (eds.) (2000) *Stories in the stepmother tongue*. Buffalo, NY: White Pine Press.

Oatley, K. (1992) *Best laid schemes: The psychology of emotions*. Cambridge: Cambridge University Press.

Oatley, K. & P. Johnson-Laird (1987) Toward a cognitive theory of emotions. *Cognition and Emotion*, 1, 29–50.

Ochs, E. & B. Schieffelin (1989) Language has a heart. *Text*, 9, 1, 7–25.

Ochsner, K. & L. Feldman Barrett (2001) A multiprocess perspective on the neuroscience of emotion. In Mayne, T. & G. Bonanno (eds.) *Emotions: Current issues and future directions*. New York/London: The Guilford Press, pp. 38–81.

Odlin, T. (1989) *Language transfer: Cross-linguistic influence in language learning*. Cambridge: Cambridge University Press.

Ogulnick, K. (ed.) (2000) *Language crossings: Negotiating the self in a multicultural world*. New York/London: Teacher's College Press.

Ohara, Y. (2001) Finding one's voice in Japanese: A study of the pitch levels of L2 users. In: Pavlenko, A., Blackledge, A., Piller, I. & M. Teutsch-Dwyer (eds.) *Multilingualism, second language learning, and gender*. Berlin/New York: Mouton de Gruyter, pp. 231–254.

O'Nell, C. (1975) An investigation of reported "fright" as a factor in the etiology of *susto*, "magical fright." *Ethos*, 3, 1, 41–63.

Ortony, A. & T. Turner (1990) What's basic about basic emotions? *Psychological Review*, 97, 3, 315–331.

Otheguy, R. & O. García (1993) Convergent conceptualizations as predictors of degree of contact in US Spanish. In Roca, A. & J. Lipski (eds.) *Spanish in the US: Linguistic contact and diversity*. Berlin: Mouton De Gruyter, pp. 135–154.

Otoya, M. (1987) *A study of personal memories of bilinguals: The role of culture and language in memory encoding and recall*. Unpublished doctoral dissertation, Harvard University.

Oxford, R. (2002) Sources of variation in language learning. In R. Kaplan (ed.) *The Oxford Handbook of Applied Linguistics*. Oxford: Oxford University Press, pp. 245–252.

Paikeday, T. (1985) *The native speaker is dead! An informal discussion of a linguistic myth with Noam Chomsky and other linguists, philosophers, psychologists, and lexicographers*. Toronto/New York: Paikeday Publishing Inc.

Panayiotou, A. (2004a) Bilingual emotions: The untranslatable self. *Estudios de Sociolingüística*, 5, 1, 1–19.

Panayiotou, A. (2004b) Switching codes, switching code: Bilinguals' emotional responses in English and Greek. *Journal of Multilingual and Multicultural Development*, 25, 2/3, 124–139.

Pang, K. (1990) *Hwabyung*: The construction of a Korean popular illness among Korean elderly immigrant women in the United States. *Culture, Medicine, and Psychiatry*, 14, 4, 495–512.

Paradis, M. (1994) Neurolinguistic aspects of implicit and explicit memory: Implications for bilingualism and SLA. In: N. Ellis (ed.) *Implicit and explicit learning of languages*. San Diego, CA: Academic Press, pp. 393–419.

Pavlenko, A. (1997) *Bilingualism and cognition*. Unpublished doctoral dissertation, Cornell University.

Pavlenko, A. (1998) Second language learning by adults: Testimonies of bilingual writers. *Issues in Applied Linguistics*, 9, 1 3–19.

Pavlenko, A. (1999) New approaches to concepts in bilingual memory. *Bilingualism: Language and Cognition*, 2, 3, 209–230.

Pavlenko, A. (2000a) L2 influence on L1 in late bilingualism. *Issues in Applied Linguistics*, 11, 2, 175–205.

Pavlenko, A. (2000b) Access to linguistic resources: Key variable in second language learning. *Estudios de Sociolingüística*, 1, 2, 85–105.

Pavlenko, A. (2001) "In the world of the tradition I was unimagined": negotiation of identities in cross-cultural autobiographies. *International Journal of Bilingualism*, 5, 3, 317–344.

Pavlenko, A. (2002a) "We have room for but one language here": Language and national identity in the US at the turn of the 20th century. *Multilingua*, 21, 2/3, 163–196.

Pavlenko, A. (2002b) Poststructuralist approaches to the study of social factors in second language learning and use. In V. Cook (ed) *Portraits of the L2 user*. Clevedon, UK: Multilingual Matters, pp. 277–302.

Pavlenko, A. (2002c) Emotions and the body in Russian and English. *Pragmatics and Cognition*, 10, 1–2, 201–236.

Pavlenko, A. (2002d) Bilingualism and emotions. *Multilingua*, 21, 1, 45–78.

Pavlenko, A. (2003a) Eyewitness memory in late bilinguals: Evidence for discursive relativity. *International Journal of Bilingualism*, 7, 3, 257–281.

Pavlenko, A. (2003b) "Language of the enemy": Foreign language education and national identity. *International Journal of Bilingual Education and Bilingualism*, 6, 5, 313–331.

Pavlenko, A. (2003c) "I feel clumsy speaking Russian": L2 influence on L1 in narratives of Russian L2 users of English. In V. Cook (ed.) *Effects of the second language on the first*. Clevedon, UK: Multilingual Matters, pp. 32–61.

Pavlenko, A. (2004a) "Stop doing that, *ia komu skazala!*": Language choice and emotions in parent-child communication. *Journal of Multilingual and Multicultural Development*, 25, 2/3, 179–203.

Pavlenko, A. (2004b) "The making of an American": negotiation of identities at the turn of the 20th century. In: Pavlenko, A. & A. Blackledge (eds) *Negotiation of identities in multilingual contexts*. Clevedon, UK: Multilingual Matters, pp. 34–67.

Pavlenko, A. (in press) Bilingual selves. In A. Pavlenko (ed.) *Bilingual minds: Emotional experience, expression, and representation*. Clevedon, UK: Multilingual Matters.

Pavlenko, A. & A. Blackledge (2004a) (eds.) *Negotiation of identities in multilingual contexts*. Clevedon, UK: Multilingual Matters.

Pavlenko, A. & A. Blackledge (2004b) Introduction: New theoretical approaches to the study of negotiation of identities in multilingual contexts. In A. Pavlenko & A. Blackledge (eds.) *Negotiation of identities in multilingual contexts*. Clevedon, UK: Multilingual Matters, pp. 1–33.

Pavlenko, A. & S. Jarvis (2002) Bidirectional transfer. *Applied Linguistics*, 23, 2, 190–214.

Pavlovitch, M. (1920) *Le langage enfantin: Acquisition du serbe et du français par un enfant serbe*. Paris.

Peck, E. (1974) The relationship of disease and other stress to second language. *Journal of Social Psychiatry*, 20, 128–133.

Pennington, M. & J. Richards (1986) Pronunciation revisited. *TESOL Quarterly*, 20, 2, 207–225.

Perdue, C. (ed.) (1993) *Adult language acquisition: Cross-linguistic perspectives.* Volume 2. The results. Cambridge: Cambridge University Press.

Pérez Firmat, G. (2003) *Tongue ties: Logo-eroticism in Anglo-Hispanic literature.* New York: Palgrave Macmillan.

Petrucelli, L. (2000) Listening for the Tao in eight tones. In Ogulnick, K. (ed.) *Language crossings: Negotiating the self in a multicultural world.* New York/London: Teacher's College Press, pp. 159–165.

Pichette, M. (2000) *The influence of gender on the acquisition of the Japanese language by white Western men and women living and working in Japan.* Unpublished manuscript, Temple University Japan.

Piller, I. (2001) Linguistic intermarriage: Language choice and negotiation of identity. In A. Pavlenko, I. Piller, A. Blackledge & M. Teutsch-Dwyer (eds.) *Multilingualism, second language learning, and gender.* Berlin/New York: Mouton de Gruyter, pp. 199–230.

Piller, I. (2002a) *Bilingual couples talk: The discursive construction of hybridity.* Amsterdam/Philadelphia: John Benjamins.

Piller, I. (2002b) Passing for a native speaker: Identity and success in second language learning. *Journal of Sociolinguistics*, 6, 2, 179–206.

Piller, I. & K. Takahashi (in press) A passion for English: Desire and the language market. In A. Pavlenko (ed.) *Bilingual minds: Emotional experience, expression, and representation.* Clevedon, UK: Multilingual Matters.

Pinker, S. (1994) *The language instinct.* New York: Harper Perennial.

Pinker, S. (1997) *How the mind works.* New York/London: W. W. Norton.

Pittam, J. & K. Scherer (1993) Vocal expression and communication of emotion. In: Lewis, M. & J. Haviland (eds.) *Handbook of emotions.* New York: Guilford, pp. 185–197.

Planalp, S. (1999) *Communicating emotion: Social, moral, and cultural processes.* Cambridge, UK: Cambridge University Press.

Planalp, S., DeFrancisco, V. & D. Rutherford (1996) Varieties of cues to emotion in naturally occurring situations. *Cognition and Emotion*, 10, 2, 137–153.

Planalp, S. & K. Knie (2002) Integrating verbal and nonverbal emotion(al) messages. In Fussell, S. (ed.) *The verbal communication of emotions: Interdisciplinary perspectives.* Mahwah, NJ: Lawrence Erlbaum, pp. 55–77.

Polanyi, L. (1995) Language learning and living abroad: Stories from the field. In Freed, B. (ed.) *Second language acquisition in a study abroad context.* Amsterdam/Philadelphia: John Benjamins, pp. 271–291.

Poole, F. (1985) Coming into social being: Cultural images of infants in Bimin-Kuskusmin folk psychology. In White, J. & J. Kirkpatrick (eds.) *Person, self, and experience: Exploring Pacific ethnopsychologies.* Berkeley, CA: University of California Press, pp. 183–242.

Precht, K. (2003) Stance moods in spoken English: Evidentiality and affect in British and American conversation. *Text*, 23, 2, 239–257.

Price, C. & I. Cuellar (1981) Effects of language and related variables on the expression of psychopathology in Mexican American psychiatric patients. *Hispanic Journal of Behavioral Sciences*, 3, 2, 145–160.

Ramaswamy, S. (1997) *Passions of the tongue: Language devotion in Tamil India*. Berkeley: University of California Press.

Richard-Amato, P. (1988) *Making it happen. Interaction in the second language classroom: From theory to practice*. New York/London: Longman.

Ries, N. (1997) *Russian talk: Culture and conversation during perestroika*. Ithaca, NY: Cornell University Press.

Riesman, P. (1977) *Freedom in Fulani social life: An introspective ethnography*. Translated by Martha Fuller. Chicago/London: The University of Chicago Press.

Riessman, C. (1987) When gender is not enough: Women interviewing women. *Gender and Society*, 1, 2, 172–207.

Rintell, E. (1984) But how did you FEEL about that? The learners' perception of emotion in speech. *Applied Linguistics*, 5, 3, 255–264.

Rintell, E. (1989) That reminds me of a story: The use of language to express emotion by second-language learners and native speakers. In M. Eisenstein (ed.) *The dynamic interlanguage: Empirical studies in second language variation*. New York/London: Plenum Press, pp. 237–257.

Rintell, E. (1990) That's incredible: Stories of emotion told by second language learners and native speakers. In: Scarcella, R., Andersen, E. & S. Krashen (eds.) *Developing communicative competence in a second language*. Boston, MA: Heinle & Heinle, pp. 75–94.

Rodriguez, R. (1997) Going home again. In J. Epstein (ed.) *The Norton book of personal essays*. New York: Norton. Originally published in The American Scholar in 1974.

Romaine, S. (1995) Bilingualism. 2nd edition. Oxford, UK: Blackwell.

Ronjat, J. (1913) *Le développement du langage observé chez un enfant bilingue*. Paris: Champion.

Rosaldo, M. (1980) *Knowledge and passion: Ilongot notions of self and social life*. Cambridge: Cambridge University Press.

Rosaldo, M. (1982) The things we do with words: Ilongot speech acts and speech act theory in philosophy. *Language in Society*, 11, 203–237.

Rosaldo, M. (1984) Toward an anthropology of self and feeling. In Shweder, R. & R. LeVine (eds.) *Culture theory: Essays on mind, self, and emotion*. NY: Cambridge University Press, pp. 137–157.

Rosario, N. (2000) On becoming. In Danquah, M. N. (Ed.) *Becoming American: Personal essays by first generation immigrant women*. New York: Hyperion, pp. 156–164.

Roseberry-McKibbin, C. & A. Brice (1998) The perception of vocal cues of emotion by Spanish-speaking limited English proficient children. *Journal of Children's Communication Development*, 20, 2, 19–24.

Ross, E., Edmondson, J. & B. Seibert (1986) The effect of affect on various acoustic measures of prosody in tone and non-tone languages: A comparison based on computer analysis of voice. *Journal of Phonetics*, 14, 283–302.

Ross, M., Xun, W. Q. E. & A. Wilson (2002) Language and the bicultural self. *Personality and Social Psychology Bulletin*, 28, 8, 1040–1050.

Rozensky, R. & M. Gomez (1983) Language switching in psychotherapy with bilinguals: Two problems, two models, and case examples. *Psychotherapy: Theory, Research and Practice*, 20, 2, 152–160.

Rusch, C. (2004) Cross-cultural variability of the semantic domain of emotion terms: An examination of English *shame* and *embarrass* with Japanese *hazukashii*. *Cross-Cultural Research*, 38, 3, 236–248.

Russell, J. (1991a) Culture and the categorization of emotions. *Psychological Bulletin*, 110, 3, 426–450.

Russell, J. (1991b) In defense of a prototype approach to emotion concepts. *Journal of Personality and Social Psychology*, 60, 37–47.

Saarni, C. (1993) Socialization of emotion. In Lewis, M. & J. Haviland (eds.) *Handbook of emotions*. New York: Guilford Press, pp. 435–446.

Saer, D. (1924) The effect of bilingualism on intelligence. *British Journal of Psychology*, 14, 25–38.

Saer, D., Smith, F. & J. Hughes (1924) *The bilingual problem: A study based upon experiments and observations in Wales*. Aberystwyth: University College of Wales.

Samarin, W. (1967) *Field linguistics: A guide to linguistic field work*. New York: Holt, Rinehart, & Winston.

Sander, F. (1934) Seelische Struktur und Sprache: Strukturpsychologisches zum Zweitsprachenproblem. *Neue Psychologische Studien*, 12, 59.

Sante, L. (1998) *The factory of facts*. New York: Pantheon Books.

Santiago-Rivera, A. & J. Altarriba (2002) The role of language in therapy with the Spanish-English bilingual client. *Professional Psychology: Research and Practice*, 33, 30–38.

Sapir, E. (1921) *Language: An introduction to the study of speech*. New York: Harcourt, Brace and World.

Sapir, E. (1927) Speech as a personality trait. *The American Journal of Sociology*, 32, 892–905.

Schachter, S. & J. Singer (1962) Cognitive, social, and physiological determinants of emotional state. *Psychological Review*, 69, 5, 379–399.

Schecter, S. & R. Bayley (1997) Language socialization practices and cultural identity: Case studies of Mexican-descent families in California and Texas. *TESOL Quarterly*, 31, 3, 513–541.

Scherer, K. (1979) Nonlinguistic vocal indicators of emotion and psychopathology. In C. Izard (ed.) *Emotions in personality and psychopathology*. New York/London: Plenum Press, pp. 495–529.

Scherer, K. (1984) Emotion as a multicomponent process: A model and some cross-cultural data. In Shaver, P. & L. Wheeler (eds.) *Review of personality and social psychology: Emotions, relationships, and health*. Vol. 5. Beverly Hills, CA: Sage, pp. 37–63.

Scherer, K. (1986) Vocal affect expression: A review and a model for future research. *Psychological Bulletin*, 99, 2, 143–165.

Scherer, K. (ed.) (1988) *Facets of emotion: Recent research*. Hillsdale, NJ: Lawrence Erlbaum.

Scherer, K. (1994) Toward a concept of "modal emotions." In Ekman, P. & R. Davidson (eds.) *The nature of emotion: Fundamental questions*. New York/Oxford: Oxford University Press, pp. 25–31.

Scherer, K., Banse, R. & H. Wallbott (2001) Emotion inferences from vocal expression correlate across languages and cultures. *Journal of Cross-Cultural Psychology, 32,* 1, 76–92.

Scherer, K., Banse, R., Wallbott, H. & T. Goldbeck (1991) Vocal cues in emotion encoding and decoding. *Motivation and Emotion, 15,* 2, 123–148.

Scherer, K., Matsumoto, D., Wallbott, H. & T. Kudoh (1988) Emotional experience in cultural context: A comparison between Europe, Japan, and the United States. In K. Scherer (ed.) *Facets of emotion: Recent research.* Hillsdale, NJ: Lawrence Erlbaum, pp. 5–30.

Scherer, K. & H. Wallbott (1994) Evidence for universality and cultural variation of differential emotion response patterning. *Journal of Personality and Social Psychology, 66,* 2, 310–328.

Scherer, K., Wallbott, H. & A. Summerfield (eds.) (1988) *Experiencing emotion: A cross-cultural study.* Cambridge: Cambridge University Press.

Scheu, D. (2000) Cultural constraints in bilinguals' codeswitching. *International Journal of Intercultural Relations, 24,* 131–150.

Schieffelin, E. (1976) *The sorrow of the lonely and the burning of the dancers.* New York: St. Martin's Press.

Schieffelin, E. (1985) Anger, grief, and shame: Toward a Kaluli ethnopsychology. In G. White & J. Kirkpatrick (eds.) *Person, self, and experience: Exploring Pacific ethnopsychologies.* Berkeley, CA: University of California Press, pp. 168–182.

Schieffelin, B. & E. Ochs (eds.) (1986) *Language socialization across cultures.* New York: Cambridge University Press.

Schieffelin, B., Woolard, K. & P. Kroskrity (eds.) (1998) *Language ideologies: Practice and theory.* New York/Oxford: Oxford University Press.

Schmid, M. (2002) *First language attrition, use and maintenance: The case of German Jews in anglophone countries.* Amsterdam/Philadelphia: John Benjamins.

Schmid, M. (2004) Identity and first language attrition: A historical approach. *Estudios de Sociolingüística, 5,* 1, 41–58.

Schmidt, Richard (1983) Interaction, acculturation, and the acquisition of communicative competence: A case study of an adult. In: N. Wolfson & E. Judd (eds.) *Sociolinguistics and Language Acquisition.* Rowley, MA: Newbury House Publishers, pp. 137–174.

Schmidt, Ronald (2000) *Language policy and identity politics in the United States.* Philadelphia: Temple University Press.

Schmidt-Atzert, L. & H. Park (1999) The Korean concepts *dapdaphada* and *uulhada:* A cross-cultural study of the meaning of emotions. *Journal of Cross-Cultural Psychology, 30,* 5, 646–654.

Schmidt-Rohr, G. (1932) *Die Sprache als Bildnerin der Völker.* München: Jena Muttersprache.

Schmidt-Rohr, G. (1933) *Mutter Sprache: vom Amt der Sprache bei der Volkwerdung.* Jena.

Schmidt-Rohr, G. (1936) Zur Frage der Zweitsprachigkeit. *Deutsche Arbeit, 36,* 408–411.

Schrauf, R. (2000) Bilingual autobiographical memory: Experimental studies and clinical cases. *Culture and Psychology, 6,* 4, 387–417.

Schrauf, R. (2002) Comparing cultures within-subjects. *Anthropological Theory, 2,* 1, 101–118.

Schrauf, R. (2003) A protocol analysis of retrieval in bilingual autobiographical memory. *International Journal of Bilingualism*, 7, 3, 235–256.

Schrauf, R., Pavlenko, A. & J.-M. Dewaele (2003) Bilingual episodic memory: An introduction. *International Journal of Bilingualism*, 7, 3, 221–233.

Schrauf, R. & D. Rubin (1998) Bilingual autobiographical memory in older adult immigrants: A test of cognitive explanations of the reminiscence bump and the linguistic encoding of memories. *Journal of Memory and Language*, 39, 437–457.

Schrauf, R. & D. Rubin (2000) Internal languages of retrieval: The bilingual encoding of memories for the personal past. *Memory and Cognition*, 28, 4, 616–623.

Schrauf, R. & D. Rubin (2003) On the bilingual's two sets of memories. In: Fivush, R. & C. Haden (eds.) *Autobiographical memory and the construction of a narrative self*. Mahwah, NJ: Lawrence Erlbaum, pp. 121–145.

Schrauf, R. & D. Rubin (2004) The 'language' and 'feel' of bilingual memory: Mnemonic traces. *Estudios de Sociolingüística*, 5, 1, 21–39.

Schumann, F. (1980) Diary of a language learner: A further analysis. In R. Scarcella & S. Krashen (eds.) *Research in second language acquisition: Selected papers of the Los Angeles Second Language Acquisition Research Forum*. Rowley, MA: Newbury House, pp. 51–57.

Schumann, J. (1978) *The pidginization process: A model for second language acquisition*. Rowley, MA: Newbury House.

Schumann, J. (1994) Where is cognition? Emotion and cognition in second language acquisition. *Studies in Second Language Acquisition*, 16, 231–242.

Schumann, J. (1997) *The neurobiology of affect in language*. University of Michigan: Blackwell.

Schumann, J. (1999) A neurobiological perspective on affect and methodology in second language learning. In Arnold, J. (ed.) *Affect in language learning*. Cambridge: Cambridge University Press, pp. 28–42.

Schumann, J. (2001) Appraisal psychology, neurobiology, and language. *Annual Review of Applied Linguistics*, 21, 23–42.

Schutz, A. & R. Baumeister (1999) The language of defense: Linguistic patterns in narratives of transgression. *Journal of Language and Social Psychology*, 18, 3, 269–286.

Scollon, R. & S. Wong-Scollon (2001) *Intercultural communication*. Second edition. Oxford: Blackwell.

Scovel, T. (1978) The effect of affect on foreign language learning: A review of the anxiety research. *Language Learning*, 28, 1, 129–142.

Selting, M. (1994) Emphatic speech style – with special focus on the prosodic signalling of heightened emotive involvement in conversation. *Journal of Pragmatics*, 22, 375–408.

Selting, M. (1996) Prosody as an activity-type distinctive cue in conversation: The case of so-called 'astonished' questions in repair initiation. In E. Couper-Kuhlen & M. Selting (eds.) *Prosody in conversation: Interactional studies*. NY: Cambridge University Press, pp. 231–270.

Semin, G., Görts, C., Nandram, Sh. & A. Semin-Goossens (2002) Cultural perspectives on the linguistic representation of emotion and emotion events. *Cognition and Emotion*, 16, 1, 11–28.

Shaver, Ph., Schwartz, J., Kirson, D. & C. O'Connor (1987) Emotion knowledge: Further exploration of a prototype approach. *Journal of Personality and Social Psychology*, 52, 6, 1061–1086.

Shweder, R. (1993) The cultural psychology of the emotions. In Lewis, M. & J. Haviland (eds.) *Handbook of emotions*. New York: Guilford Press, pp. 417–433.

Shweder, R. (1994) "You're not sick, you're just in love": Emotion as an interpretive system. In Ekman, P. & R. Davidson (eds.) *The nature of emotion: Fundamental questions*. New York/Oxford: Oxford University Press, pp. 32–44.

Siegal, M. (1996) The role of learner subjectivity in second language sociolinguistic competency: Western women learning Japanese. *Applied Linguistics*, 17, 356–382.

Slobin, D. (1996) From "thought and language" to "thinking for speaking". In J. Gumperz & S. Levinson (eds.), *Rethinking linguistic relativity*. Cambridge: Cambridge University Press, pp. 70–96.

Smith, F. (1923) Bilingualism and mental development. *British Journal of Psychology*, 13, 271–282.

Smith, M. (1931) A study of five bilingual children from the same family. *Child Development*, 2, 184–187.

Smith, M. (1939) Some light on the problem of bilingualism as found from a study of the progress in mastery of English among pre-school children of non-American ancestry in Hawaii. *Genetic Psychology Monographs*, 21, 119–284.

Solomon, D. & F. Ali (1975) Influence of verbal content and intonation on meaning attributions of first- and second-language speakers. *Journal of Social Psychology*, 95, 3–9.

Sparks, R. & L. Ganshow (2001) Aptitude for learning a foreign language. *Annual Review of Applied Linguistics*, 21, 90–111.

Spoerl, D. (1943) Bilinguality and emotional adjustment. *Journal of Abnormal and Social Psychology*, 38, 35–57.

Spolsky, B. & E. Shohamy (1999) *The languages of Israel: Policy, ideology, and practice*. Clevedon, UK: Multilingual Matters.

Stankiewicz, E. (1964) Problems of emotive language. In Sebeok, T. (ed.) *Approaches to semiotics*. The Hague: Mouton, pp. 239–264.

Stearns, P. (1993) History of emotions: The issue of change. In M. Lewis & J. Haviland (eds.) *Handbook of emotions*. New York: Guilford Press, pp. 17–28.

Stearns, P. (1994) *American cool: Constructing a twentieth-century emotional style*. New York: New York University Press.

Stearns, C. & P. Stearns (1986) Anger: *The struggle for emotional control in America's history*. Chicago, IL: University of Chicago Press.

Stengel, E. (1939) On learning a new language. *International Journal of Psychoanalysis*, 20, 471–479.

Stepanova, O. & J. Coley (2002) The Green Eyed Monster: Linguistic influences on concepts of envy and jealousy in Russian and English. *Journal of Cognition and Culture*, 2, 4, 235–262.

Strauss, H. (ed.) (1986) *Jewish immigrants in the Nazi period in the USA. Volume 5. The individual and collective experience of German-Jewish immigrants 1933–1984*. New York/München: K. G. Saur.

Strongman, K. (1996) *The psychology of emotion: Theories of emotion in perspective.* 4th edition. New York: John Wiley & Sons.

Stroud, C. (1998) Perspectives on cultural variability of discourse and some implications for code-switching. In Auer, P. (ed.) *Code-switching in conversation: Language, interaction, and identity.* London/New York: Routledge, pp. 321–348.

Swan, M. & B. Smith (2001) *Learner English. A teacher's guide to interference and other problems.* Second edition. Cambridge, UK: Cambridge University Press.

Talburt, S. & M. Stewart (1999) What's the subject of study abroad?: Race, gender, and "living culture". *The Modern Language Journal,* 83, 2, 163–175.

Tannen, D. (1982) Ethnic style in male-female conversation. In Gumperz, J. (ed.) *Language and social identity.* New York: Cambridge University Press, pp. 217–231.

Tannen, D. (1984) *Conversational style: Analyzing talk among friends.* Ablex.

Tannen, D. (1989) *Talking voices: Repetition, dialogue, and imagery in conversational discourse.* Cambridge, UK: Cambridge University Press.

Tannen, D. (1993) The relativity of linguistic strategies: Rethinking power and solidarity in gender and dominance. In Tannen, D. (ed.) *Gender and conversational interaction.* New York/Oxford: Oxford University Press, pp. 165–188.

Tapia, M. (2001) Measuring emotional intelligence. *Psychological Reports,* 88, 353–364.

Te amaré en silencio (2002) Director: Andre Zinca, produced by Univision.

Teicholz, T. (ed.) (1993) *Conversations with Jerzy Kosinski.* Jackson: University Press of Mississippi.

Todorov, T. (1994) Dialogism and schizophrenia. In Arteaga, A. (ed.) *An other tongue. Nation and ethnicity in the linguistic borderlands.* Durham & London: Duke University Press, pp. 203–214.

Tomiyama, M. (1999) The first stage of second language attrition: A case study of a Japanese returnee. In Hansen, L. (ed.) *Second language attrition in Japanese contexts.* New York/Oxford: Oxford University Press, pp. 59–79.

Toya, M. & M. Kodis (1996) But I don't want to be rude: On learning how to express anger in the L2. *JALT Journal,* 18, 2, 279–295.

Twombly, S. (1995) Piropos and friendships: Gender and culture clash in study abroad. *Frontiers: The Interdisciplinary Journal of Study Abroad,* 1, 1–27.

Uhlman, F. (1960) *The making of an Englishman.* London: Victor Gollancz.

Ungerer, F. & H.-J. Schmid (1996) *An introduction to cognitive linguistics.* New York/London: Longman.

Valdes, G. (2003) *Expanding definitions of giftedness: The case of young interpreters from immigrant communities.* Mahwah, NJ: Lawrence Erlbaum.

Valentine, C. & B. Saint Damian (1988) Gender and culture as determinants of the 'ideal voice.' *Semiotica,* 71, 3/4, 285–303.

van Bezooijen (van Bezooyen), R. (1984) *Characteristics and recognizability of vocal expressions of emotion.* Dordrecht, Holland: Foris Publications.

van Bezooijen, R. (1995) Sociocultural aspects of pitch differences between Japanese and Dutch women. *Language and Speech,* 38, 3, 253–265.

van Bezooijen, R. (1996) The effect of pitch on the attribution of gender-related personality traits. In Warner, N., Ahlers, J., Bilmes, L., Oliver, M., Wertheim, S. &

M. Chen (eds.) *Gender and Belief Systems. Proceedings of the Fourth Berkeley Women and Language Conference*, April 19–21, 1996, pp. 755–766.

van Bezooijen, R., Otto, S. & T. Heenan (1983) Recognition of vocal expressions of emotion: A three-nation study to identify universal characteristics. *Journal of Cross-Cultural Psychology*, 14, 4, 387–406.

van Eemeren, F., van Grootendorst, R., Jackson, S. & S. Jacobs (1993) *Reconstructing argumentative discourse*. Tuscaloosa: University of Alabama Press.

van Hell, J. & T. Dijkstra (2002) Foreign language knowledge can influence native language performance in exclusively native contexts. *Psychonomic Bulletin and Review*, 9, 4.

Vasquez, C. & R. Javier (1991) The problem with interpreters: Communicating with Spanish-speaking patients. *Hospital and Community Psychiatry*, 42, 163–165.

Vaux, B. & J. Cooper (1999) *Introduction to linguistic field methods*. Muenchen: Lincom Europa.

Vázquez, C. (1982a) Research on the psychiatric evaluation of the bilingual patient: A methodological critique. *Hispanic Journal of Behavioral Sciences*, 4, 1, 75–80.

Vázquez, C. (1982b) Reply to Cuellar and Price. *Hispanic Journal of Behavioral Sciences*, 4, 1, 85–88.

Velikovsky, I. (1934) Can a newly acquired language become the speech of the unconscious? *Psychoanalytic Review*, 21, 329–335.

Venkateswaran, P. (2000) Language, exile, and discovery. In Ogulnick, K. (ed.) *Language crossings: Negotiating the self in a multicultural world*. New York: Teacher's College Press, pp. 59–63.

Vildomec, V. (1963) *Multilingualism*. Leyden: A. W. Sythoff.

Waas, M. (1996) *Language attrition downunder: German speakers in Australia*. Frankfurt/New York: Peter Lang.

Wallace, A. & M. Carson (1973) Sharing and diversity in emotion terminology. *Ethos*, 1, 1, 1–29.

Wallbott, H. & K. Scherer (1986) Cues and channels in emotion recognition. *Journal of Personality and Social Psychology*, 51, 4, 690–699.

Walton, D. (1998) *The new dialectic: Conversational contexts of argument*. Toronto: University of Toronto Press.

Watson, R. (1995) *The Philosopher's Demise: Learning French*. Columbia, MO: University of Missouri Press.

Weinreich, U. (1953) *Languages in contact: Findings and problems*. Publications of the Linguistic Circle of New York. New York.

Weisgerber, L. (1929) *Muttersprache und Geistesbildung*. Göttingen: Vandenhoek & Ruprecht.

Weisgerber, L. (1933) Die Stellung der Sprache im Aufbau der Gesamtkultur. *Wörter und Sachen*, 15, 134–224; 16, 97–236.

Weller, S., Baer, R., Garcia, J., Glazer, M., Trotter, R., Pachter, L. & R. Klein (2002) Regional variation in Latino descriptions of *susto*. *Culture, Medicine, and Psychiatry*, 26, 4, 449–472.

White, G. (1990) Moral discourse and the rhetoric of emotion. In C. Lutz & A. Abu-Lughod (eds.) *Language and the politics of emotion*. Cambridge: Cambridge University Press.

White, G. (1993) Emotions inside out: The anthropology of affect. In M. Lewis & J. Haviland (eds.) *Handbook of emotions*. New York: Guilford Press, pp. 29–39.

White, L. & F. Genesee (1996) How native is near-native? The issue of ultimate attainment in adult second language acquisition. *Second Language Research*, 12, 3, 233–265.

Whitney, M. (1918) National ideals and the teaching of modern languages. *Modern Language Journal*, 3, 1, 5–13.

Wierzbicka, A. (1985) Different cultures, different languages, different speech acts: Polish vs. English. *Journal of Pragmatics*, 9, 145–178.

Wierzbicka, A. (1986) Human emotions: Universal or culture-specific? *American Anthropologist*, 88, 3, 584–594.

Wierzbicka, A. (1991) *Cross-cultural pragmatics: The semantics of human interaction.* Berlin/New York: Mouton de Gruyter.

Wierzbicka, A. (1992) *Semantics, culture, and cognition: Universal human concepts in culture-specific configurations.* New York: Oxford University Press.

Wierzbicka, A. (1994) Emotion, language, and cultural scripts. In Kitayama, S. & H. Markus (eds.) *Emotion and culture: Empirical studies of mutual influence.* Washington, DC: American Psychological Association, pp. 133–196.

Wierzbicka, A. (1995) Everyday conceptions of emotion: A semantic perspective. In Russell, J., Fernández-Dols, J., Manstead, A. & J. Wellenkamp (eds.) *Everyday conceptions of emotion: An introduction to the psychology, anthropology, and linguistics of emotion.* Dodrecht: Kluwer Academic, pp. 117–47.

Wierzbicka, A. (1997) The double life of a bilingual: A cross-cultural perspective. In M. Bond (ed.) *Working at the interface of cultures: Eighteen lives in social science.* London: Routledge, pp. 113–125.

Wierzbicka, A. (1998) Russian emotional expression. *Ethos*, 26, 4, 456–483.

Wierzbicka, A. (1999) *Emotions across languages and cultures: Diversity and universals.* Cambridge: Cambridge University Press.

Wierzbicka, A. (2003) Emotion and culture: Arguing with Martha Nussbaum. *Ethos*, 31, 4, 577–600.

Wierzbicka, A. (2004) Preface: Bilingual lives, bilingual experience. Special issue of the *Journal of Multilingual and Multicultural Development*, 25, 2/3, 94–104.

Wierzbicka, A. (in press) Universal human concepts as a tool for exploring bilingual lives. *International Journal of Bilingualism.*

Wikan, U. (1990) *Managing turbulent hearts: A Balinese formula for living.* Chicago, IL: Chicago University Press.

Wikan, U. (1993) Beyond the words: The power of resonance. In G. Pálsson (ed.) *Beyond boundaries: Understanding, translation and anthropological discourse.* Oxford: Berg, pp. 184–209.

Williams, C. & K. Stevens (1972) Emotions and speech: Some acoustical correlates. *Journal of the Acoustic Society of America*, 52, 4, 1238–1250.

Williams, C. & K. Stevens (1981) Vocal correlates of emotional states. In J. Darby (ed.) *Speech evaluation in psychiatry.* New York: Grune & Stratton, pp. 221–240.

Yoshioka, J. (1929) A study of bilingualism. *Journal of Genetic Psychology*, 36, 473–479.

Young, R. & A. W. He (eds.) (1998) *Talking and testing: Discourse approaches to the assessment of oral proficiency.* Amsterdam/Philadelphia: John Benjamins.

Yuasa, I. (2002) Empiricism and emotion: Representing and interpreting pitch ranges. In S. Benor, M. Rose, D. Sharma, J. Sweetland, & Quing Zhang (eds.) *Gendered practices in language.* Stanford, CA: CSLI Publications, pp. 193–209.

Zac de Filc, S. (1992) Psychic change in the analyst. *International Journal of Psycho-analysis*, 73, 323–328.

Zentella, A. (1997) *Growing up bilingual: Puerto Rican children in New York*. Oxford: Blackwell.

Zhengdao Ye, V. (2004) La double vie de Veronica: Reflections on my life as a Chinese migrant in Australia. *Life Writing*, 1, 1, 133–145.

Author Index

Subject Index

Made in the USA
Lexington, KY
14 July 2013